My Special One

1

**VOLUME
ONE**

STORY & ART BY

MOMOKO KODA

CONTENTS

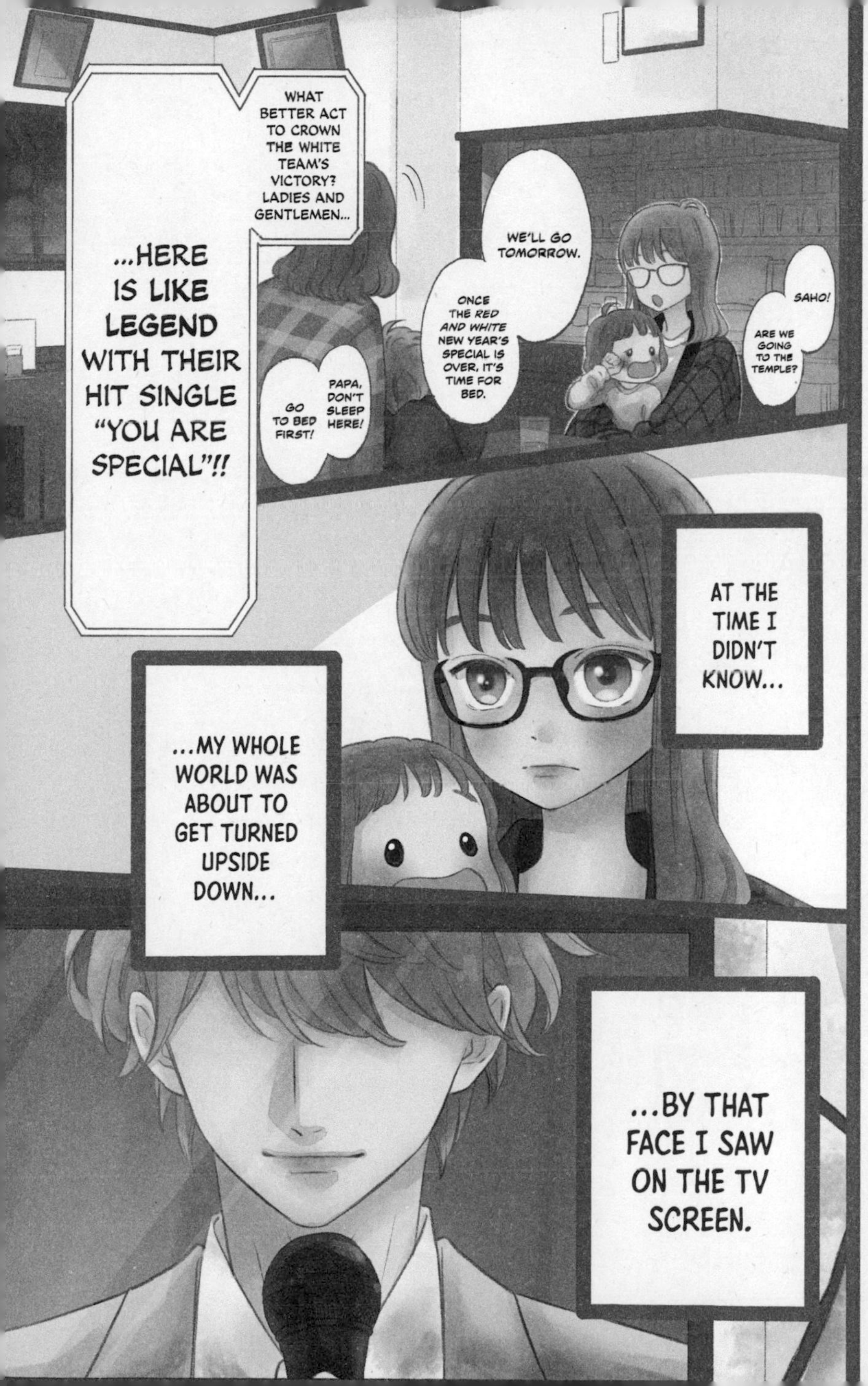
SAHO!
ARE WE GOING TO THE TEMPLE?
WE'LL GO TOMORROW.
ONCE THE RED AND WHITE NEW YEAR'S SPECIAL IS OVER, IT'S TIME FOR BED.
PAPA, DON'T SLEEP HERE!
GO TO BED FIRST!
WHAT BETTER ACT TO CROWN THE WHITE TEAM'S VICTORY? LADIES AND GENTLEMEN...
...HERE IS LIKE LEGEND WITH THEIR HIT SINGLE "YOU ARE SPECIAL"!!
AT THE TIME I DIDN'T KNOW...
...MY WHOLE WORLD WAS ABOUT TO GET TURNED UPSIDE DOWN...
...BY THAT FACE I SAW ON THE TV SCREEN.

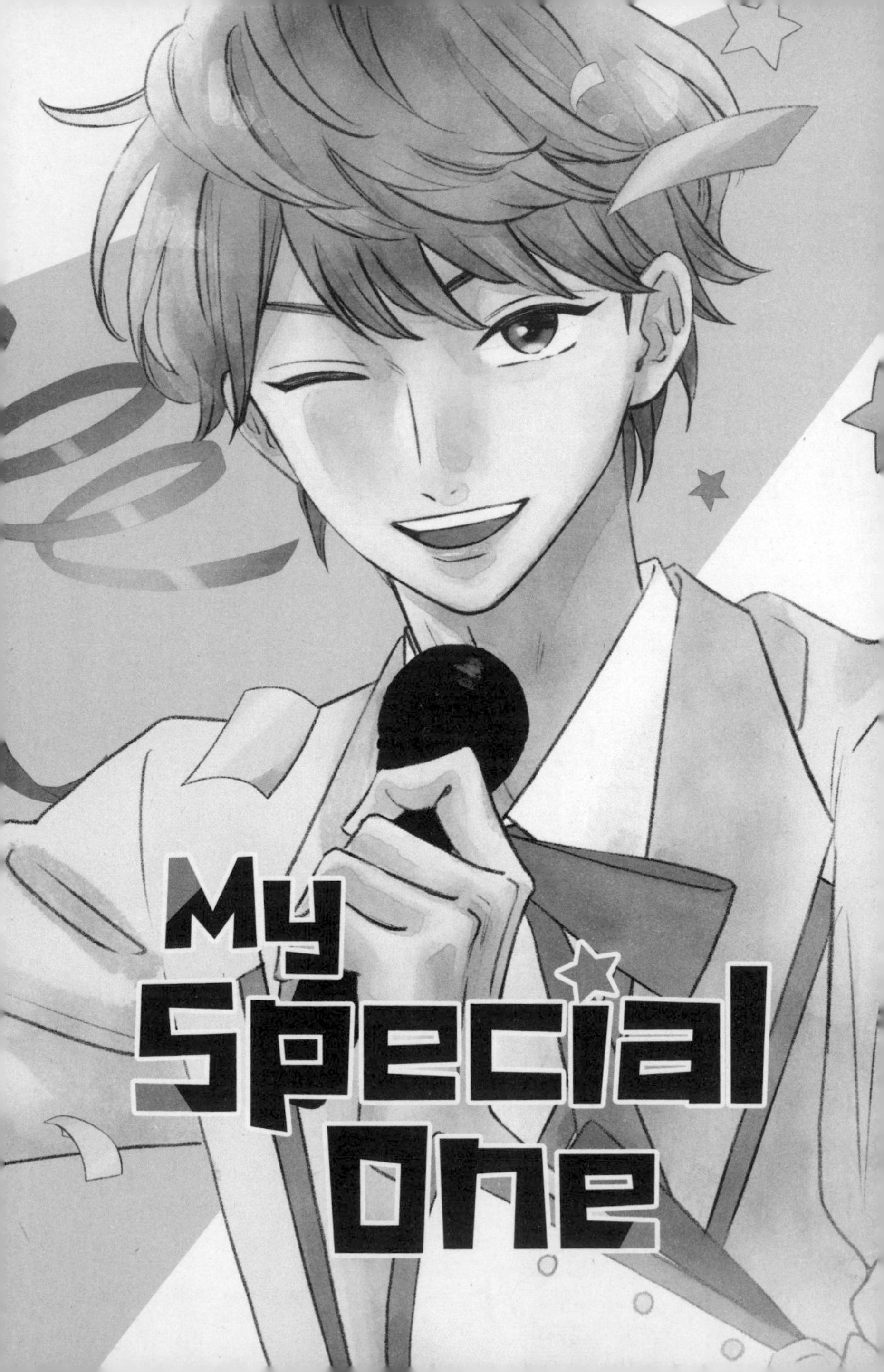
My Special One

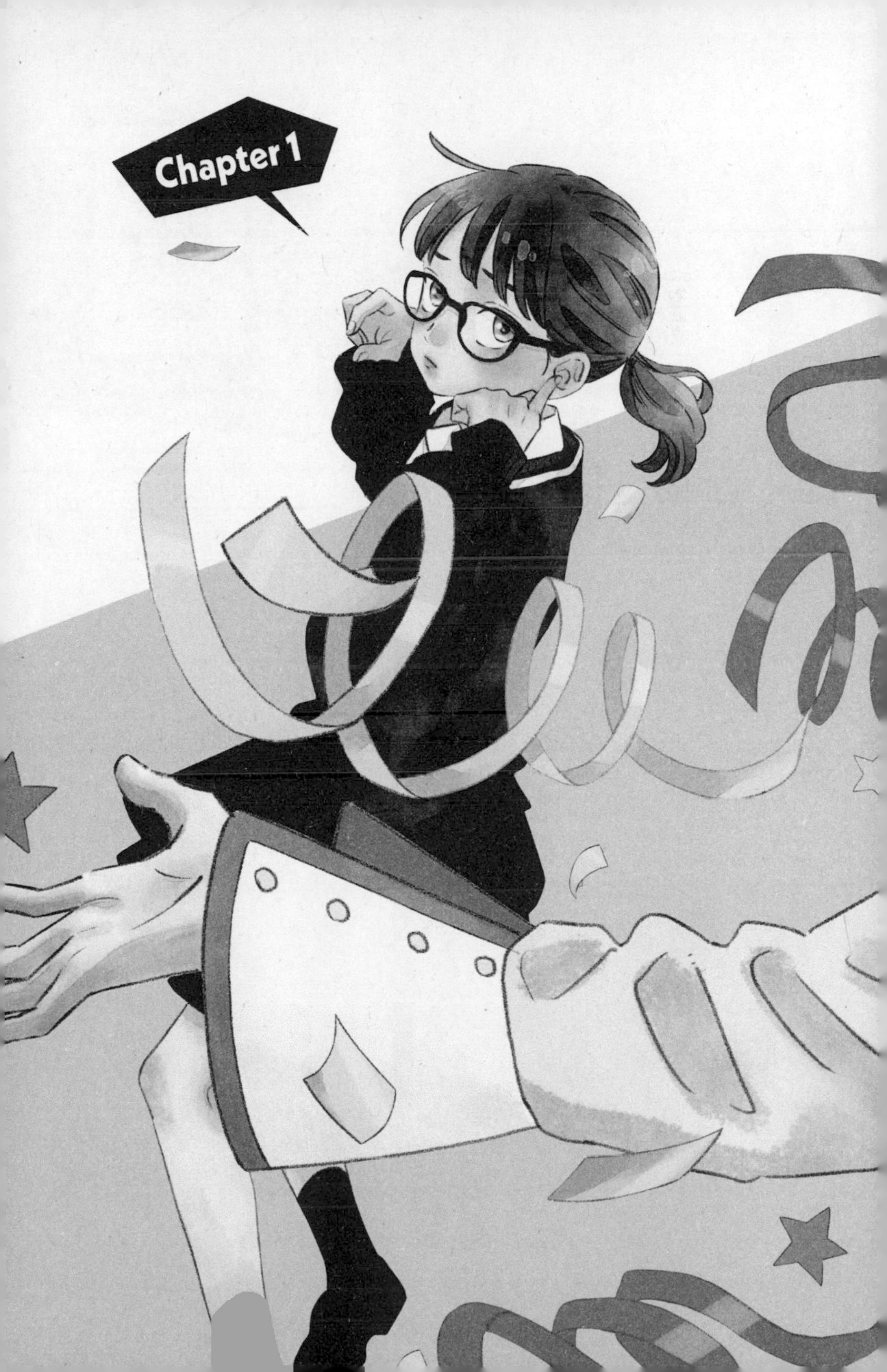
Chapter 1

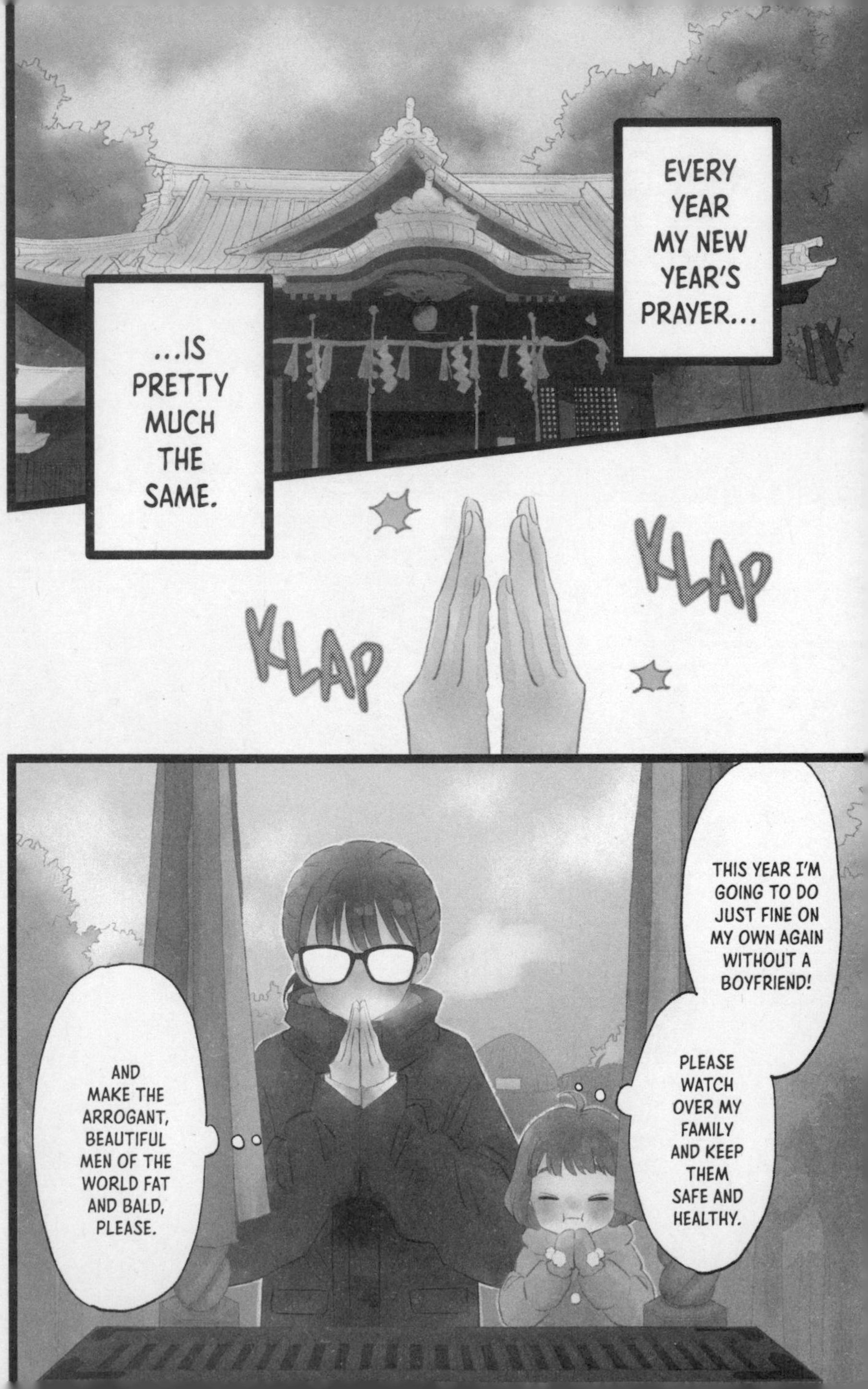
EVERY YEAR MY NEW YEAR'S PRAYER...
...IS PRETTY MUCH THE SAME.
KLAP
KLAP
THIS YEAR I'M GOING TO DO JUST FINE ON MY OWN AGAIN WITHOUT A BOYFRIEND!
PLEASE WATCH OVER MY FAMILY AND KEEP THEM SAFE AND HEALTHY.
AND MAKE THE ARROGANT, BEAUTIFUL MEN OF THE WORLD FAT AND BALD, PLEASE.

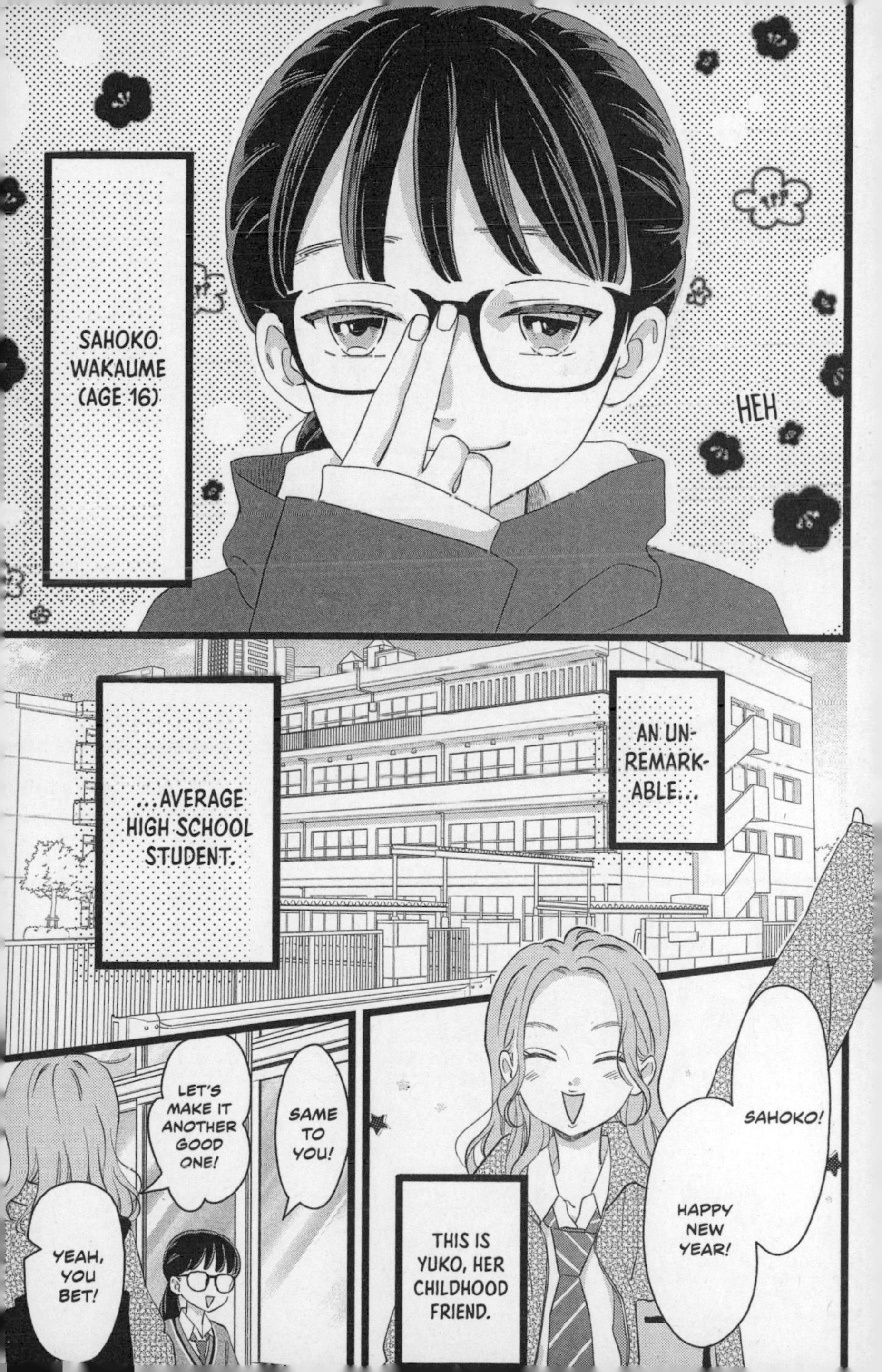
SAHOKO WAKAUME (AGE 16)
HEH
AN UN-REMARK-ABLE...
...AVERAGE HIGH SCHOOL STUDENT.
SAHOKO!
HAPPY NEW YEAR!
THIS IS YUKO, HER CHILDHOOD FRIEND.
SAME TO YOU!
LET'S MAKE IT ANOTHER GOOD ONE!
YEAH, YOU BET!

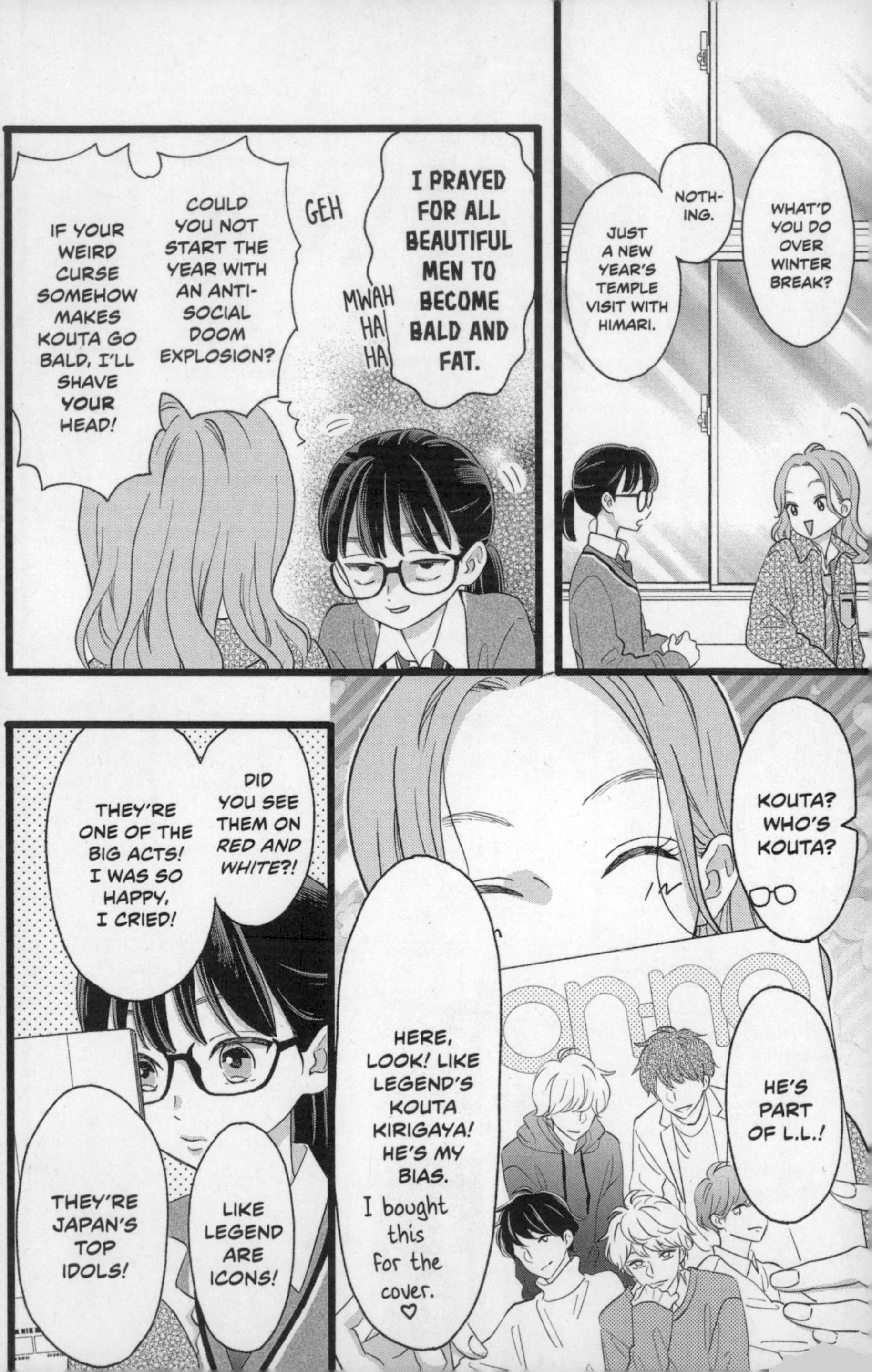
WHAT'D YOU DO OVER WINTER BREAK?
NOTH-ING.
JUST A NEW YEAR'S TEMPLE VISIT WITH HIMARI.
I PRAYED FOR ALL BEAUTIFUL MEN TO BECOME BALD AND FAT.
MWAH HA HA
GEH
COULD YOU NOT START THE YEAR WITH AN ANTI-SOCIAL DOOM EXPLOSION?
IF YOUR WEIRD CURSE SOMEHOW MAKES KOUTA GO BALD, I'LL SHAVE YOUR HEAD!
KOUTA? WHO'S KOUTA?
HE'S PART OF L.L.!
HERE, LOOK! LIKE LEGEND'S KOUTA KIRIGAYA! HE'S MY BIAS.
I bought this for the cover. ♡
DID YOU SEE THEM ON RED AND WHITE?!
THEY'RE ONE OF THE BIG ACTS! I WAS SO HAPPY, I CRIED!
LIKE LEGEND ARE ICONS!
THEY'RE JAPAN'S TOP IDOLS!

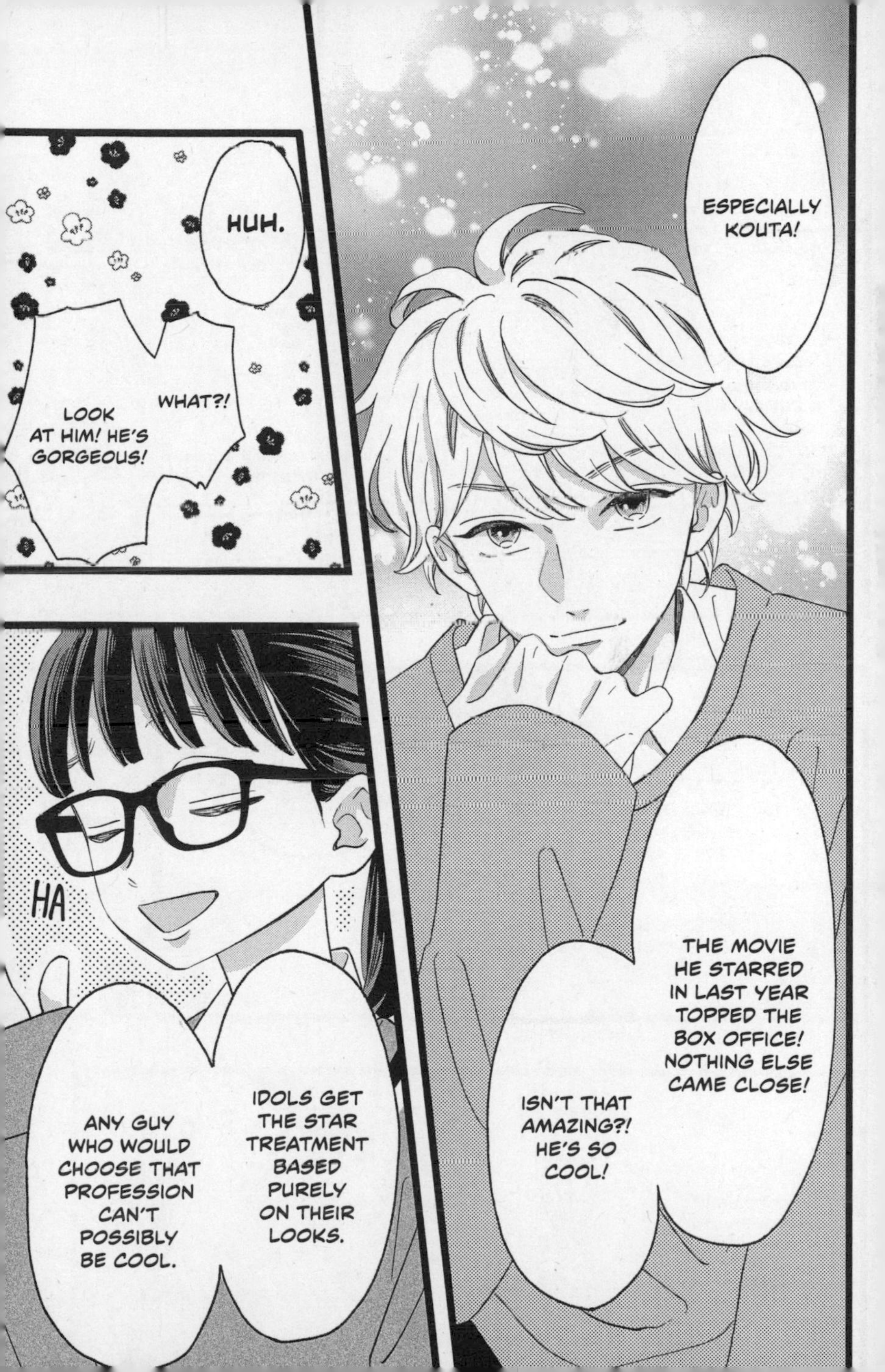
ESPECIALLY KOUTA!
THE MOVIE HE STARRED IN LAST YEAR TOPPED THE BOX OFFICE! NOTHING ELSE CAME CLOSE!
ISN'T THAT AMAZING?! HE'S SO COOL!
HUH.
WHAT?!
LOOK AT HIM! HE'S GORGEOUS!
HA
IDOLS GET THE STAR TREATMENT BASED PURELY ON THEIR LOOKS.
ANY GUY WHO WOULD CHOOSE THAT PROFESSION CAN'T POSSIBLY BE COOL.

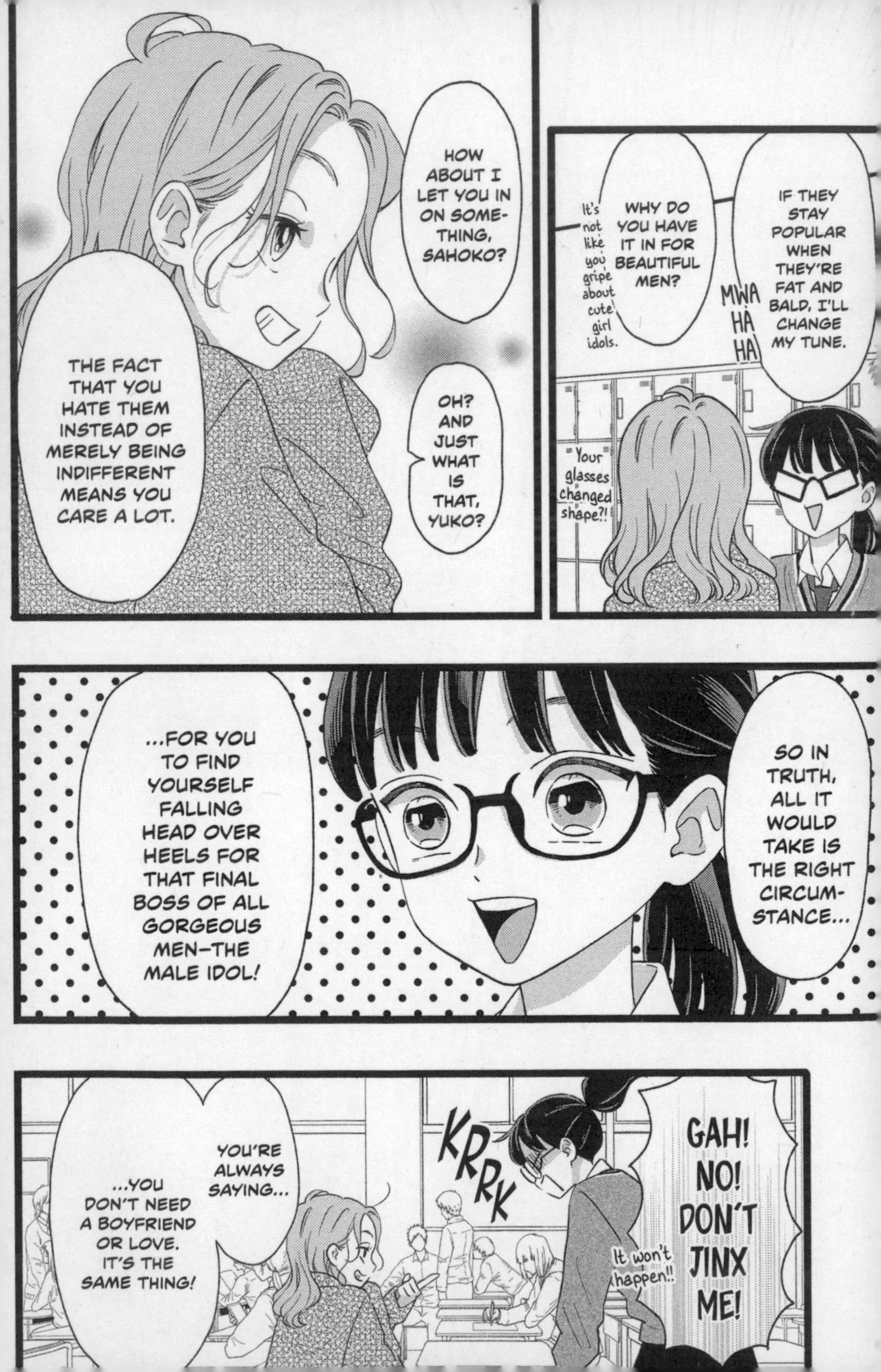
IF THEY STAY POPULAR WHEN THEY'RE FAT AND BALD, I'LL CHANGE MY TUNE.
MWA HA HA
WHY DO YOU HAVE IT IN FOR BEAUTIFUL MEN?
It's not like you gripe about cute girl idols.
Your glasses changed shape?!
HOW ABOUT I LET YOU IN ON SOME-THING, SAHOKO?
OH? AND JUST WHAT IS THAT, YUKO?
THE FACT THAT YOU HATE THEM INSTEAD OF MERELY BEING INDIFFERENT MEANS YOU CARE A LOT.
SO IN TRUTH, ALL IT WOULD TAKE IS THE RIGHT CIRCUM-STANCE...
...FOR YOU TO FIND YOURSELF FALLING HEAD OVER HEELS FOR THAT FINAL BOSS OF ALL GORGEOUS MEN—THE MALE IDOL!
GAH! NO! DON'T JINX ME!
It won't happen!!
KRRK
YOU'RE ALWAYS SAYING...
...YOU DON'T NEED A BOYFRIEND OR LOVE. IT'S THE SAME THING!

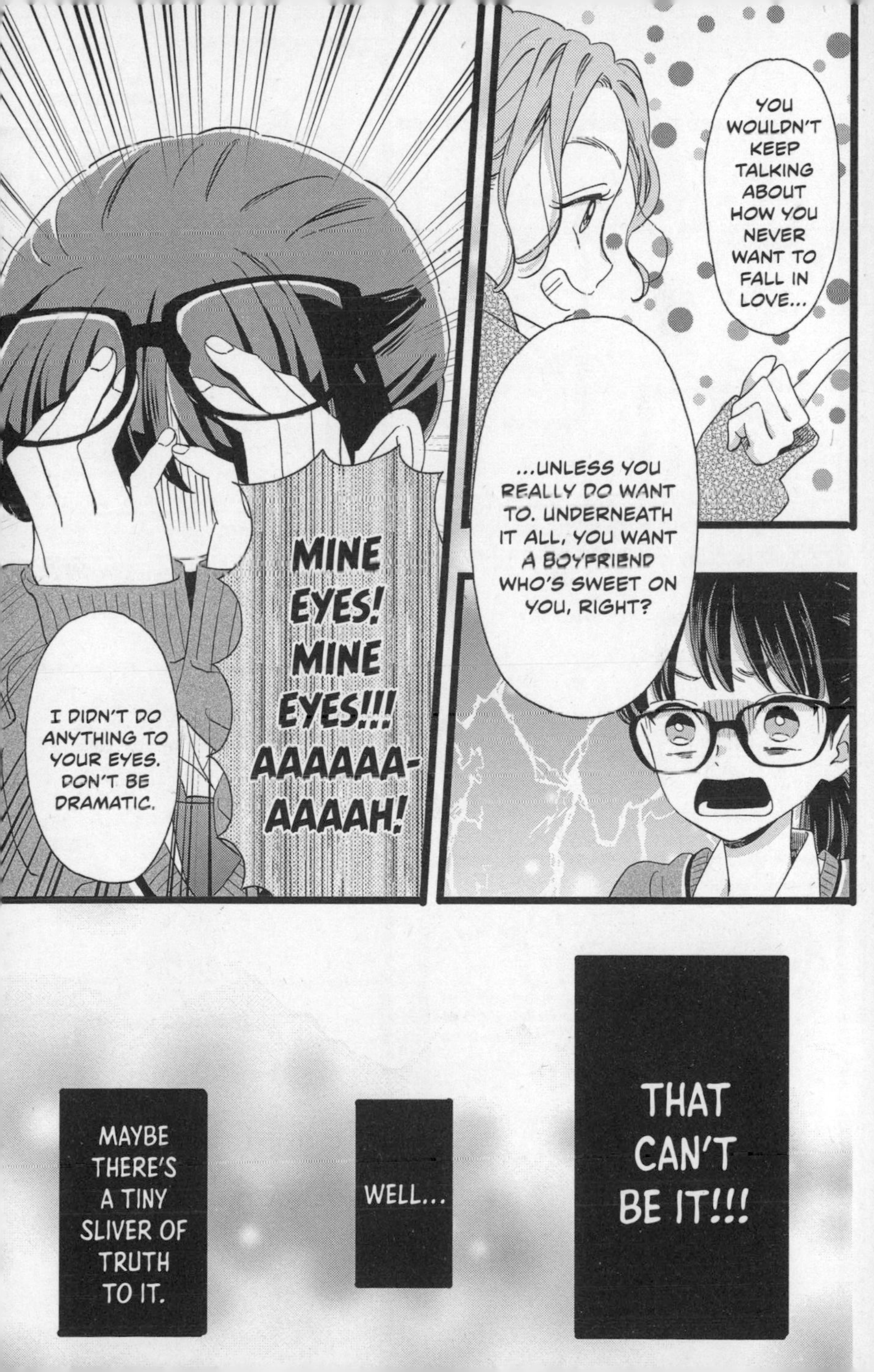

YOU WOULDN'T KEEP TALKING ABOUT HOW YOU NEVER WANT TO FALL IN LOVE...
...UNLESS YOU REALLY DO WANT TO. UNDERNEATH IT ALL, YOU WANT A BOYFRIEND WHO'S SWEET ON YOU, RIGHT?
MINE EYES! MINE EYES!!! AAAAAA-AAAAH!
I DIDN'T DO ANYTHING TO YOUR EYES. DON'T BE DRAMATIC.
THAT CAN'T BE IT!!!
WELL...
MAYBE THERE'S A TINY SLIVER OF TRUTH TO IT.

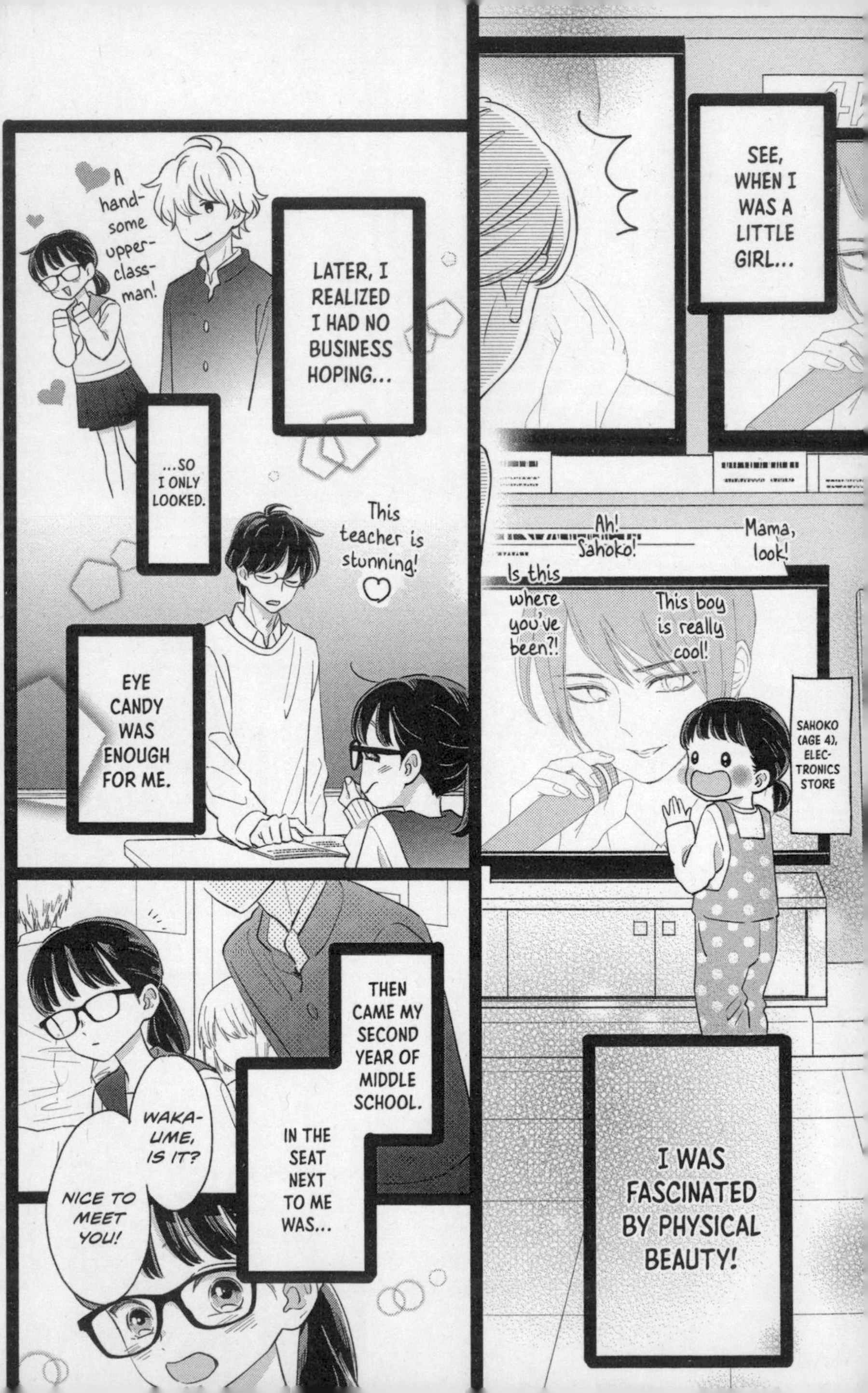
SEE, WHEN I WAS A LITTLE GIRL...
Mama, look!
This boy is really cool!
Ah! Sahoko!
Is this where you've been?!
SAHOKO (AGE 4), ELECTRONICS STORE
I WAS FASCINATED BY PHYSICAL BEAUTY!
LATER, I REALIZED I HAD NO BUSINESS HOPING...
A handsome upperclassman!
...SO I ONLY LOOKED.
This teacher is stunning!
EYE CANDY WAS ENOUGH FOR ME.
THEN CAME MY SECOND YEAR OF MIDDLE SCHOOL.
IN THE SEAT NEXT TO ME WAS...
WAKAUME, IS IT?
NICE TO MEET YOU!

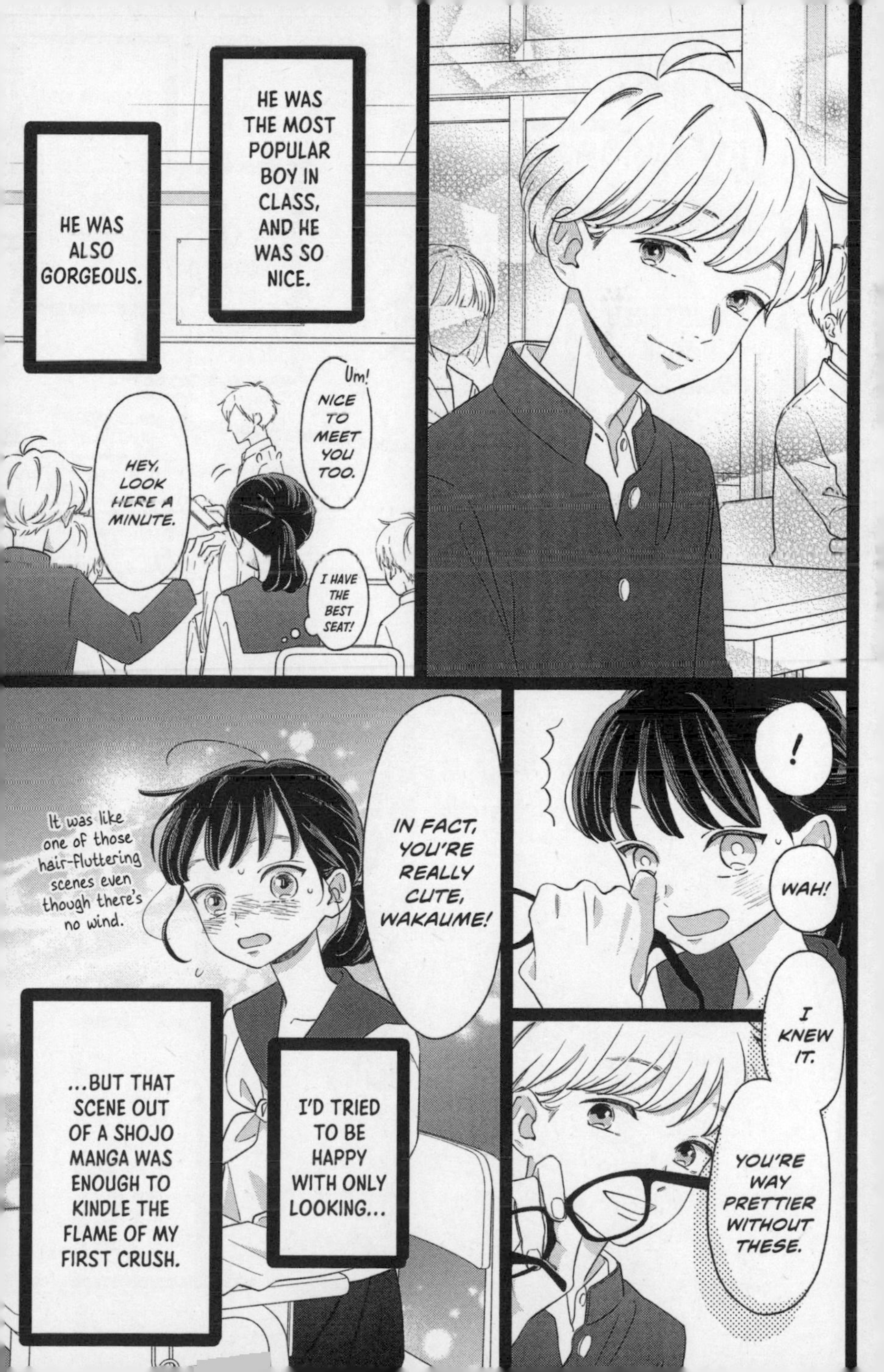
HE WAS THE MOST POPULAR BOY IN CLASS, AND HE WAS SO NICE.
HE WAS ALSO GORGEOUS.
Um! NICE TO MEET YOU TOO.
HEY, LOOK HERE A MINUTE.
I HAVE THE BEST SEAT!
!
WAH!
I KNEW IT.
YOU'RE WAY PRETTIER WITHOUT THESE.
IN FACT, YOU'RE REALLY CUTE, WAKAUME!
It was like one of those hair-fluttering scenes even though there's no wind.
I'D TRIED TO BE HAPPY WITH ONLY LOOKING...
...BUT THAT SCENE OUT OF A SHOJO MANGA WAS ENOUGH TO KINDLE THE FLAME OF MY FIRST CRUSH.

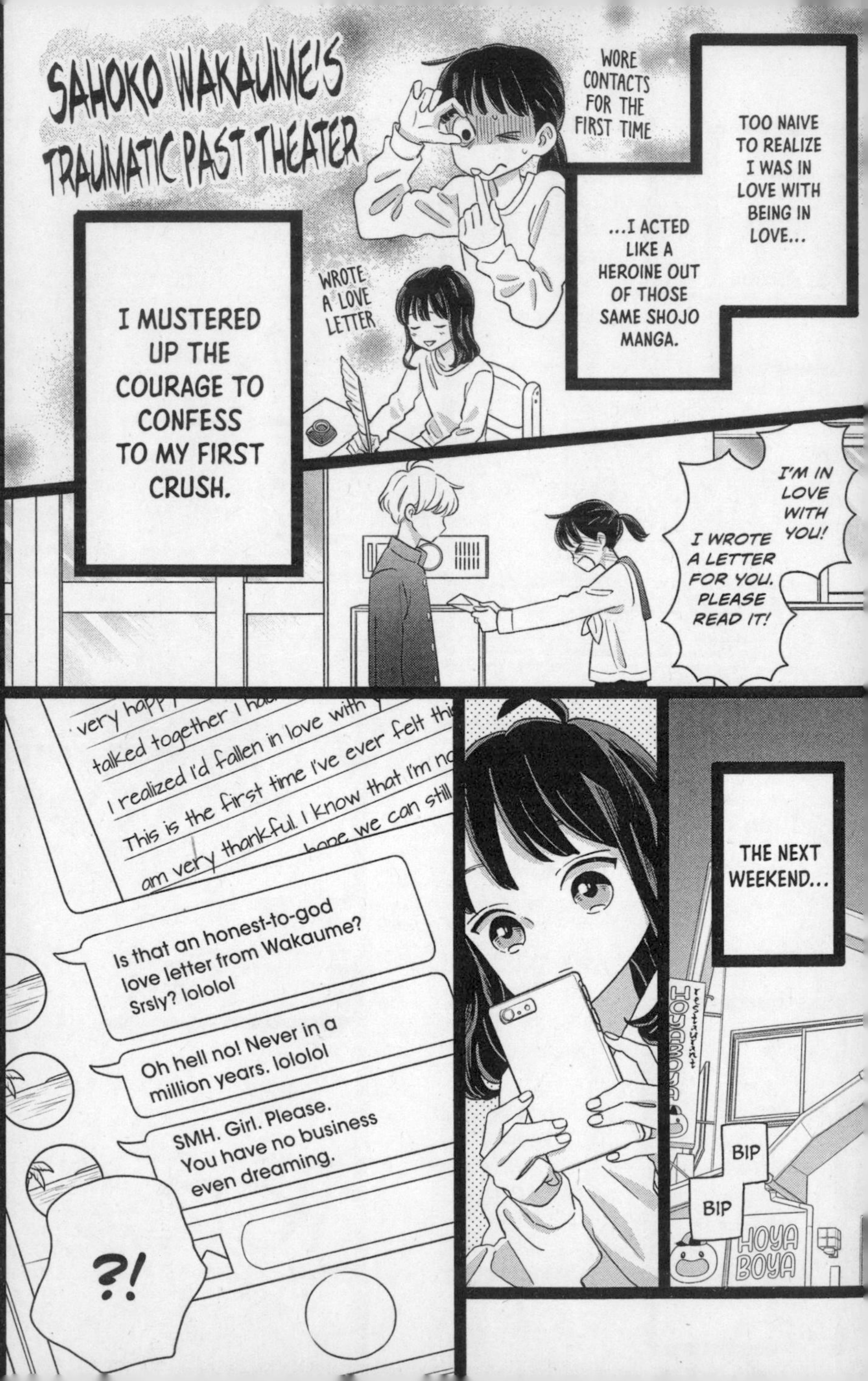
TOO NAIVE TO REALIZE I WAS IN LOVE WITH BEING IN LOVE...
...I ACTED LIKE A HEROINE OUT OF THOSE SAME SHOJO MANGA.
WORE CONTACTS FOR THE FIRST TIME
SAHOKO WAKAUME'S TRAUMATIC PAST THEATER
WROTE A LOVE LETTER
I MUSTERED UP THE COURAGE TO CONFESS TO MY FIRST CRUSH.
I'M IN LOVE WITH YOU!
I WROTE A LETTER FOR YOU. PLEASE READ IT!
THE NEXT WEEKEND...
BIP
BIP
HOYA BOYA
very
talked together
I realized I'd fallen in love with
This is the first time I've ever felt
am very thankful. I know that I'm
we can still
Is that an honest-to-god love letter from Wakaume? Srsly? lololol
Oh hell no! Never in a million years. lololol
SMH. Girl. Please. You have no business even dreaming.
?!

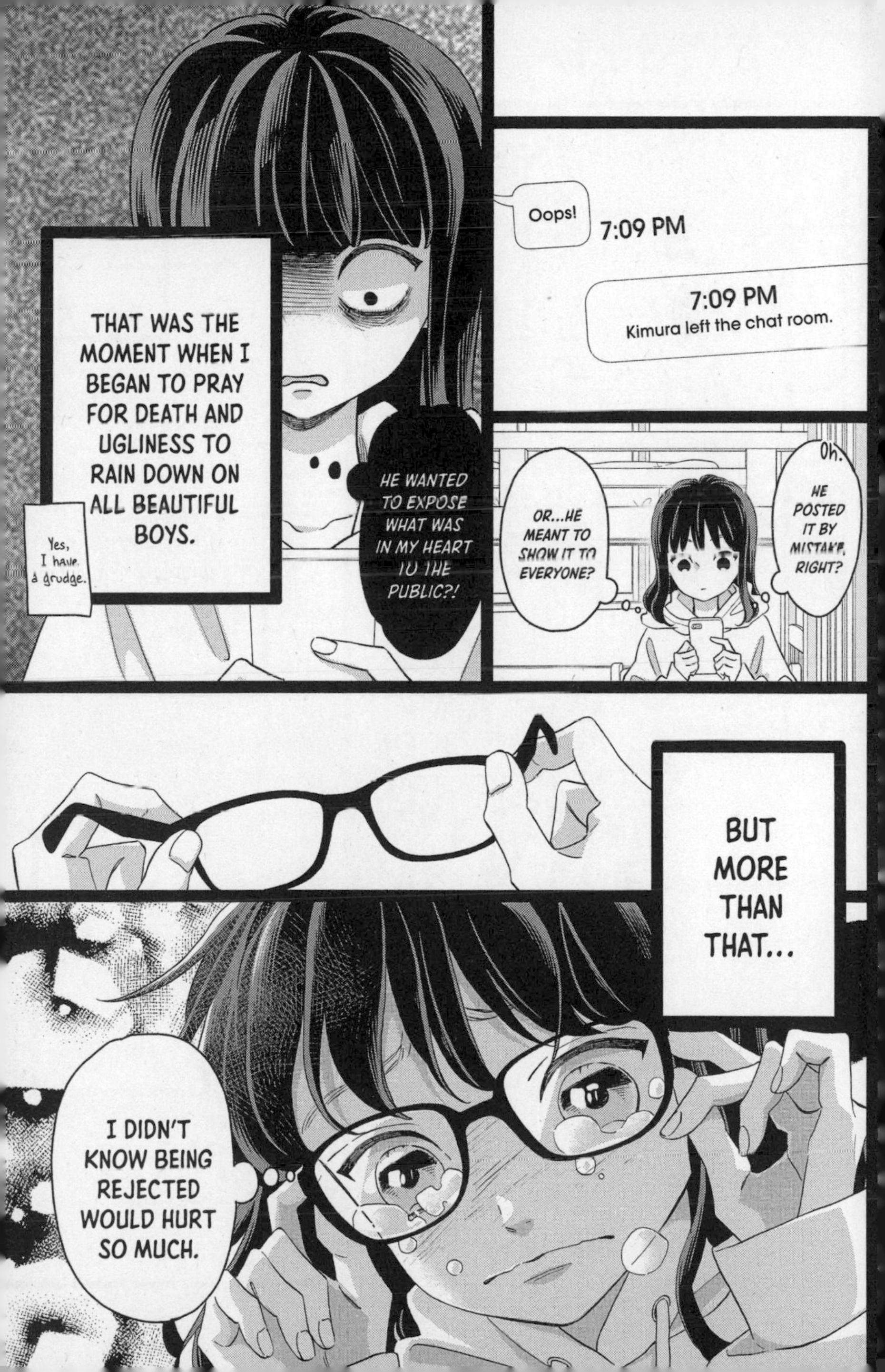
Oops!
7:09 PM
7:09 PM
Kimura left the chat room.
Oh.
HE POSTED IT BY MISTAKE, RIGHT?
OR...HE MEANT TO SHOW IT TO EVERYONE?
HE WANTED TO EXPOSE WHAT WAS IN MY HEART TO THE PUBLIC?!
THAT WAS THE MOMENT WHEN I BEGAN TO PRAY FOR DEATH AND UGLINESS TO RAIN DOWN ON ALL BEAUTIFUL BOYS.
Yes, I have a grudge.
BUT MORE THAN THAT...
I DIDN'T KNOW BEING REJECTED WOULD HURT SO MUCH.

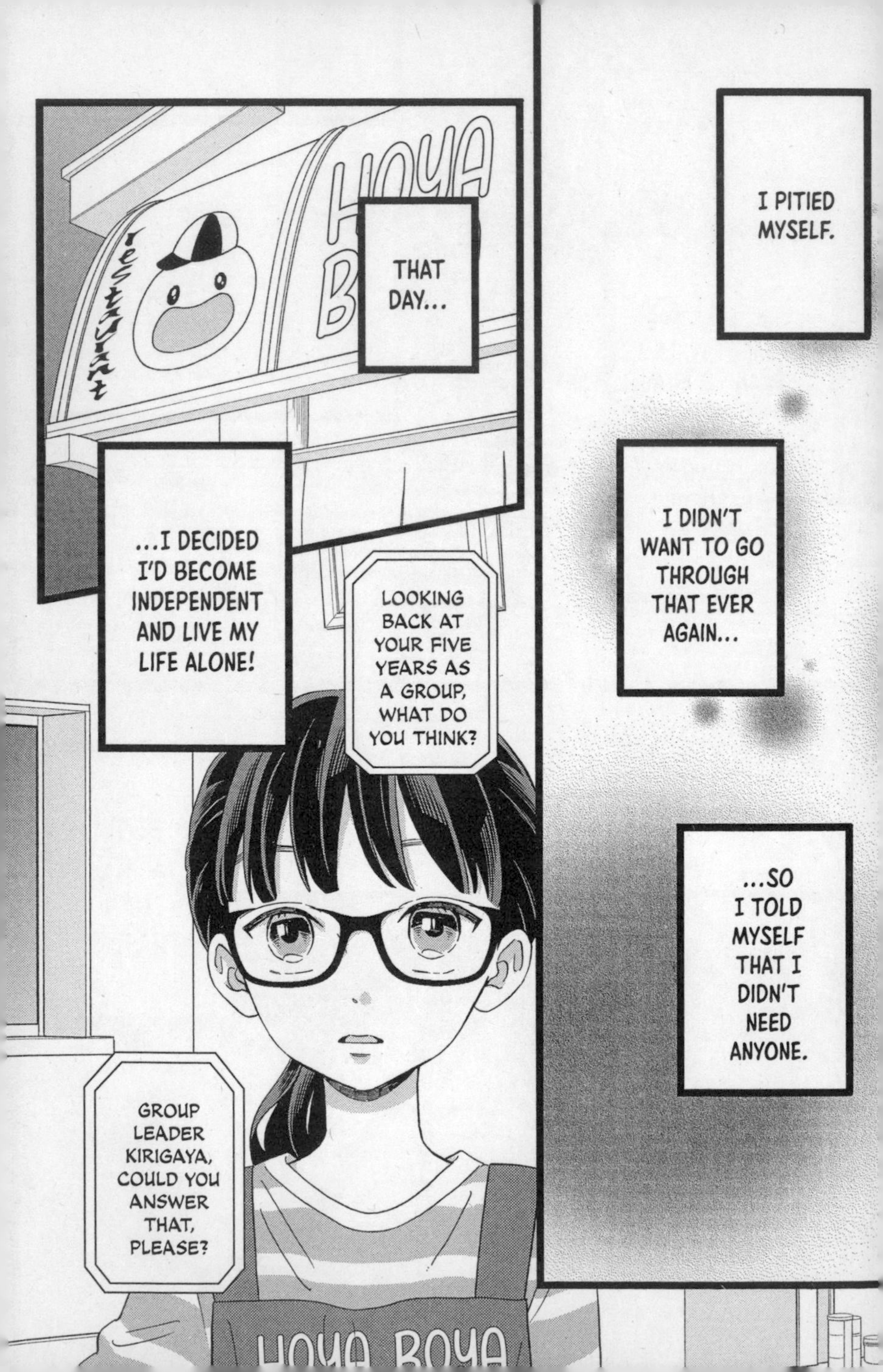
I PITIED MYSELF.
I DIDN'T WANT TO GO THROUGH THAT EVER AGAIN...
...SO I TOLD MYSELF THAT I DIDN'T NEED ANYONE.
THAT DAY...
...I DECIDED I'D BECOME INDEPENDENT AND LIVE MY LIFE ALONE!
LOOKING BACK AT YOUR FIVE YEARS AS A GROUP, WHAT DO YOU THINK?
GROUP LEADER KIRIGAYA, COULD YOU ANSWER THAT, PLEASE?
HOYA BOYA

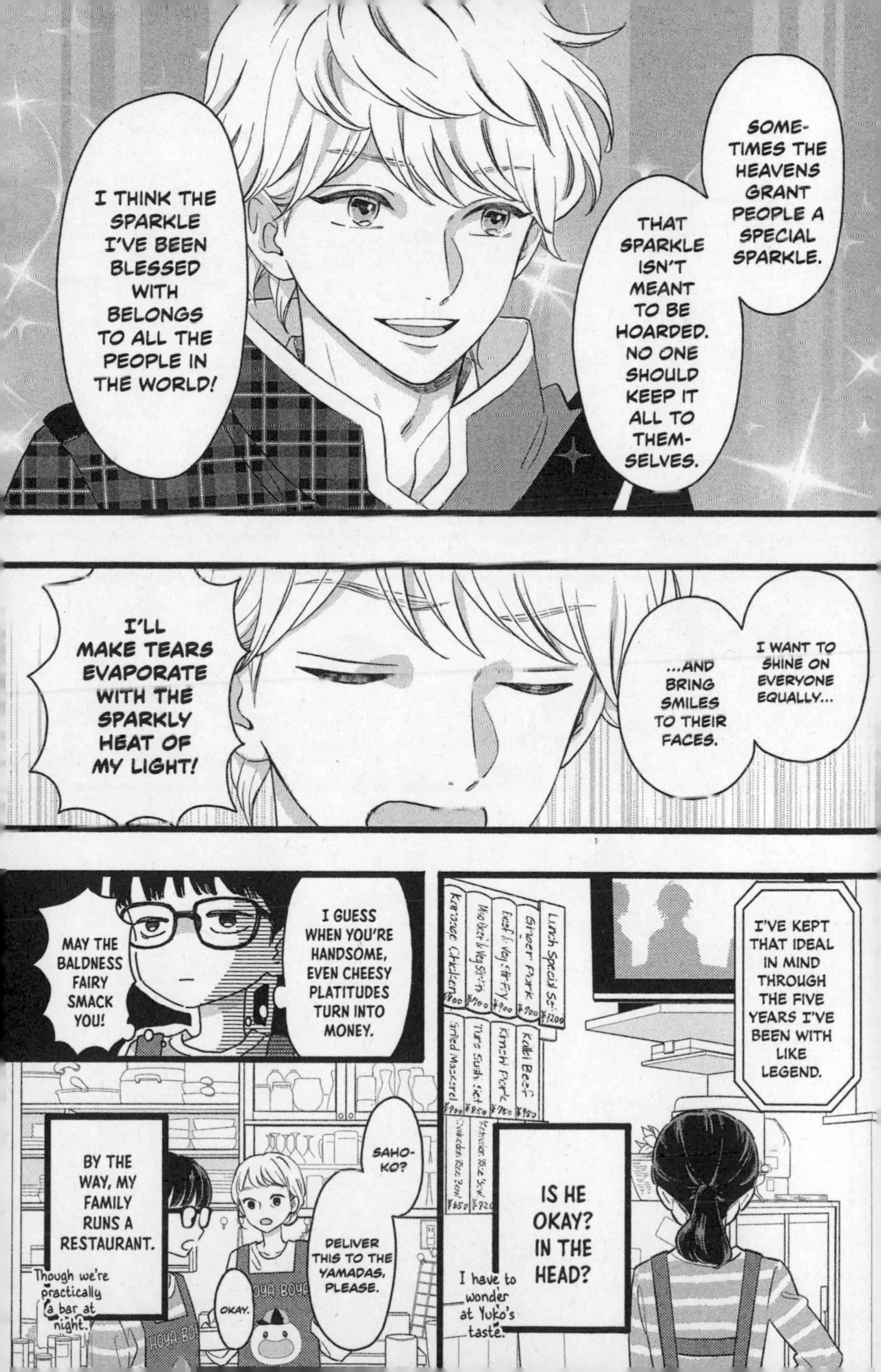
SOME-TIMES THE HEAVENS GRANT PEOPLE A SPECIAL SPARKLE.
THAT SPARKLE ISN'T MEANT TO BE HOARDED. NO ONE SHOULD KEEP IT ALL TO THEM-SELVES.
I THINK THE SPARKLE I'VE BEEN BLESSED WITH BELONGS TO ALL THE PEOPLE IN THE WORLD!
I WANT TO SHINE ON EVERYONE EQUALLY...
...AND BRING SMILES TO THEIR FACES.
I'LL MAKE TEARS EVAPORATE WITH THE SPARKLY HEAT OF MY LIGHT!
I'VE KEPT THAT IDEAL IN MIND THROUGH THE FIVE YEARS I'VE BEEN WITH LIKE LEGEND.
Ginger Pork ¥900
Kalbi Beef ¥950
Kimchi Pork ¥750
IS HE OKAY? IN THE HEAD?
I have to wonder at Yuko's taste.
I GUESS WHEN YOU'RE HANDSOME, EVEN CHEESY PLATITUDES TURN INTO MONEY.
MAY THE BALDNESS FAIRY SMACK YOU!
SAHO-KO?
BY THE WAY, MY FAMILY RUNS A RESTAURANT.
DELIVER THIS TO THE YAMADAS, PLEASE.
Though we're practically a bar at night.
OKAY.

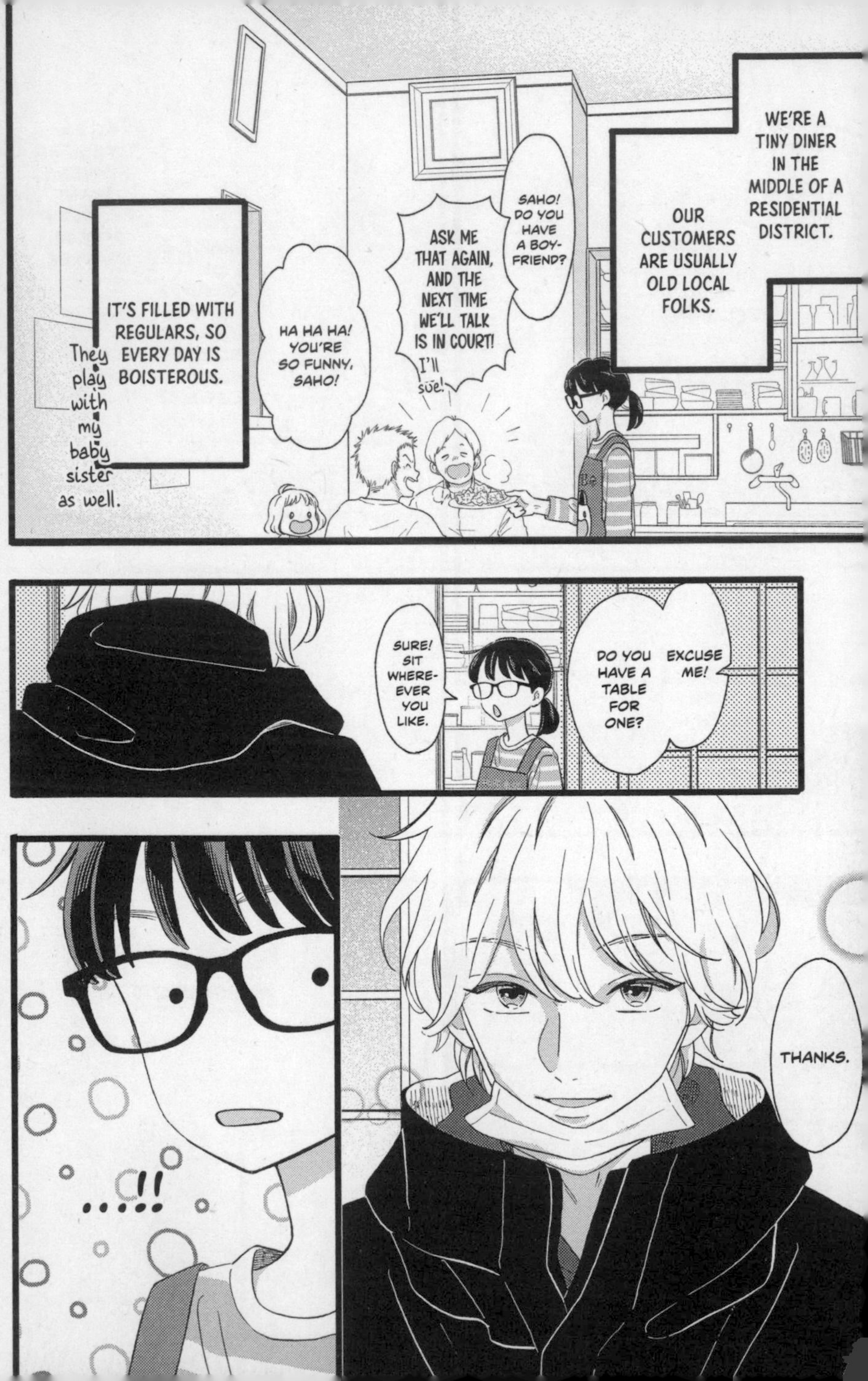
WE'RE A TINY DINER IN THE MIDDLE OF A RESIDENTIAL DISTRICT.
OUR CUSTOMERS ARE USUALLY OLD LOCAL FOLKS.
SAHO! DO YOU HAVE A BOY-FRIEND?
ASK ME THAT AGAIN, AND THE NEXT TIME WE'LL TALK IS IN COURT!
I'll sue!
HA HA HA! YOU'RE SO FUNNY, SAHO!
IT'S FILLED WITH REGULARS, SO EVERY DAY IS BOISTEROUS.
They play with my baby sister as well.
EXCUSE ME!
DO YOU HAVE A TABLE FOR ONE?
SURE! SIT WHERE-EVER YOU LIKE.
THANKS.
...!!

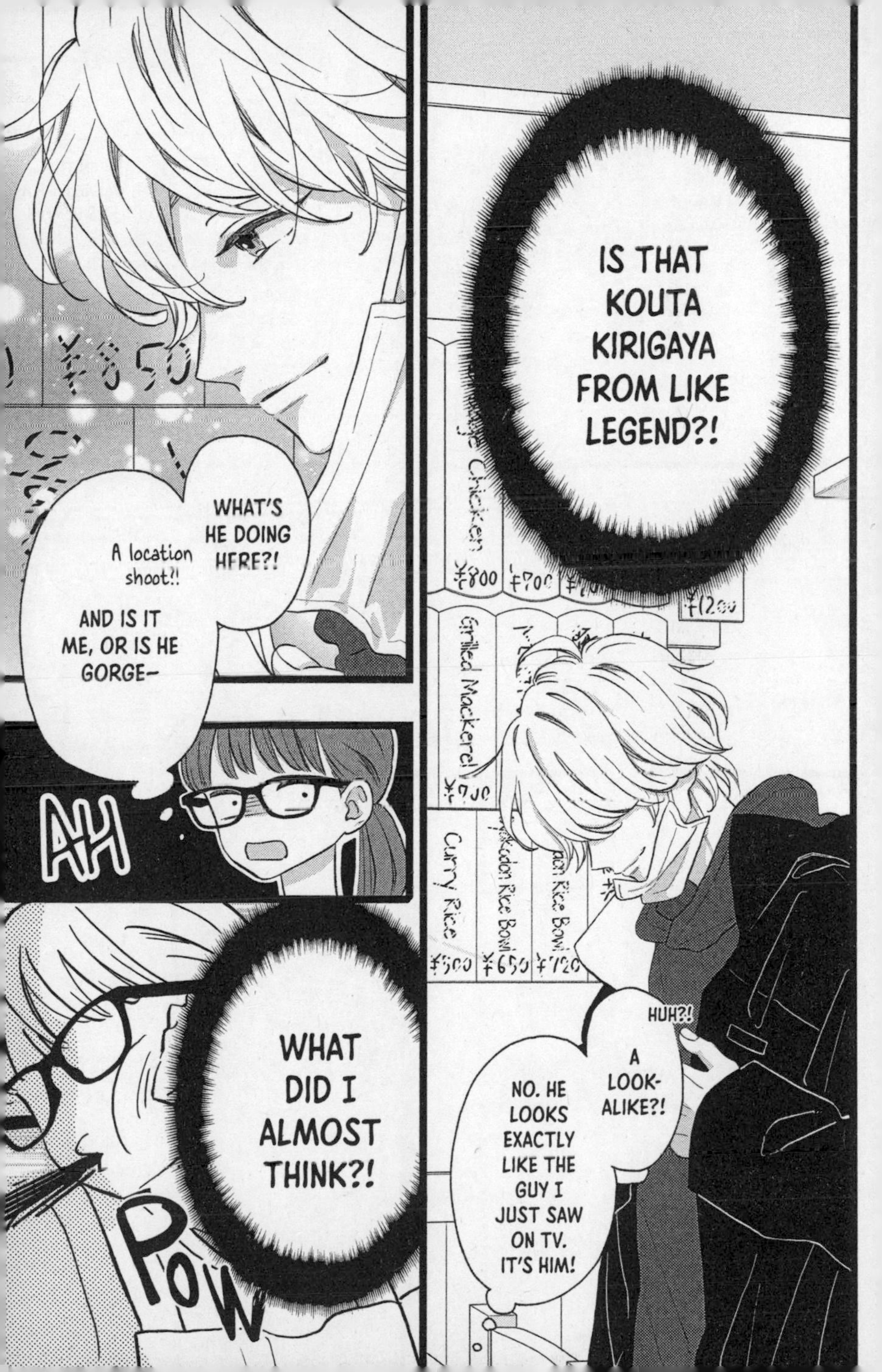
IS THAT KOUTA KIRIGAYA FROM LIKE LEGEND?!
¥800
Grilled Mackerel
Curry Rice
¥500
¥650
¥720
HUH?!
A LOOK-ALIKE?!
NO. HE LOOKS EXACTLY LIKE THE GUY I JUST SAW ON TV. IT'S HIM!
¥850
WHAT'S HE DOING HERE?!
A location shoot?!
AND IS IT ME, OR IS HE GORGE–
AH
WHAT DID I ALMOST THINK?!
POW

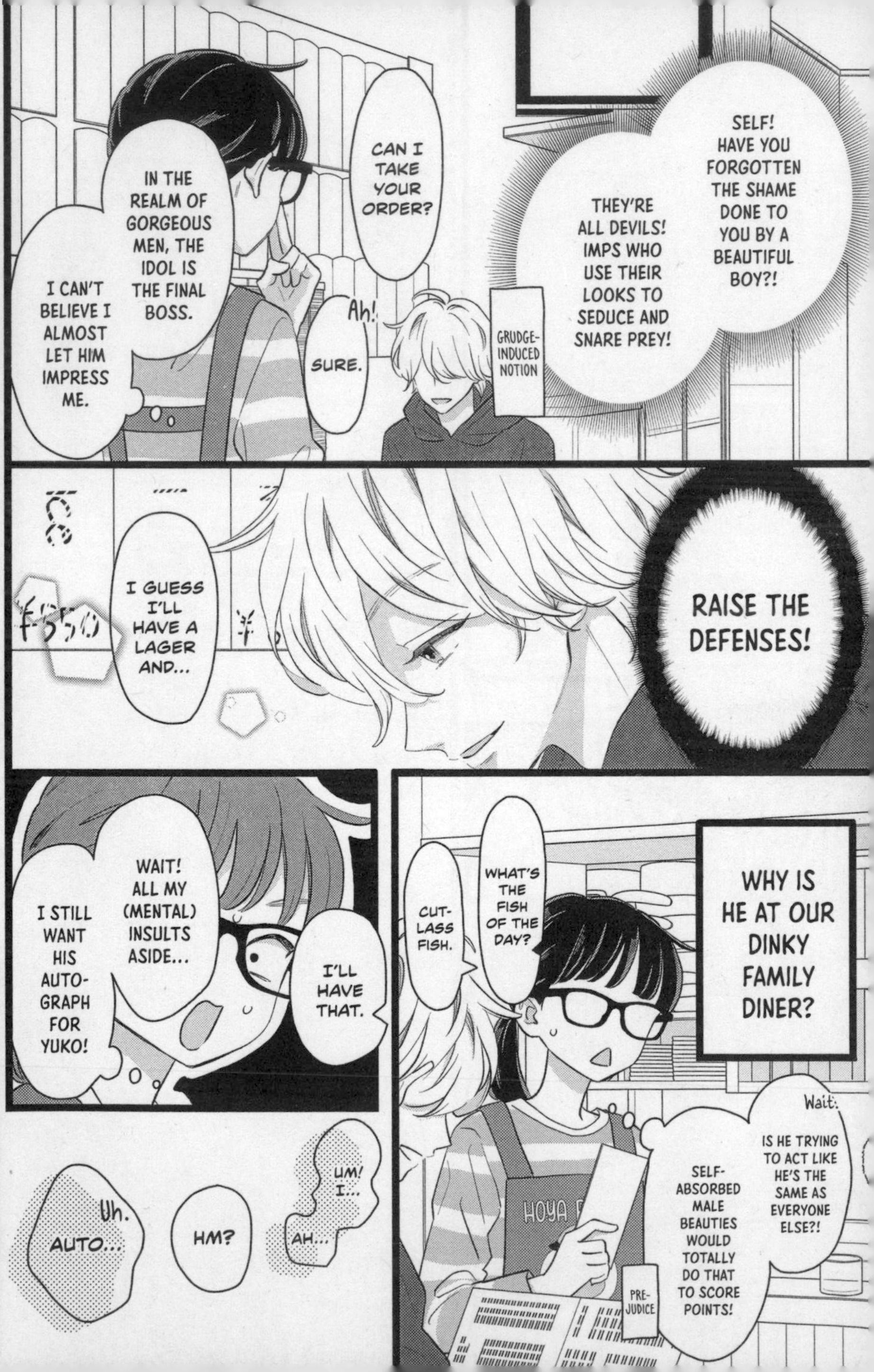
SELF! HAVE YOU FORGOTTEN THE SHAME DONE TO YOU BY A BEAUTIFUL BOY?!
THEY'RE ALL DEVILS! IMPS WHO USE THEIR LOOKS TO SEDUCE AND SNARE PREY!
GRUDGE-INDUCED NOTION
CAN I TAKE YOUR ORDER?
Ah!
SURE.
IN THE REALM OF GORGEOUS MEN, THE IDOL IS THE FINAL BOSS.
I CAN'T BELIEVE I ALMOST LET HIM IMPRESS ME.
RAISE THE DEFENSES!
I GUESS I'LL HAVE A LAGER AND...
WHY IS HE AT OUR DINKY FAMILY DINER?
WHAT'S THE FISH OF THE DAY?
CUT-LASS FISH.
Wait.
IS HE TRYING TO ACT LIKE HE'S THE SAME AS EVERYONE ELSE?!
SELF-ABSORBED MALE BEAUTIES WOULD TOTALLY DO THAT TO SCORE POINTS!
PRE-JUDICE
HOYA
I'LL HAVE THAT.
WAIT! ALL MY (MENTAL) INSULTS ASIDE...
I STILL WANT HIS AUTO-GRAPH FOR YUKO!
UM! I...
AH...
HM?
Uh.
AUTO...

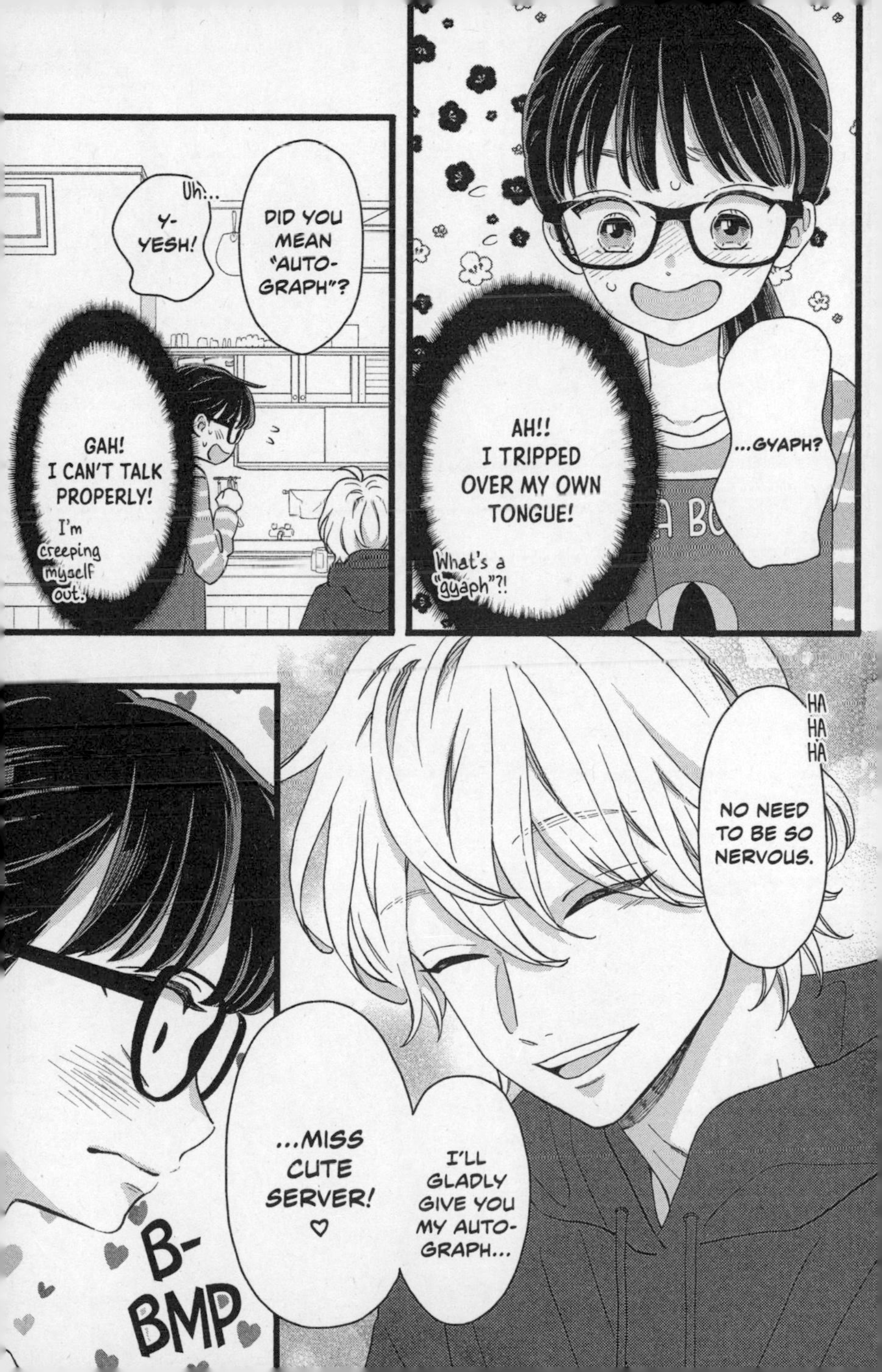
...GYAPH?
AH!! I TRIPPED OVER MY OWN TONGUE!
What's a "gyaph"?!
DID YOU MEAN "AUTO-GRAPH"?
Uh...
Y-YESH!
GAH! I CAN'T TALK PROPERLY!
I'm creeping myself out.
HA HA HA
NO NEED TO BE SO NERVOUS.
I'LL GLADLY GIVE YOU MY AUTO-GRAPH...
...MISS CUTE SERVER! ♡
B-BMP

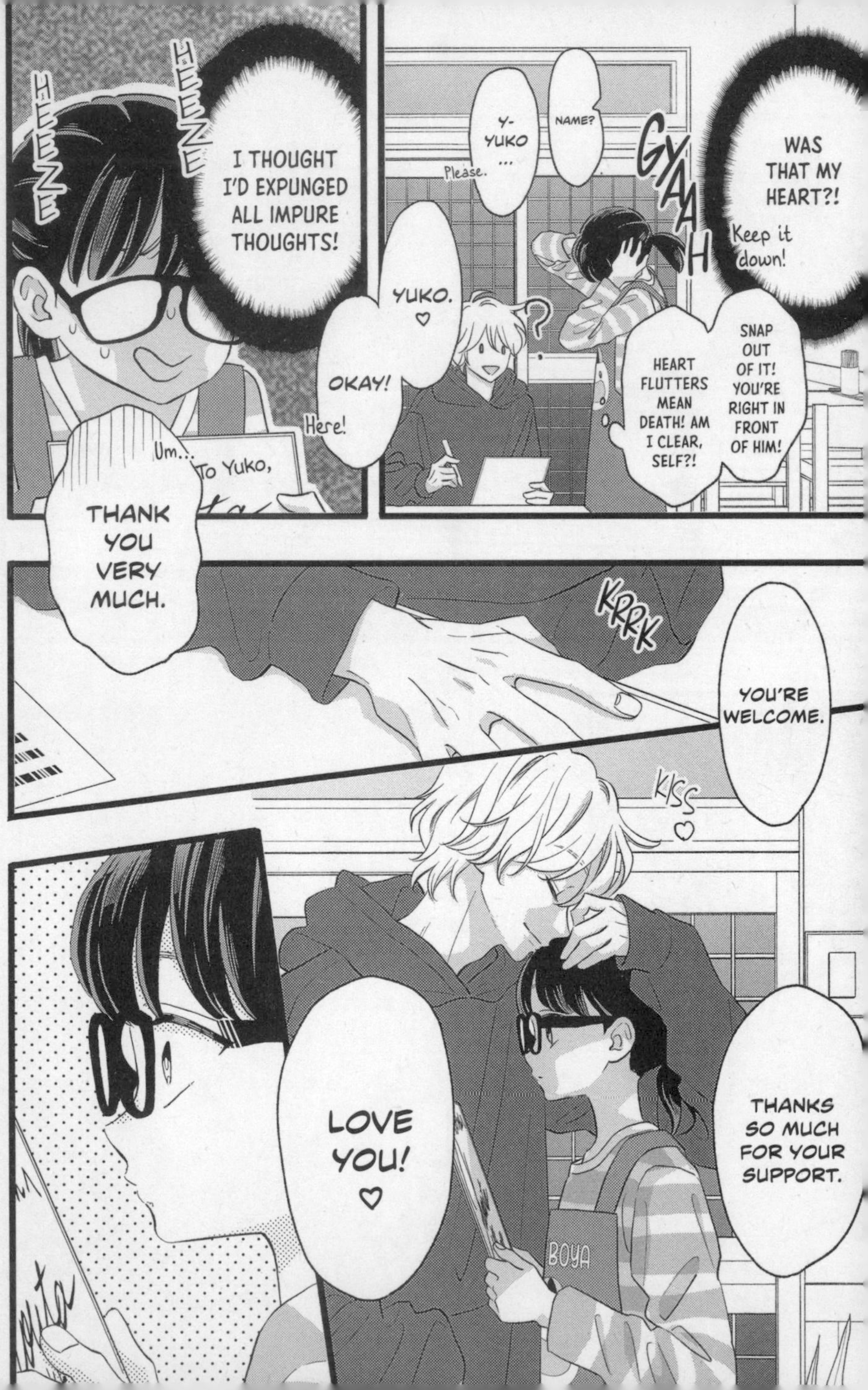
WAS THAT MY HEART?!
Keep it down!
GYAAAH
NAME?
Y-YUKO...
Please.
SNAP OUT OF IT! YOU'RE RIGHT IN FRONT OF HIM!
HEART FLUTTERS MEAN DEATH! AM I CLEAR, SELF?!
YUKO. ♡
OKAY!
Here!
I THOUGHT I'D EXPUNGED ALL IMPURE THOUGHTS!
HEEZE
HEEZE
Um...
To Yuko,
THANK YOU VERY MUCH.
KRRK
YOU'RE WELCOME.
KISS ♡
THANKS SO MUCH FOR YOUR SUPPORT.
LOVE YOU! ♡
BOYA

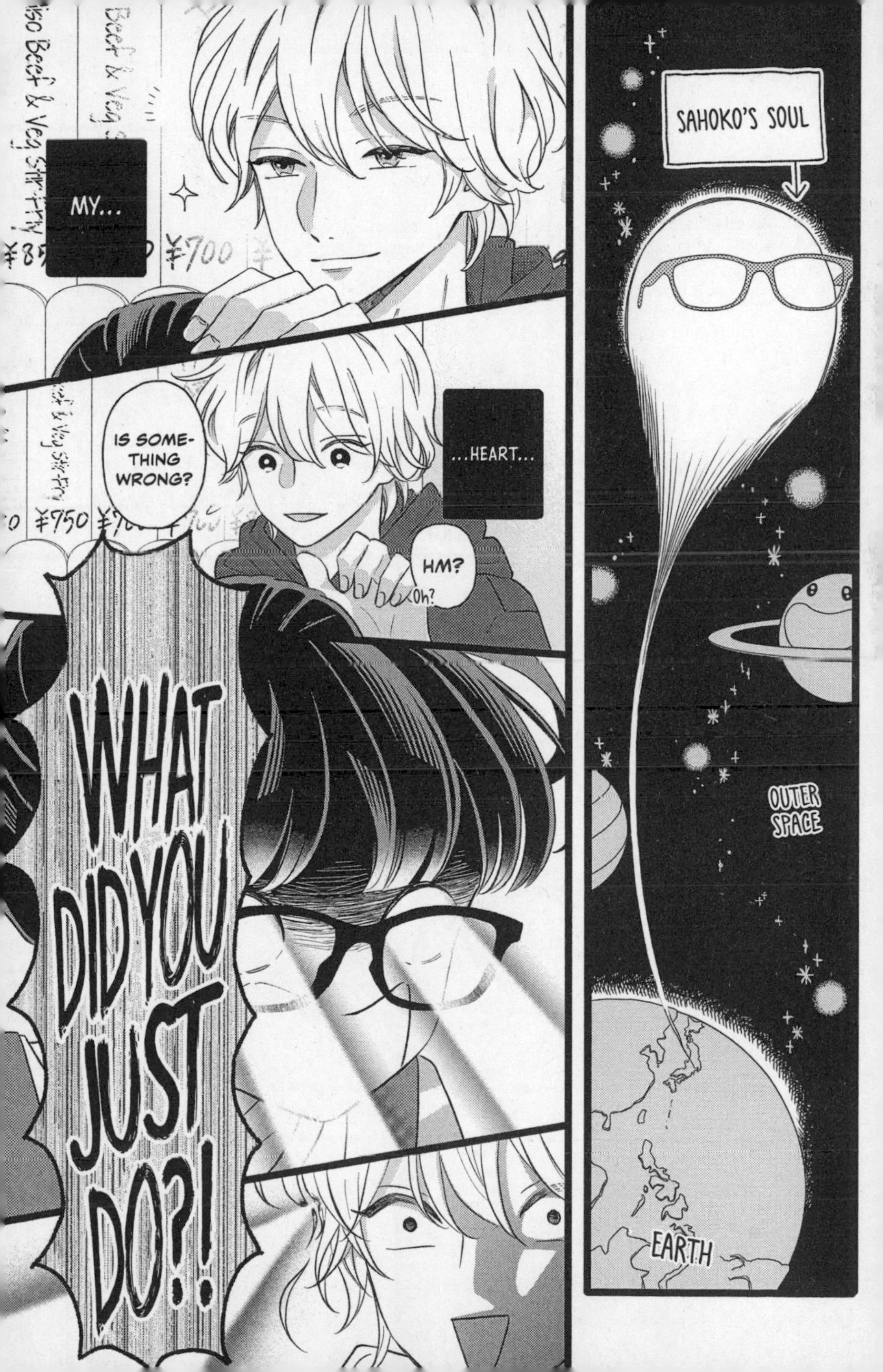
SAHOKO'S SOUL
OUTER SPACE
EARTH
MY...
...HEART...
HM?
Oh?
IS SOME-THING WRONG?
WHAT DID YOU JUST DO?!

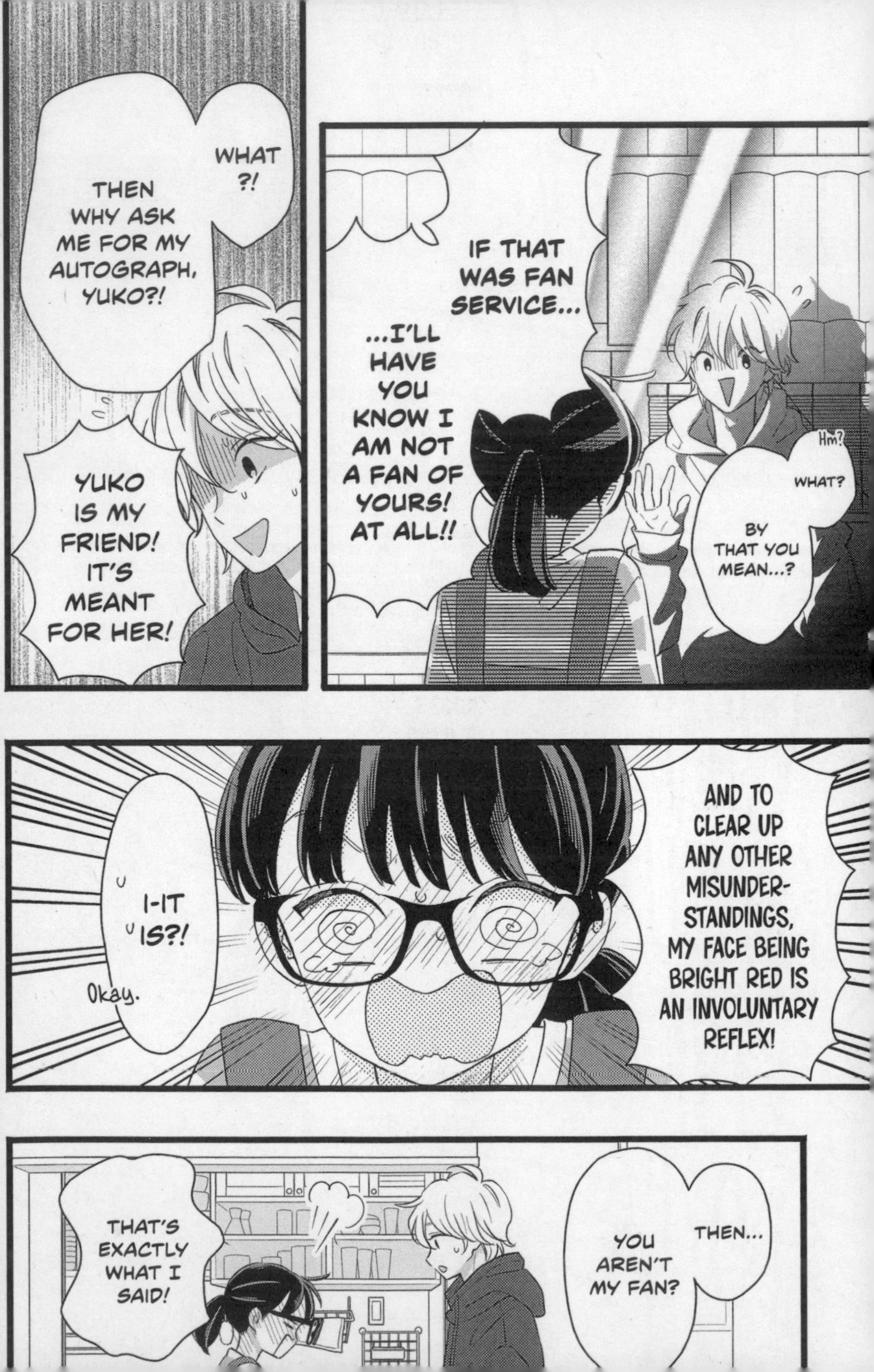
IF THAT WAS FAN SERVICE...
...I'LL HAVE YOU KNOW I AM NOT A FAN OF YOURS! AT ALL!!
Hm?
WHAT?
BY THAT YOU MEAN...?
WHAT?!
THEN WHY ASK ME FOR MY AUTOGRAPH, YUKO?!
YUKO IS MY FRIEND! IT'S MEANT FOR HER!
AND TO CLEAR UP ANY OTHER MISUNDER-STANDINGS, MY FACE BEING BRIGHT RED IS AN INVOLUNTARY REFLEX!
I-IT IS?!
Okay.
THEN...
YOU AREN'T MY FAN?
THAT'S EXACTLY WHAT I SAID!

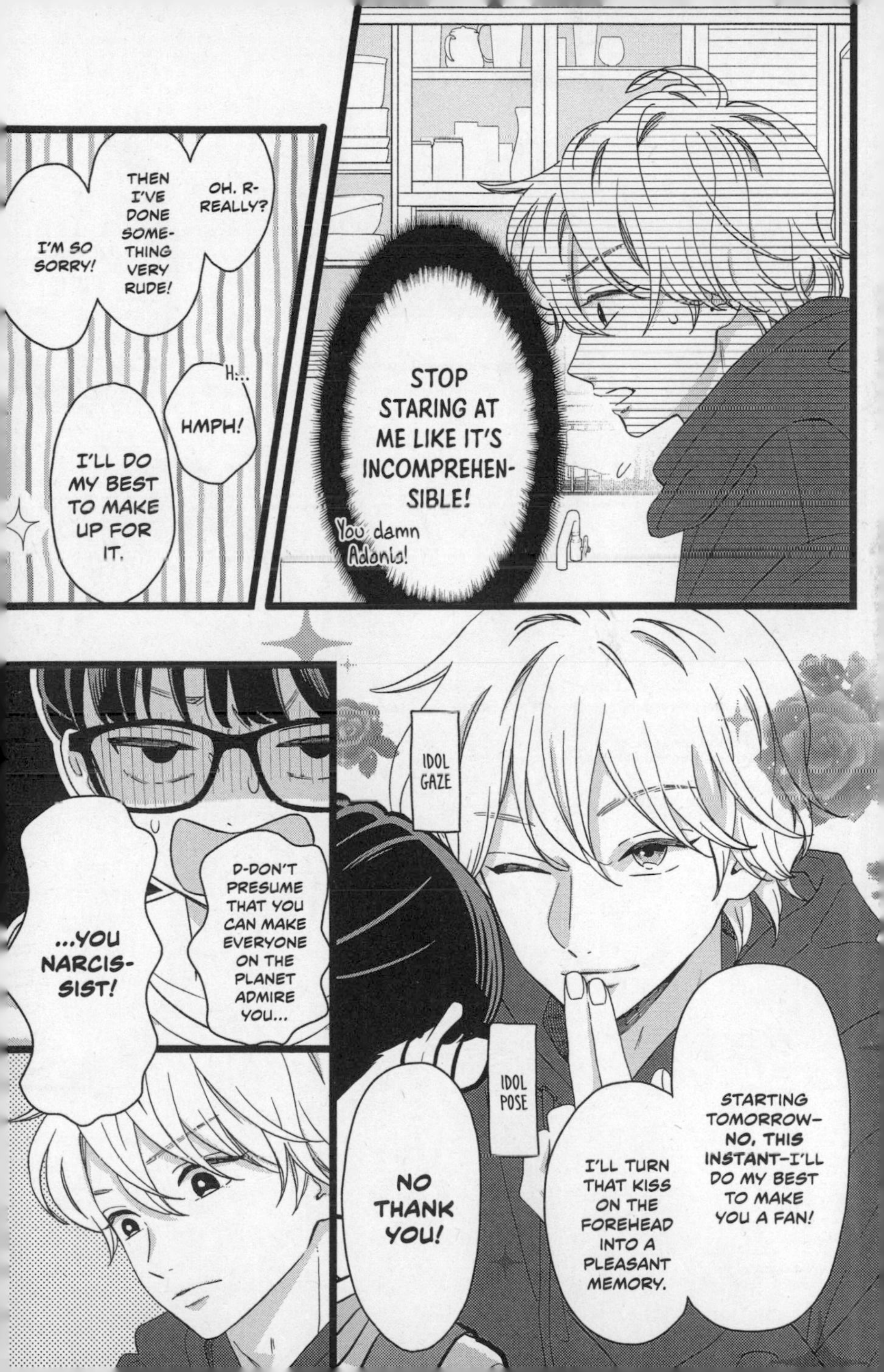
STOP STARING AT ME LIKE IT'S INCOMPREHENSIBLE!
You damn Adonis!
OH. R-REALLY?
THEN I'VE DONE SOMETHING VERY RUDE!
I'M SO SORRY!
H...
HMPH!
I'LL DO MY BEST TO MAKE UP FOR IT.
IDOL GAZE
STARTING TOMORROW—NO, THIS INSTANT—I'LL DO MY BEST TO MAKE YOU A FAN!
I'LL TURN THAT KISS ON THE FOREHEAD INTO A PLEASANT MEMORY.
IDOL POSE
NO THANK YOU!
D-DON'T PRESUME THAT YOU CAN MAKE EVERYONE ON THE PLANET ADMIRE YOU...
...YOU NARCISSIST!

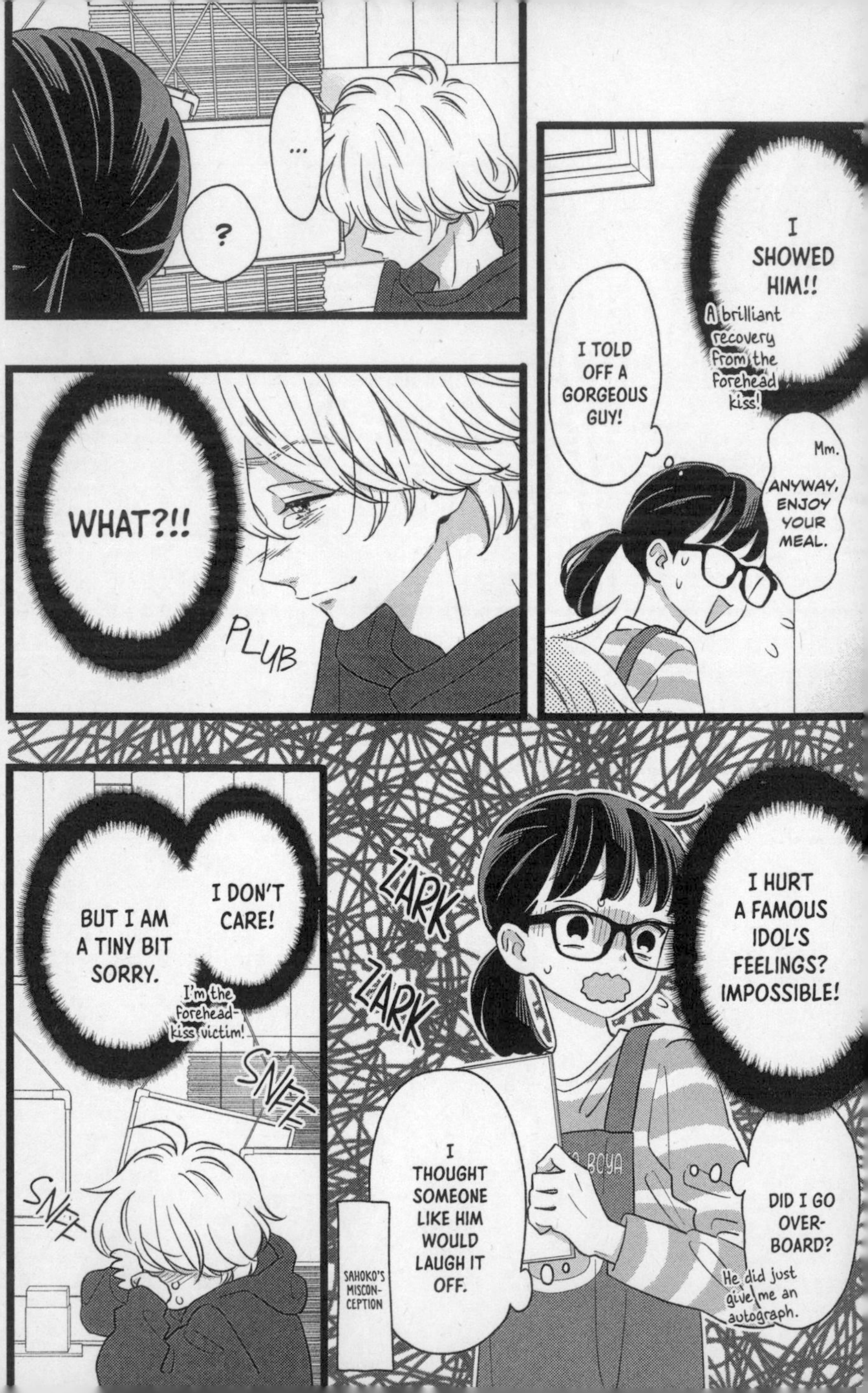
I SHOWED HIM!!
A brilliant recovery from the forehead kiss!
I TOLD OFF A GORGEOUS GUY!
Mm.
ANYWAY, ENJOY YOUR MEAL.
...
?
WHAT?!!
PLUB
I HURT A FAMOUS IDOL'S FEELINGS? IMPOSSIBLE!
ZARK
ZARK
DID I GO OVER-BOARD?
He did just give me an autograph.
I THOUGHT SOMEONE LIKE HIM WOULD LAUGH IT OFF.
SAHOKO'S MISCON-CEPTION
I DON'T CARE!
BUT I AM A TINY BIT SORRY.
I'm the forehead-kiss victim!
SNFF
SNFF

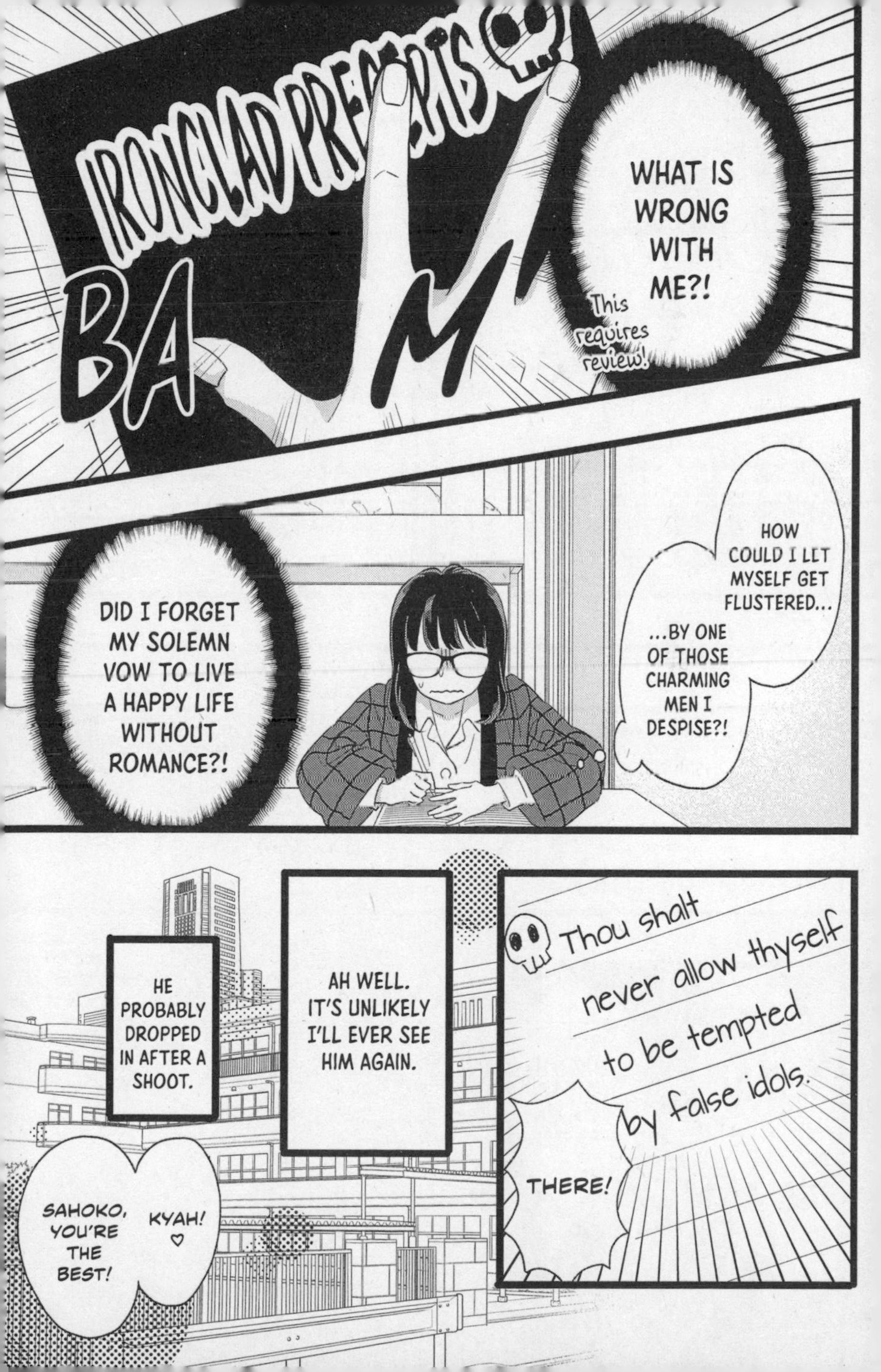
WHAT IS WRONG WITH ME?!
This requires review!
IRONCLAD PRECEPTS
BAM
HOW COULD I LET MYSELF GET FLUSTERED...
...BY ONE OF THOSE CHARMING MEN I DESPISE?!
DID I FORGET MY SOLEMN VOW TO LIVE A HAPPY LIFE WITHOUT ROMANCE?!
Thou shalt never allow thyself to be tempted by false idols.
THERE!
AH WELL. IT'S UNLIKELY I'LL EVER SEE HIM AGAIN.
HE PROBABLY DROPPED IN AFTER A SHOOT.
KYAH! ♡
SAHOKO, YOU'RE THE BEST!

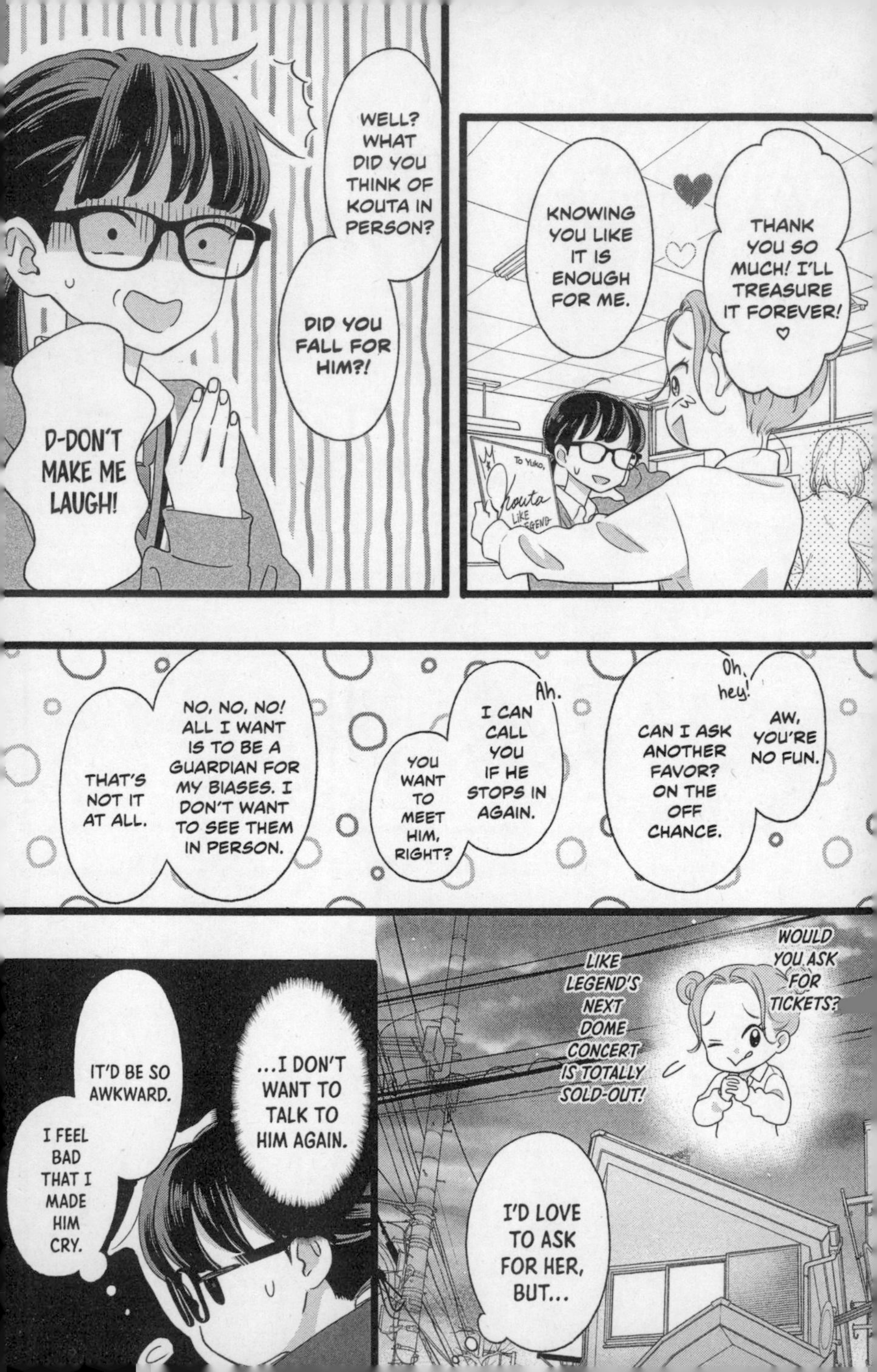
THANK YOU SO MUCH! I'LL TREASURE IT FOREVER! ♡
KNOWING YOU LIKE IT IS ENOUGH FOR ME.
To Yuko, Kouta LIKE LEGEND
WELL? WHAT DID YOU THINK OF KOUTA IN PERSON?
DID YOU FALL FOR HIM?!
D-DON'T MAKE ME LAUGH!
Oh, hey!
AW, YOU'RE NO FUN.
CAN I ASK ANOTHER FAVOR? ON THE OFF CHANCE.
Ah.
I CAN CALL YOU IF HE STOPS IN AGAIN.
YOU WANT TO MEET HIM, RIGHT?
NO, NO, NO! ALL I WANT IS TO BE A GUARDIAN FOR MY BIASES. I DON'T WANT TO SEE THEM IN PERSON.
THAT'S NOT IT AT ALL.
WOULD YOU ASK FOR TICKETS?
LIKE LEGEND'S NEXT DOME CONCERT IS TOTALLY SOLD-OUT!
I'D LOVE TO ASK FOR HER, BUT...
...I DON'T WANT TO TALK TO HIM AGAIN.
IT'D BE SO AWKWARD.
I FEEL BAD THAT I MADE HIM CRY.

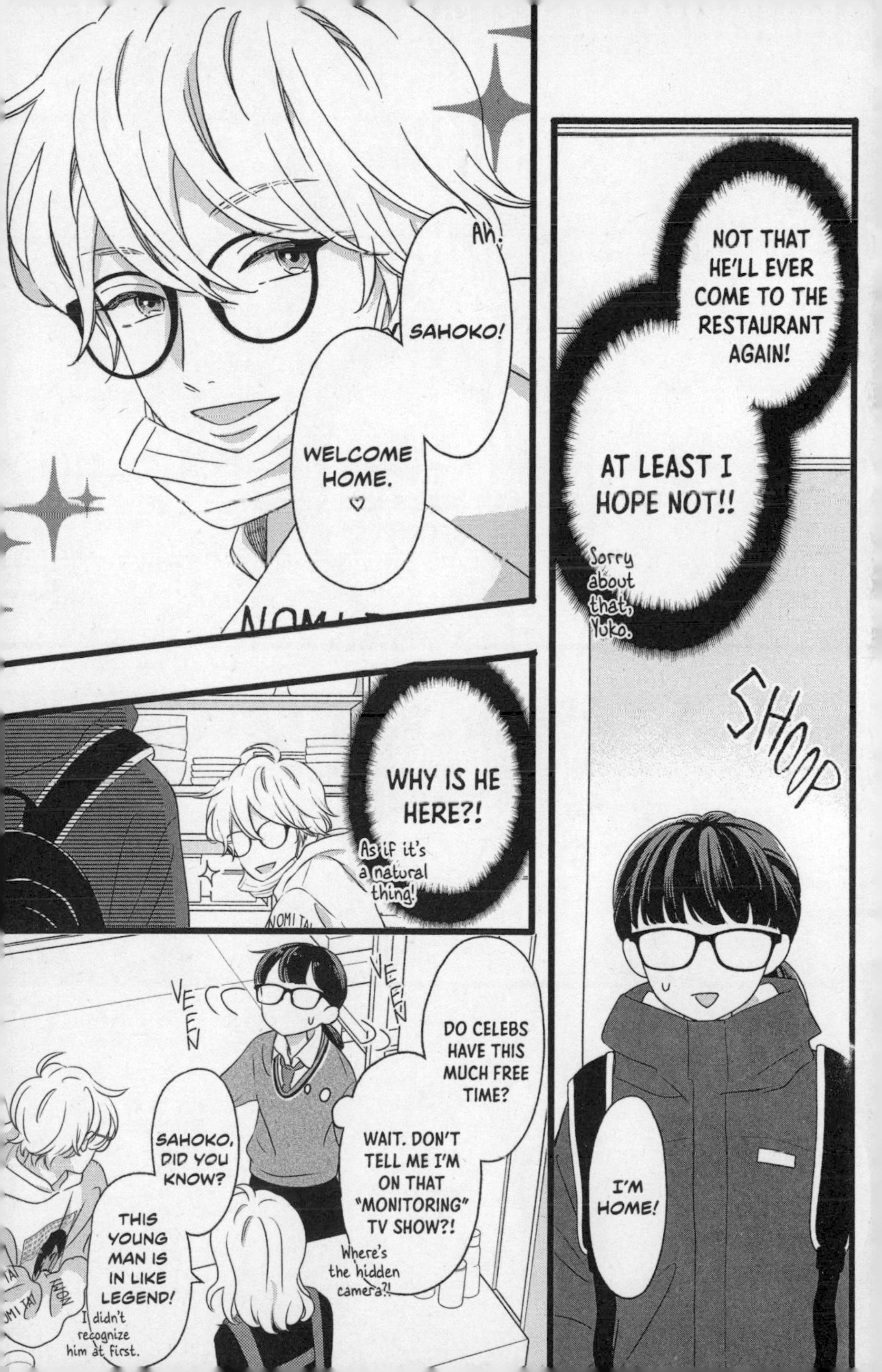
NOT THAT HE'LL EVER COME TO THE RESTAURANT AGAIN!
AT LEAST I HOPE NOT!!
Sorry about that, Yuko.
SHOOP
I'M HOME!
Ah.
SAHOKO!
WELCOME HOME. ♡
WHY IS HE HERE?!
As if it's a natural thing!
NOMI TAI
DO CELEBS HAVE THIS MUCH FREE TIME?
VEEN
VEEN
WAIT. DON'T TELL ME I'M ON THAT "MONITORING" TV SHOW?!
Where's the hidden camera?!
SAHOKO, DID YOU KNOW?
THIS YOUNG MAN IS IN LIKE LEGEND!
I didn't recognize him at first.

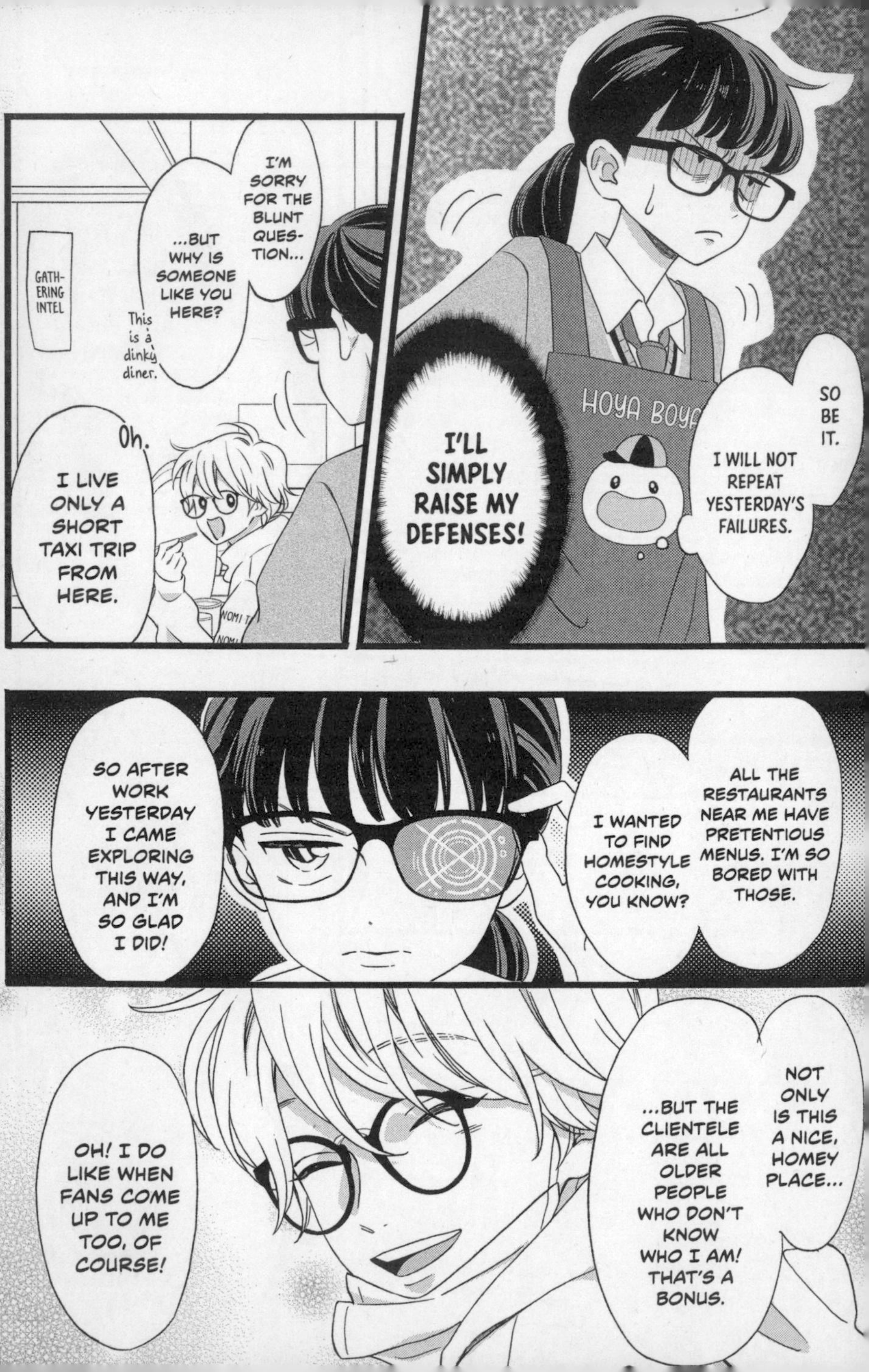

SO BE IT.
I WILL NOT REPEAT YESTERDAY'S FAILURES.
I'LL SIMPLY RAISE MY DEFENSES!
HOYA BOYA
I'M SORRY FOR THE BLUNT QUES-TION...
...BUT WHY IS SOMEONE LIKE YOU HERE?
This is a dinky diner.
GATH-ERING INTEL
Oh.
I LIVE ONLY A SHORT TAXI TRIP FROM HERE.
ALL THE RESTAURANTS NEAR ME HAVE PRETENTIOUS MENUS. I'M SO BORED WITH THOSE.
I WANTED TO FIND HOMESTYLE COOKING, YOU KNOW?
SO AFTER WORK YESTERDAY I CAME EXPLORING THIS WAY, AND I'M SO GLAD I DID!
NOT ONLY IS THIS A NICE, HOMEY PLACE...
...BUT THE CLIENTELE ARE ALL OLDER PEOPLE WHO DON'T KNOW WHO I AM! THAT'S A BONUS.
OH! I DO LIKE WHEN FANS COME UP TO ME TOO, OF COURSE!

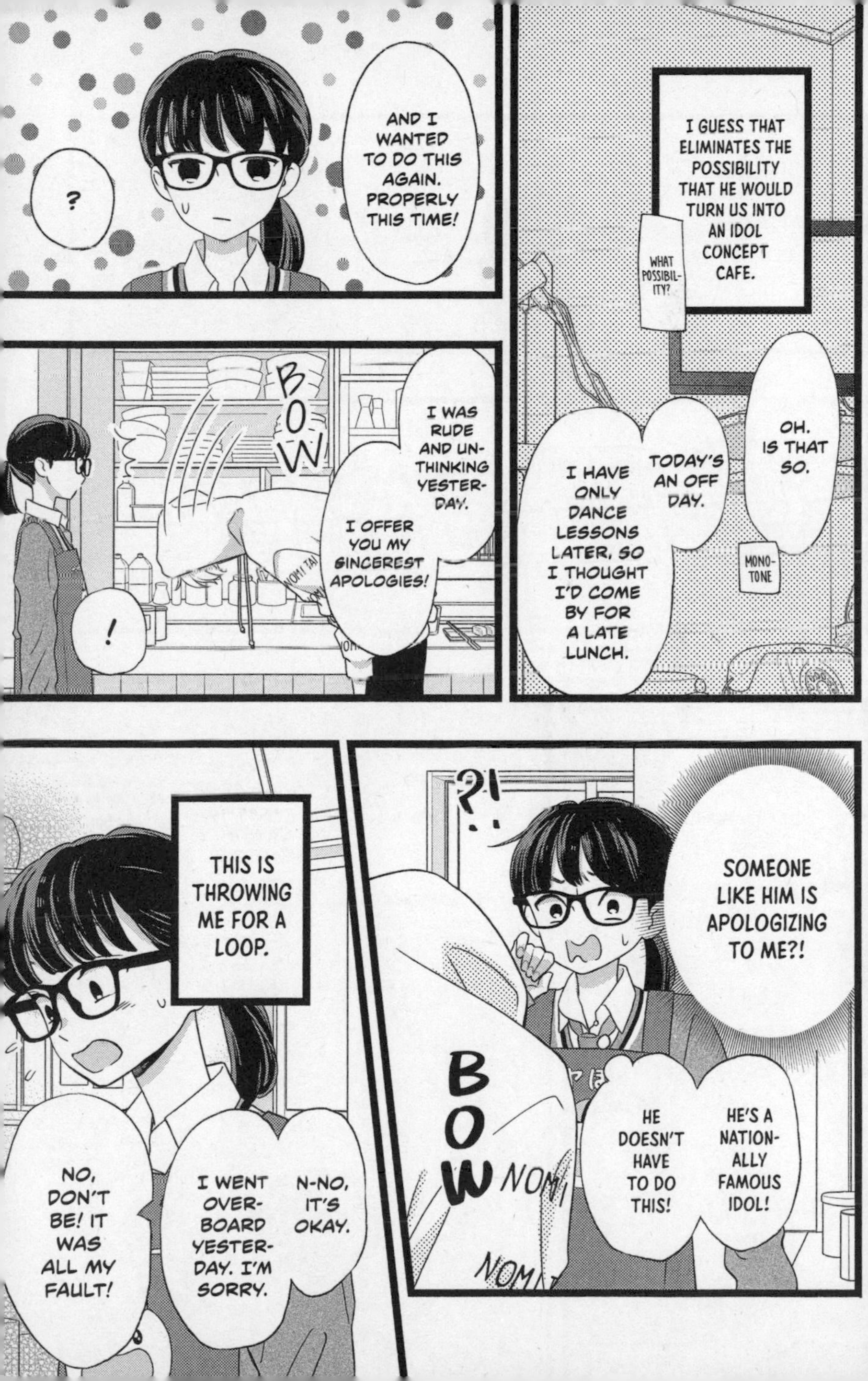
I GUESS THAT ELIMINATES THE POSSIBILITY THAT HE WOULD TURN US INTO AN IDOL CONCEPT CAFE.
WHAT POSSIBIL-ITY?
OH. IS THAT SO.
MONO-TONE
TODAY'S AN OFF DAY.
I HAVE ONLY DANCE LESSONS LATER, SO I THOUGHT I'D COME BY FOR A LATE LUNCH.
AND I WANTED TO DO THIS AGAIN. PROPERLY THIS TIME!
?
BOW
I WAS RUDE AND UN-THINKING YESTER-DAY.
I OFFER YOU MY SINCEREST APOLOGIES!
NOMI TAI
!
?!
SOMEONE LIKE HIM IS APOLOGIZING TO ME?!
HE'S A NATION-ALLY FAMOUS IDOL!
HE DOESN'T HAVE TO DO THIS!
BOW
NOMI
NOMI
THIS IS THROWING ME FOR A LOOP.
N-NO, IT'S OKAY.
I WENT OVER-BOARD YESTER-DAY. I'M SORRY.
NO, DON'T BE! IT WAS ALL MY FAULT!

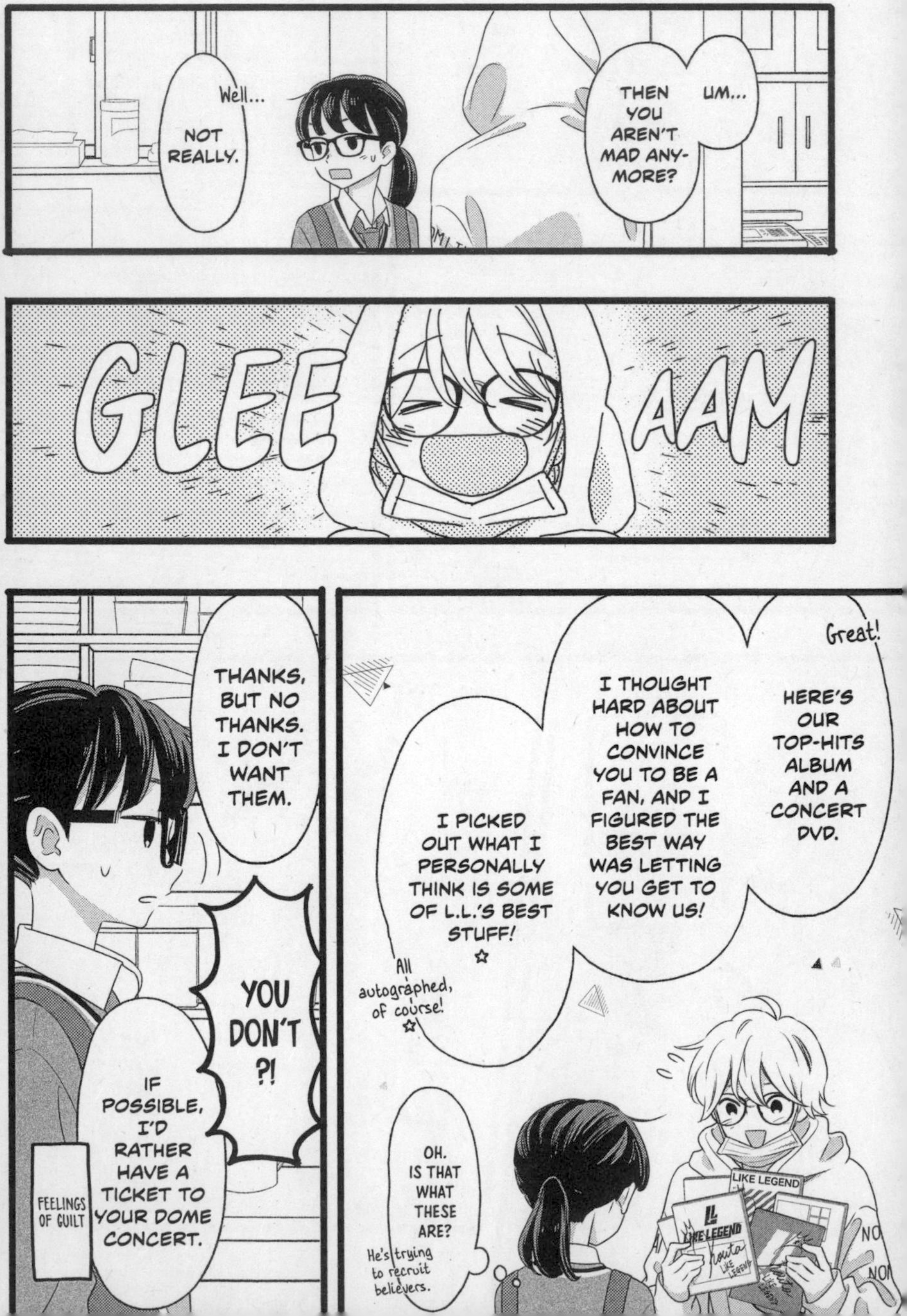
UM... THEN YOU AREN'T MAD ANYMORE?
Well... NOT REALLY.
GLEE AAM
Great!
HERE'S OUR TOP-HITS ALBUM AND A CONCERT DVD.
I THOUGHT HARD ABOUT HOW TO CONVINCE YOU TO BE A FAN, AND I FIGURED THE BEST WAY WAS LETTING YOU GET TO KNOW US!
I PICKED OUT WHAT I PERSONALLY THINK IS SOME OF L.L.'S BEST STUFF! ☆
All autographed, of course! ☆
LIKE LEGEND
LIKE LEGEND
OH. IS THAT WHAT THESE ARE?
He's trying to recruit believers.
THANKS, BUT NO THANKS. I DON'T WANT THEM.
YOU DON'T ?!
IF POSSIBLE, I'D RATHER HAVE A TICKET TO YOUR DOME CONCERT.
FEELINGS OF GUILT

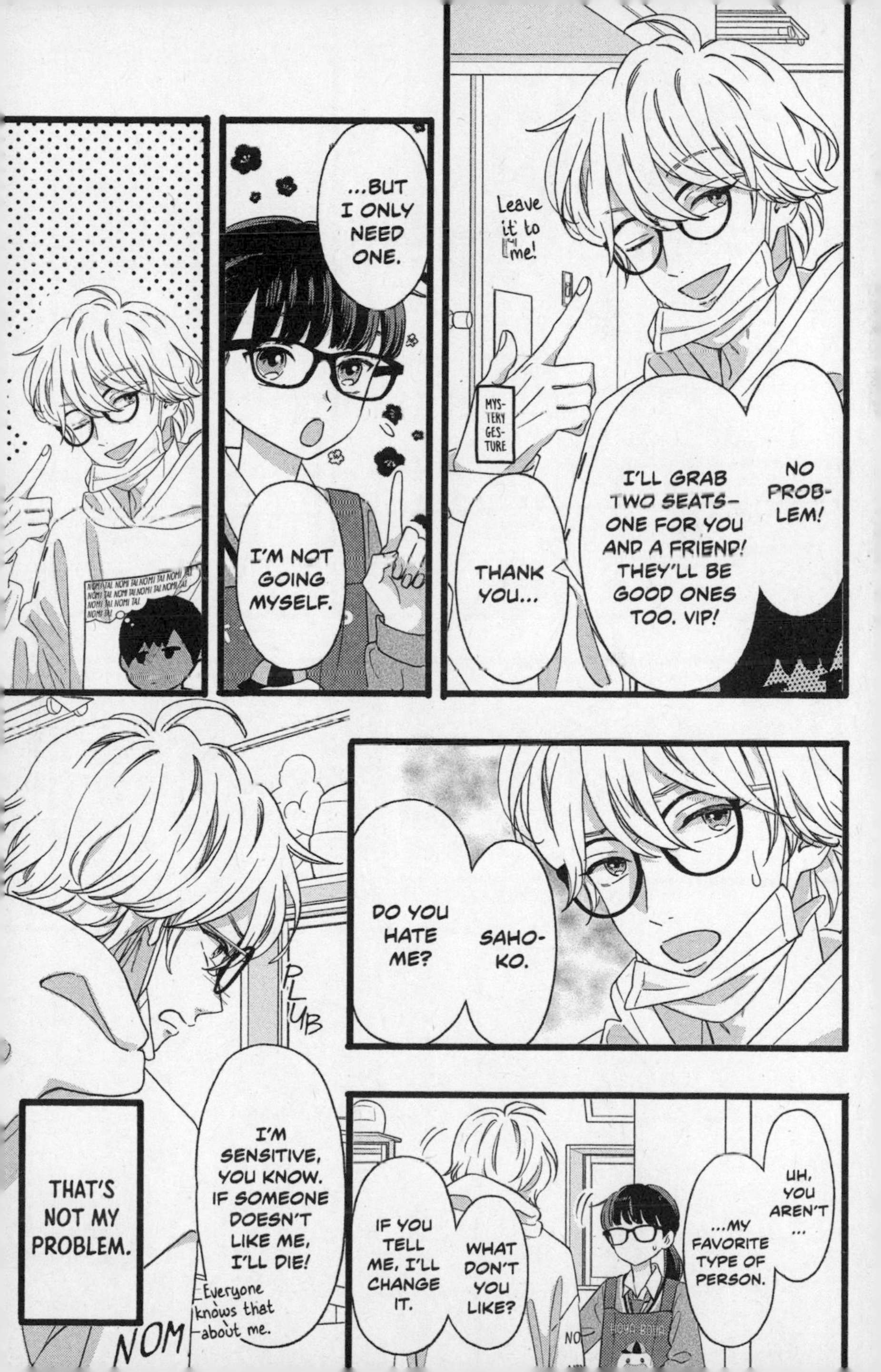
Leave it to me!
MYSTERY GESTURE
NO PROBLEM!
I'LL GRAB TWO SEATS— ONE FOR YOU AND A FRIEND! THEY'LL BE GOOD ONES TOO. VIP!
THANK YOU...
...BUT I ONLY NEED ONE.
I'M NOT GOING MYSELF.
SAHOKO.
DO YOU HATE ME?
PLUB
UH, YOU AREN'T ...
...MY FAVORITE TYPE OF PERSON.
WHAT DON'T YOU LIKE?
IF YOU TELL ME, I'LL CHANGE IT.
I'M SENSITIVE, YOU KNOW. IF SOMEONE DOESN'T LIKE ME, I'LL DIE!
Everyone knows that about me.
THAT'S NOT MY PROBLEM.
NOM

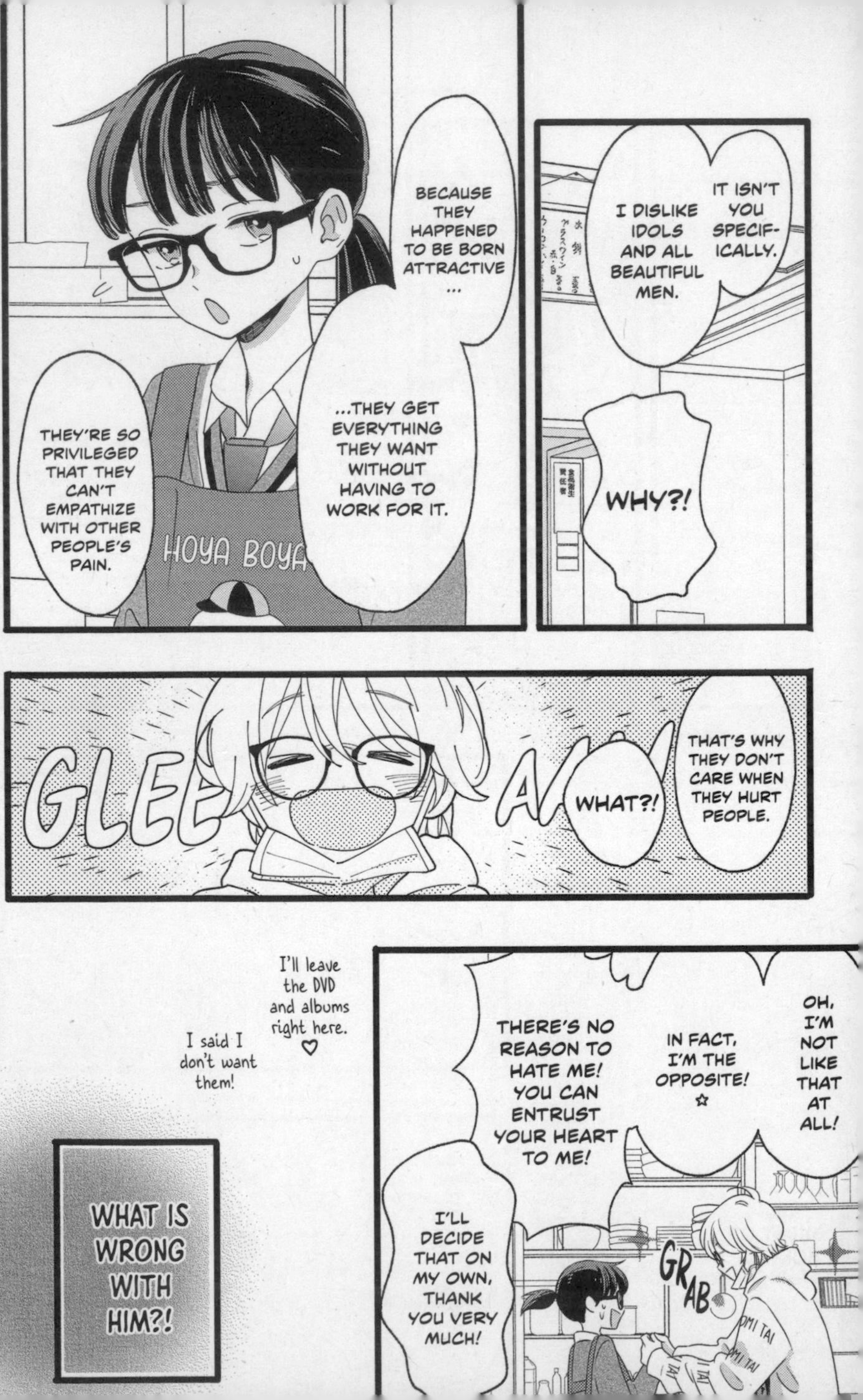
IT ISN'T YOU SPECIFICALLY.
I DISLIKE IDOLS AND ALL BEAUTIFUL MEN.
WHY?!
BECAUSE THEY HAPPENED TO BE BORN ATTRACTIVE ...
...THEY GET EVERYTHING THEY WANT WITHOUT HAVING TO WORK FOR IT.
THEY'RE SO PRIVILEGED THAT THEY CAN'T EMPATHIZE WITH OTHER PEOPLE'S PAIN.
HOYA BOYA
THAT'S WHY THEY DON'T CARE WHEN THEY HURT PEOPLE.
WHAT?!
GLEE
A
OH, I'M NOT LIKE THAT AT ALL!
IN FACT, I'M THE OPPOSITE! ☆
THERE'S NO REASON TO HATE ME! YOU CAN ENTRUST YOUR HEART TO ME!
I'LL DECIDE THAT ON MY OWN, THANK YOU VERY MUCH!
GRAB
I'll leave the DVD and albums right here. ♡
I said I don't want them!
WHAT IS WRONG WITH HIM?!

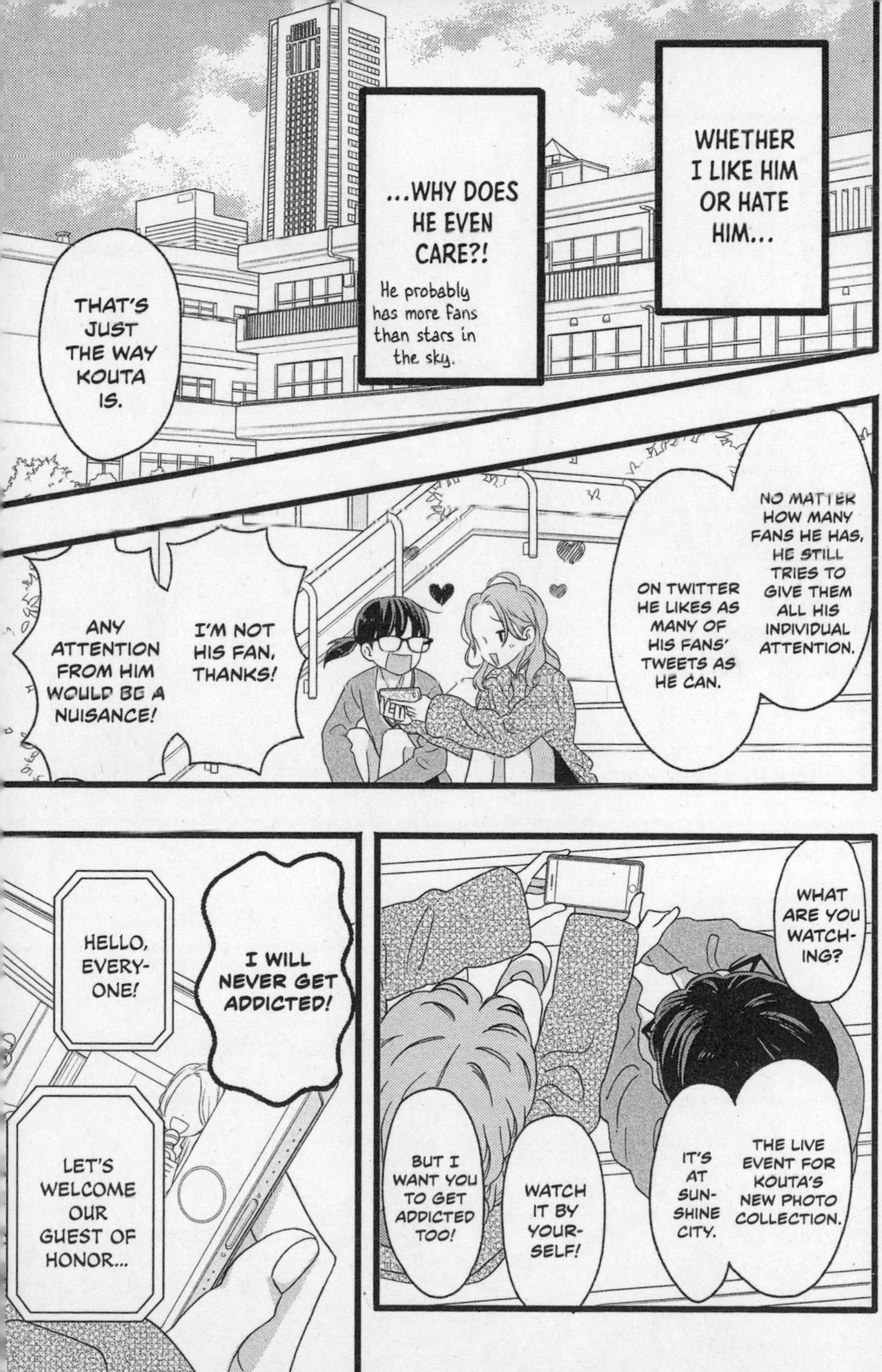
WHETHER I LIKE HIM OR HATE HIM...
...WHY DOES HE EVEN CARE?!
He probably has more fans than stars in the sky.
THAT'S JUST THE WAY KOUTA IS.
NO MATTER HOW MANY FANS HE HAS, HE STILL TRIES TO GIVE THEM ALL HIS INDIVIDUAL ATTENTION.
ON TWITTER HE LIKES AS MANY OF HIS FANS' TWEETS AS HE CAN.
I'M NOT HIS FAN, THANKS!
ANY ATTENTION FROM HIM WOULD BE A NUISANCE!
WHAT ARE YOU WATCHING?
THE LIVE EVENT FOR KOUTA'S NEW PHOTO COLLECTION.
IT'S AT SUNSHINE CITY.
WATCH IT BY YOURSELF!
BUT I WANT YOU TO GET ADDICTED TOO!
I WILL NEVER GET ADDICTED!
HELLO, EVERYONE!
LET'S WELCOME OUR GUEST OF HONOR...

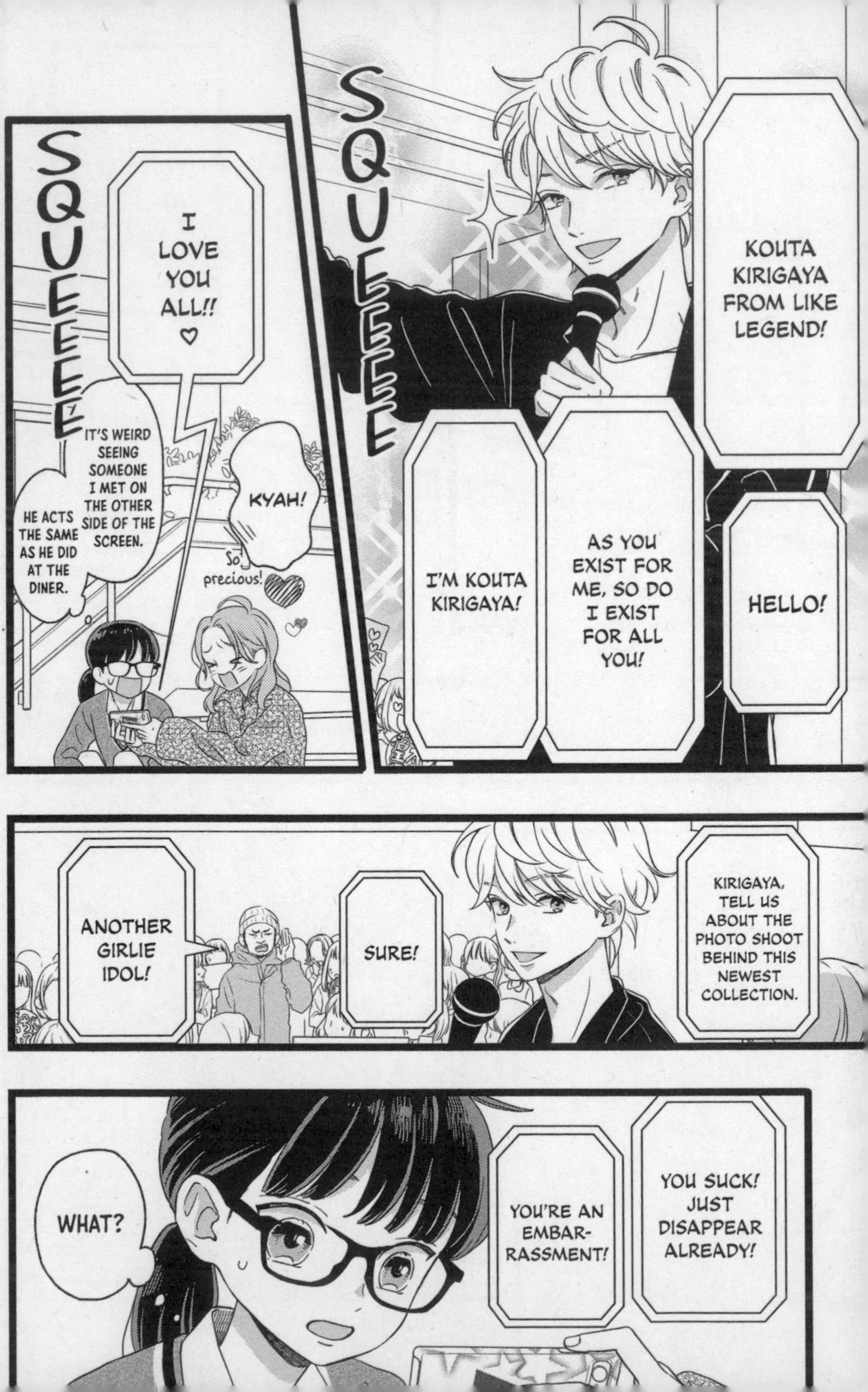
KOUTA KIRIGAYA FROM LIKE LEGEND!
HELLO!
AS YOU EXIST FOR ME, SO DO I EXIST FOR ALL YOU!
I'M KOUTA KIRIGAYA!
SQUEEEE
SQUEEEE
I LOVE YOU ALL!! ♡
KYAH!
So precious!
IT'S WEIRD SEEING SOMEONE I MET ON THE OTHER SIDE OF THE SCREEN.
HE ACTS THE SAME AS HE DID AT THE DINER.
KIRIGAYA, TELL US ABOUT THE PHOTO SHOOT BEHIND THIS NEWEST COLLECTION.
SURE!
ANOTHER GIRLIE IDOL!
YOU SUCK! JUST DISAPPEAR ALREADY!
YOU'RE AN EMBAR-RASSMENT!
WHAT?

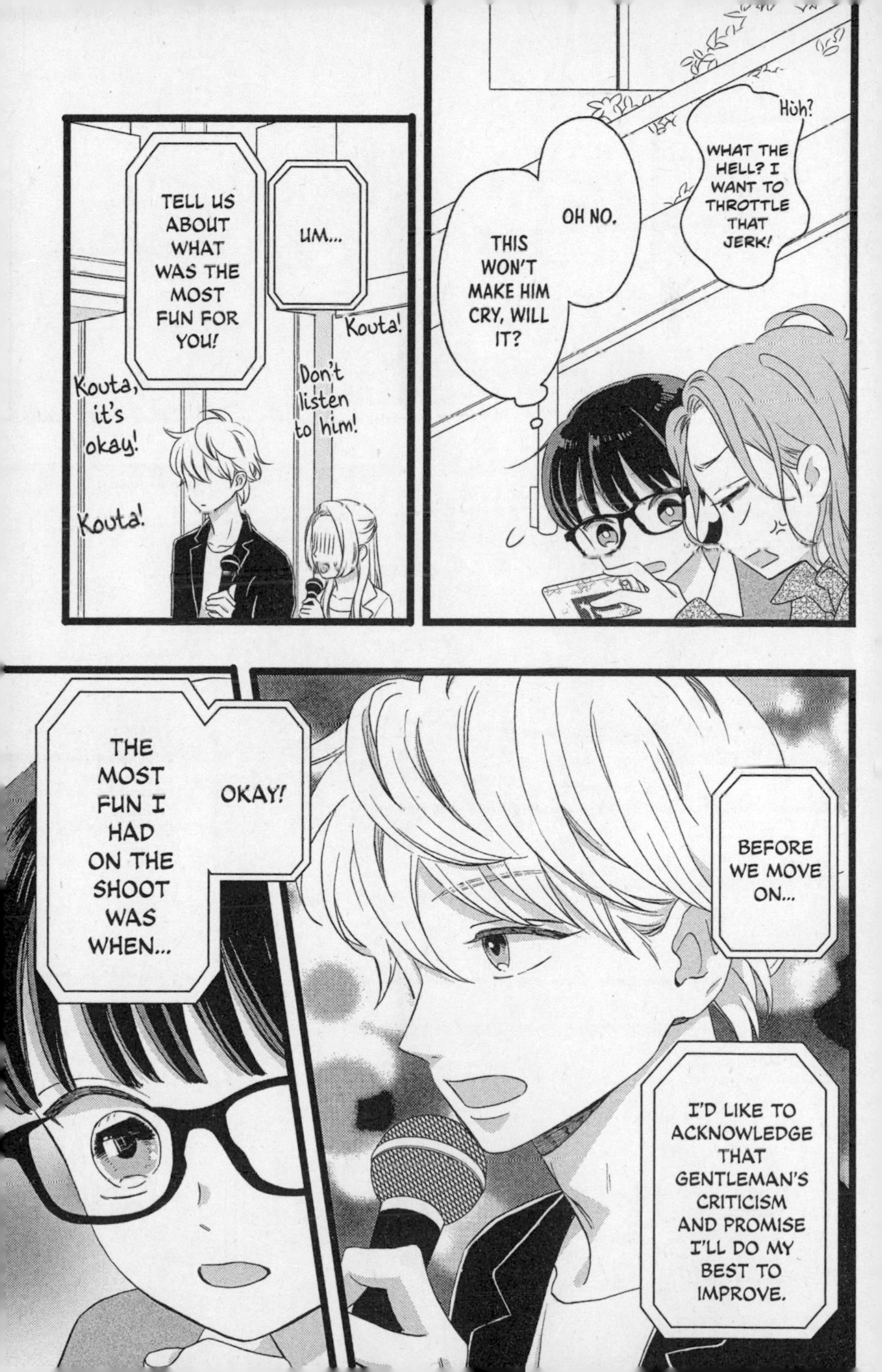
Huh?
WHAT THE HELL? I WANT TO THROTTLE THAT JERK!
OH NO.
THIS WON'T MAKE HIM CRY, WILL IT?
TELL US ABOUT WHAT WAS THE MOST FUN FOR YOU!
UM...
Kouta!
Don't listen to him!
Kouta, it's okay!
Kouta!
BEFORE WE MOVE ON...
I'D LIKE TO ACKNOWLEDGE THAT GENTLEMAN'S CRITICISM AND PROMISE I'LL DO MY BEST TO IMPROVE.
OKAY!
THE MOST FUN I HAD ON THE SHOOT WAS WHEN...

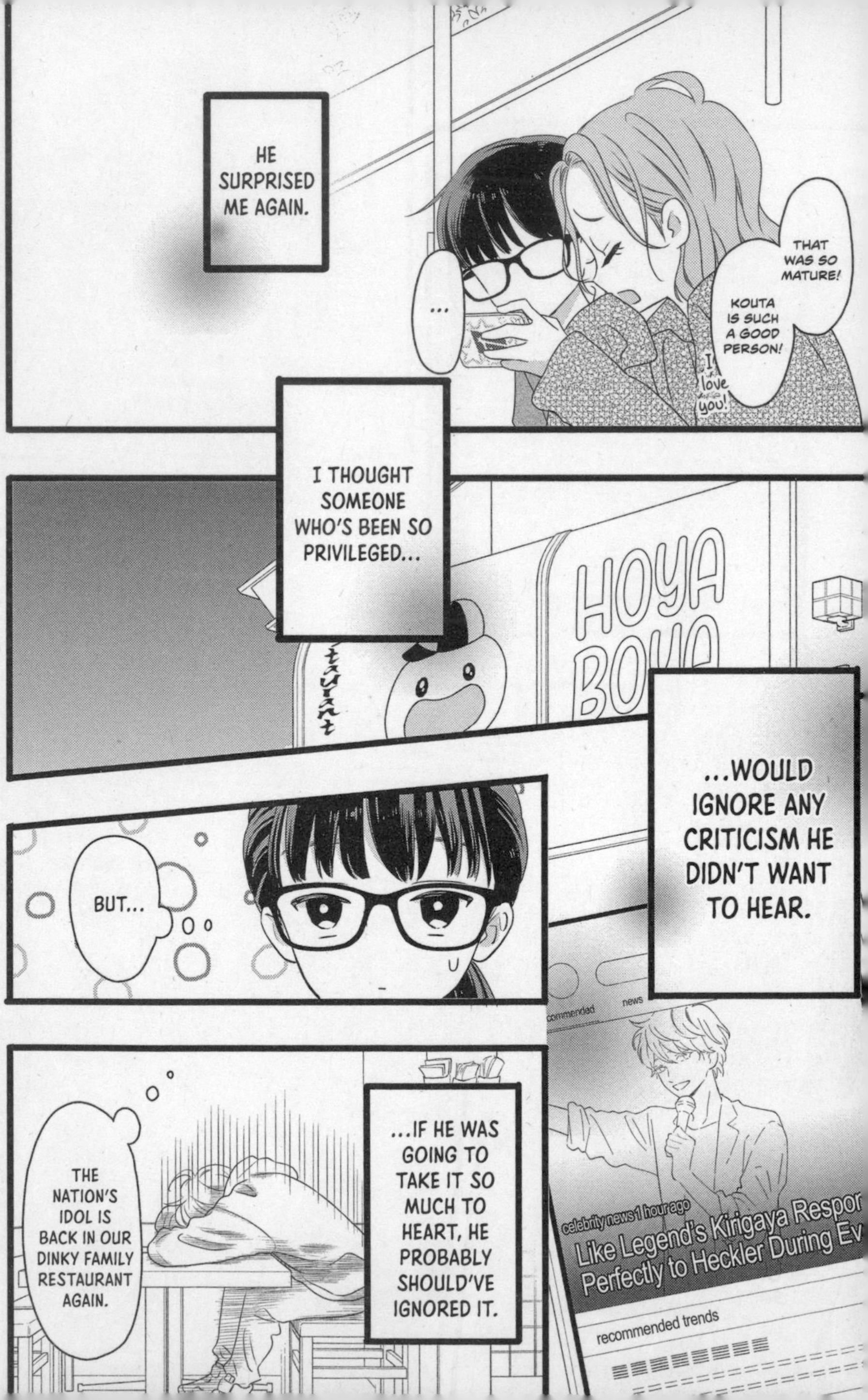
THAT WAS SO MATURE!
KOUTA IS SUCH A GOOD PERSON!
I love you!
...
HE SURPRISED ME AGAIN.
I THOUGHT SOMEONE WHO'S BEEN SO PRIVILEGED...
HOYA BOYA
...WOULD IGNORE ANY CRITICISM HE DIDN'T WANT TO HEAR.
BUT...
news
celebrity news 1 hour ago
Like Legend's Kirigaya Respor
Perfectly to Heckler During Ev
recommended trends
...IF HE WAS GOING TO TAKE IT SO MUCH TO HEART, HE PROBABLY SHOULD'VE IGNORED IT.
THE NATION'S IDOL IS BACK IN OUR DINKY FAMILY RESTAURANT AGAIN.

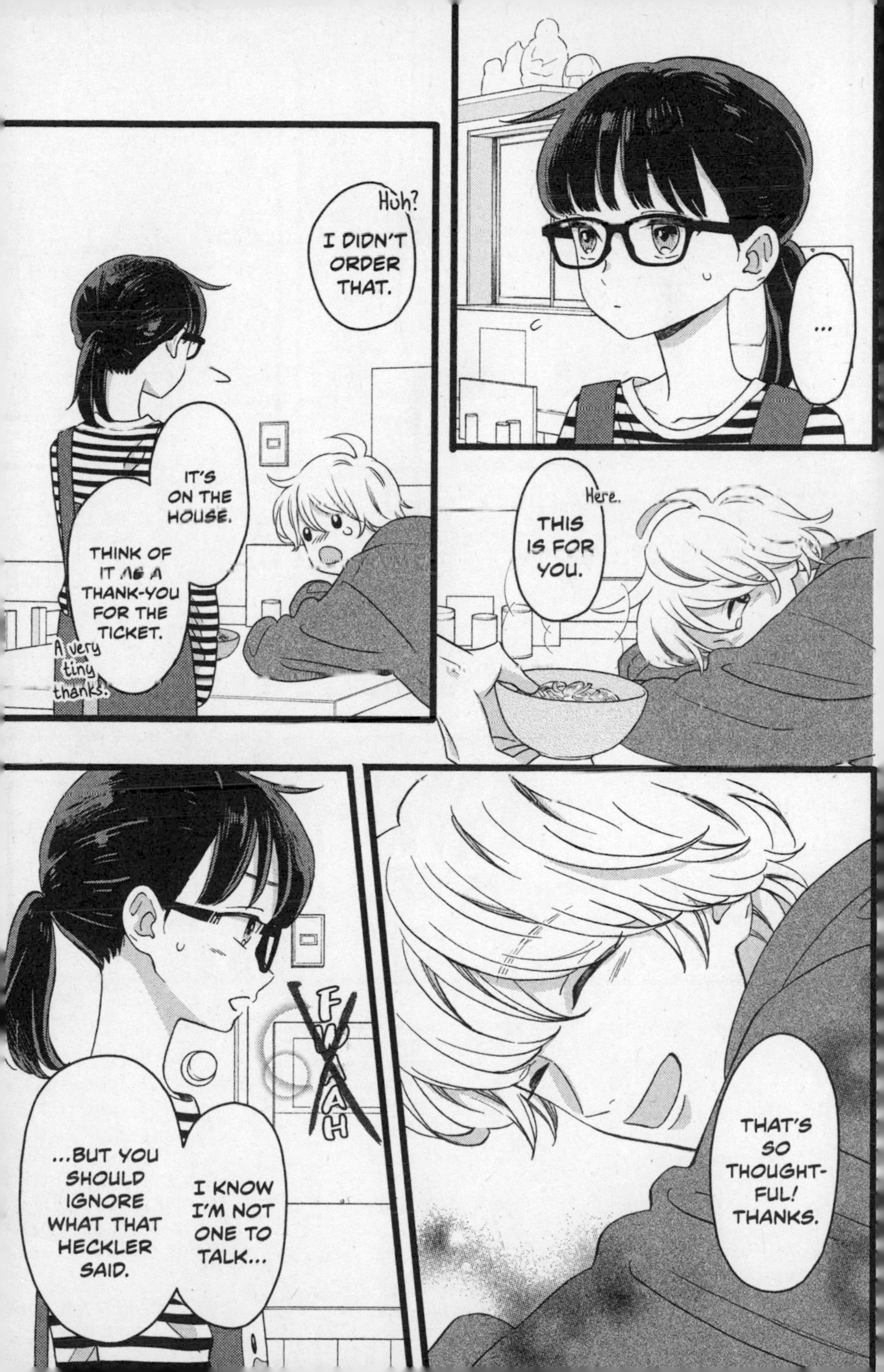
...
Here.
THIS IS FOR YOU.
Huh?
I DIDN'T ORDER THAT.
IT'S ON THE HOUSE.
THINK OF IT AS A THANK-YOU FOR THE TICKET.
A very tiny thanks!
THAT'S SO THOUGHTFUL! THANKS.
FWAH
I KNOW I'M NOT ONE TO TALK...
...BUT YOU SHOULD IGNORE WHAT THAT HECKLER SAID.

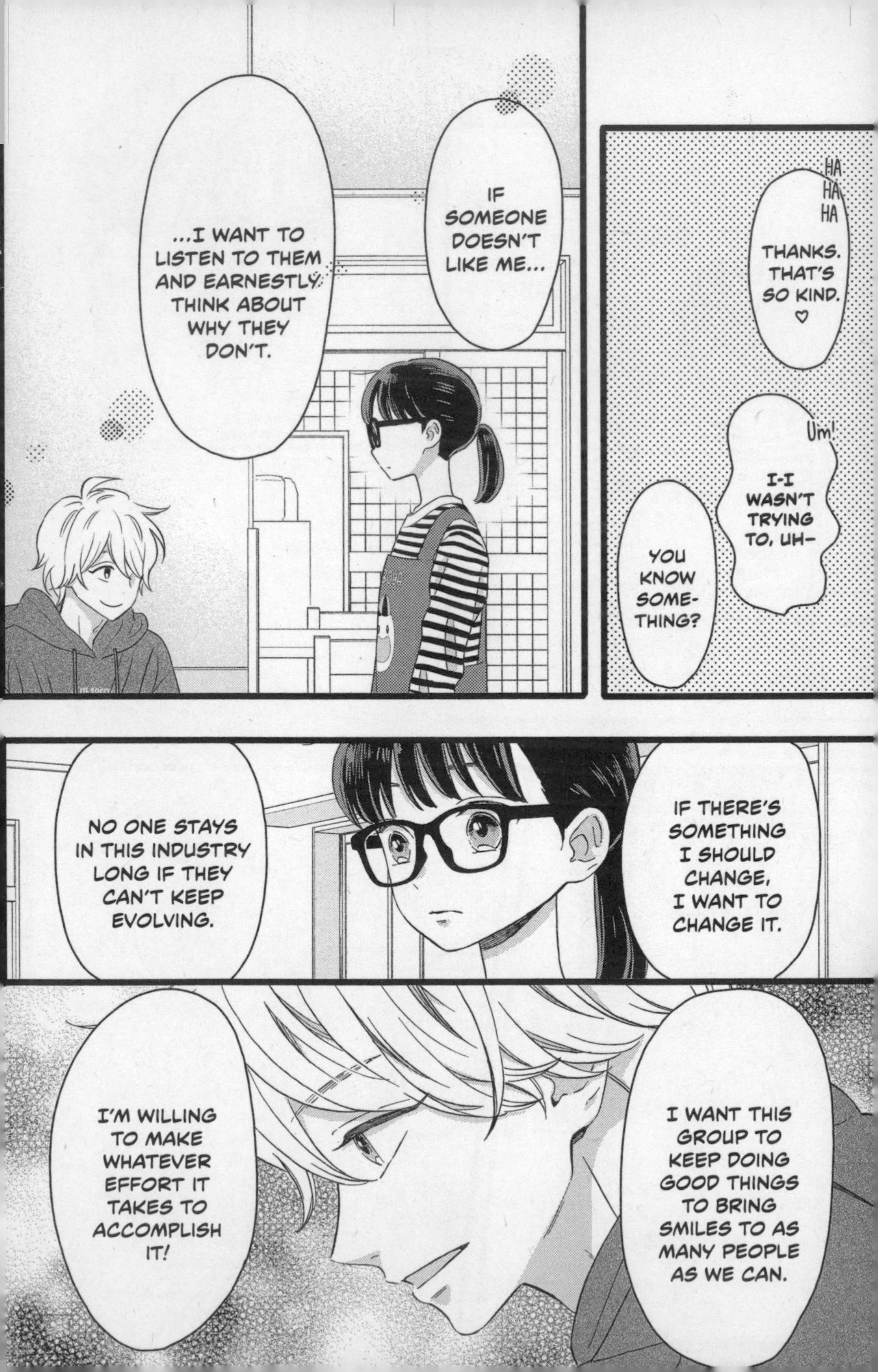
HA HA HA
THANKS. THAT'S SO KIND. ♡
Um!
I-I WASN'T TRYING TO, UH-
YOU KNOW SOME-THING?
IF SOMEONE DOESN'T LIKE ME...
...I WANT TO LISTEN TO THEM AND EARNESTLY THINK ABOUT WHY THEY DON'T.
IF THERE'S SOMETHING I SHOULD CHANGE, I WANT TO CHANGE IT.
NO ONE STAYS IN THIS INDUSTRY LONG IF THEY CAN'T KEEP EVOLVING.
I WANT THIS GROUP TO KEEP DOING GOOD THINGS TO BRING SMILES TO AS MANY PEOPLE AS WE CAN.
I'M WILLING TO MAKE WHATEVER EFFORT IT TAKES TO ACCOMPLISH IT!

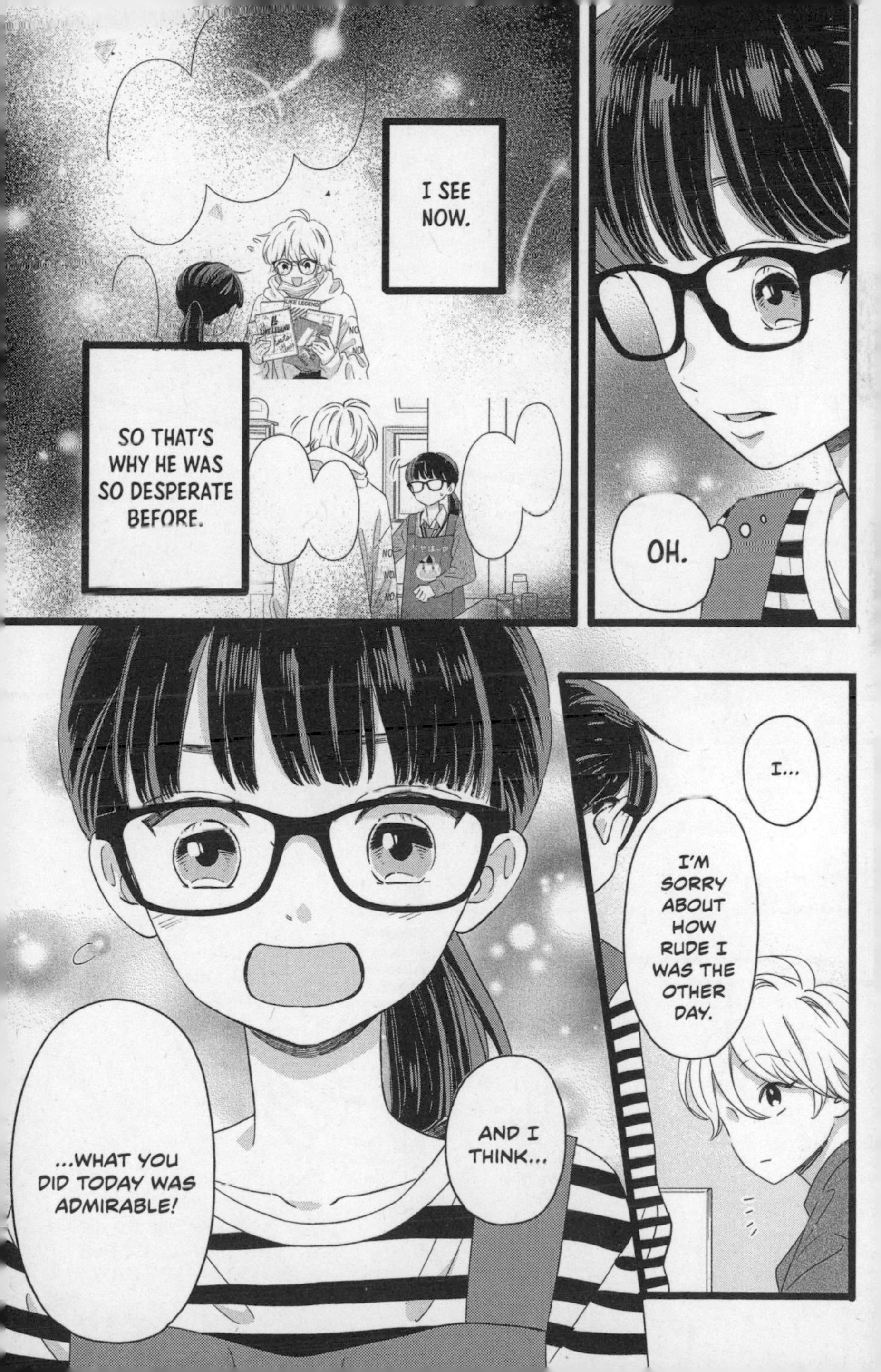
OH.
I SEE NOW.
SO THAT'S WHY HE WAS SO DESPERATE BEFORE.
I...
I'M SORRY ABOUT HOW RUDE I WAS THE OTHER DAY.
AND I THINK...
...WHAT YOU DID TODAY WAS ADMIRABLE!

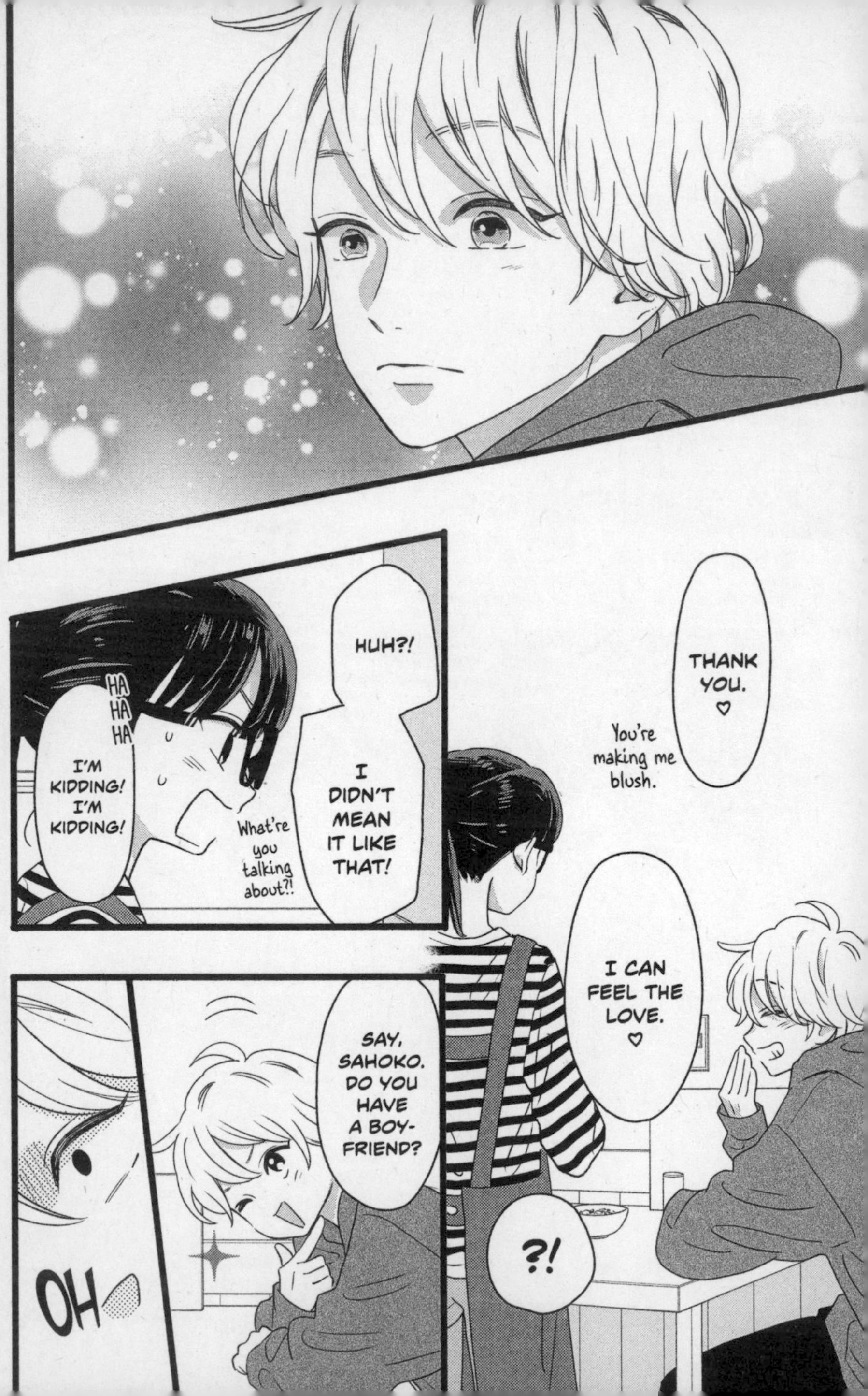
THANK YOU. ♡
You're making me blush.
I CAN FEEL THE LOVE. ♡
?!
HUH?!
I DIDN'T MEAN IT LIKE THAT!
What're you talking about?!
HA HA HA
I'M KIDDING! I'M KIDDING!
SAY, SAHOKO. DO YOU HAVE A BOY-FRIEND?
OH

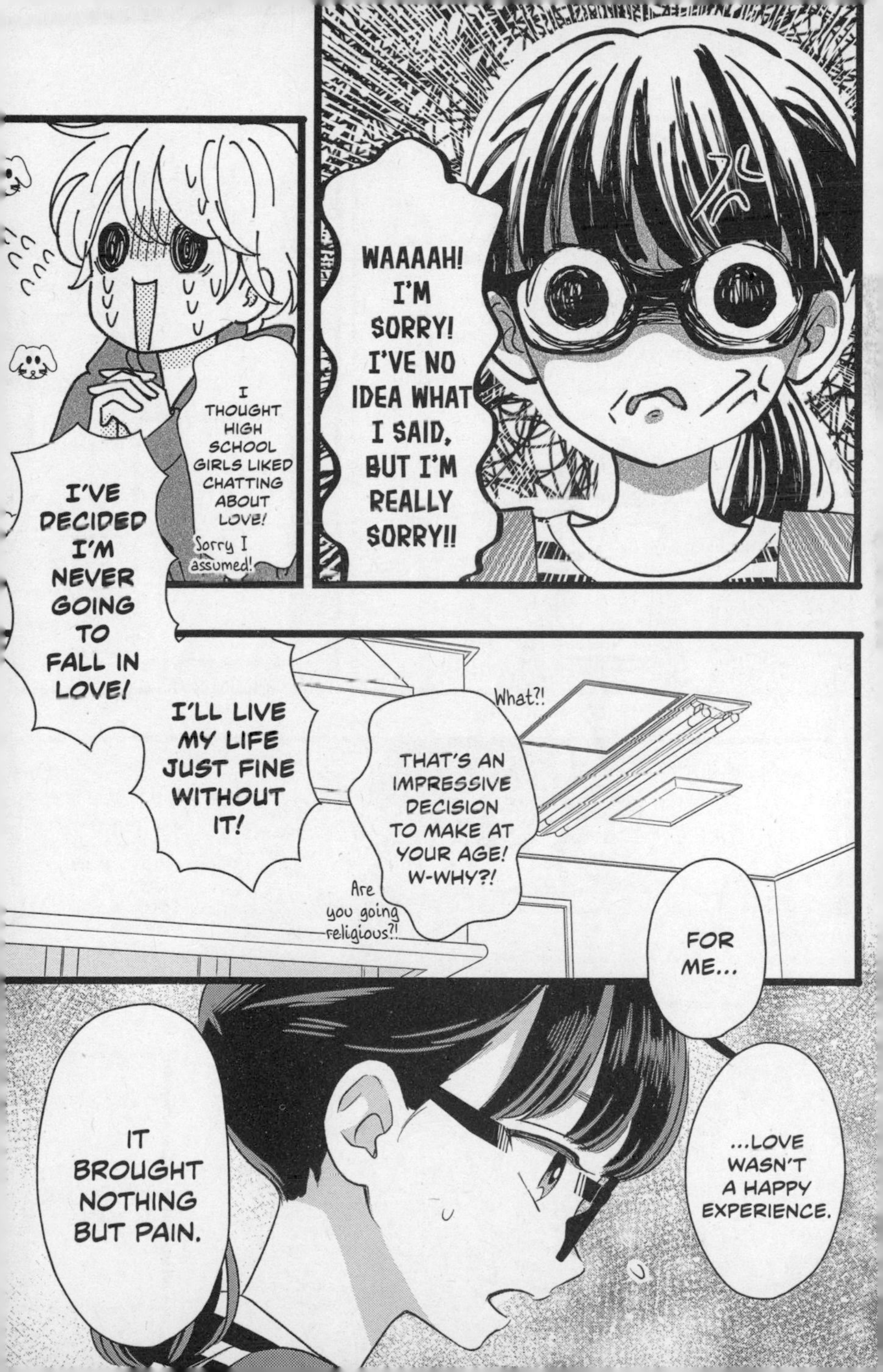
WAAAAH! I'M SORRY! I'VE NO IDEA WHAT I SAID, BUT I'M REALLY SORRY!!
I THOUGHT HIGH SCHOOL GIRLS LIKED CHATTING ABOUT LOVE!
Sorry I assumed!
I'VE DECIDED I'M NEVER GOING TO FALL IN LOVE!
I'LL LIVE MY LIFE JUST FINE WITHOUT IT!
What?!
THAT'S AN IMPRESSIVE DECISION TO MAKE AT YOUR AGE! W-WHY?!
Are you going religious?!
FOR ME...
...LOVE WASN'T A HAPPY EXPERIENCE.
IT BROUGHT NOTHING BUT PAIN.

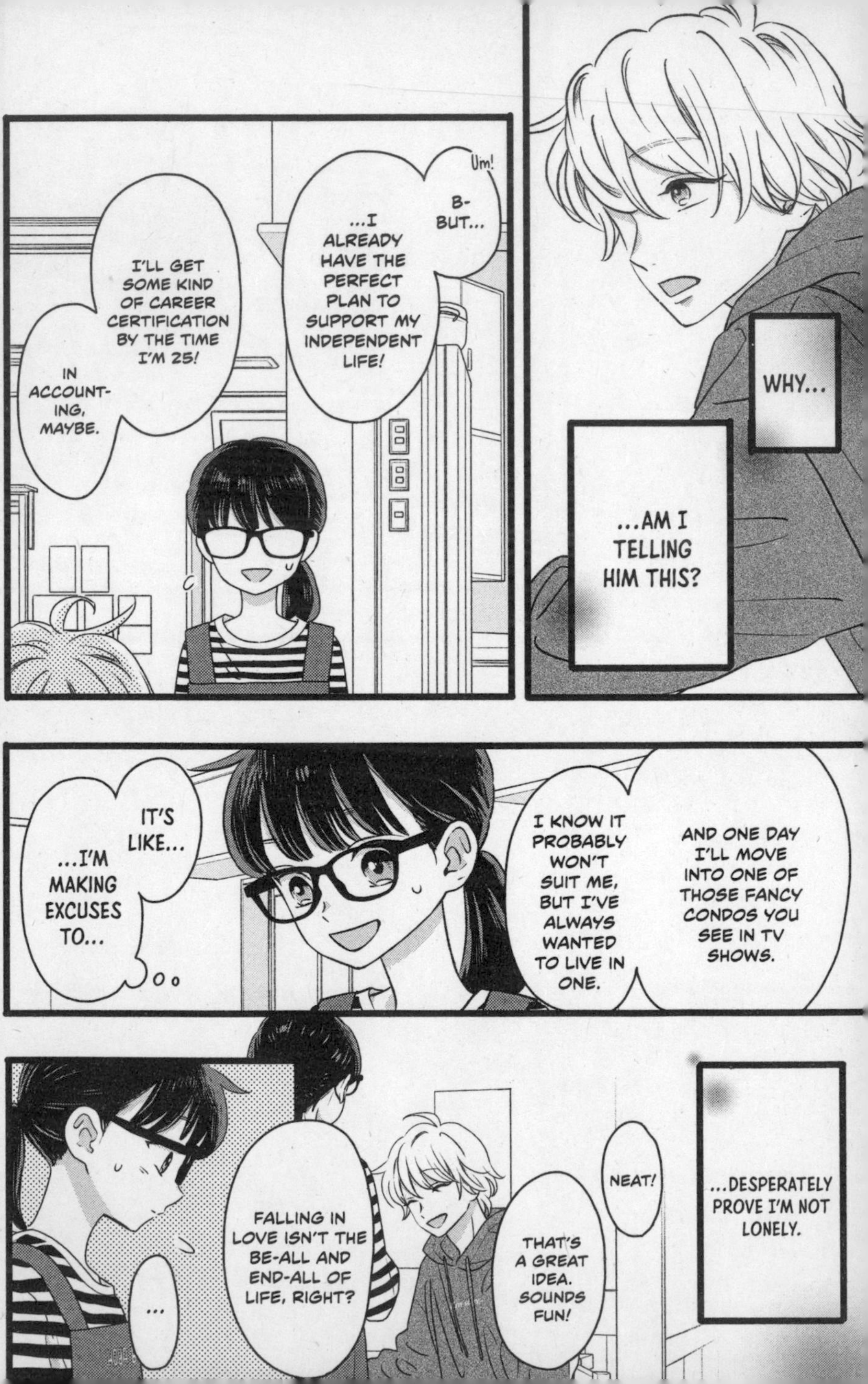
WHY...
...AM I TELLING HIM THIS?
Um!
B-BUT...
...I ALREADY HAVE THE PERFECT PLAN TO SUPPORT MY INDEPENDENT LIFE!
I'LL GET SOME KIND OF CAREER CERTIFICATION BY THE TIME I'M 25!
IN ACCOUNTING, MAYBE.
AND ONE DAY I'LL MOVE INTO ONE OF THOSE FANCY CONDOS YOU SEE IN TV SHOWS.
I KNOW IT PROBABLY WON'T SUIT ME, BUT I'VE ALWAYS WANTED TO LIVE IN ONE.
IT'S LIKE...
...I'M MAKING EXCUSES TO...
...DESPERATELY PROVE I'M NOT LONELY.
NEAT!
THAT'S A GREAT IDEA. SOUNDS FUN!
FALLING IN LOVE ISN'T THE BE-ALL AND END-ALL OF LIFE, RIGHT?
...

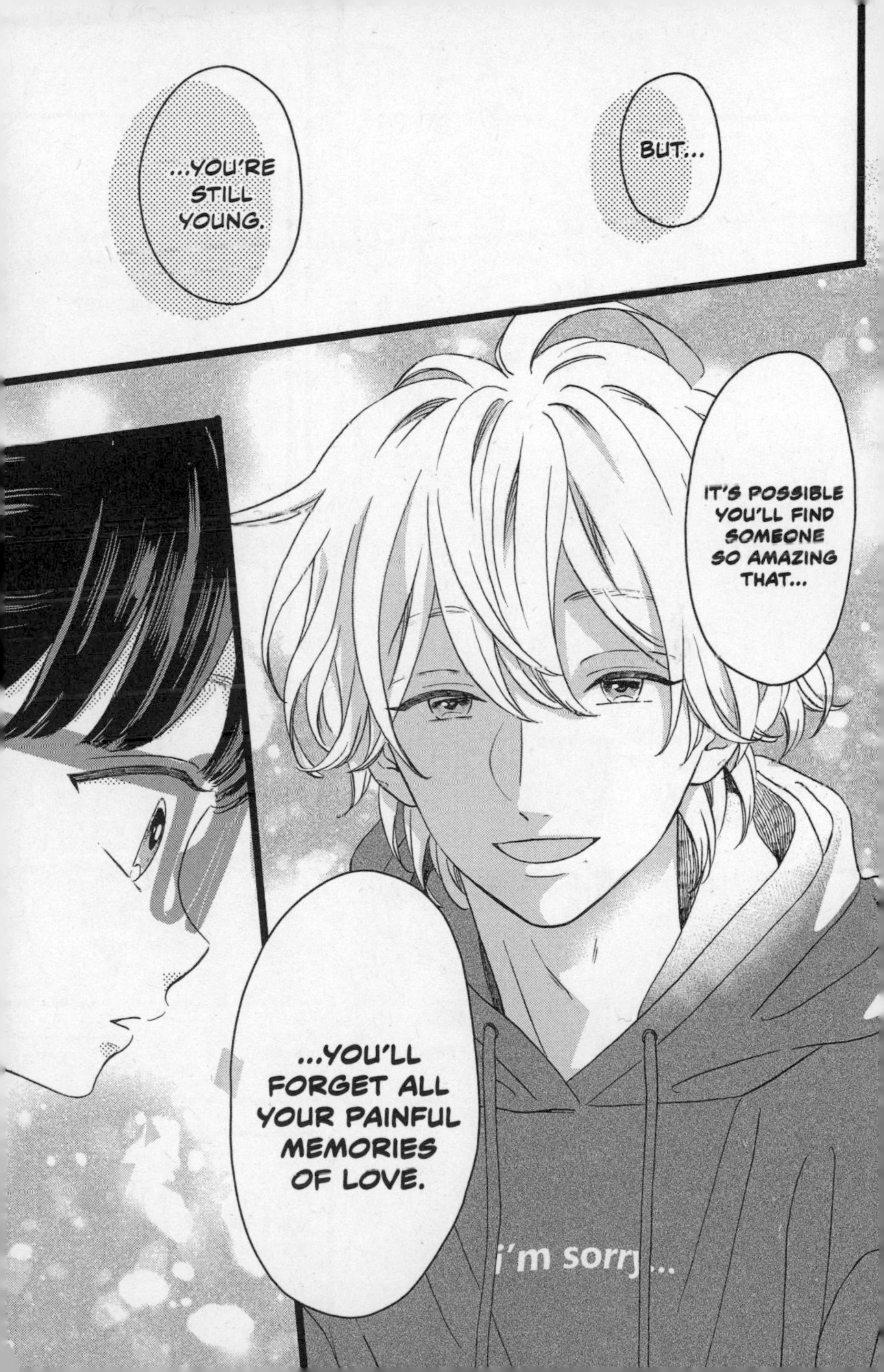
BUT...
...YOU'RE STILL YOUNG.
IT'S POSSIBLE YOU'LL FIND SOMEONE SO AMAZING THAT...
...YOU'LL FORGET ALL YOUR PAINFUL MEMORIES OF LOVE.
i'm sorry...

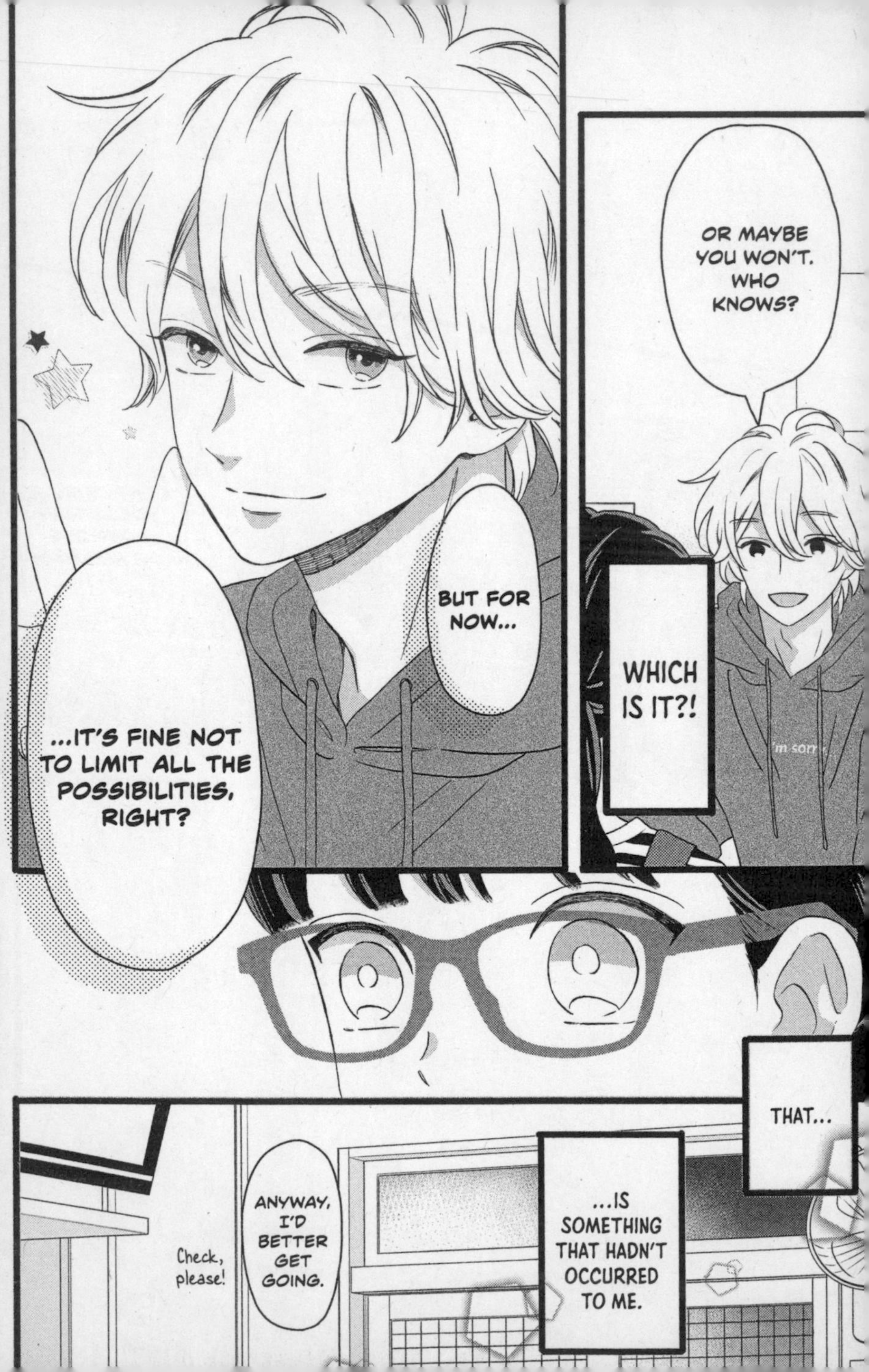
OR MAYBE YOU WON'T. WHO KNOWS?
WHICH IS IT?!
BUT FOR NOW...
...IT'S FINE NOT TO LIMIT ALL THE POSSIBILITIES, RIGHT?
THAT...
...IS SOMETHING THAT HADN'T OCCURRED TO ME.
ANYWAY, I'D BETTER GET GOING.
Check, please!

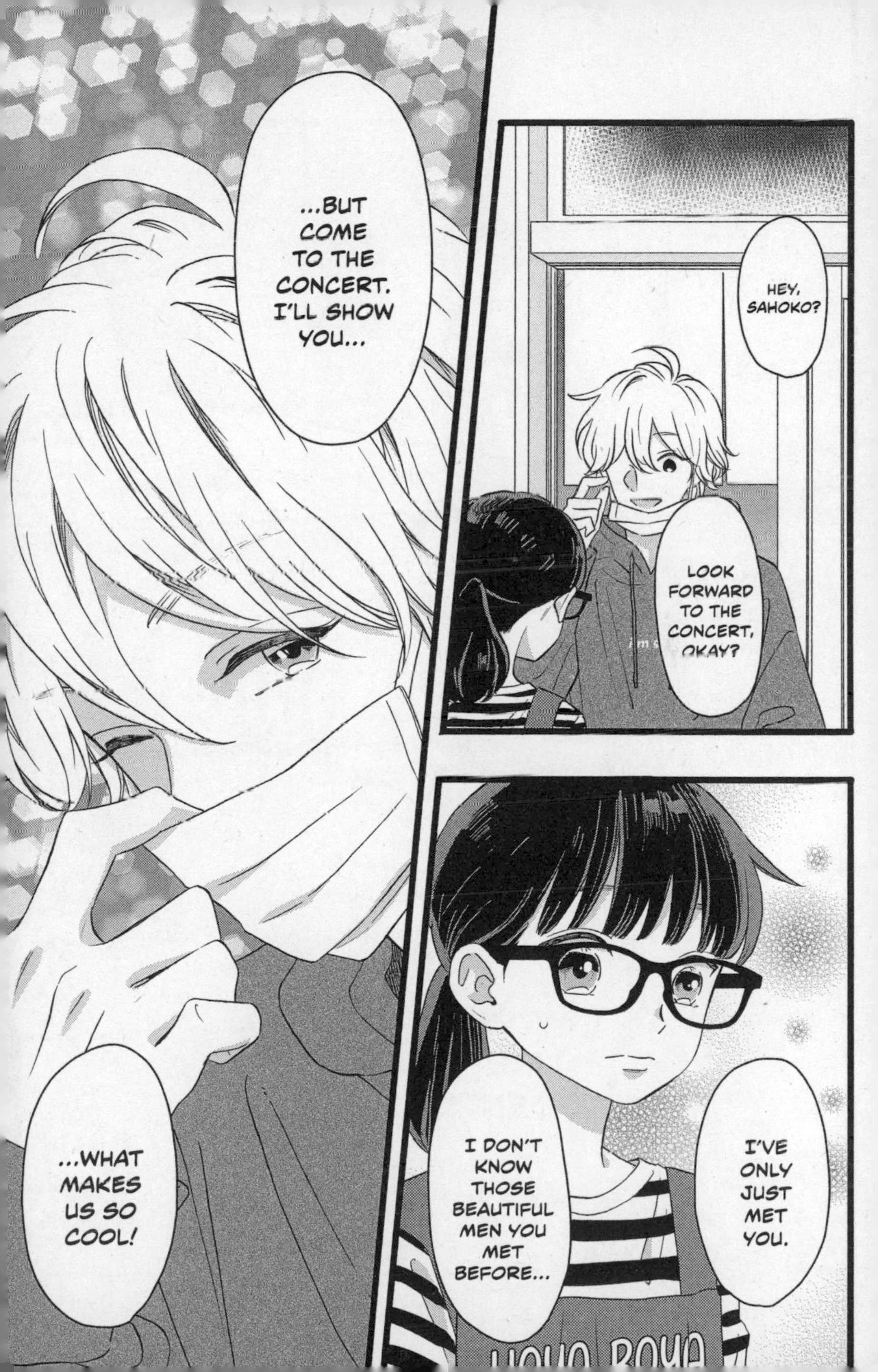
HEY, SAHOKO?
LOOK FORWARD TO THE CONCERT, OKAY?
I'VE ONLY JUST MET YOU.
I DON'T KNOW THOSE BEAUTIFUL MEN YOU MET BEFORE...
...BUT COME TO THE CONCERT. I'LL SHOW YOU...
...WHAT MAKES US SO COOL!

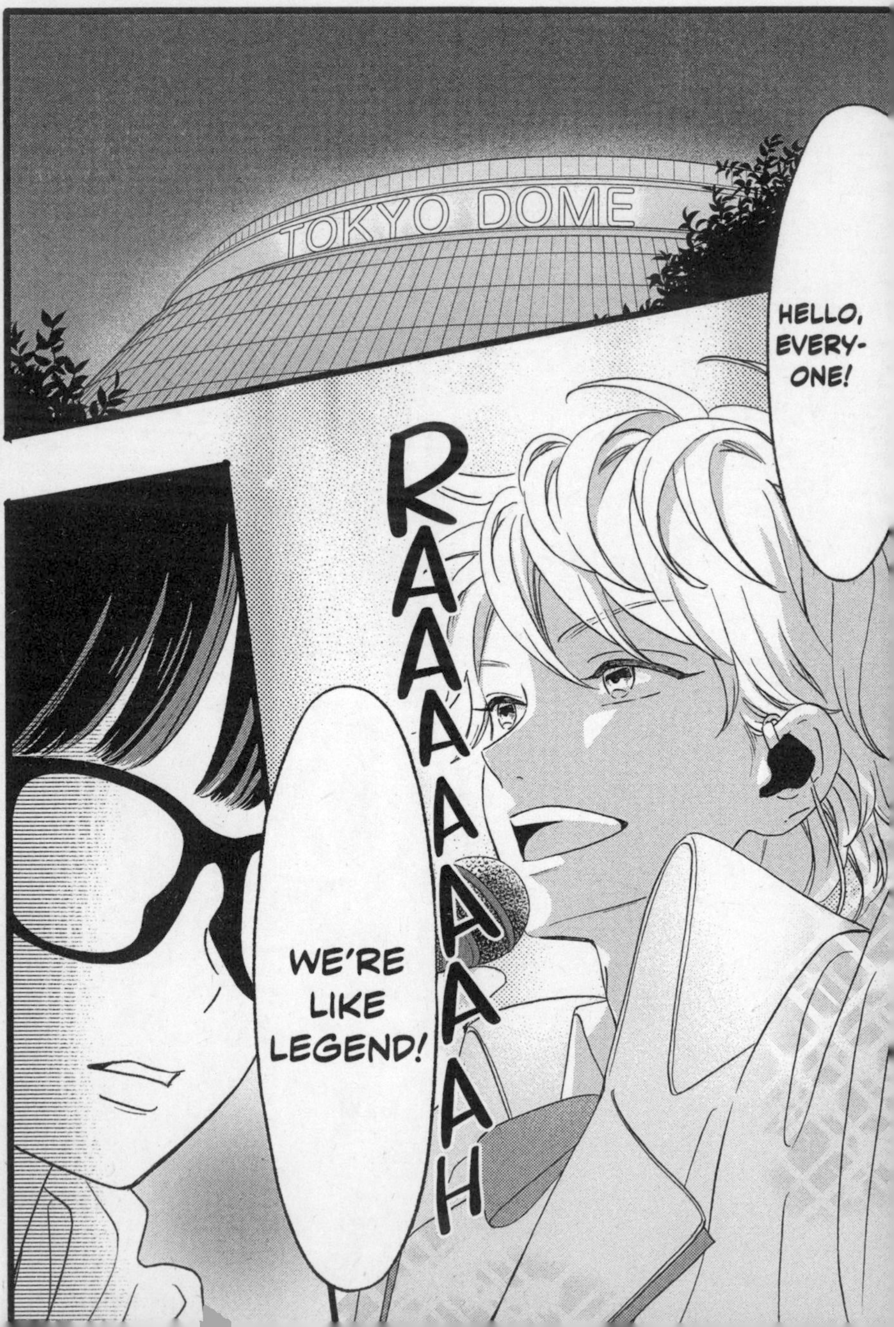
TOKYO DOME
HELLO, EVERY-ONE!
RAAAAAAAH
WE'RE LIKE LEGEND!

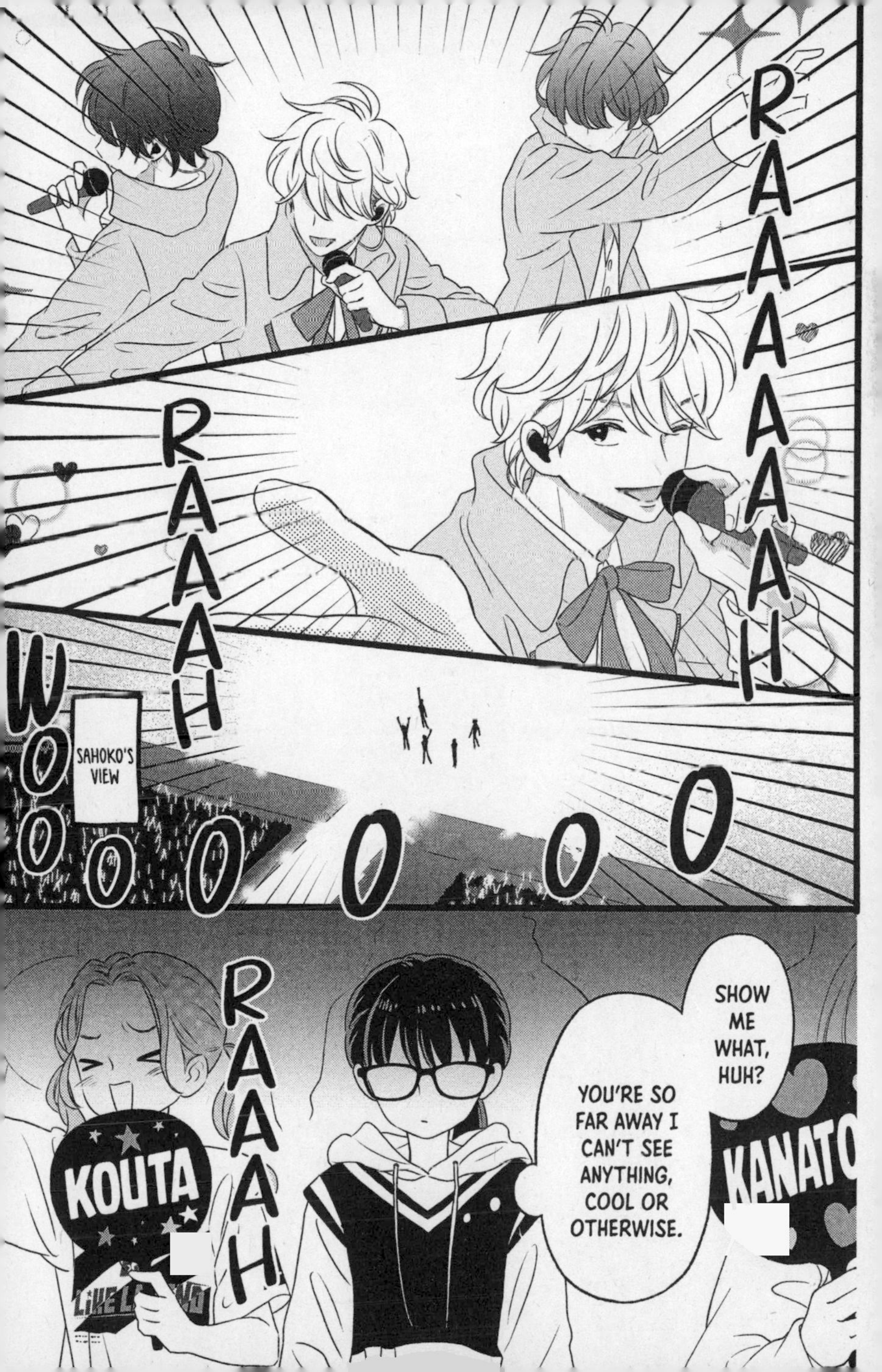
RAAAAAAH
RAAAAH
WOOOOOOO
SAHOKO'S VIEW
SHOW ME WHAT, HUH?
YOU'RE SO FAR AWAY I CAN'T SEE ANYTHING, COOL OR OTHERWISE.
KANATO
RAAAAH
KOUTA

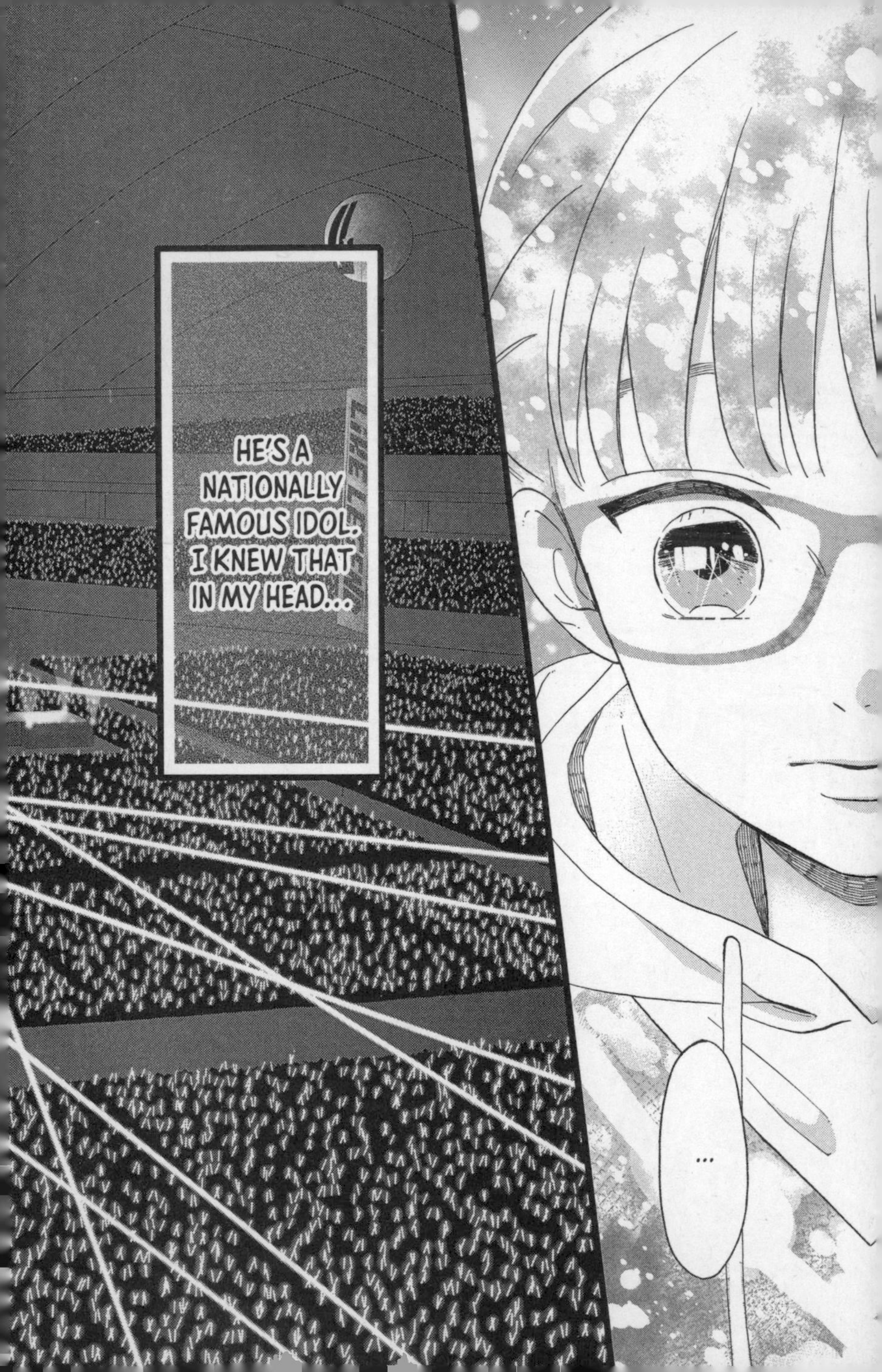
...
HE'S A NATIONALLY FAMOUS IDOL. I KNEW THAT IN MY HEAD...

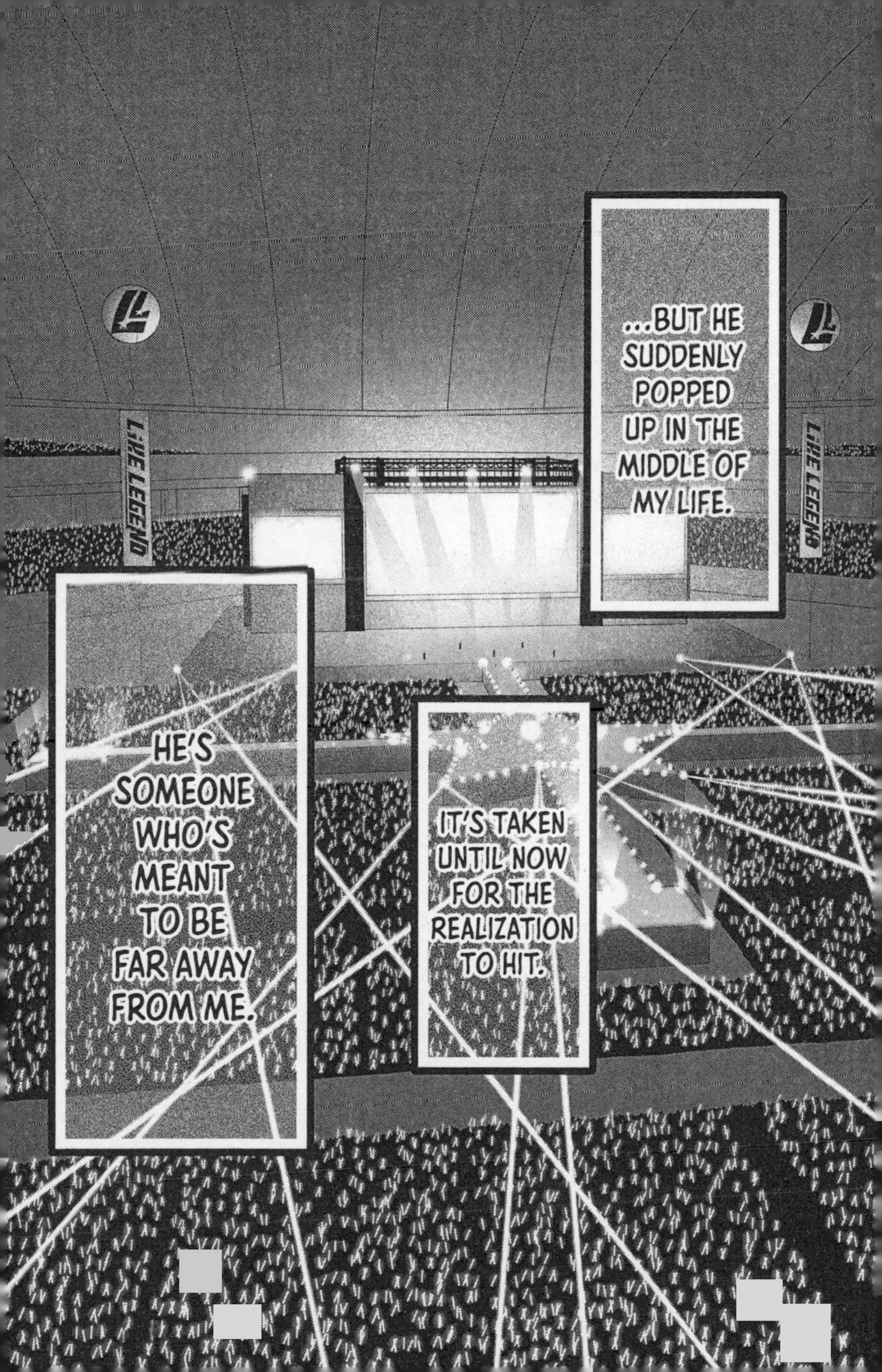

...BUT HE SUDDENLY POPPED UP IN THE MIDDLE OF MY LIFE.
HE'S SOMEONE WHO'S MEANT TO BE FAR AWAY FROM ME.
IT'S TAKEN UNTIL NOW FOR THE REALIZATION TO HIT.
LiKE LEGEND
LiKE LEGEND

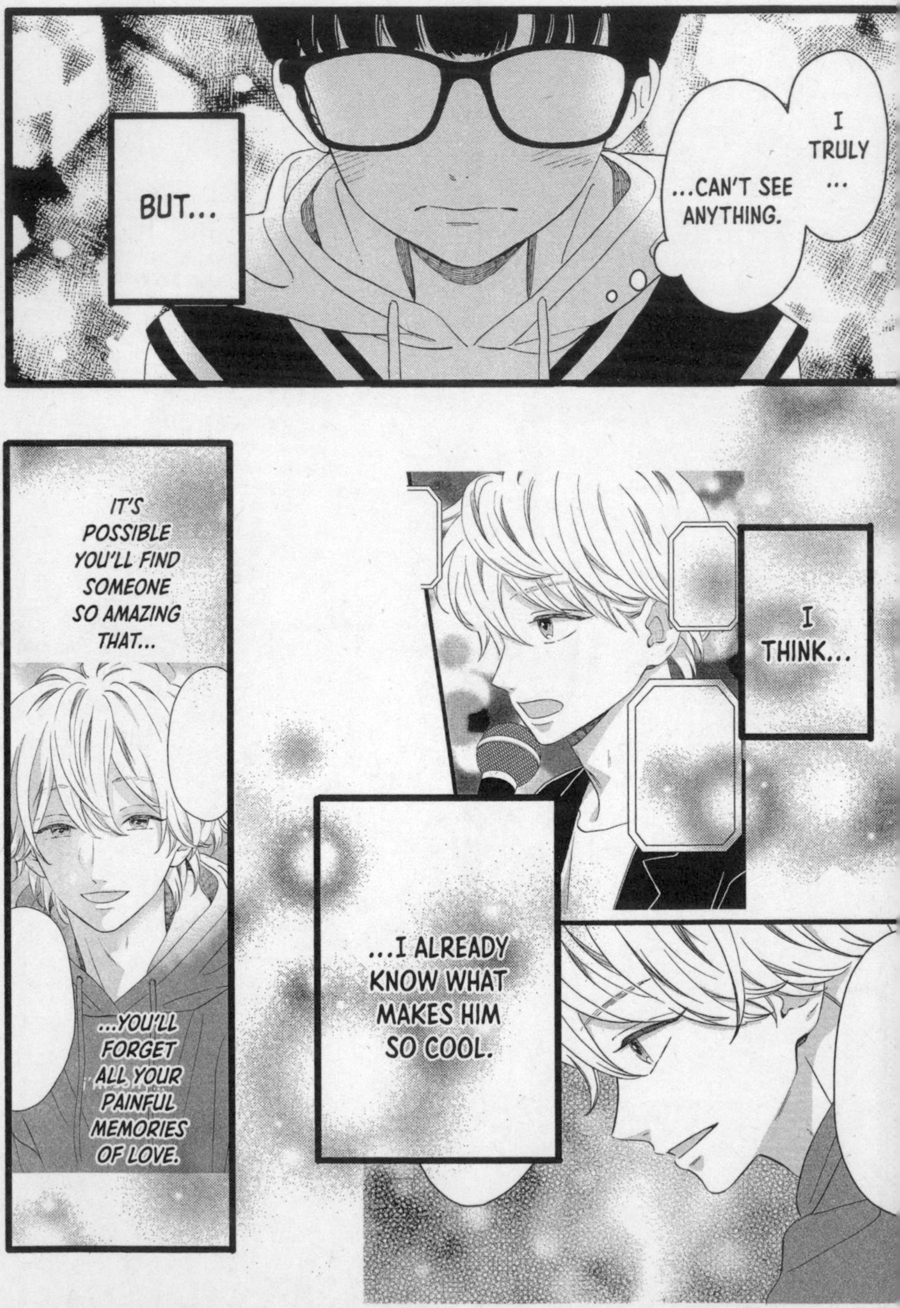
I TRULY ...
...CAN'T SEE ANYTHING.
BUT...
I THINK...
...I ALREADY KNOW WHAT MAKES HIM SO COOL.
IT'S POSSIBLE YOU'LL FIND SOMEONE SO AMAZING THAT...
...YOU'LL FORGET ALL YOUR PAINFUL MEMORIES OF LOVE.

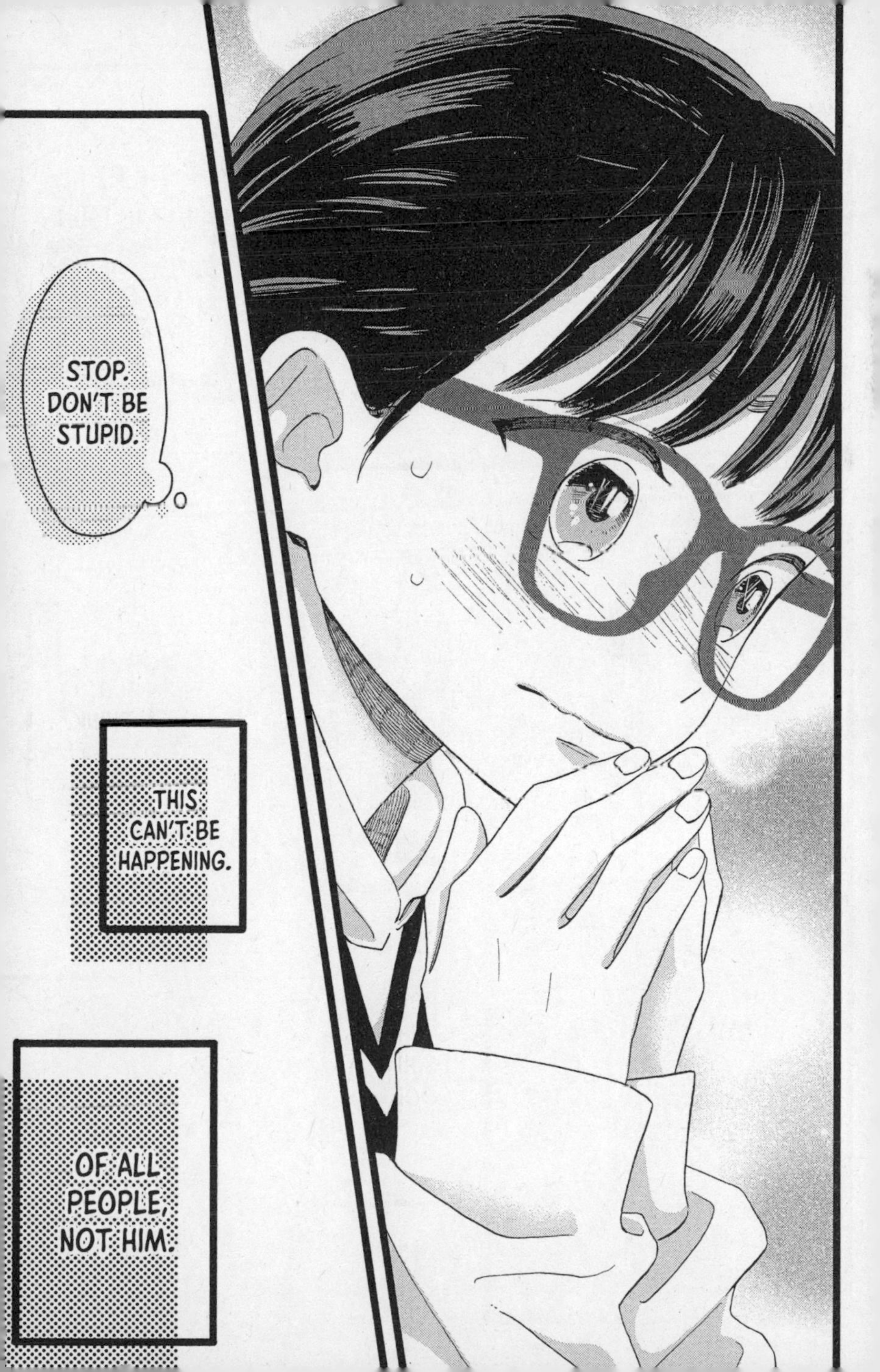
STOP. DON'T BE STUPID.
THIS CAN'T BE HAPPENING.
OF ALL PEOPLE, NOT HIM.

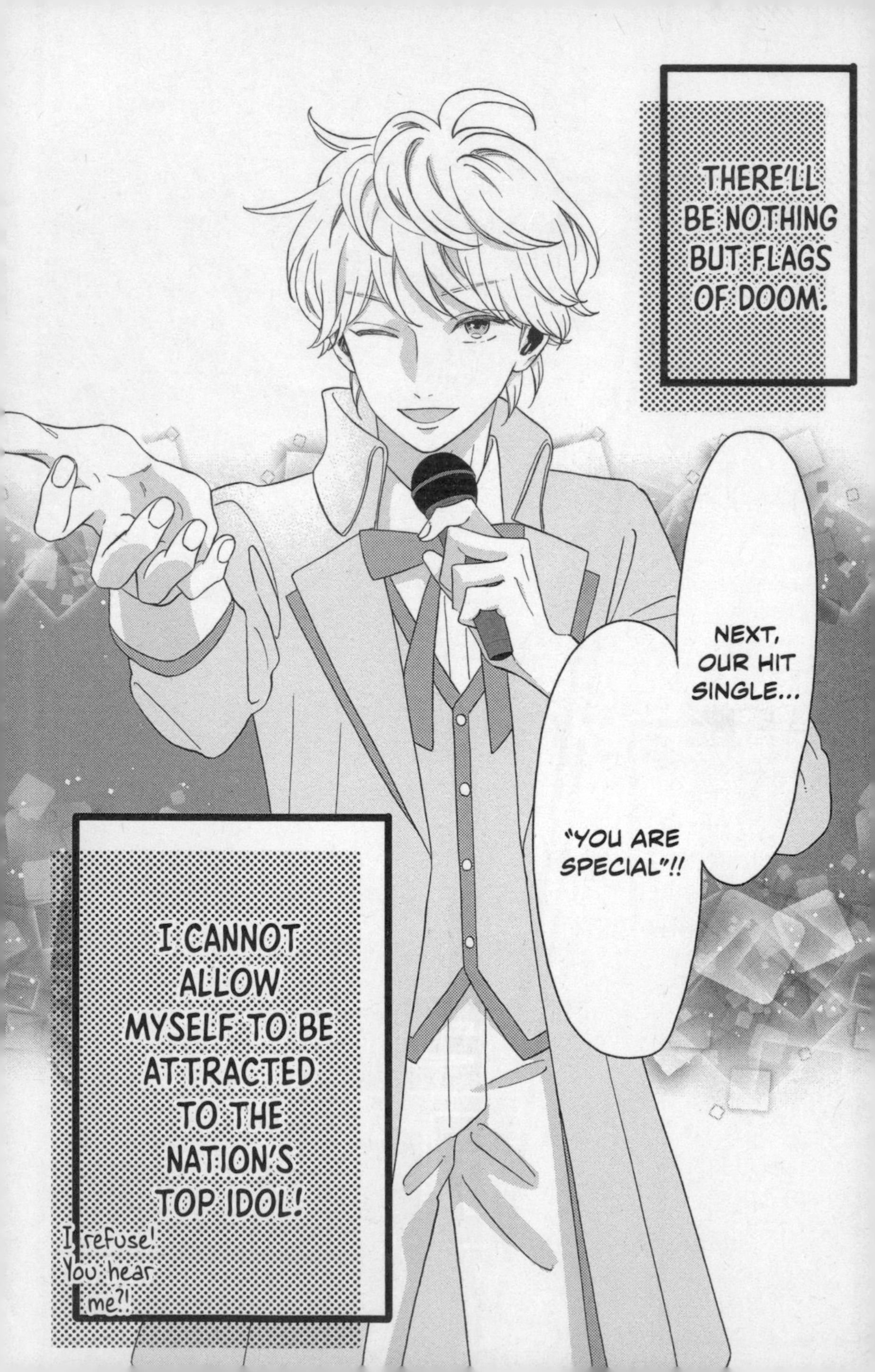
THERE'LL BE NOTHING BUT FLAGS OF DOOM.
NEXT, OUR HIT SINGLE... "YOU ARE SPECIAL"!!
I CANNOT ALLOW MYSELF TO BE ATTRACTED TO THE NATION'S TOP IDOL!
I refuse! You hear me?!

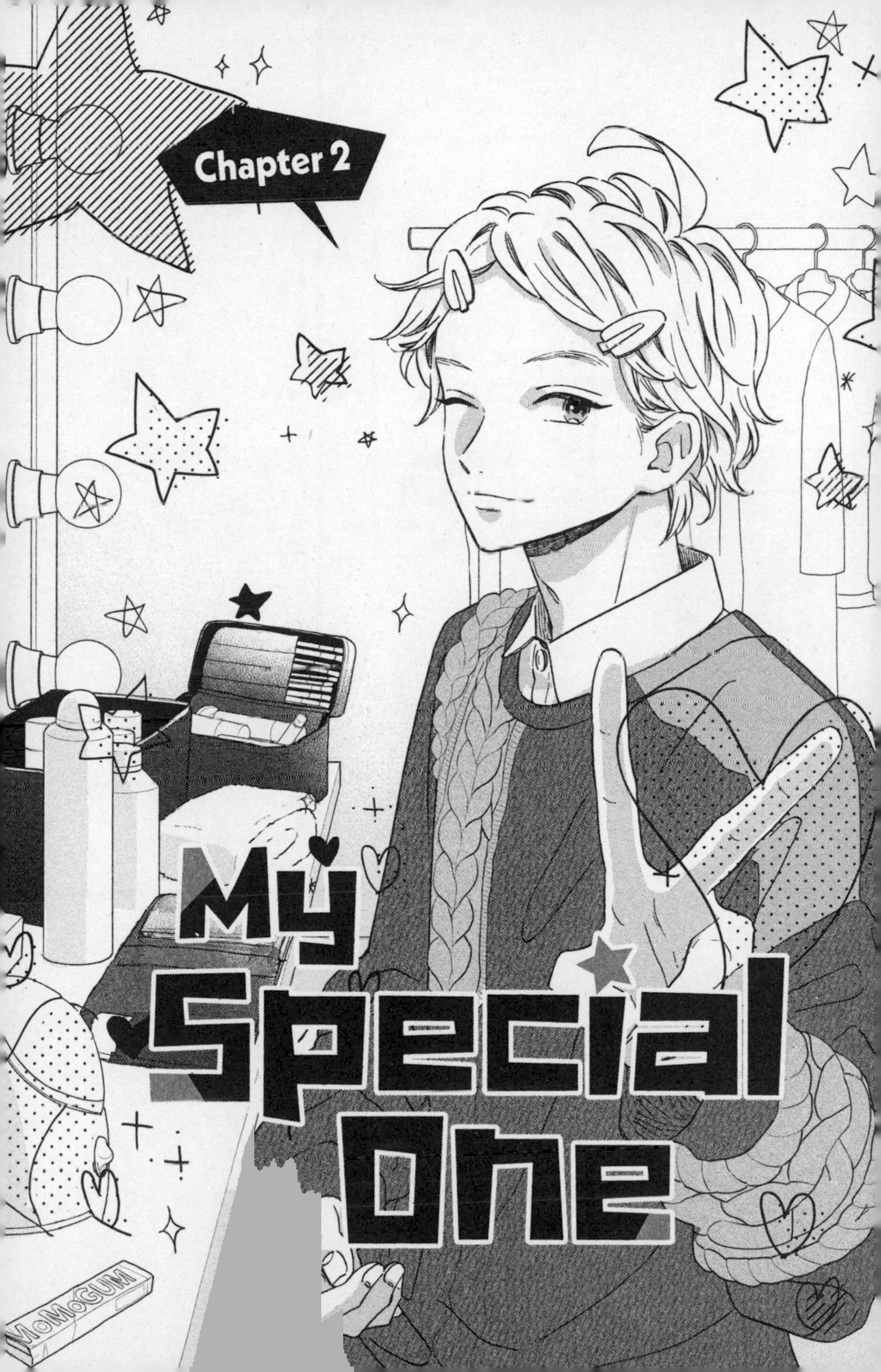

Chapter 2
My Special One
MoMoGUM

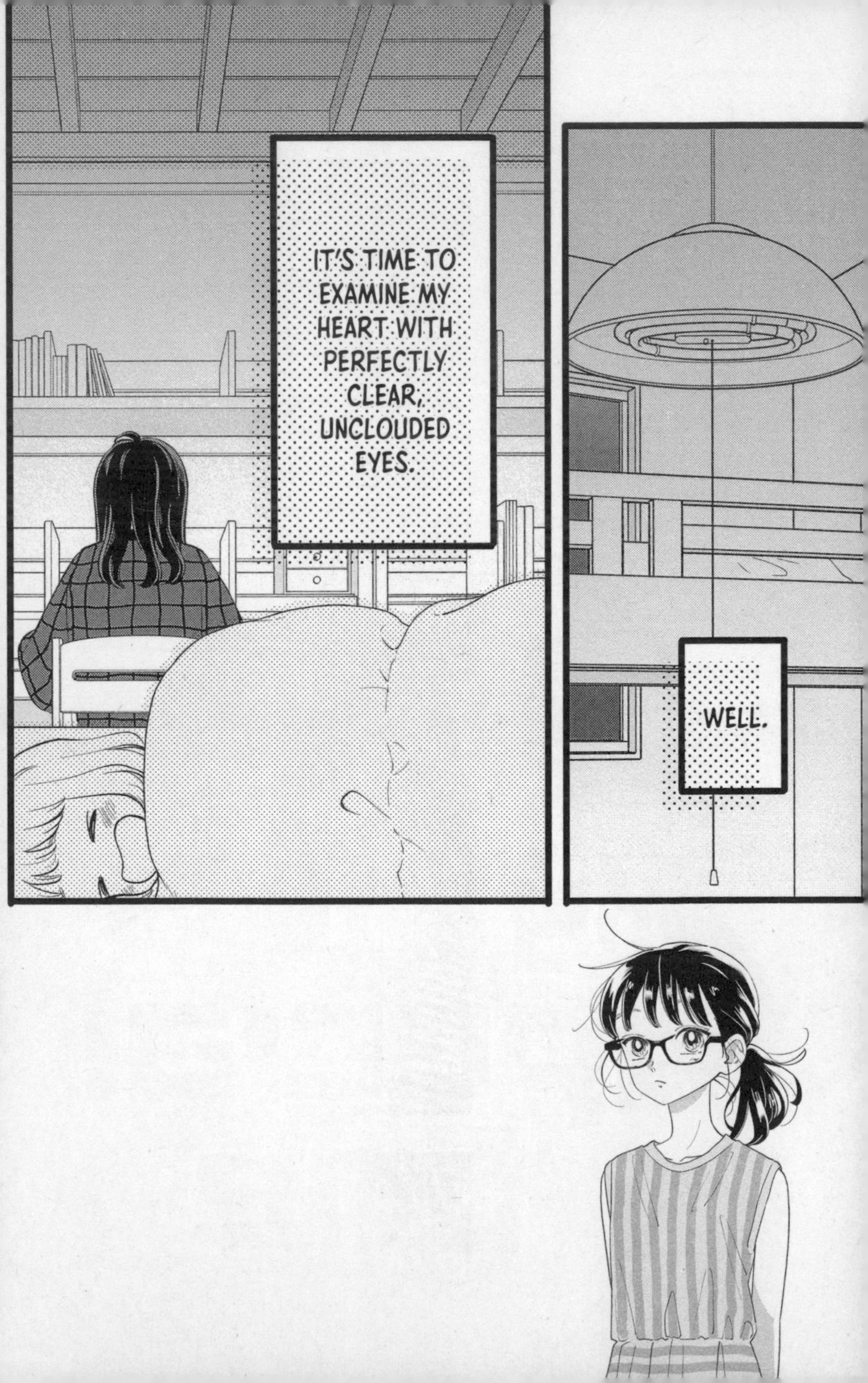
WELL.
IT'S TIME TO EXAMINE MY HEART WITH PERFECTLY CLEAR, UNCLOUDED EYES.

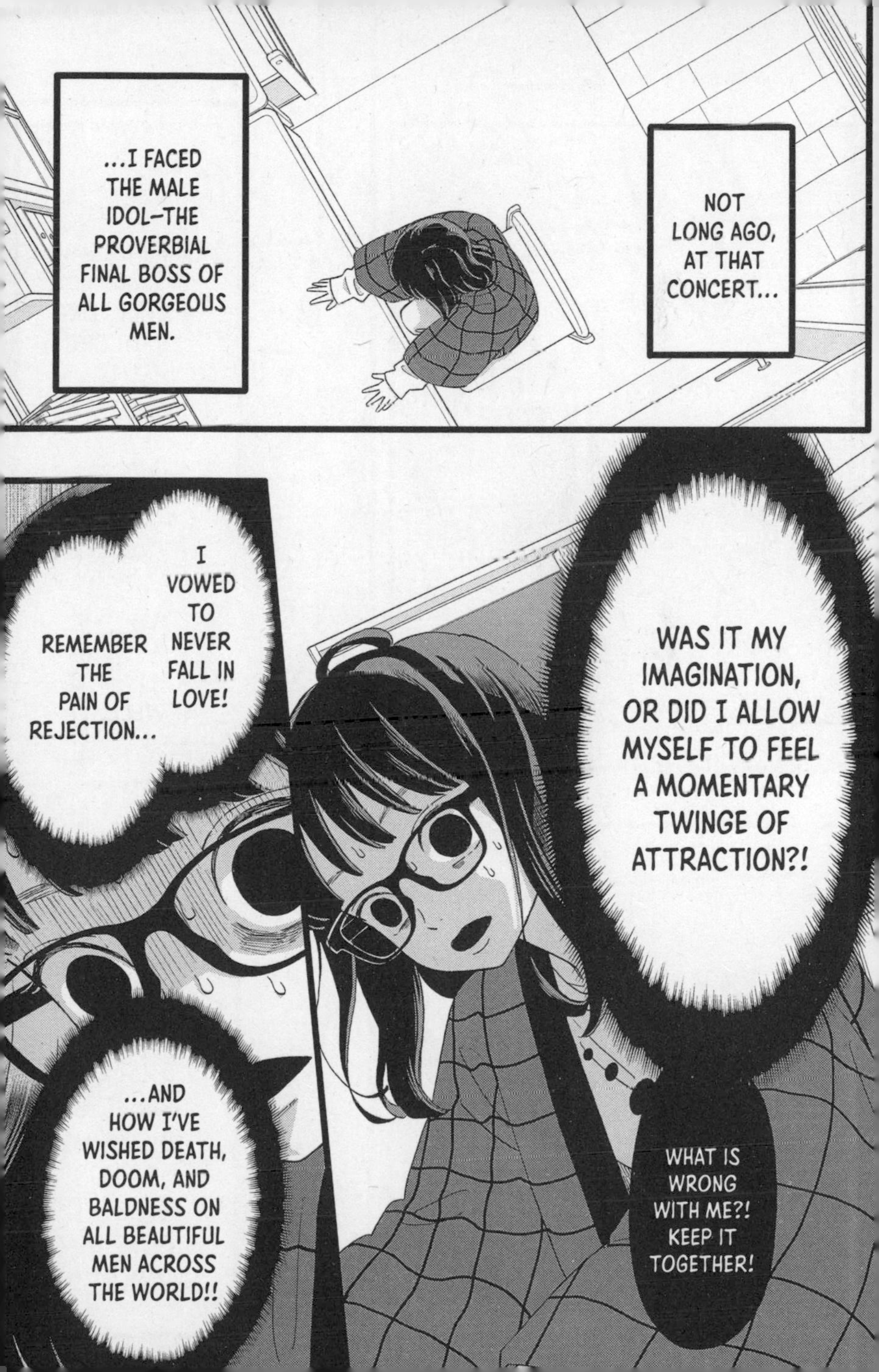
NOT LONG AGO, AT THAT CONCERT...
...I FACED THE MALE IDOL—THE PROVERBIAL FINAL BOSS OF ALL GORGEOUS MEN.
WAS IT MY IMAGINATION, OR DID I ALLOW MYSELF TO FEEL A MOMENTARY TWINGE OF ATTRACTION?!
I VOWED TO NEVER FALL IN LOVE!
REMEMBER THE PAIN OF REJECTION...
...AND HOW I'VE WISHED DEATH, DOOM, AND BALDNESS ON ALL BEAUTIFUL MEN ACROSS THE WORLD!!
WHAT IS WRONG WITH ME?! KEEP IT TOGETHER!

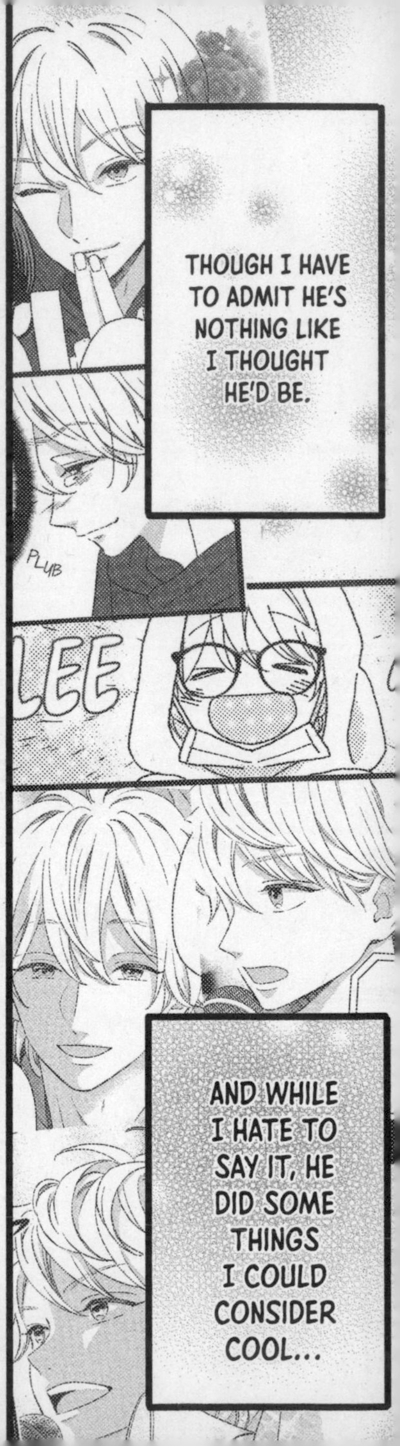
THOUGH I HAVE TO ADMIT HE'S NOTHING LIKE I THOUGHT HE'D BE.
PLUB
AND WHILE I HATE TO SAY IT, HE DID SOME THINGS I COULD CONSIDER COOL...
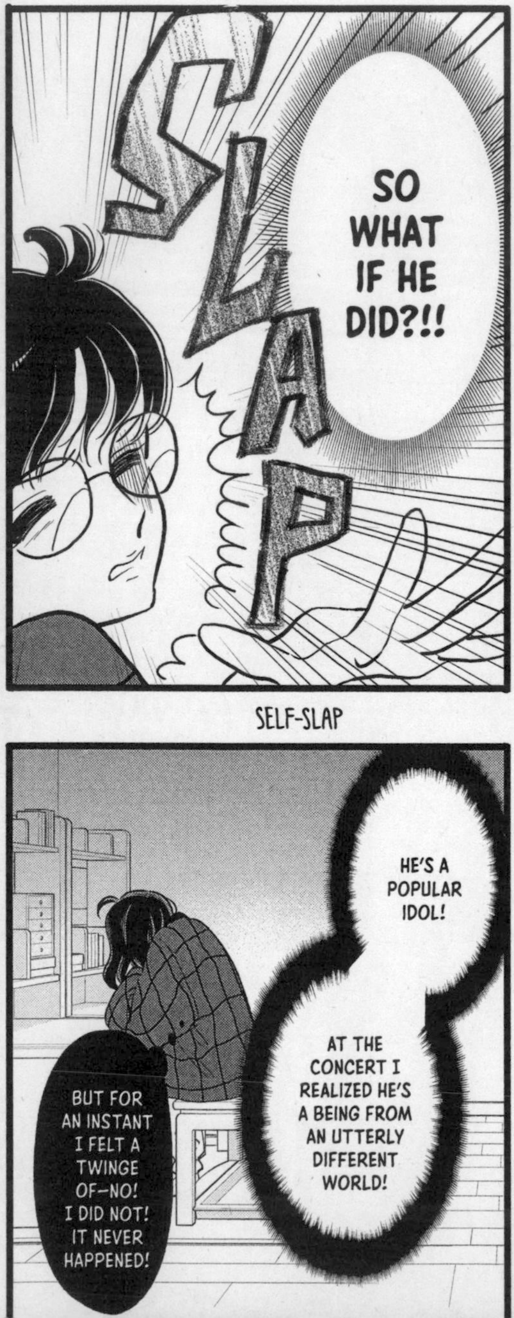
SO WHAT IF HE DID?!!
SLAP
SELF-SLAP
HE'S A POPULAR IDOL!
AT THE CONCERT I REALIZED HE'S A BEING FROM AN UTTERLY DIFFERENT WORLD!
BUT FOR AN INSTANT I FELT A TWINGE OF—NO! I DID NOT! IT NEVER HAPPENED!

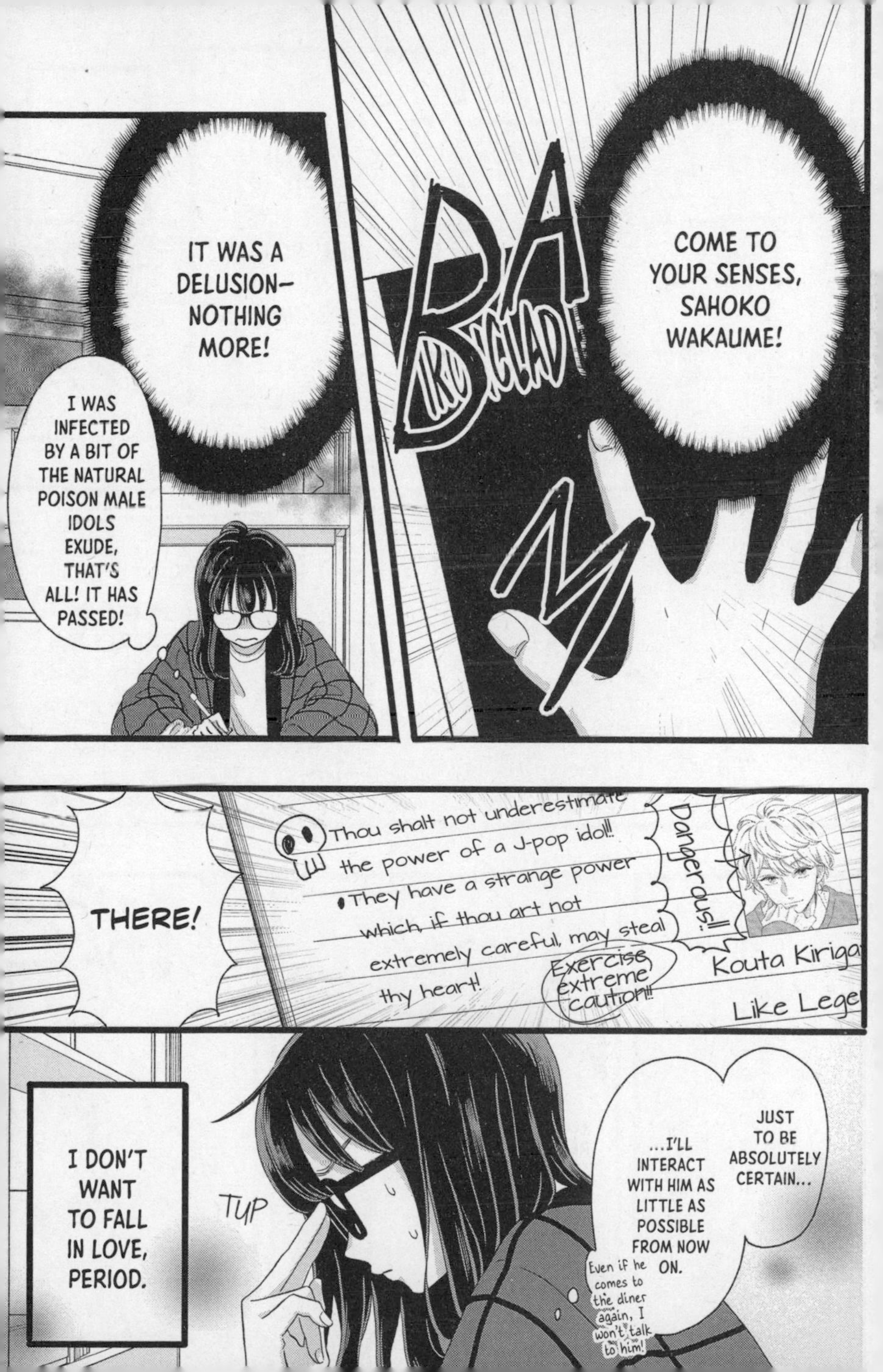
BAM
COME TO YOUR SENSES, SAHOKO WAKAUME!
IT WAS A DELUSION—NOTHING MORE!
I WAS INFECTED BY A BIT OF THE NATURAL POISON MALE IDOLS EXUDE, THAT'S ALL! IT HAS PASSED!
Dangerous!!
Kouta Kiriga
Like Lege
Thou shalt not underestimate the power of a J-pop idol!!
• They have a strange power which, if thou art not extremely careful, may steal thy heart!
Exercise extreme caution!!
THERE!
JUST TO BE ABSOLUTELY CERTAIN...
...I'LL INTERACT WITH HIM AS LITTLE AS POSSIBLE FROM NOW ON.
Even if he comes to the diner again, I won't talk to him!
TUP
I DON'T WANT TO FALL IN LOVE, PERIOD.

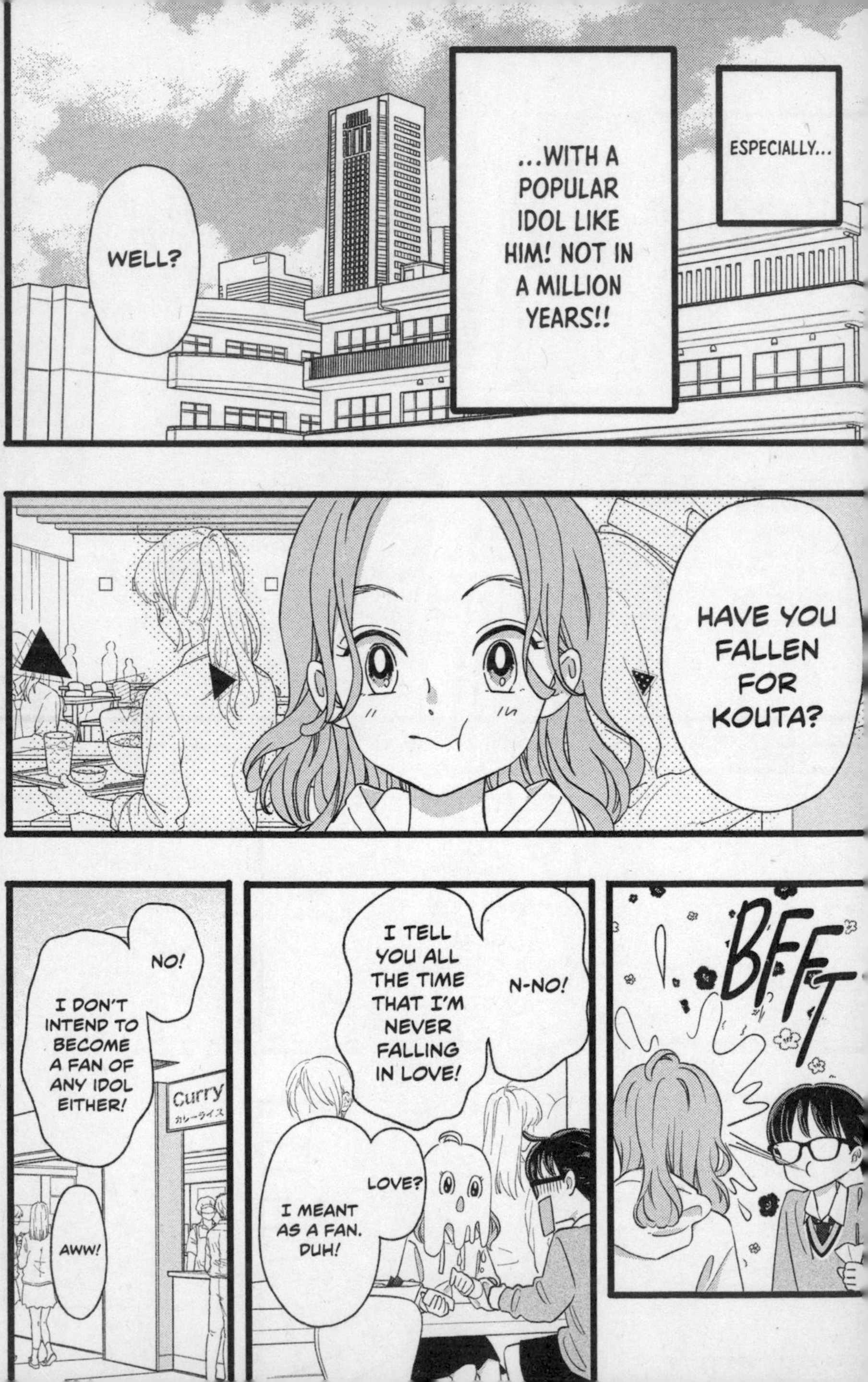
ESPECIALLY...
...WITH A POPULAR IDOL LIKE HIM! NOT IN A MILLION YEARS!!
WELL?
HAVE YOU FALLEN FOR KOUTA?
BFFT
N-NO!
I TELL YOU ALL THE TIME THAT I'M NEVER FALLING IN LOVE!
LOVE?
I MEANT AS A FAN. DUH!
NO!
I DON'T INTEND TO BECOME A FAN OF ANY IDOL EITHER!
Curry
カレーライス
AWW!

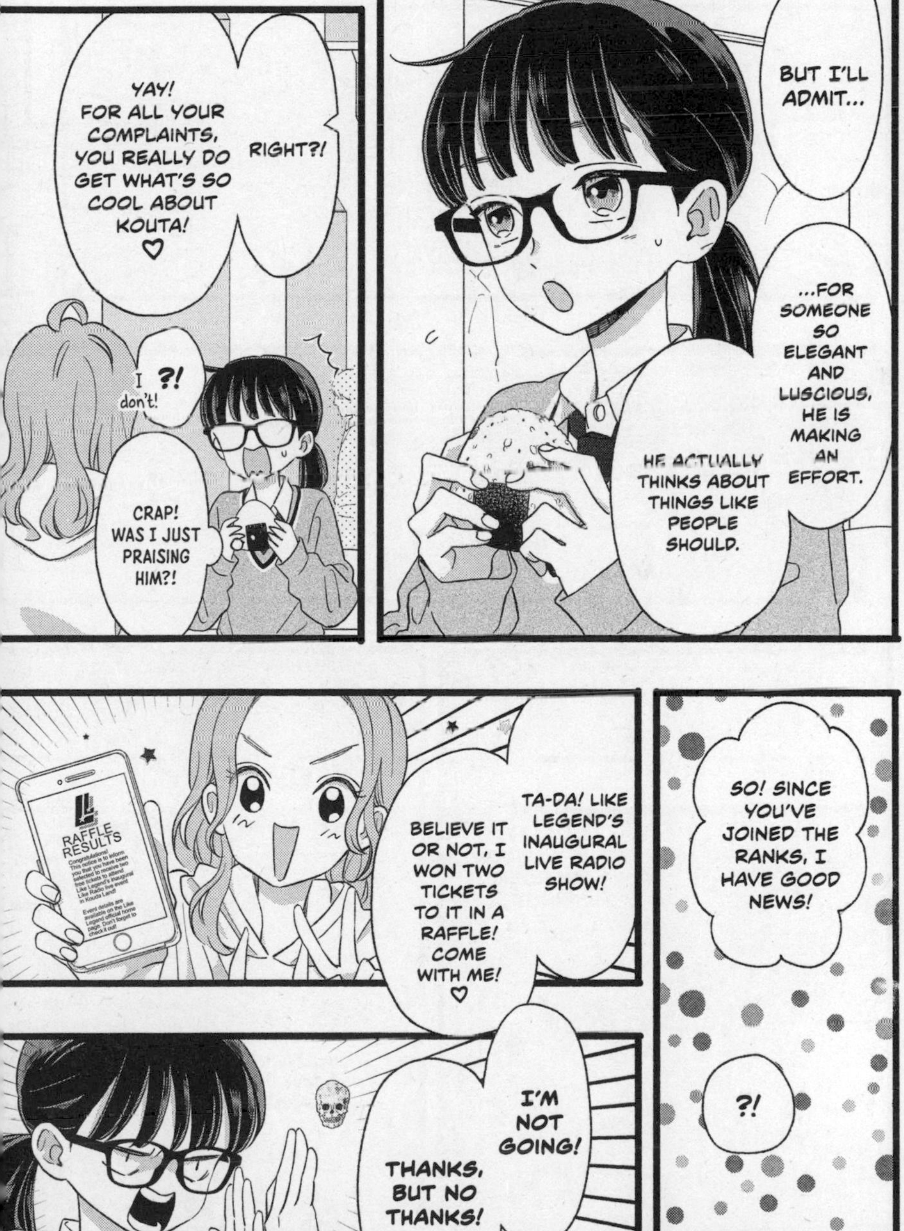
BUT I'LL ADMIT...
...FOR SOMEONE SO ELEGANT AND LUSCIOUS, HE IS MAKING AN EFFORT.
HE ACTUALLY THINKS ABOUT THINGS LIKE PEOPLE SHOULD.
YAY! FOR ALL YOUR COMPLAINTS, YOU REALLY DO GET WHAT'S SO COOL ABOUT KOUTA! ♡
RIGHT?!
?!
I don't!
CRAP! WAS I JUST PRAISING HIM?!
SO! SINCE YOU'VE JOINED THE RANKS, I HAVE GOOD NEWS!
?!
TA-DA! LIKE LEGEND'S INAUGURAL LIVE RADIO SHOW!
BELIEVE IT OR NOT, I WON TWO TICKETS TO IT IN A RAFFLE! COME WITH ME! ♡
RAFFLE RESULTS
Congratulations! This notice is to inform you that you have been selected to receive two free tickets to attend Like Legend's inaugural Like Radio live event in Kouda Land!
Event details are available on the Like Legend official home page. Don't forget to check it out!
I'M NOT GOING!
THANKS, BUT NO THANKS!

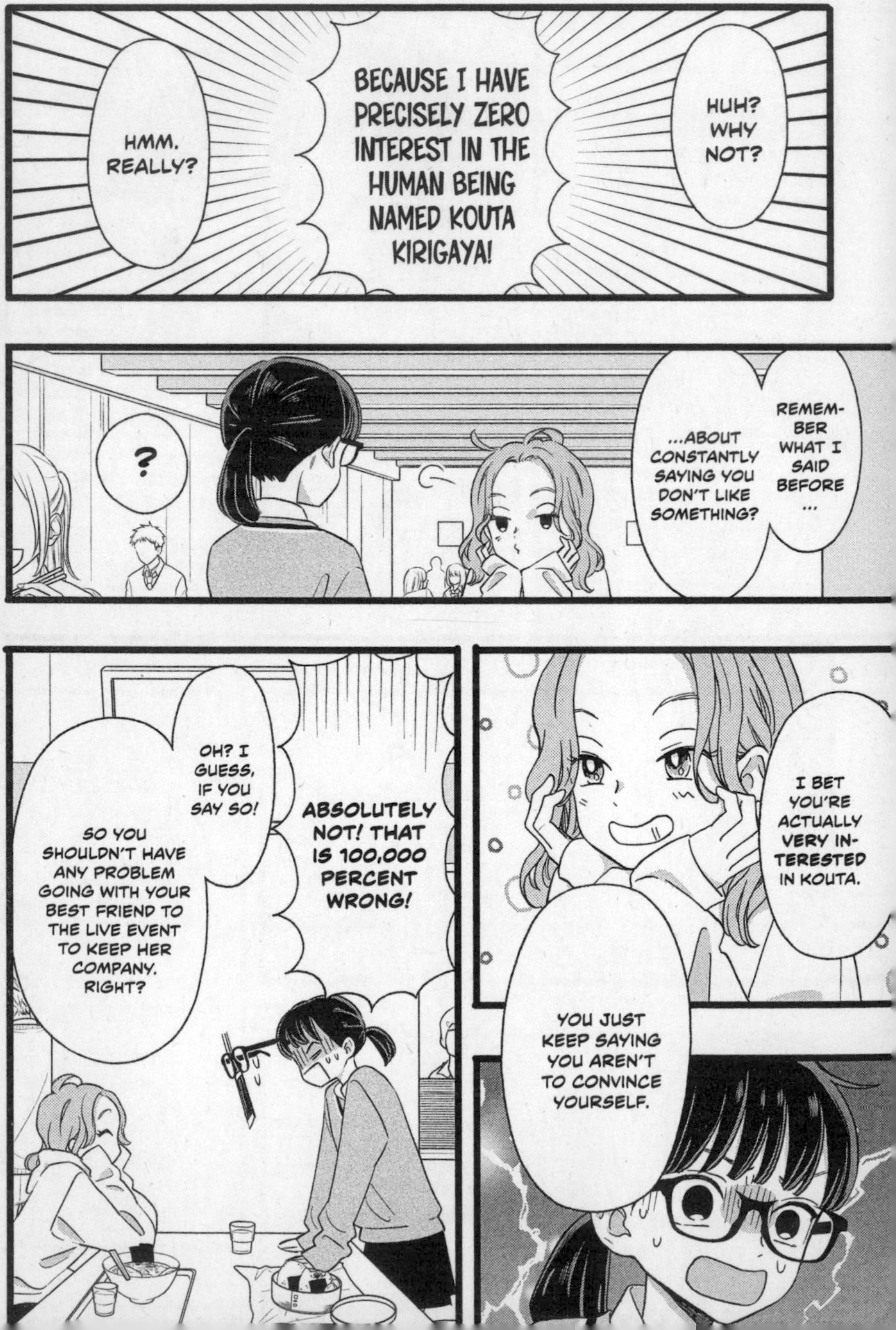
HUH? WHY NOT?
BECAUSE I HAVE PRECISELY ZERO INTEREST IN THE HUMAN BEING NAMED KOUTA KIRIGAYA!
HMM. REALLY?
REMEMBER WHAT I SAID BEFORE...
...ABOUT CONSTANTLY SAYING YOU DON'T LIKE SOMETHING?
?
I BET YOU'RE ACTUALLY VERY INTERESTED IN KOUTA.
YOU JUST KEEP SAYING YOU AREN'T TO CONVINCE YOURSELF.
ABSOLUTELY NOT! THAT IS 100,000 PERCENT WRONG!
OH? I GUESS, IF YOU SAY SO!
SO YOU SHOULDN'T HAVE ANY PROBLEM GOING WITH YOUR BEST FRIEND TO THE LIVE EVENT TO KEEP HER COMPANY. RIGHT?

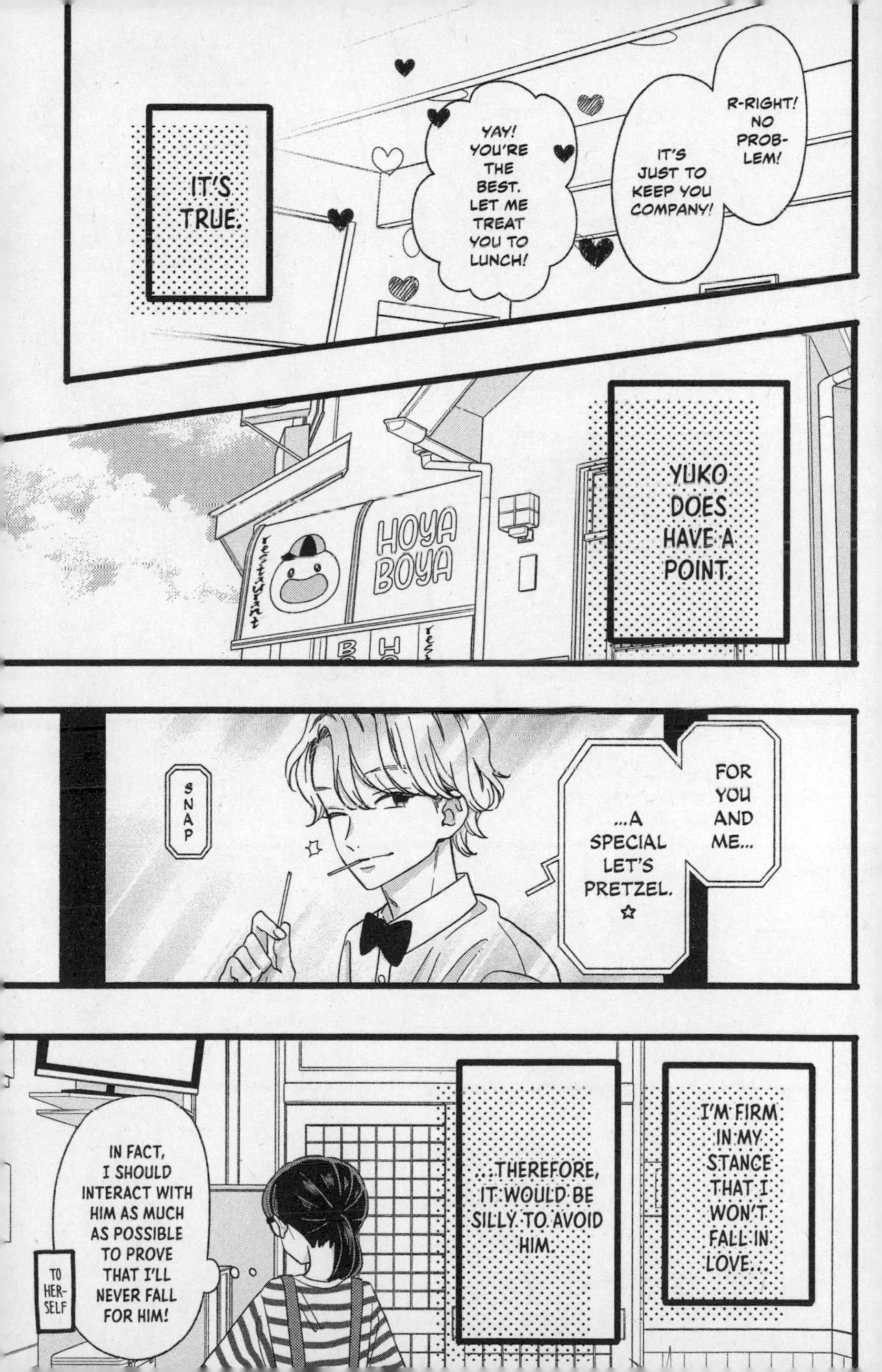
R-RIGHT! NO PROBLEM!
IT'S JUST TO KEEP YOU COMPANY!
YAY! YOU'RE THE BEST. LET ME TREAT YOU TO LUNCH!
IT'S TRUE.
YUKO DOES HAVE A POINT.
HOYA BOYA
FOR YOU AND ME...
...A SPECIAL LET'S PRETZEL. ☆
SNAP
I'M FIRM IN MY STANCE THAT I WON'T FALL IN LOVE...
...THEREFORE, IT WOULD BE SILLY TO AVOID HIM.
IN FACT, I SHOULD INTERACT WITH HIM AS MUCH AS POSSIBLE TO PROVE THAT I'LL NEVER FALL FOR HIM!
TO HERSELF

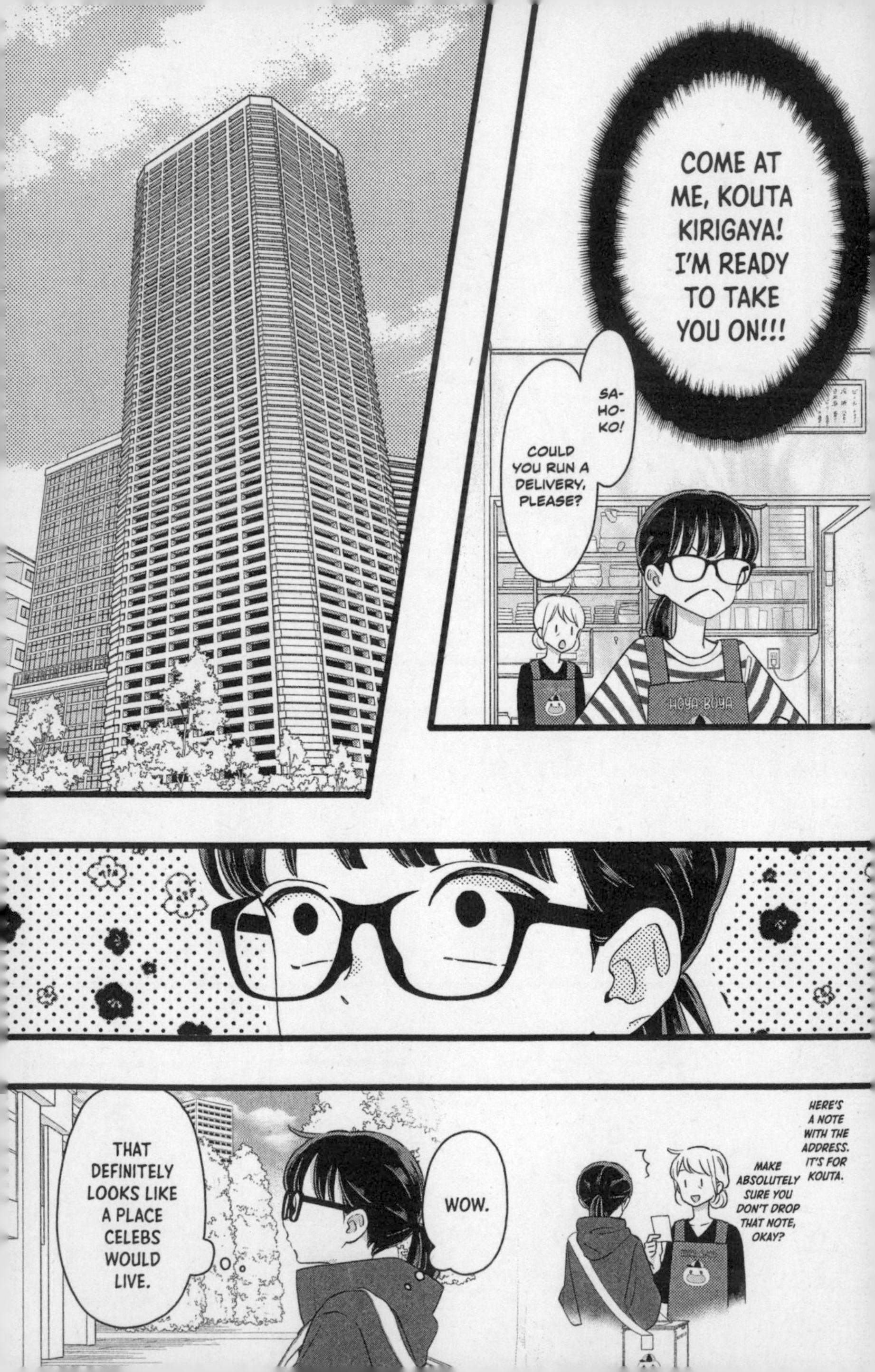
COME AT ME, KOUTA KIRIGAYA! I'M READY TO TAKE YOU ON!!!
SA-HO-KO!
COULD YOU RUN A DELIVERY, PLEASE?
HOYA BOYA
HERE'S A NOTE WITH THE ADDRESS. IT'S FOR KOUTA.
MAKE ABSOLUTELY SURE YOU DON'T DROP THAT NOTE, OKAY?
WOW.
THAT DEFINITELY LOOKS LIKE A PLACE CELEBS WOULD LIVE.

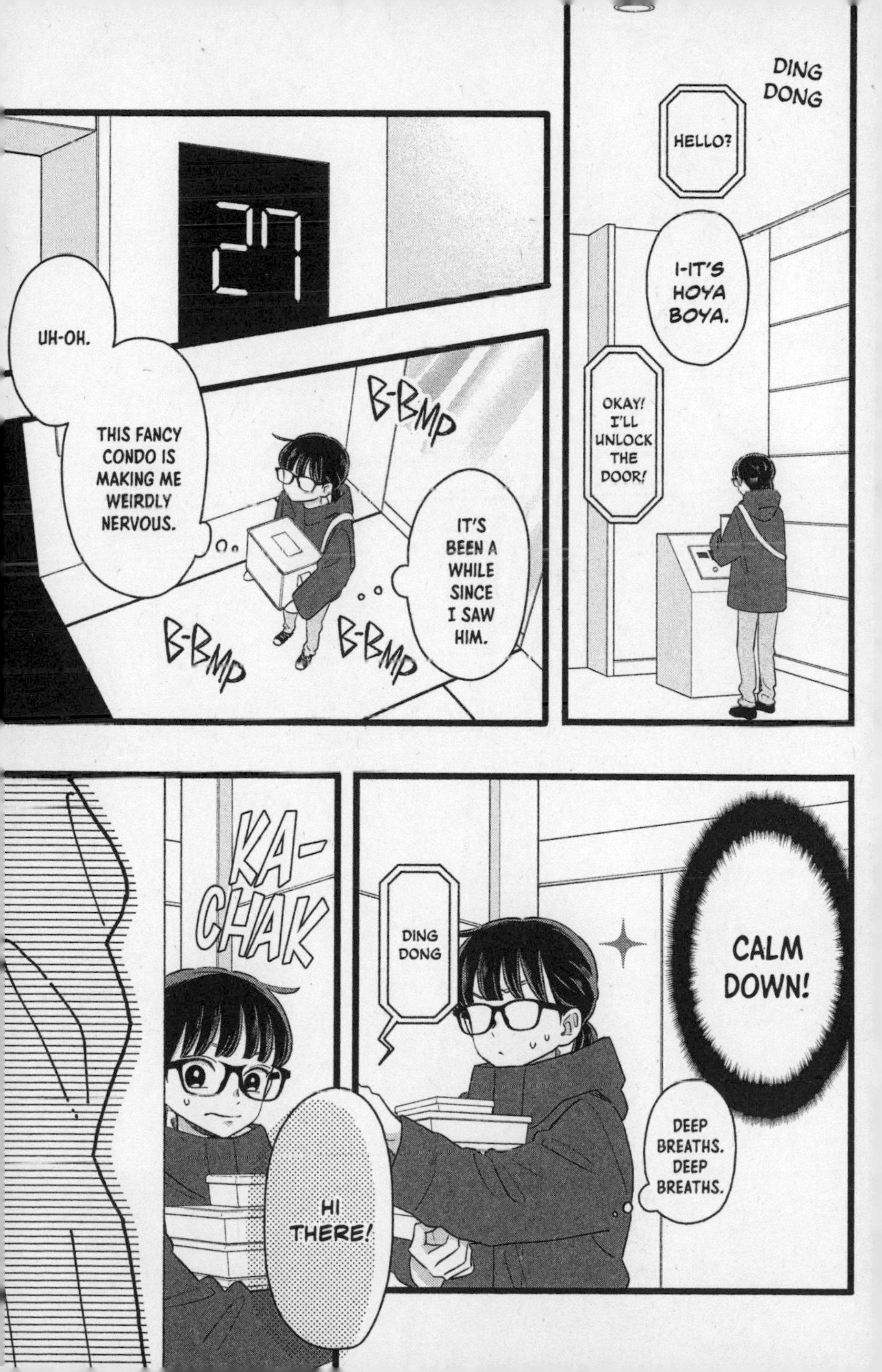
DING DONG
HELLO?
I-IT'S HOYA BOYA.
OKAY! I'LL UNLOCK THE DOOR!
UH-OH.
B-BMP
IT'S BEEN A WHILE SINCE I SAW HIM.
THIS FANCY CONDO IS MAKING ME WEIRDLY NERVOUS.
B-BMP
B-BMP
CALM DOWN!
DING DONG
DEEP BREATHS. DEEP BREATHS.
KA-CHAK
HI THERE!

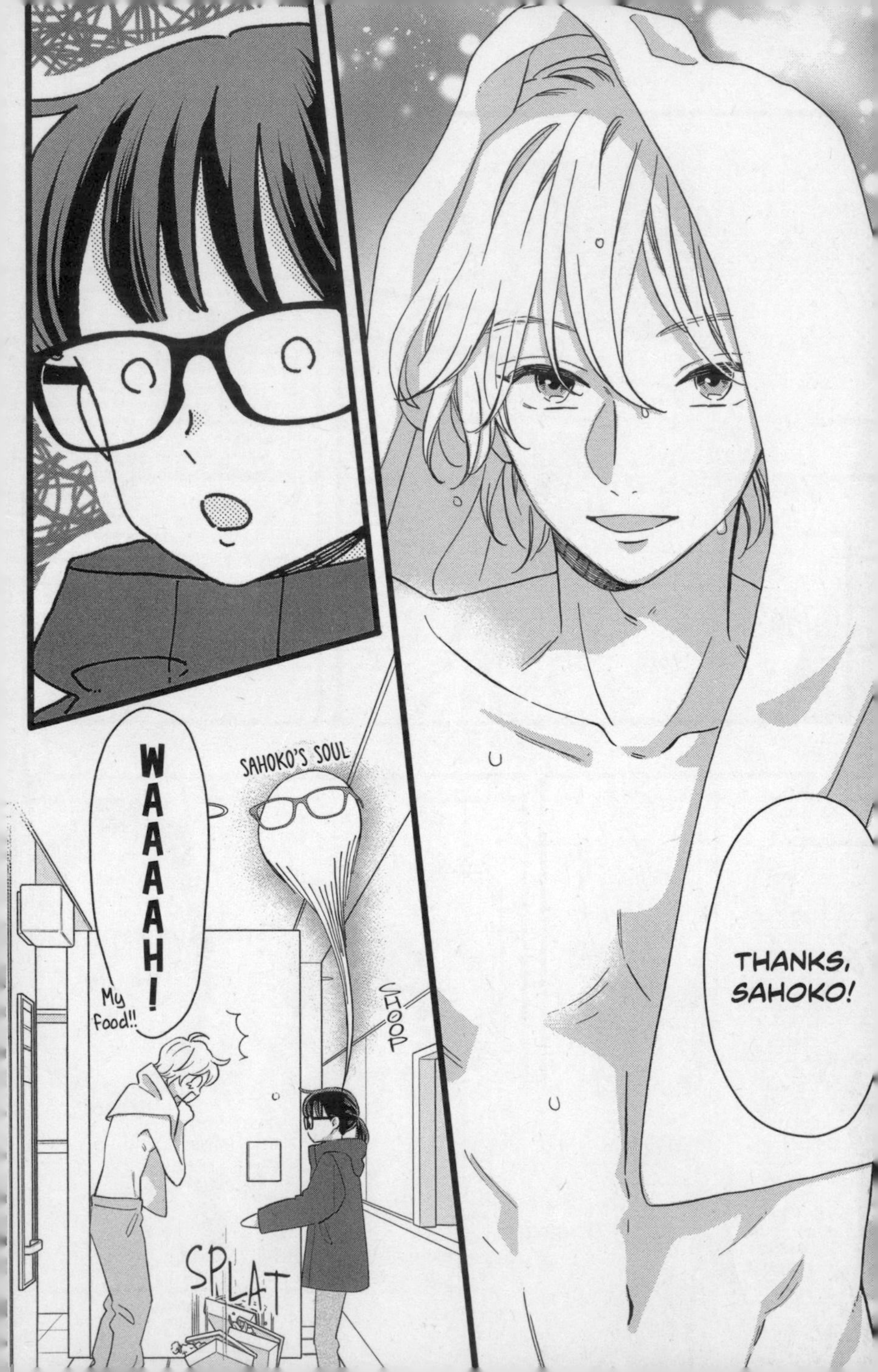
THANKS, SAHOKO!
WAAAAAH!
My food!!
SAHOKO'S SOUL
SHOOP
SPLAT

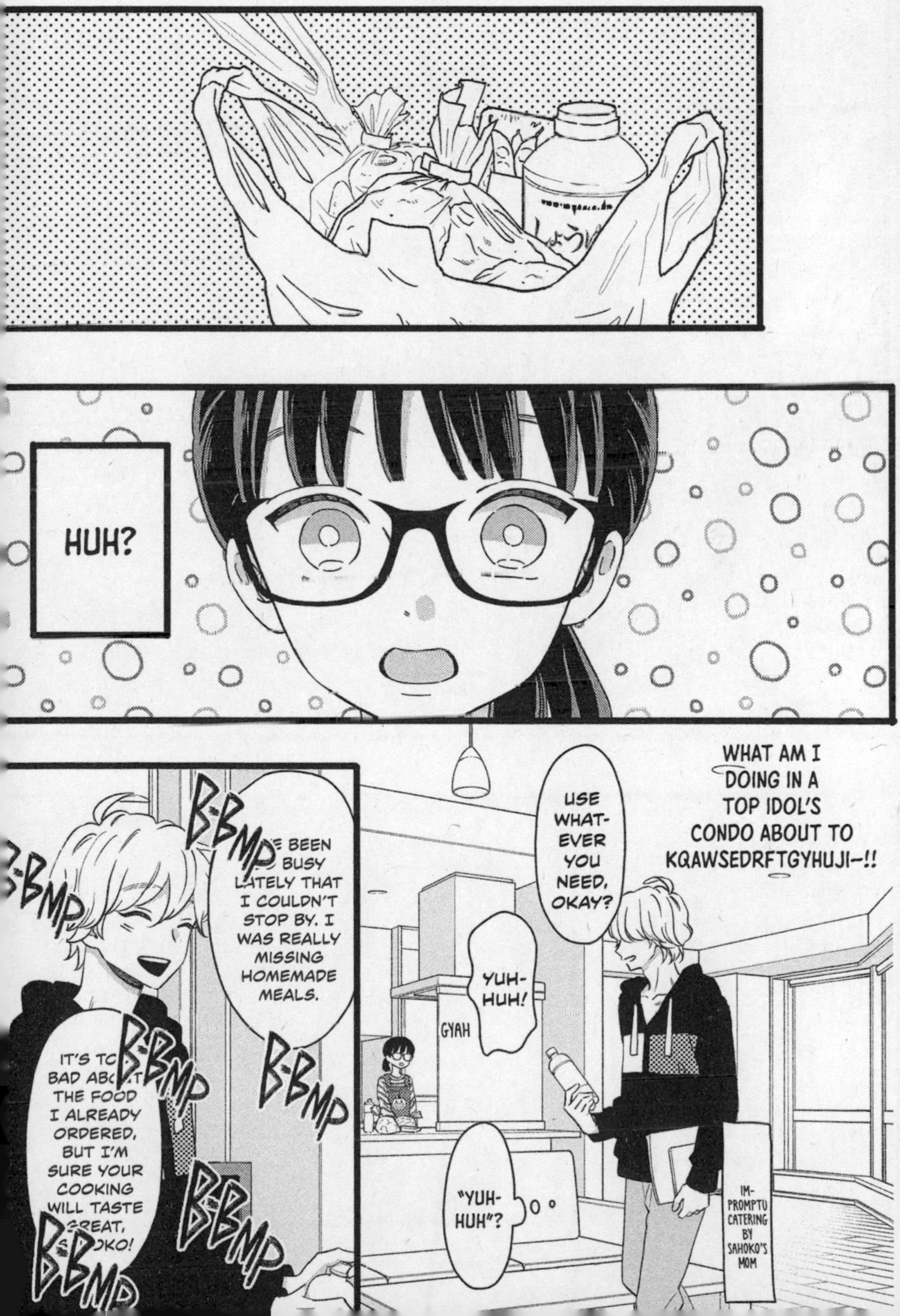
HUH?
WHAT AM I DOING IN A TOP IDOL'S CONDO ABOUT TO KQAWSEDRFTGYHUJI–!!
USE WHAT-EVER YOU NEED, OKAY?
YUH-HUH!
GYAH
"YUH-HUH"?
IM-PROMPTU CATERING BY SAHOKO'S MOM
B-BMP
B-BMP
E BEEN BUSY LATELY THAT I COULDN'T STOP BY. I WAS REALLY MISSING HOMEMADE MEALS.
B-BMP
B-BMP
IT'S TO BAD ABO THE FOOD I ALREADY ORDERED, BUT I'M SURE YOUR COOKING WILL TASTE GREAT,
B-BMP
B-BMP

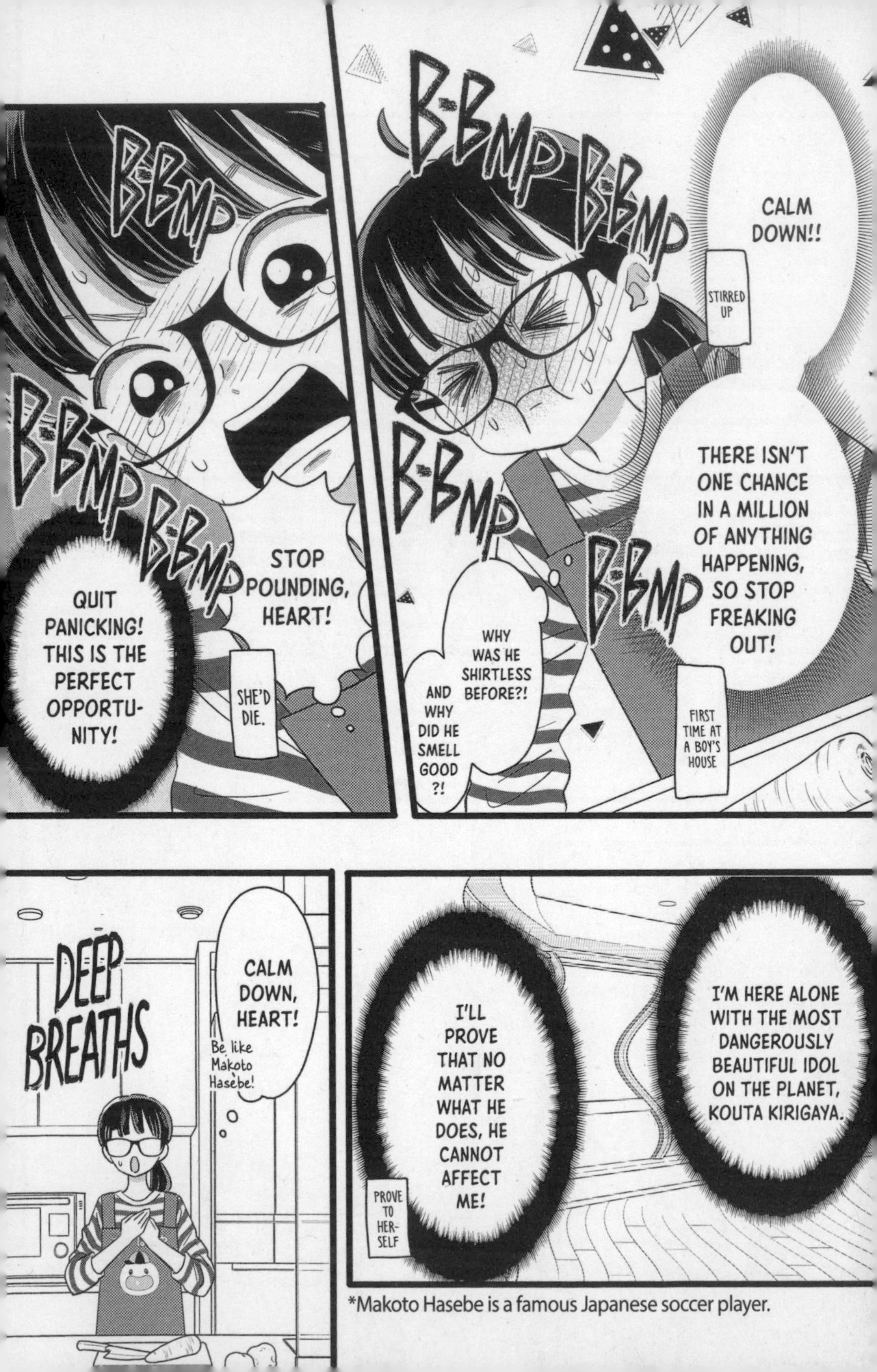
B-BMP B-BMP
CALM DOWN!!
STIRRED UP
B-BMP
B-BMP
THERE ISN'T ONE CHANCE IN A MILLION OF ANYTHING HAPPENING, SO STOP FREAKING OUT!
FIRST TIME AT A BOY'S HOUSE
WHY WAS HE SHIRTLESS BEFORE?!
AND WHY DID HE SMELL GOOD?!
B-BMP
STOP POUNDING, HEART!
B-BMP B-BMP
QUIT PANICKING! THIS IS THE PERFECT OPPORTU-NITY!
SHE'D DIE.
I'M HERE ALONE WITH THE MOST DANGEROUSLY BEAUTIFUL IDOL ON THE PLANET, KOUTA KIRIGAYA.
I'LL PROVE THAT NO MATTER WHAT HE DOES, HE CANNOT AFFECT ME!
PROVE TO HER-SELF
CALM DOWN, HEART!
Be like Makoto Hasebe!
DEEP BREATHS

*Makoto Hasebe is a famous Japanese soccer player.

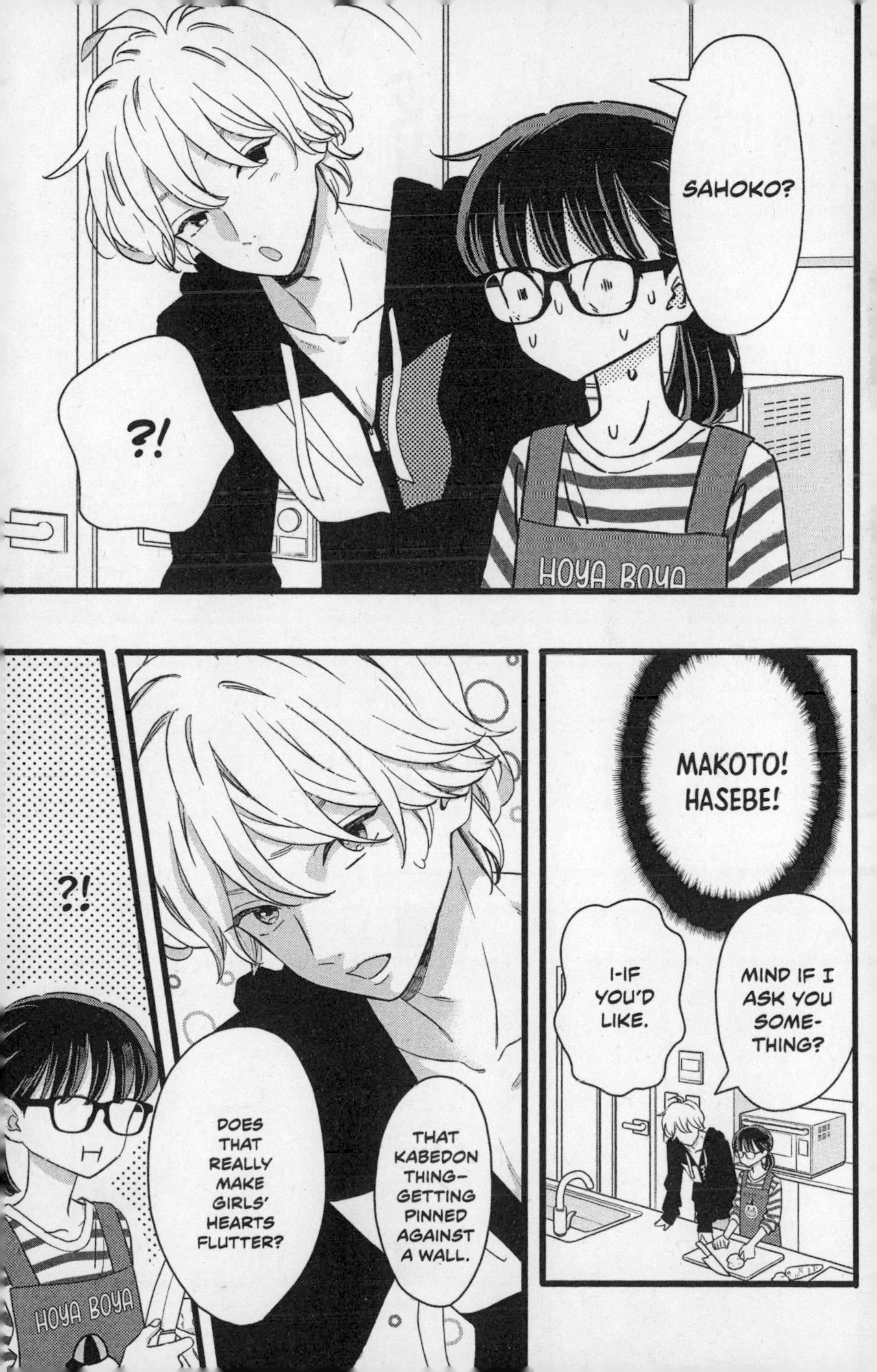
SAHOKO?
?!
HOYA BOYA
MAKOTO! HASEBE!
MIND IF I ASK YOU SOMETHING?
I-IF YOU'D LIKE.
THAT KABEDON THING—GETTING PINNED AGAINST A WALL.
DOES THAT REALLY MAKE GIRLS' HEARTS FLUTTER?
?!
HOYA BOYA

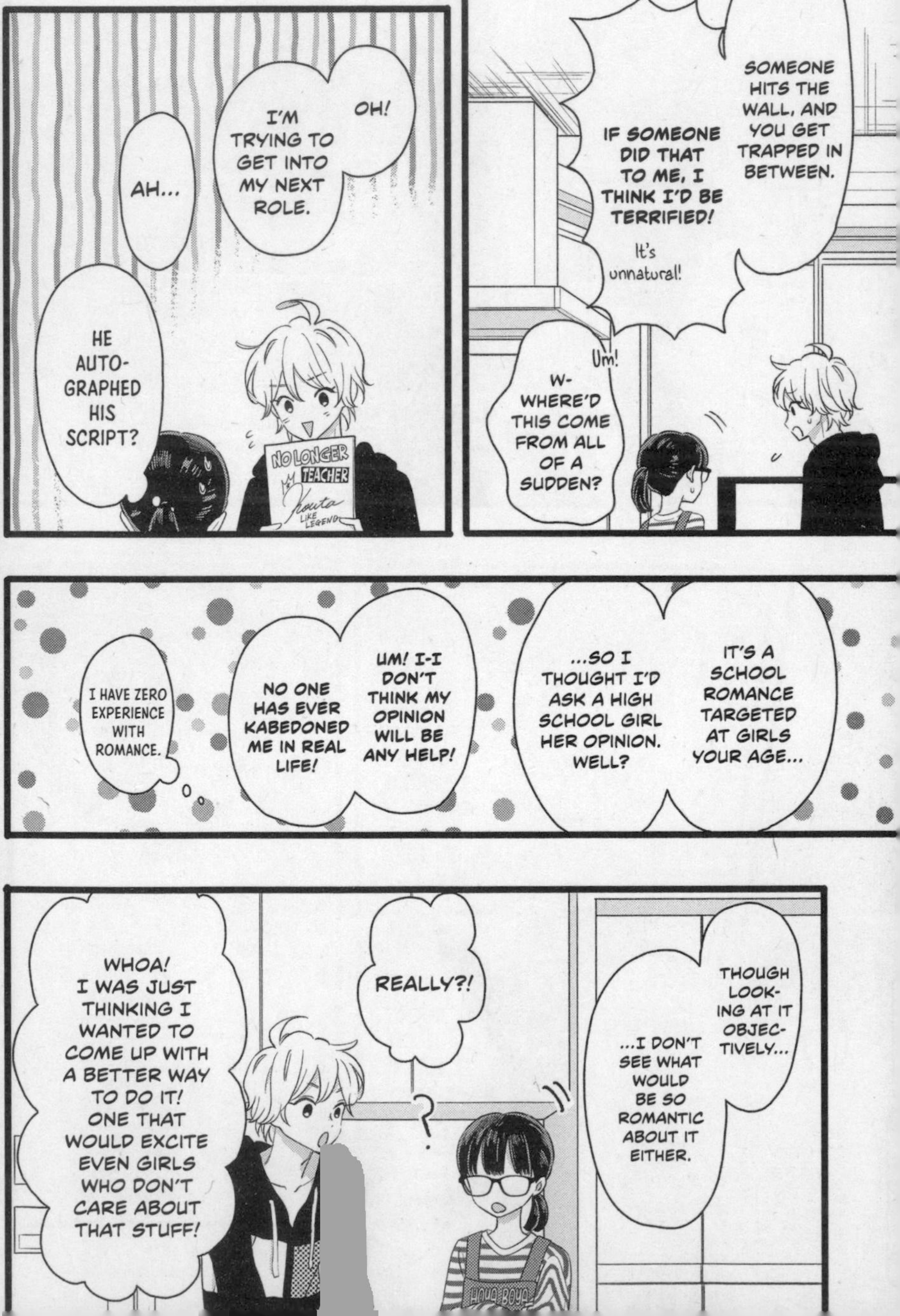
SOMEONE HITS THE WALL, AND YOU GET TRAPPED IN BETWEEN.
IF SOMEONE DID THAT TO ME, I THINK I'D BE TERRIFIED!
It's unnatural!
Um!
W-WHERE'D THIS COME FROM ALL OF A SUDDEN?
OH!
I'M TRYING TO GET INTO MY NEXT ROLE.
AH...
HE AUTOGRAPHED HIS SCRIPT?
NO LONGER TEACHER
IT'S A SCHOOL ROMANCE TARGETED AT GIRLS YOUR AGE...
...SO I THOUGHT I'D ASK A HIGH SCHOOL GIRL HER OPINION. WELL?
UM! I-I DON'T THINK MY OPINION WILL BE ANY HELP!
NO ONE HAS EVER KABEDONED ME IN REAL LIFE!
I HAVE ZERO EXPERIENCE WITH ROMANCE.
THOUGH LOOKING AT IT OBJECTIVELY...
...I DON'T SEE WHAT WOULD BE SO ROMANTIC ABOUT IT EITHER.
REALLY?!
WHOA! I WAS JUST THINKING I WANTED TO COME UP WITH A BETTER WAY TO DO IT! ONE THAT WOULD EXCITE EVEN GIRLS WHO DON'T CARE ABOUT THAT STUFF!

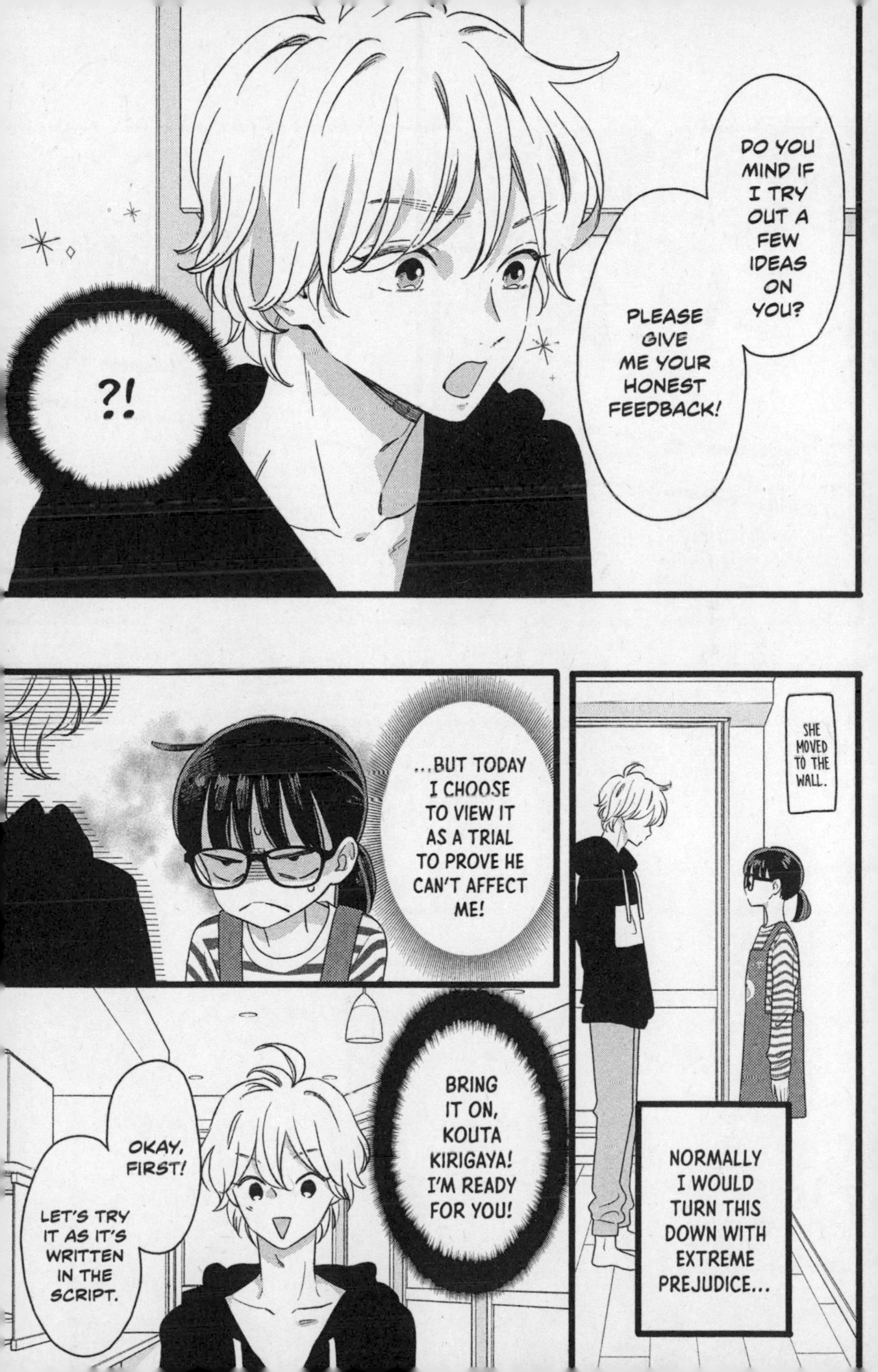
DO YOU MIND IF I TRY OUT A FEW IDEAS ON YOU?
PLEASE GIVE ME YOUR HONEST FEEDBACK!
?!
SHE MOVED TO THE WALL.
NORMALLY I WOULD TURN THIS DOWN WITH EXTREME PREJUDICE...
...BUT TODAY I CHOOSE TO VIEW IT AS A TRIAL TO PROVE HE CAN'T AFFECT ME!
BRING IT ON, KOUTA KIRIGAYA! I'M READY FOR YOU!
OKAY, FIRST!
LET'S TRY IT AS IT'S WRITTEN IN THE SCRIPT.

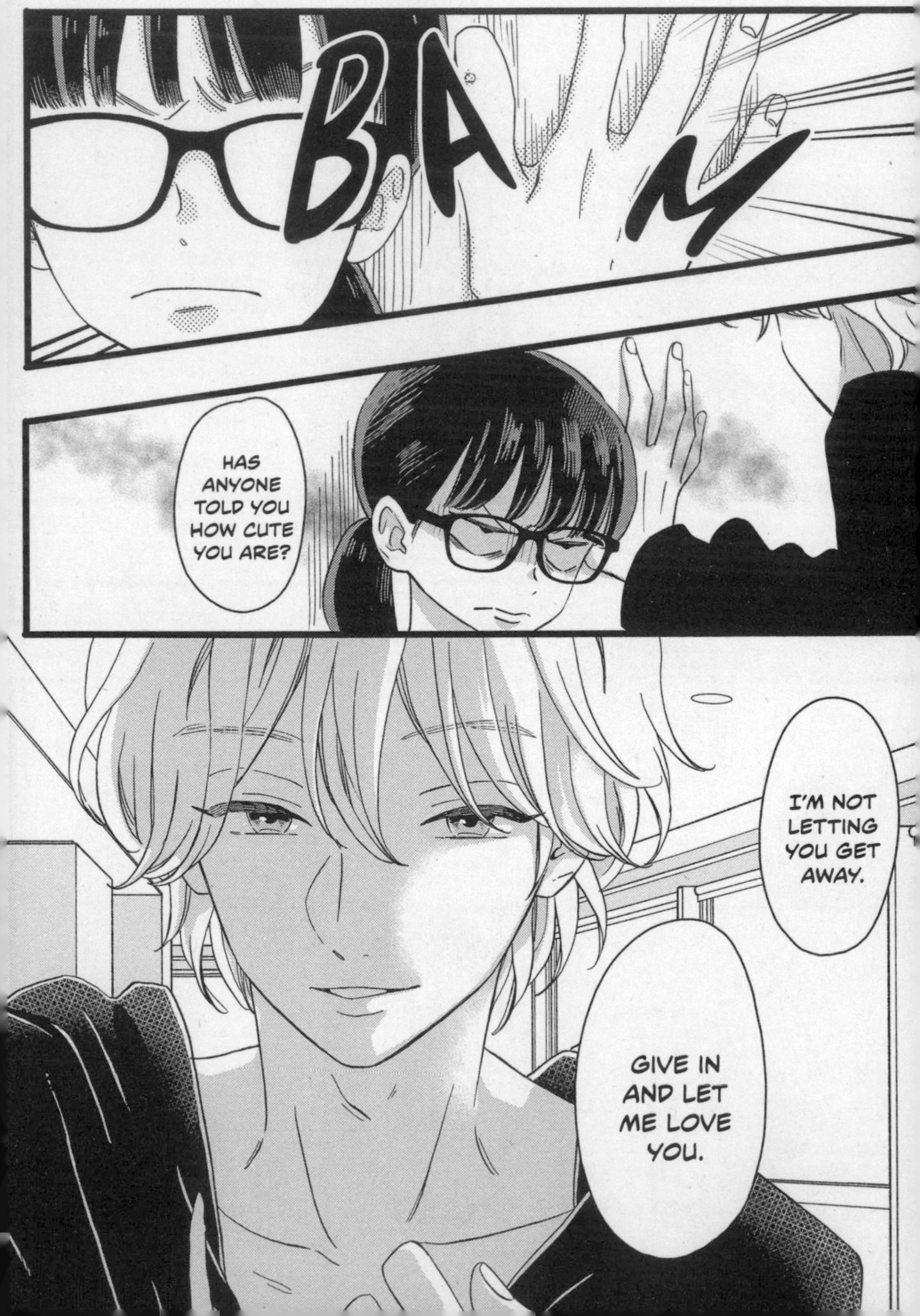
BAM
HAS ANYONE TOLD YOU HOW CUTE YOU ARE?
I'M NOT LETTING YOU GET AWAY.
GIVE IN AND LET ME LOVE YOU.

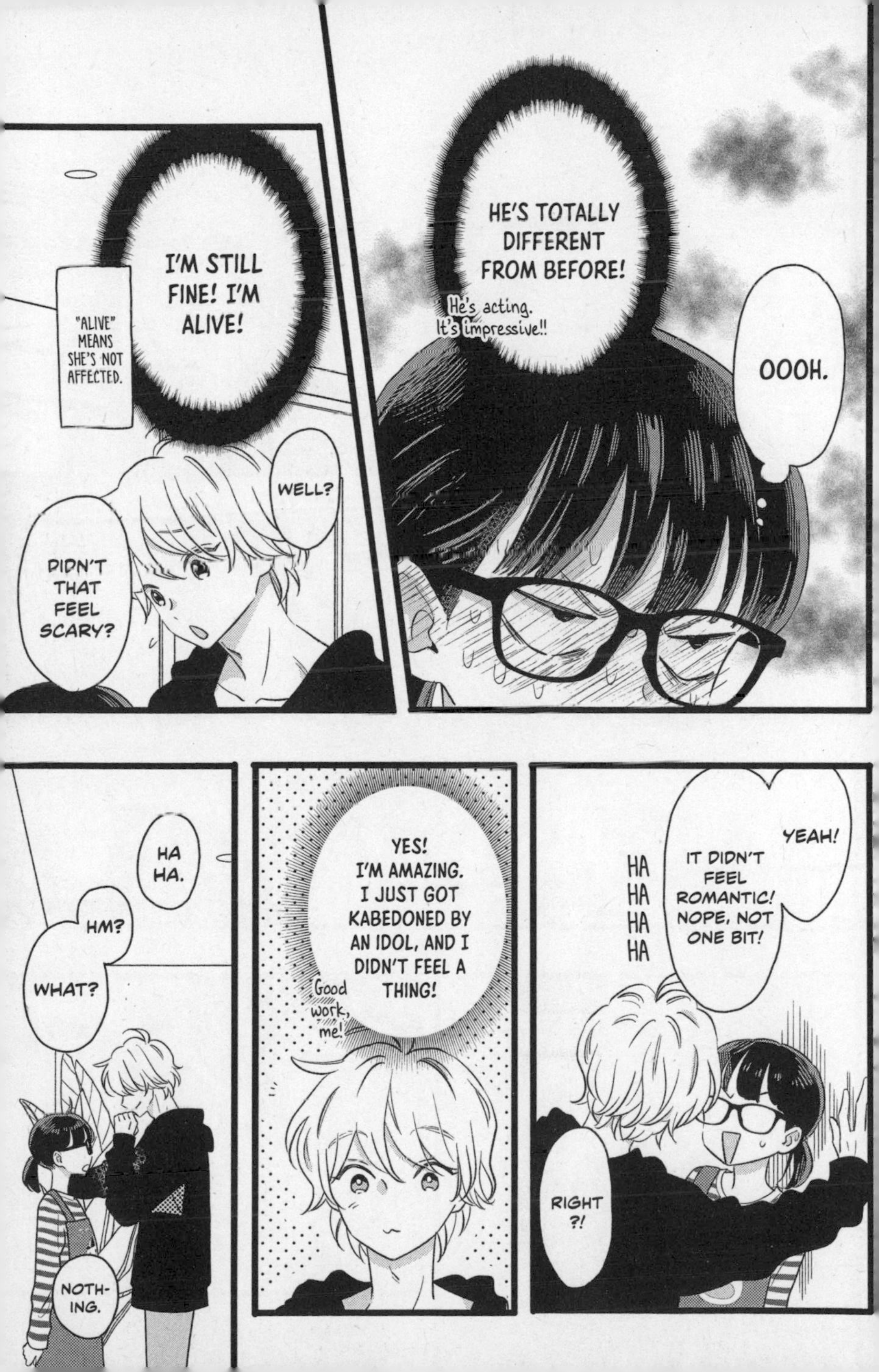
HE'S TOTALLY DIFFERENT FROM BEFORE!
He's acting. It's impressive!!
OOOH.
I'M STILL FINE! I'M ALIVE!
"ALIVE" MEANS SHE'S NOT AFFECTED.
WELL?
DIDN'T THAT FEEL SCARY?
YEAH!
IT DIDN'T FEEL ROMANTIC! NOPE, NOT ONE BIT!
HA HA HA HA
RIGHT ?!
YES! I'M AMAZING. I JUST GOT KABEDONED BY AN IDOL, AND I DIDN'T FEEL A THING!
Good work, me!
HA HA.
HM?
WHAT?
NOTH-ING.

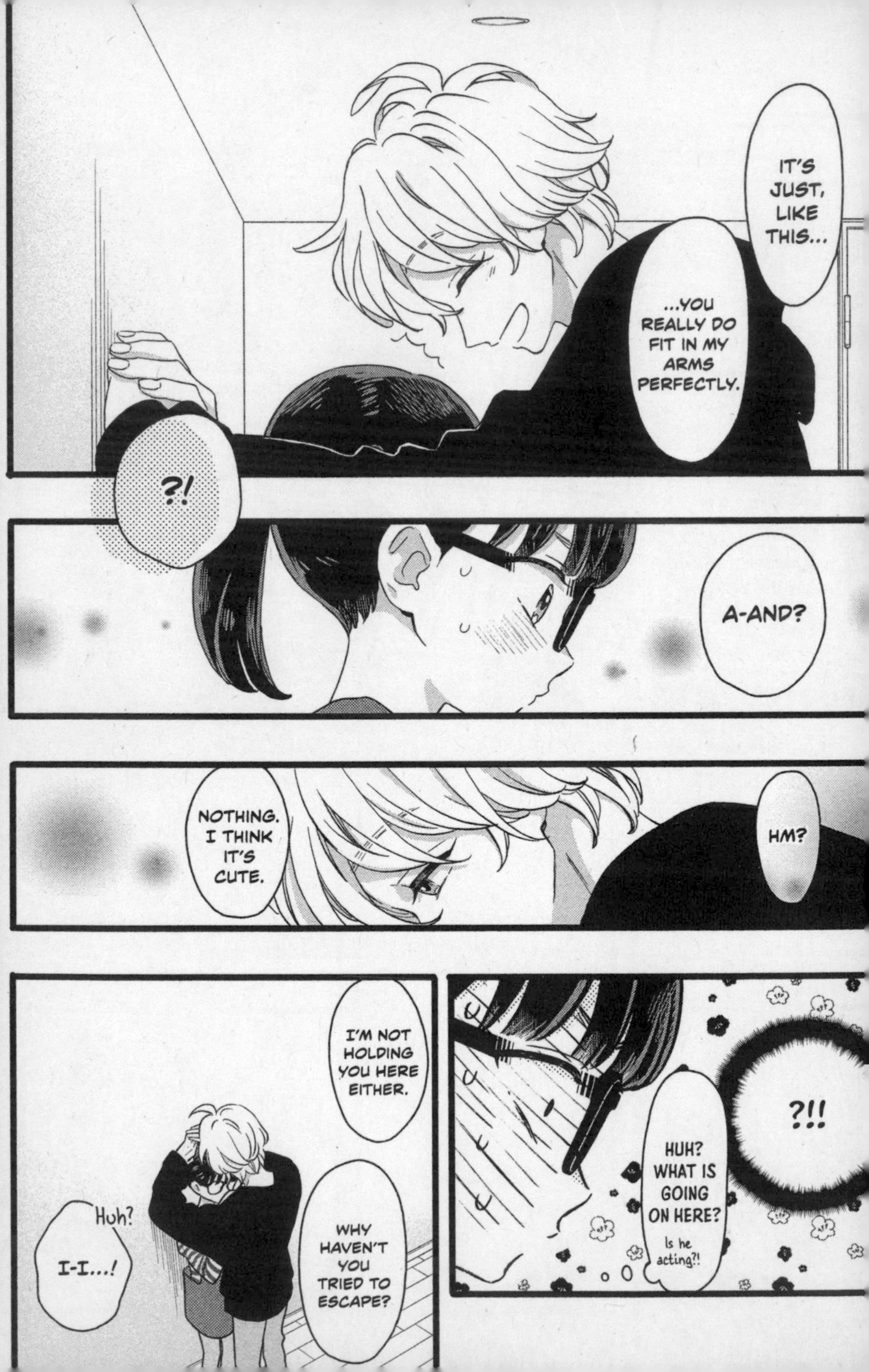
IT'S JUST, LIKE THIS...
...YOU REALLY DO FIT IN MY ARMS PERFECTLY.
?!
A-AND?
HM?
NOTHING. I THINK IT'S CUTE.
?!!
HUH? WHAT IS GOING ON HERE?
Is he acting?!
I'M NOT HOLDING YOU HERE EITHER.
WHY HAVEN'T YOU TRIED TO ESCAPE?
Huh?
I-I...!

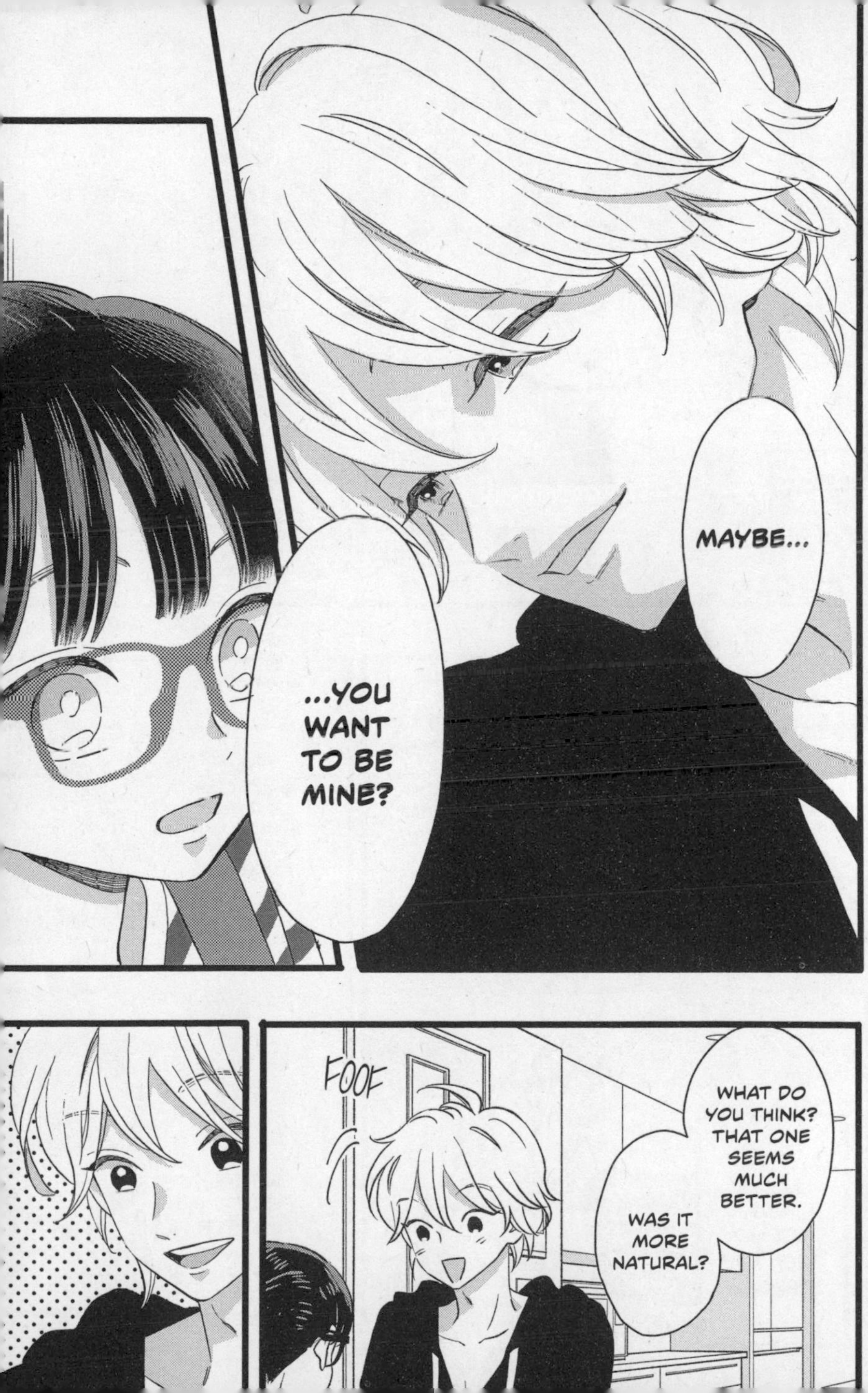
MAYBE...
...YOU WANT TO BE MINE?
WHAT DO YOU THINK? THAT ONE SEEMS MUCH BETTER.
WAS IT MORE NATURAL?
FOOF

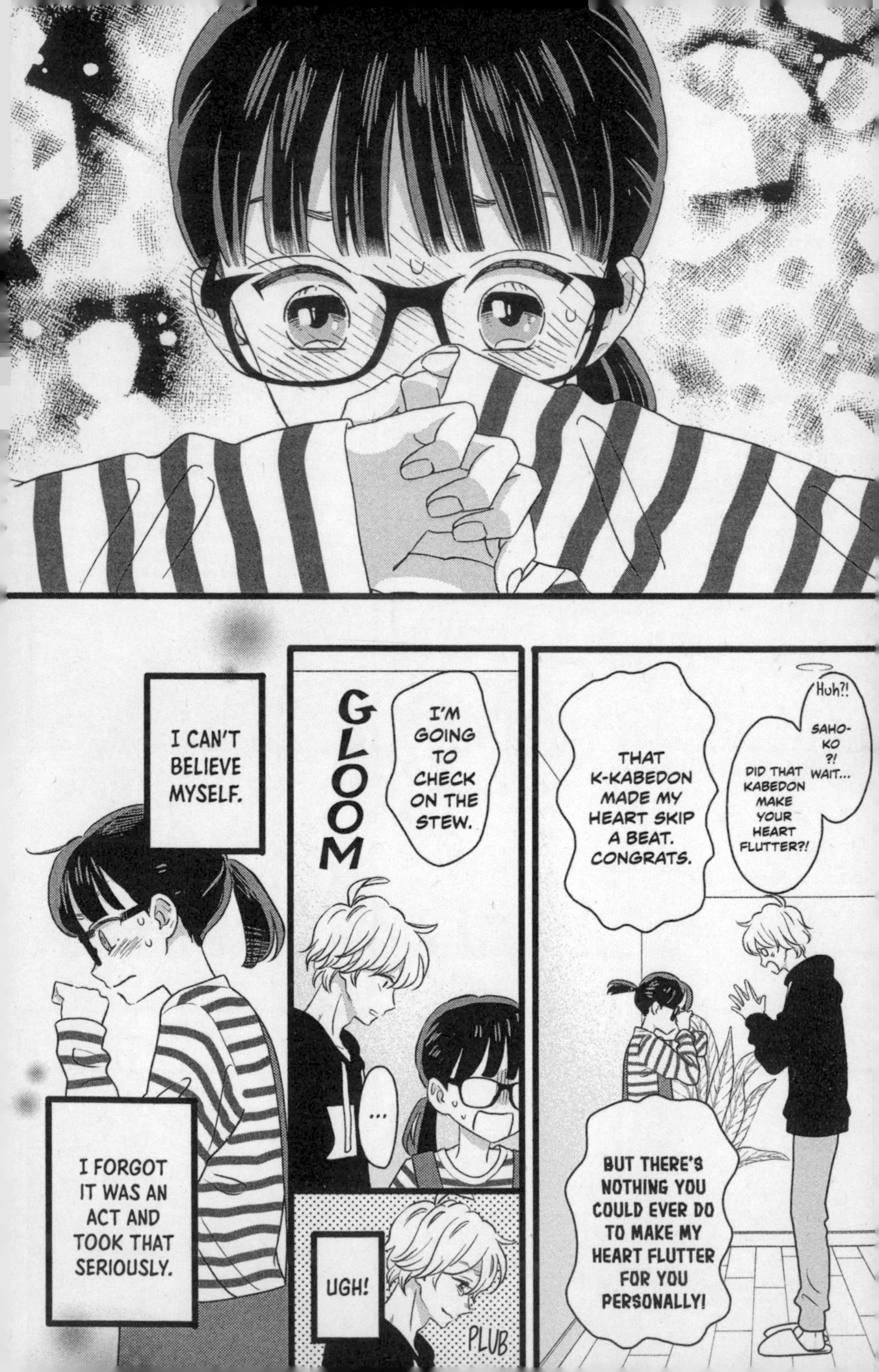
Huh?!
SAHO-KO ?! WAIT...
DID THAT KABEDON MAKE YOUR HEART FLUTTER?!
THAT K-KABEDON MADE MY HEART SKIP A BEAT. CONGRATS.
BUT THERE'S NOTHING YOU COULD EVER DO TO MAKE MY HEART FLUTTER FOR YOU PERSONALLY!
I'M GOING TO CHECK ON THE STEW.
GLOOM
...
UGH!
PLUB
I CAN'T BELIEVE MYSELF.
I FORGOT IT WAS AN ACT AND TOOK THAT SERIOUSLY.

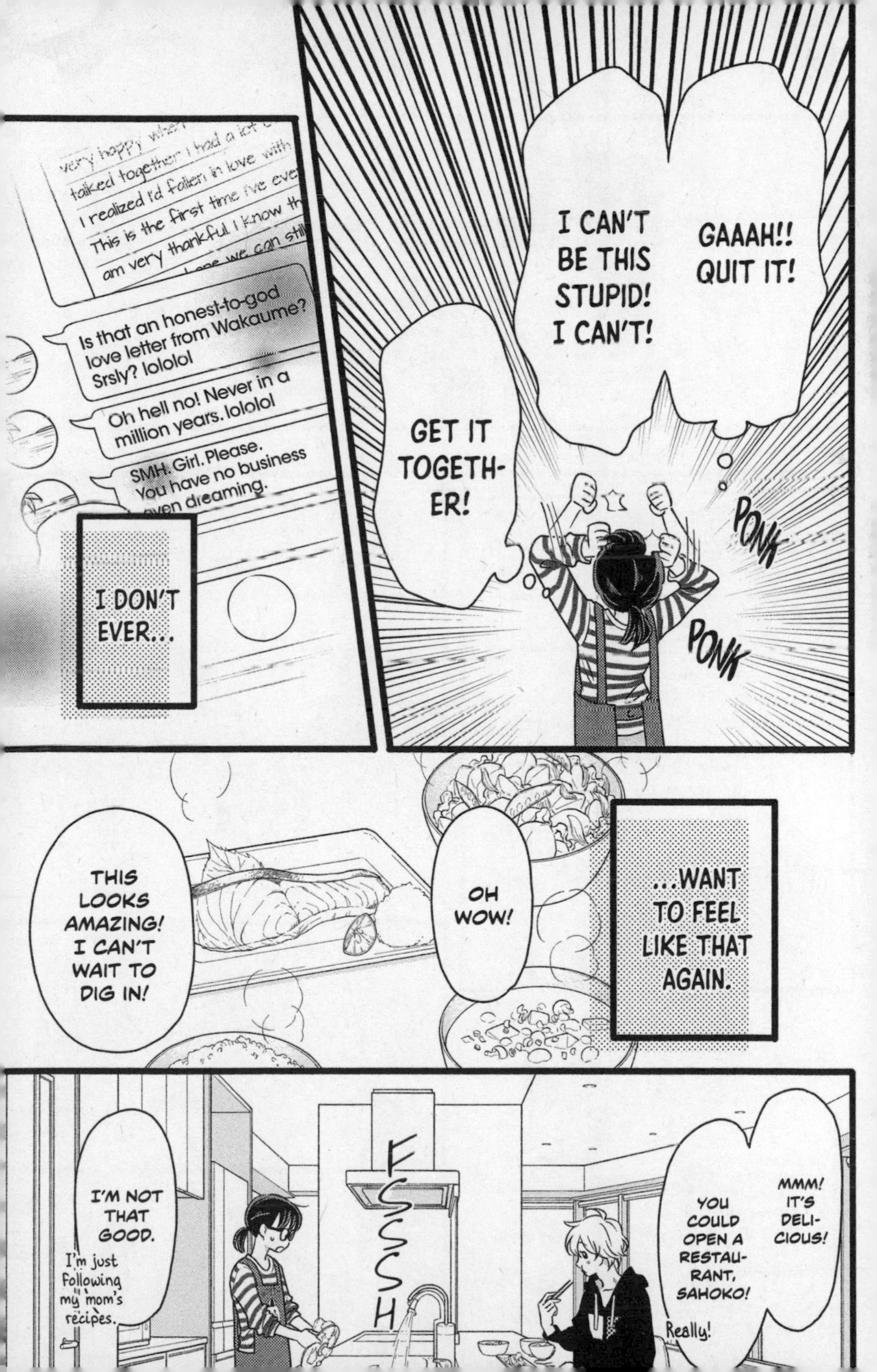
GAAAH!! QUIT IT!
I CAN'T BE THIS STUPID! I CAN'T!
GET IT TOGETH-ER!
PONK
PONK
talked together I had a lot
I realized I'd fallen in love with
This is the first time I've ever
am very thankful. I know th
Is that an honest-to-god love letter from Wakaume? Srsly? lololol
Oh hell no! Never in a million years. lololol
SMH. Girl. Please. You have no business even dreaming.
I DON'T EVER...
...WANT TO FEEL LIKE THAT AGAIN.
OH WOW!
THIS LOOKS AMAZING! I CAN'T WAIT TO DIG IN!
MMM! IT'S DELI-CIOUS!
YOU COULD OPEN A RESTAU-RANT, SAHOKO!
Really!
FSSSH
I'M NOT THAT GOOD.
I'm just following my mom's recipes.

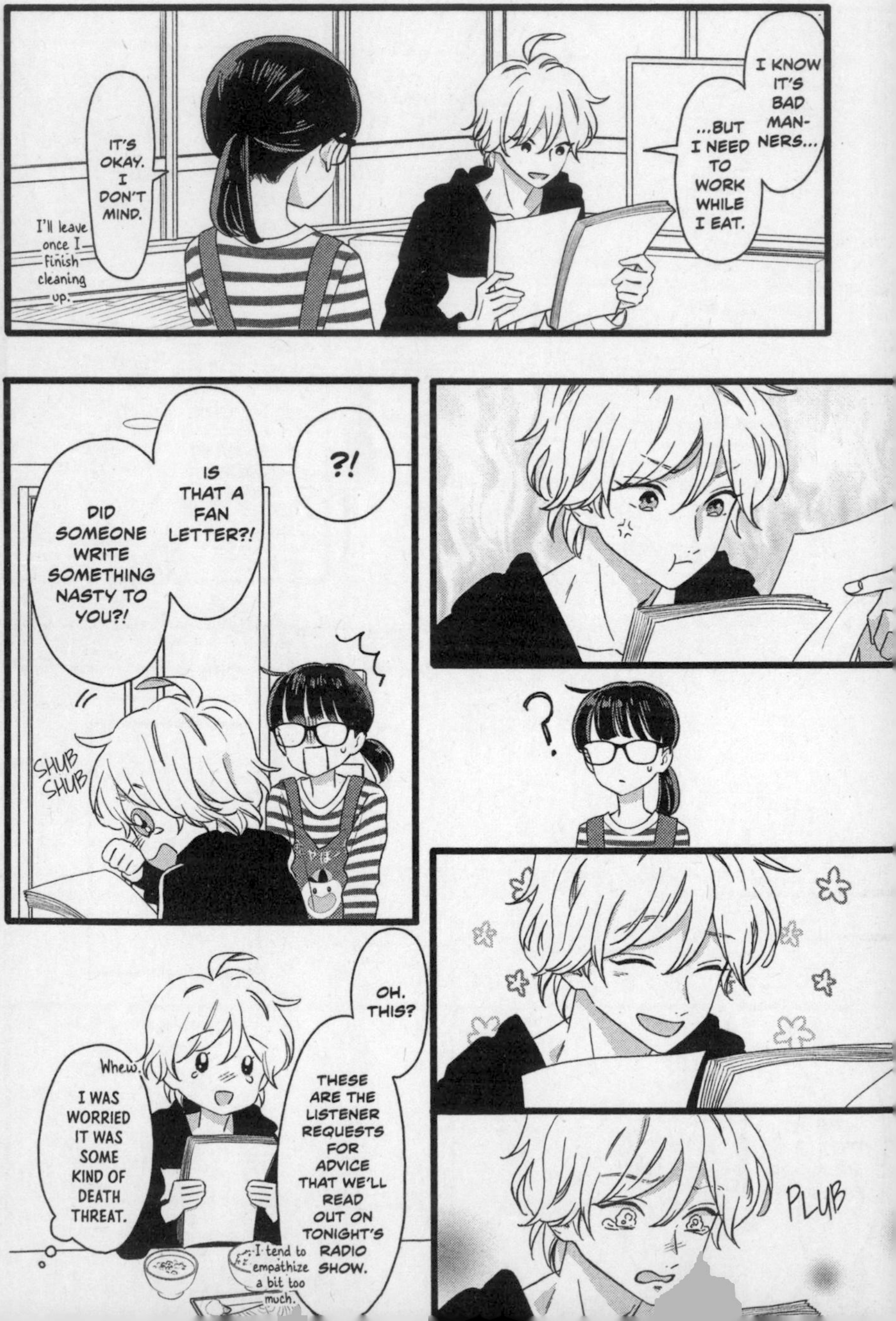
I KNOW IT'S BAD MANNERS...
...BUT I NEED TO WORK WHILE I EAT.
IT'S OKAY. I DON'T MIND.
I'll leave once I finish cleaning up.
?
?!
IS THAT A FAN LETTER?!
DID SOMEONE WRITE SOMETHING NASTY TO YOU?!
SHUB SHUB
OH. THIS?
THESE ARE THE LISTENER REQUESTS FOR ADVICE THAT WE'LL READ OUT ON TONIGHT'S RADIO SHOW.
Whew.
I WAS WORRIED IT WAS SOME KIND OF DEATH THREAT.
PLUB
I tend to empathize a bit too much.

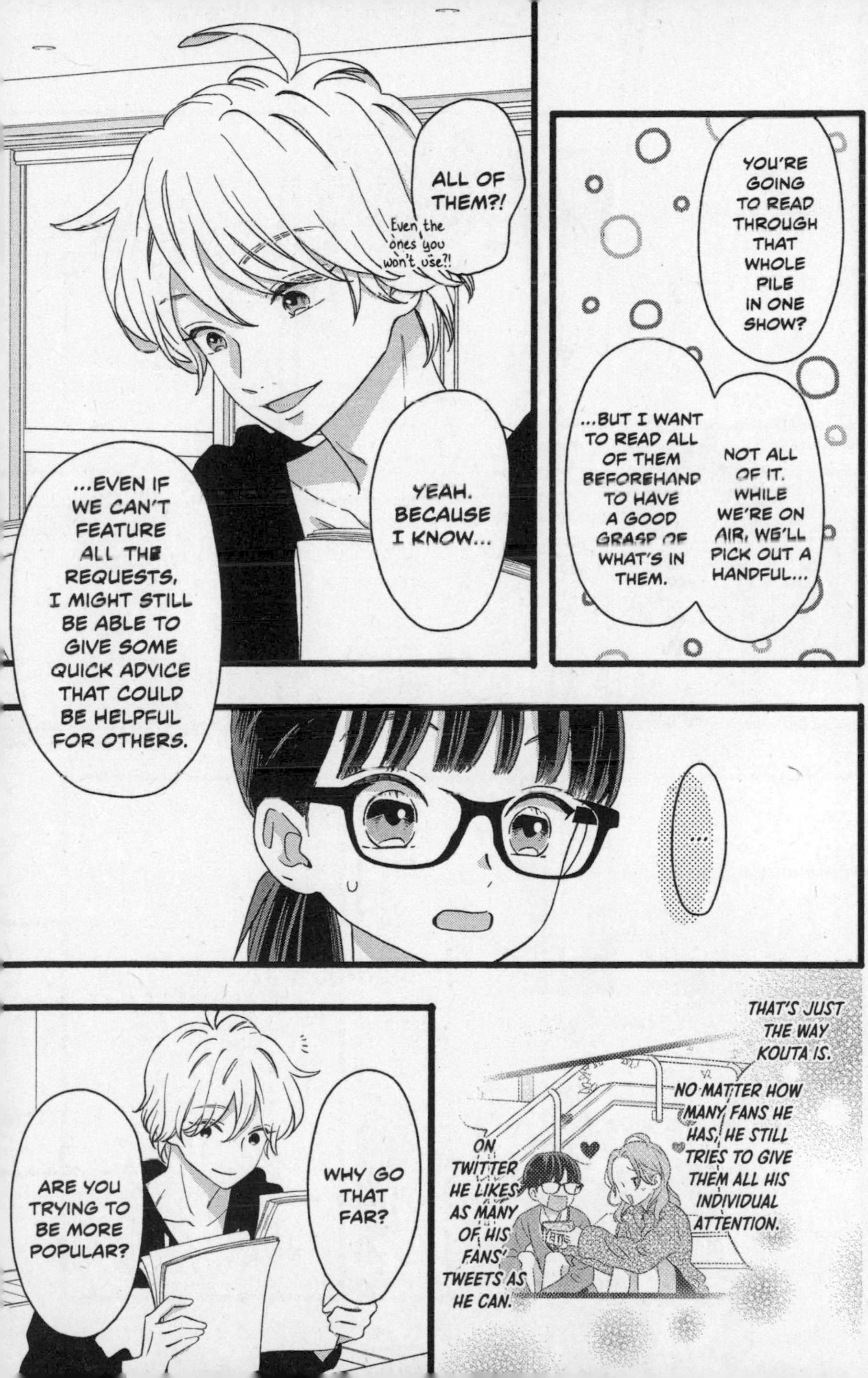
YOU'RE GOING TO READ THROUGH THAT WHOLE PILE IN ONE SHOW?
NOT ALL OF IT. WHILE WE'RE ON AIR, WE'LL PICK OUT A HANDFUL...
...BUT I WANT TO READ ALL OF THEM BEFOREHAND TO HAVE A GOOD GRASP OF WHAT'S IN THEM.
ALL OF THEM?!
Even the ones you won't use?!
YEAH. BECAUSE I KNOW...
...EVEN IF WE CAN'T FEATURE ALL THE REQUESTS, I MIGHT STILL BE ABLE TO GIVE SOME QUICK ADVICE THAT COULD BE HELPFUL FOR OTHERS.
...
THAT'S JUST THE WAY KOUTA IS.
NO MATTER HOW MANY FANS HE HAS, HE STILL TRIES TO GIVE THEM ALL HIS INDIVIDUAL ATTENTION.
ON TWITTER HE LIKES AS MANY OF HIS FANS' TWEETS AS HE CAN.
WHY GO THAT FAR?
ARE YOU TRYING TO BE MORE POPULAR?

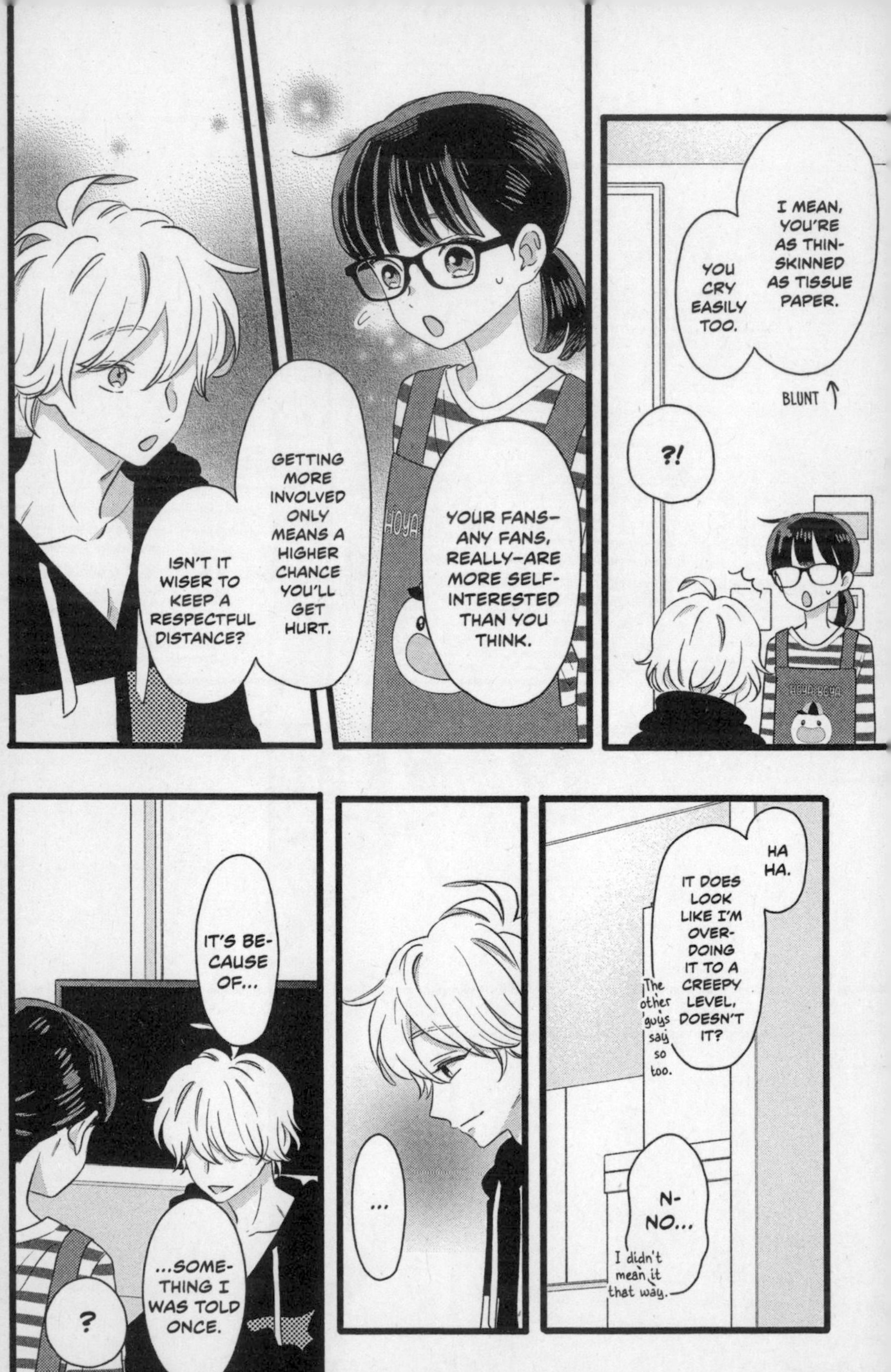
I MEAN, YOU'RE AS THIN-SKINNED AS TISSUE PAPER.
YOU CRY EASILY TOO.
BLUNT
?!
YOUR FANS—ANY FANS, REALLY—ARE MORE SELF-INTERESTED THAN YOU THINK.
GETTING MORE INVOLVED ONLY MEANS A HIGHER CHANCE YOU'LL GET HURT.
ISN'T IT WISER TO KEEP A RESPECTFUL DISTANCE?
HA HA.
IT DOES LOOK LIKE I'M OVER-DOING IT TO A CREEPY LEVEL, DOESN'T IT?
The other guys say so too.
N-NO...
I didn't mean it that way.
...
IT'S BE-CAUSE OF...
...SOME-THING I WAS TOLD ONCE.
?

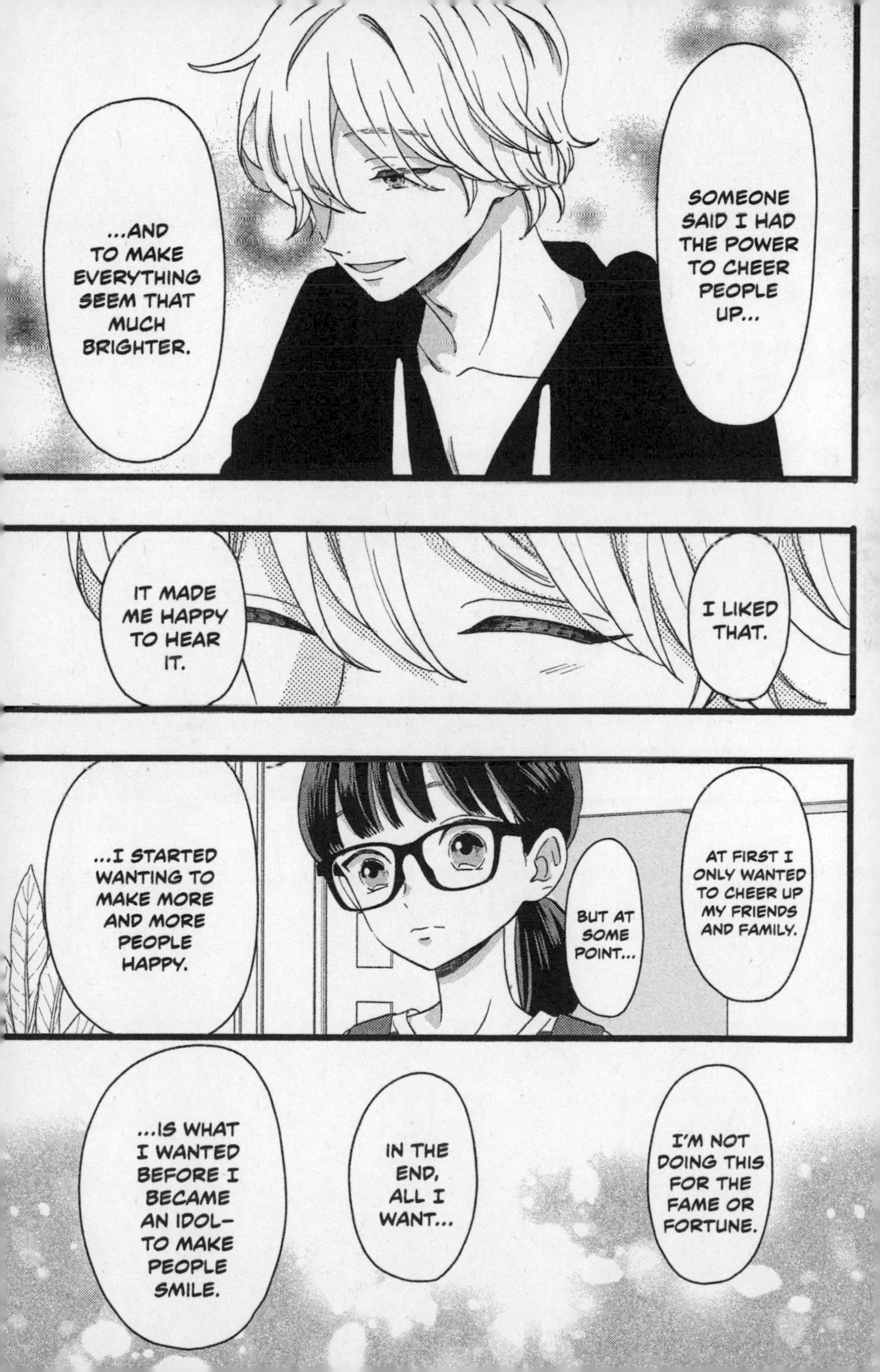
SOMEONE SAID I HAD THE POWER TO CHEER PEOPLE UP...
...AND TO MAKE EVERYTHING SEEM THAT MUCH BRIGHTER.
I LIKED THAT.
IT MADE ME HAPPY TO HEAR IT.
AT FIRST I ONLY WANTED TO CHEER UP MY FRIENDS AND FAMILY.
BUT AT SOME POINT...
...I STARTED WANTING TO MAKE MORE AND MORE PEOPLE HAPPY.
I'M NOT DOING THIS FOR THE FAME OR FORTUNE.
IN THE END, ALL I WANT...
...IS WHAT I WANTED BEFORE I BECAME AN IDOL—TO MAKE PEOPLE SMILE.

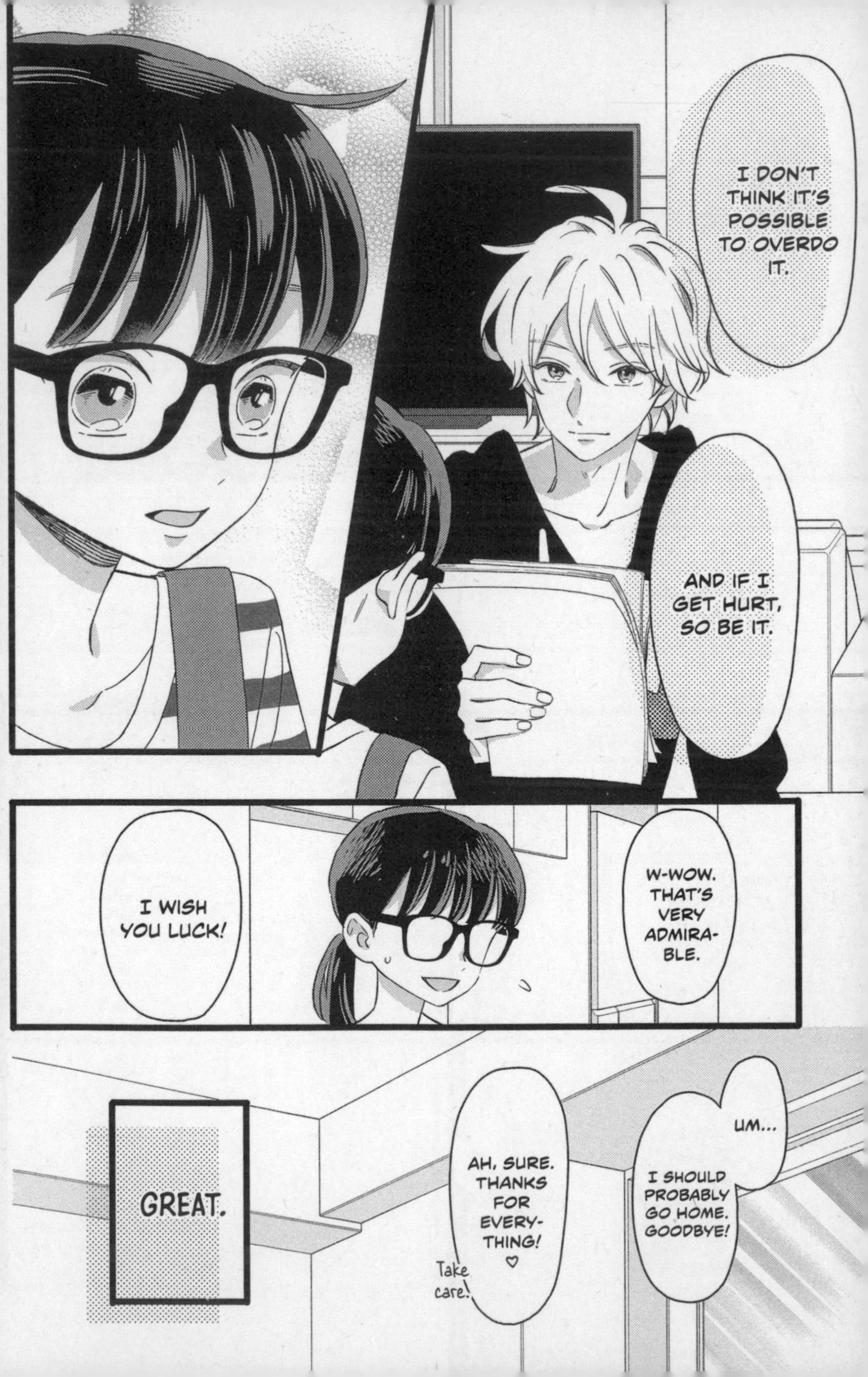
I DON'T THINK IT'S POSSIBLE TO OVERDO IT.
AND IF I GET HURT, SO BE IT.
W-WOW. THAT'S VERY ADMIRA-BLE.
I WISH YOU LUCK!
UM...
I SHOULD PROBABLY GO HOME. GOODBYE!
AH, SURE. THANKS FOR EVERY-THING! ♡
Take care!
GREAT.

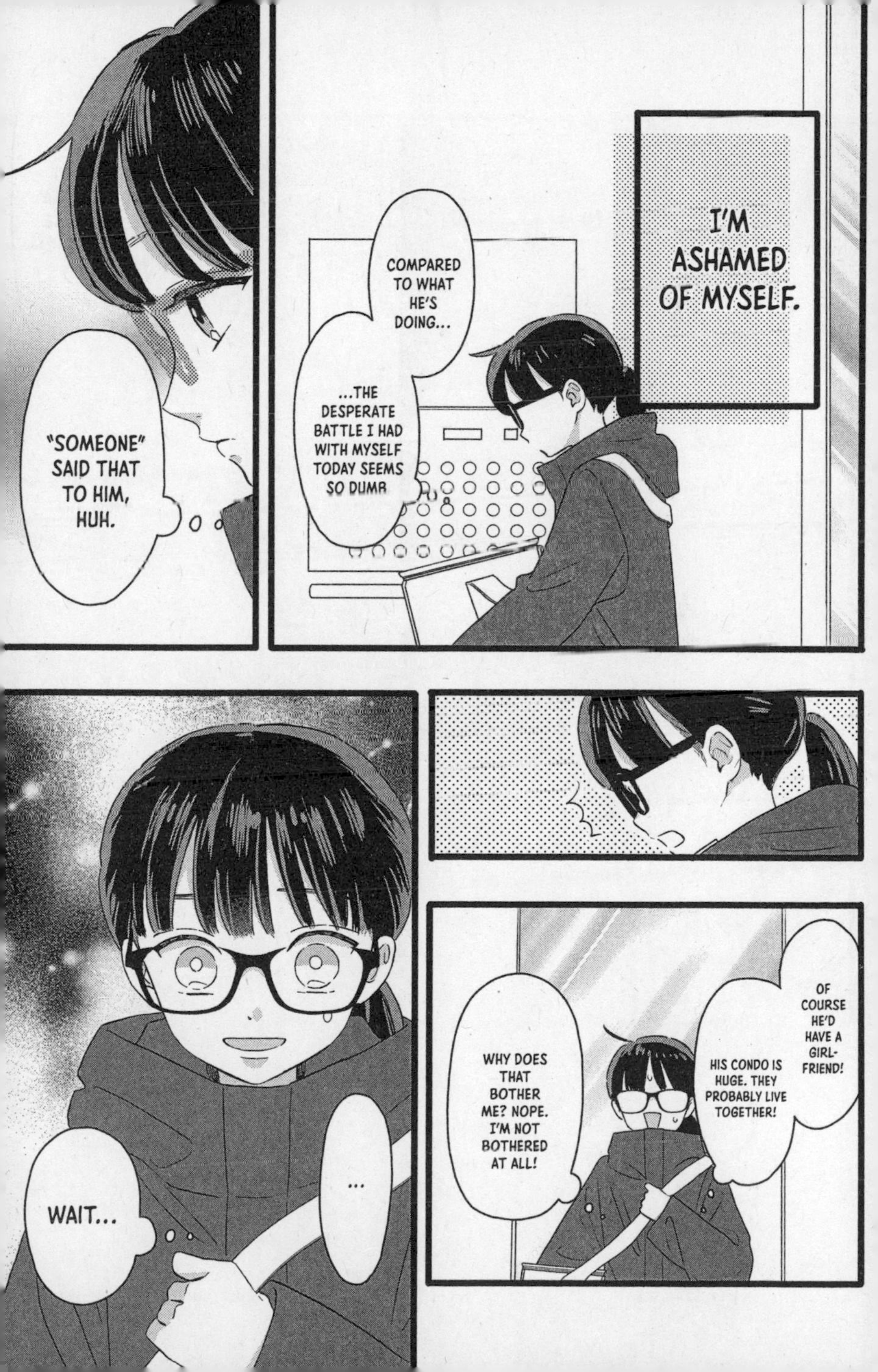
I'M ASHAMED OF MYSELF.
COMPARED TO WHAT HE'S DOING...
...THE DESPERATE BATTLE I HAD WITH MYSELF TODAY SEEMS SO DUMB
"SOMEONE" SAID THAT TO HIM, HUH.
OF COURSE HE'D HAVE A GIRL-FRIEND!
HIS CONDO IS HUGE. THEY PROBABLY LIVE TOGETHER!
WHY DOES THAT BOTHER ME? NOPE. I'M NOT BOTHERED AT ALL!
...
WAIT...

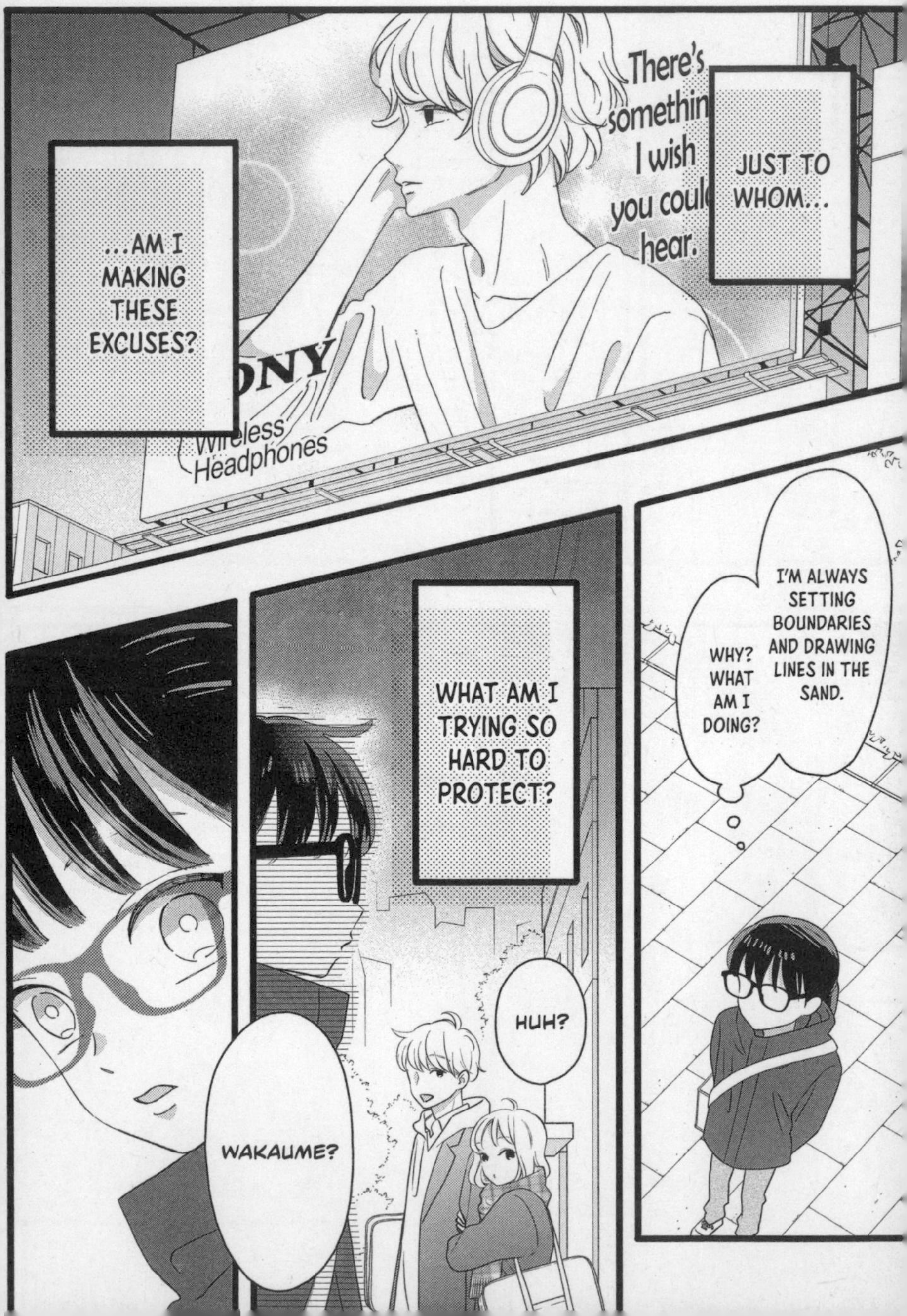
JUST TO WHOM...
There's somethin I wish you coul hear.
...AM I MAKING THESE EXCUSES?
ONY
Wireless Headphones
I'M ALWAYS SETTING BOUNDARIES AND DRAWING LINES IN THE SAND.
WHY? WHAT AM I DOING?
WHAT AM I TRYING SO HARD TO PROTECT?
HUH?
WAKAUME?

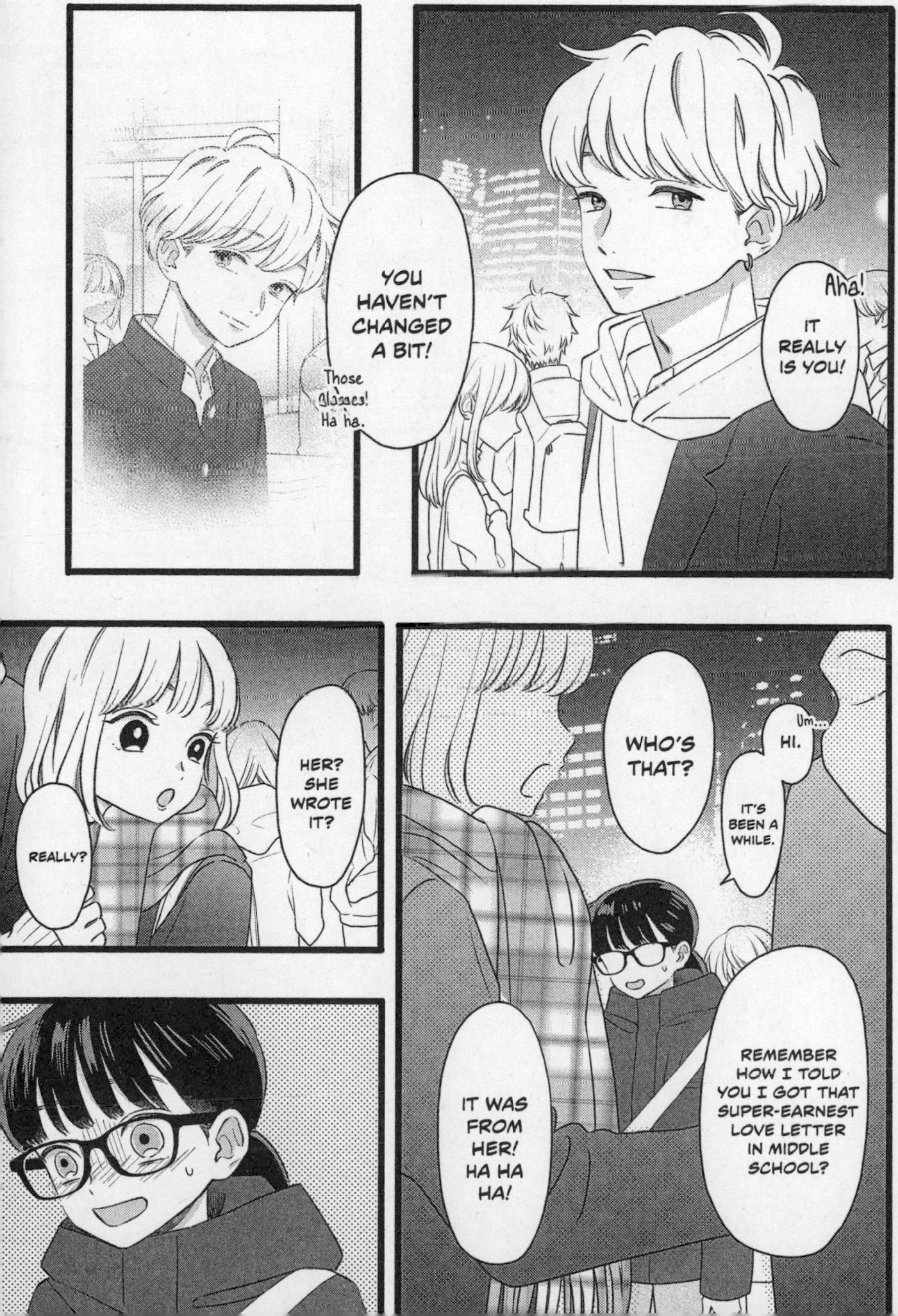
Aha!
IT REALLY IS YOU!
YOU HAVEN'T CHANGED A BIT!
Those glasses! Ha ha.
Um... HI.
IT'S BEEN A WHILE.
WHO'S THAT?
REMEMBER HOW I TOLD YOU I GOT THAT SUPER-EARNEST LOVE LETTER IN MIDDLE SCHOOL?
IT WAS FROM HER! HA HA HA!
HER? SHE WROTE IT?
REALLY?

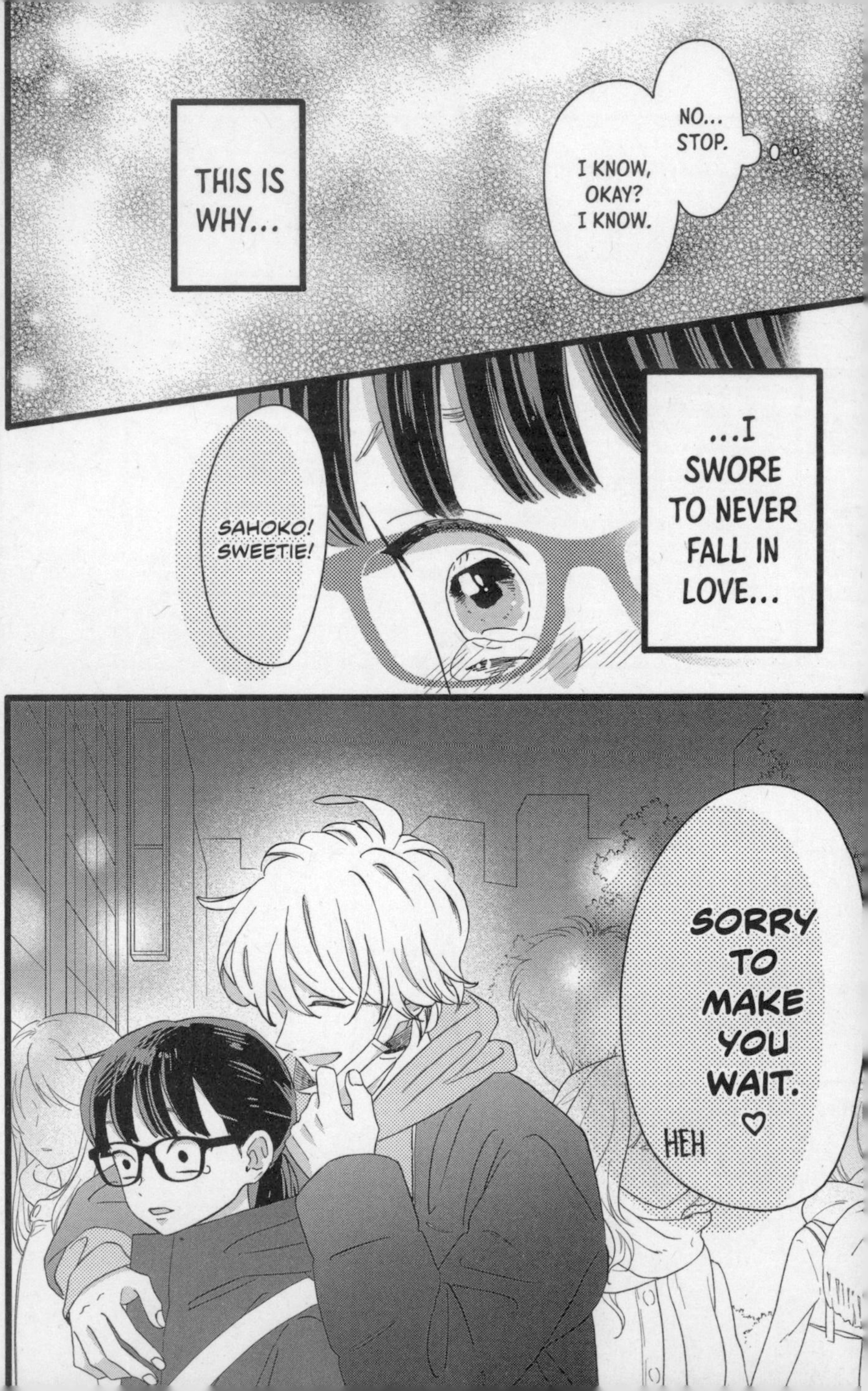
NO... STOP.
I KNOW, OKAY? I KNOW.
THIS IS WHY...
...I SWORE TO NEVER FALL IN LOVE...
SAHOKO! SWEETIE!
SORRY TO MAKE YOU WAIT. ♡
HEH

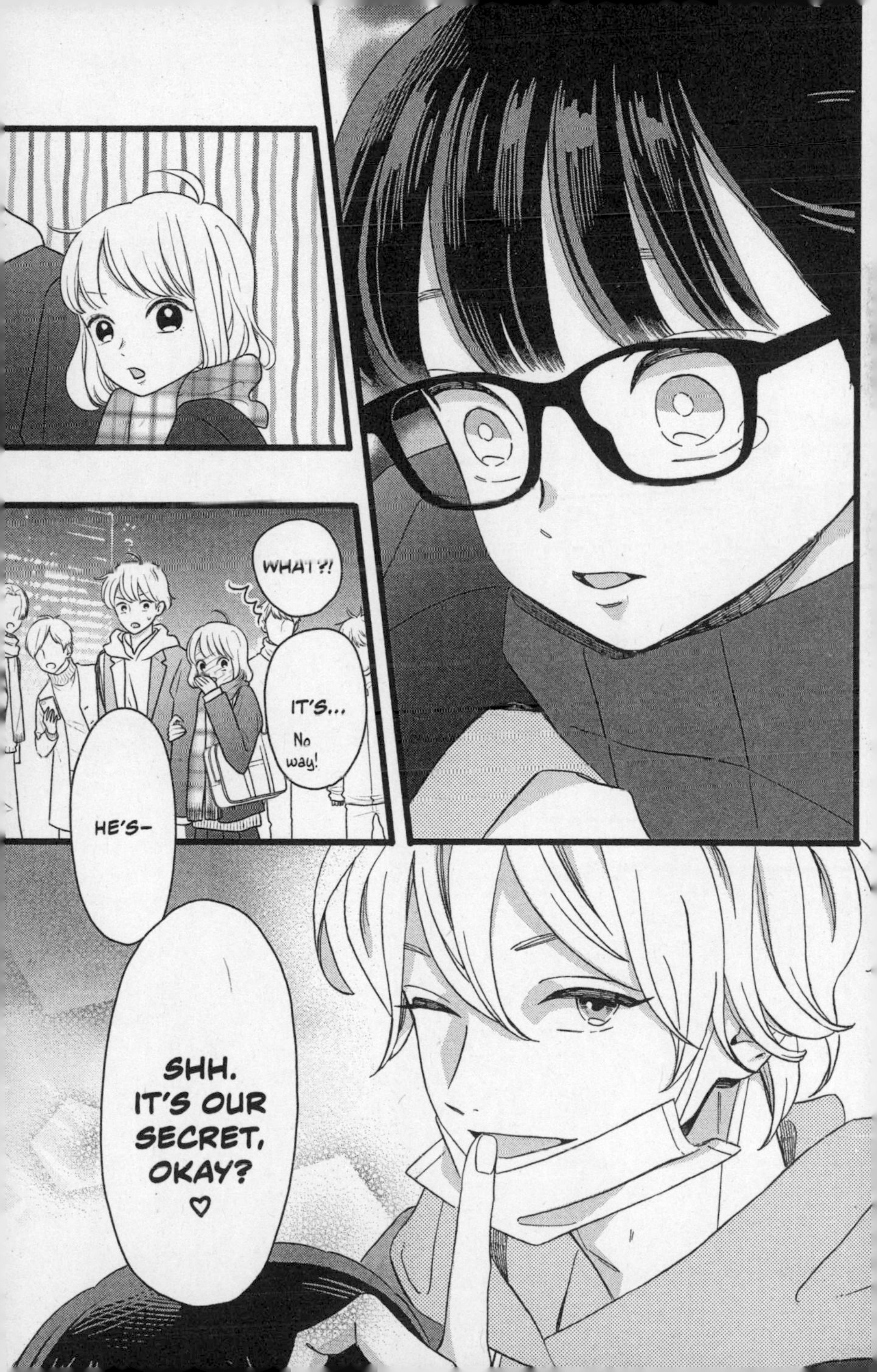
WHAT?!
IT'S...
No way!
HE'S-
SHH. IT'S OUR SECRET, OKAY? ♡

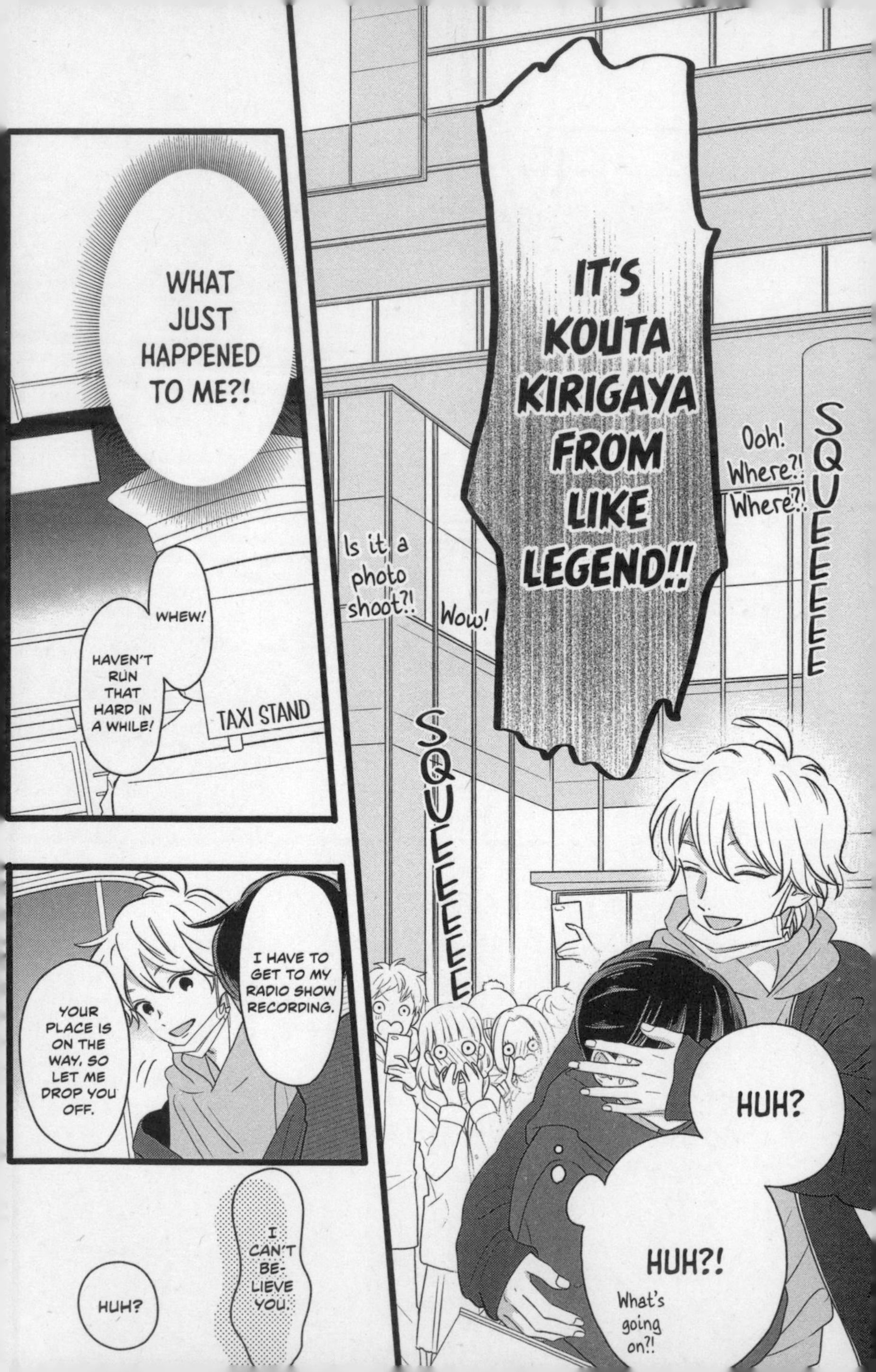
SQUEEEEE
Ooh! Where?! Where?!
IT'S KOUTA KIRIGAYA FROM LIKE LEGEND!!
Wow!
Is it a photo shoot?!
SQUEEEEE
HUH?
HUH?!
What's going on?!
WHAT JUST HAPPENED TO ME?!
WHEW!
HAVEN'T RUN THAT HARD IN A WHILE!
TAXI STAND
I HAVE TO GET TO MY RADIO SHOW RECORDING.
YOUR PLACE IS ON THE WAY, SO LET ME DROP YOU OFF.
I CAN'T BE-LIEVE YOU.
HUH?

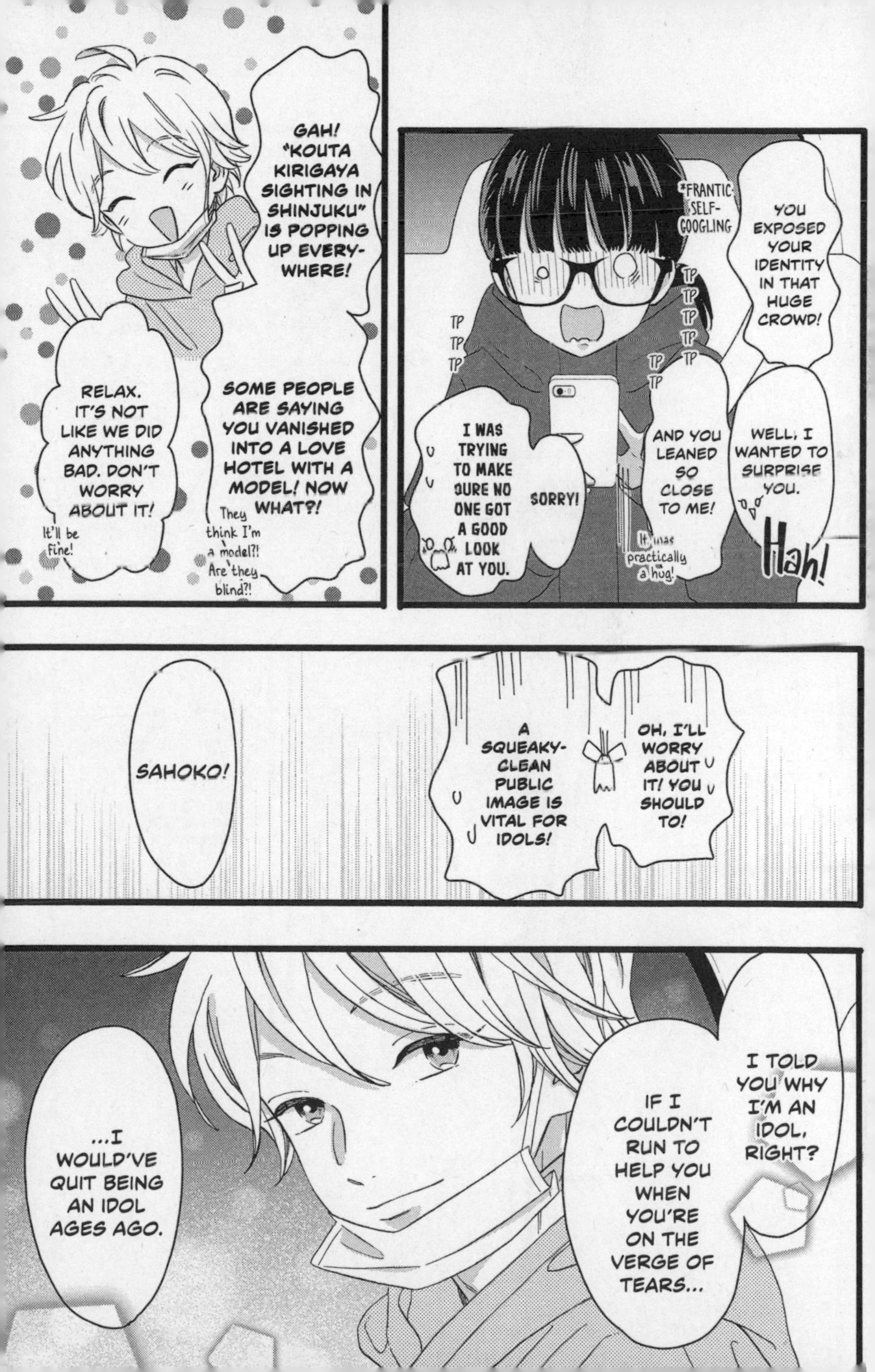
YOU EXPOSED YOUR IDENTITY IN THAT HUGE CROWD!
*FRANTIC SELF-GOOGLING
TP TP TP TP TP
TP TP TP
TP TP
WELL, I WANTED TO SURPRISE YOU.
Hah!
AND YOU LEANED SO CLOSE TO ME!
It was practically a hug!
SORRY!
I WAS TRYING TO MAKE SURE NO ONE GOT A GOOD LOOK AT YOU.
GAH! "KOUTA KIRIGAYA SIGHTING IN SHINJUKU" IS POPPING UP EVERY-WHERE!
SOME PEOPLE ARE SAYING YOU VANISHED INTO A LOVE HOTEL WITH A MODEL! NOW WHAT?!
They think I'm a model?! Are they blind?!
RELAX. IT'S NOT LIKE WE DID ANYTHING BAD. DON'T WORRY ABOUT IT!
It'll be fine!
OH, I'LL WORRY ABOUT IT! YOU SHOULD TO!
A SQUEAKY-CLEAN PUBLIC IMAGE IS VITAL FOR IDOLS!
SAHOKO!
I TOLD YOU WHY I'M AN IDOL, RIGHT?
IF I COULDN'T RUN TO HELP YOU WHEN YOU'RE ON THE VERGE OF TEARS...
...I WOULD'VE QUIT BEING AN IDOL AGES AGO.

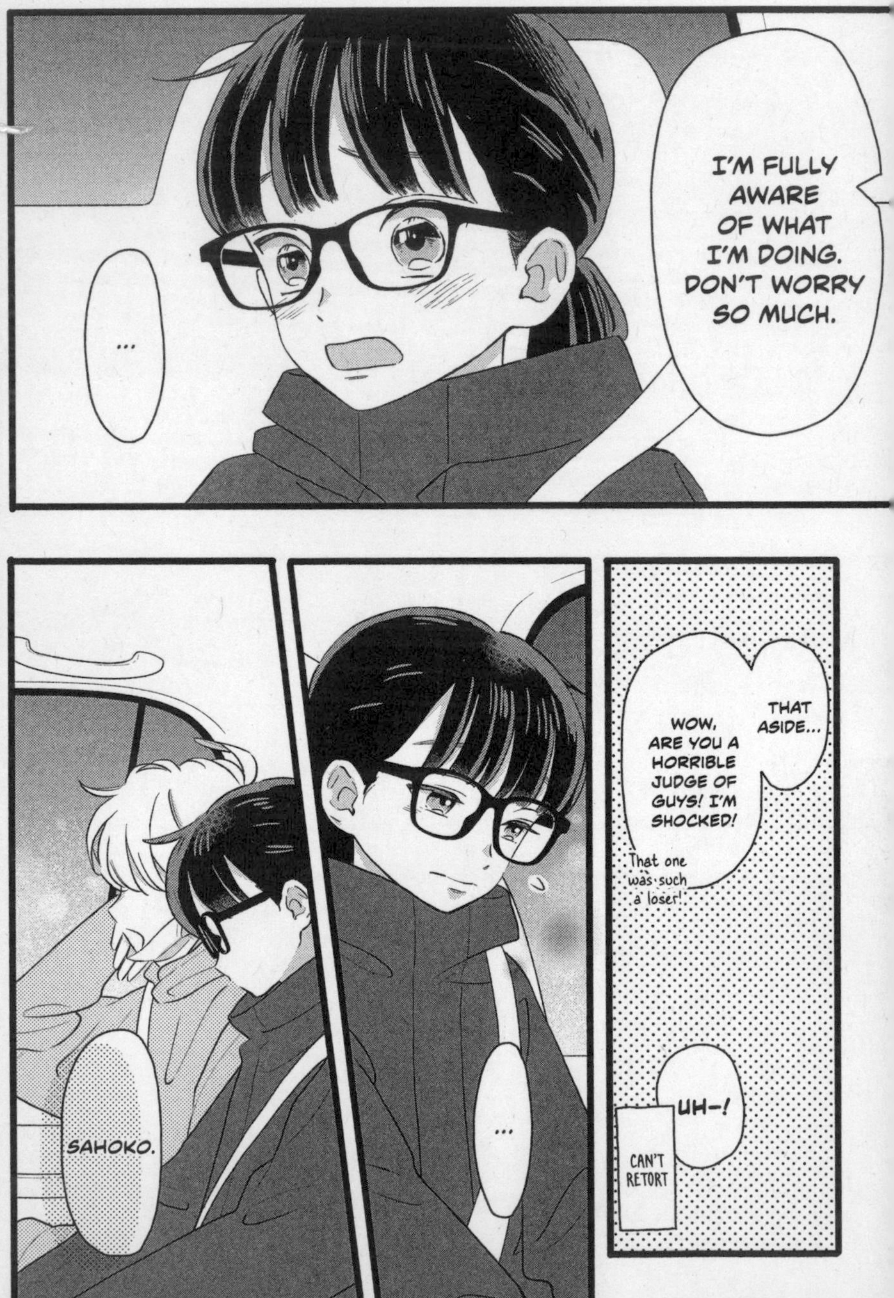
I'M FULLY AWARE OF WHAT I'M DOING. DON'T WORRY SO MUCH.
...
THAT ASIDE...
WOW, ARE YOU A HORRIBLE JUDGE OF GUYS! I'M SHOCKED!
That one was such a loser!
UH-!
CAN'T RETORT
...
SAHOKO.

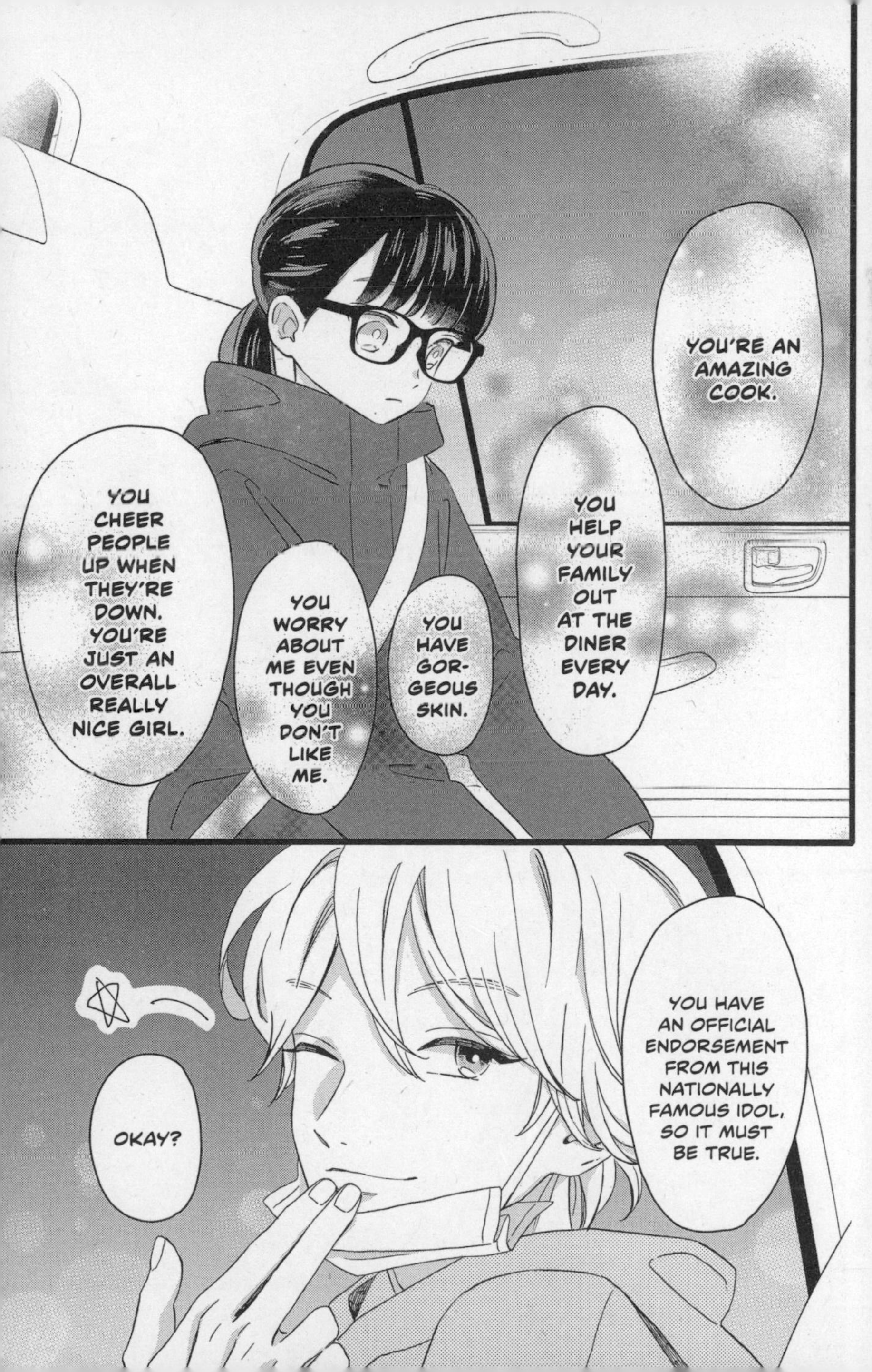
YOU'RE AN AMAZING COOK.
YOU HELP YOUR FAMILY OUT AT THE DINER EVERY DAY.
YOU HAVE GOR-GEOUS SKIN.
YOU WORRY ABOUT ME EVEN THOUGH YOU DON'T LIKE ME.
YOU CHEER PEOPLE UP WHEN THEY'RE DOWN. YOU'RE JUST AN OVERALL REALLY NICE GIRL.
YOU HAVE AN OFFICIAL ENDORSEMENT FROM THIS NATIONALLY FAMOUS IDOL, SO IT MUST BE TRUE.
OKAY?

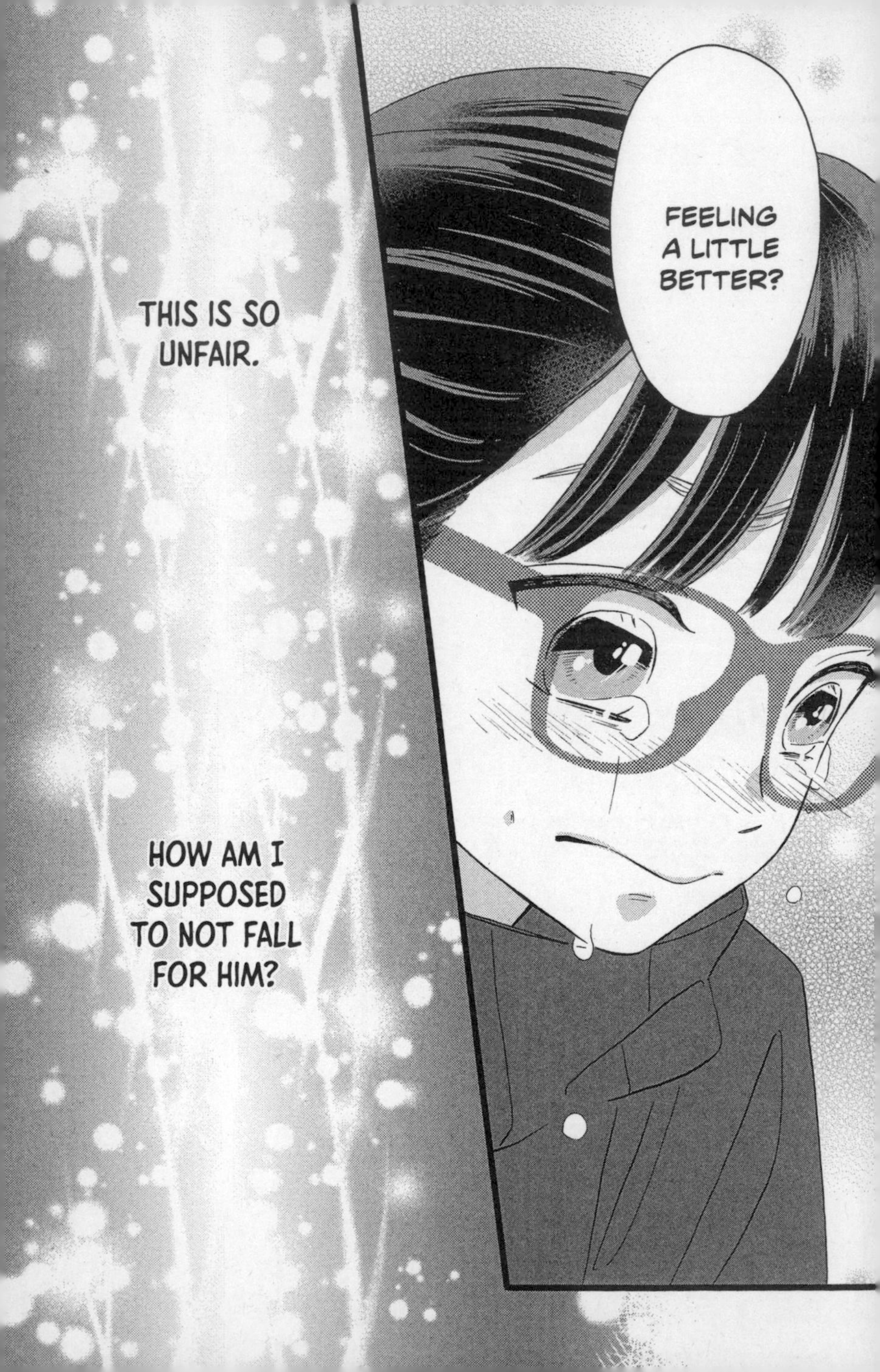
FEELING A LITTLE BETTER?
THIS IS SO UNFAIR.
HOW AM I SUPPOSED TO NOT FALL FOR HIM?

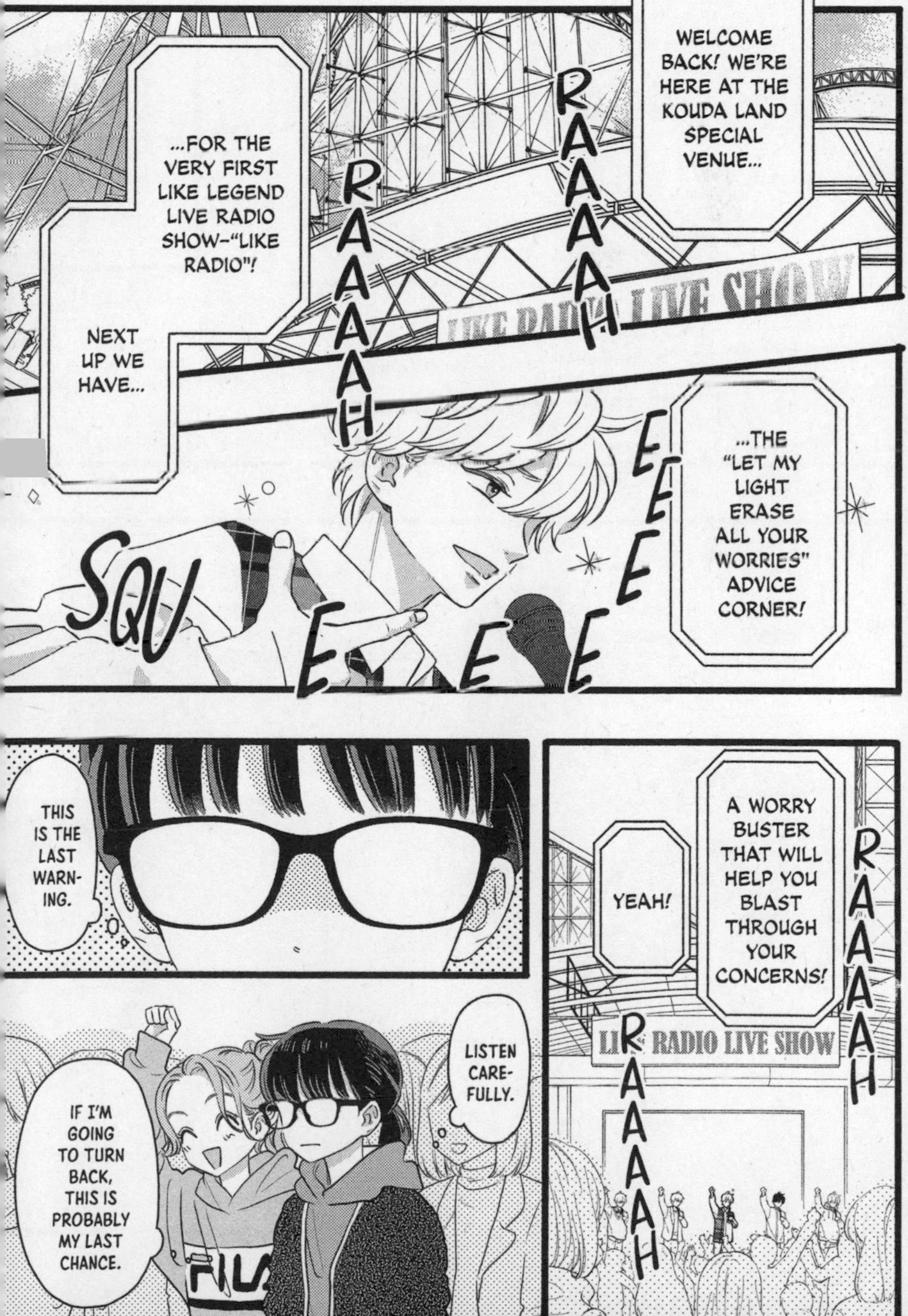
WELCOME BACK! WE'RE HERE AT THE KOUDA LAND SPECIAL VENUE...
RAAAAH
RAAAAH
...FOR THE VERY FIRST LIKE LEGEND LIVE RADIO SHOW—"LIKE RADIO"!
LIKE RADIO LIVE SHOW
NEXT UP WE HAVE...
...THE "LET MY LIGHT ERASE ALL YOUR WORRIES" ADVICE CORNER!
SQUEEEEEE
A WORRY BUSTER THAT WILL HELP YOU BLAST THROUGH YOUR CONCERNS!
YEAH!
RAAAAH
LI RADIO LIVE SHOW
RAAAAH
THIS IS THE LAST WARNING.
LISTEN CAREFULLY.
IF I'M GOING TO TURN BACK, THIS IS PROBABLY MY LAST CHANCE.
FILA

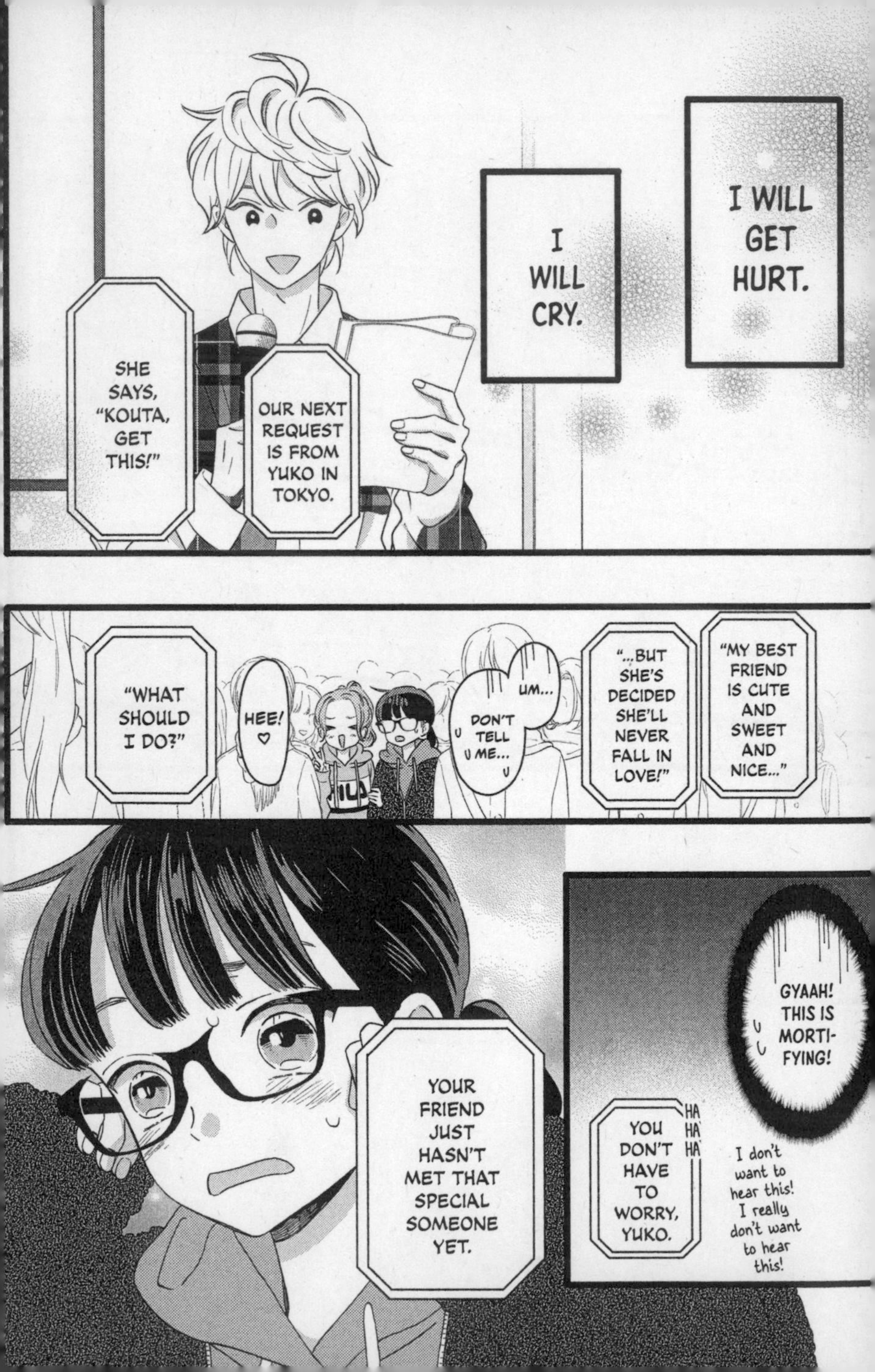
I WILL GET HURT.
I WILL CRY.
OUR NEXT REQUEST IS FROM YUKO IN TOKYO.
SHE SAYS, "KOUTA, GET THIS!"
"MY BEST FRIEND IS CUTE AND SWEET AND NICE..."
"...BUT SHE'S DECIDED SHE'LL NEVER FALL IN LOVE!"
UM... DON'T TELL ME...
HEE! ♡
"WHAT SHOULD I DO?"
GYAAH! THIS IS MORTIFYING!
I don't want to hear this! I really don't want to hear this!
HA HA HA
YOU DON'T HAVE TO WORRY, YUKO.
YOUR FRIEND JUST HASN'T MET THAT SPECIAL SOMEONE YET.

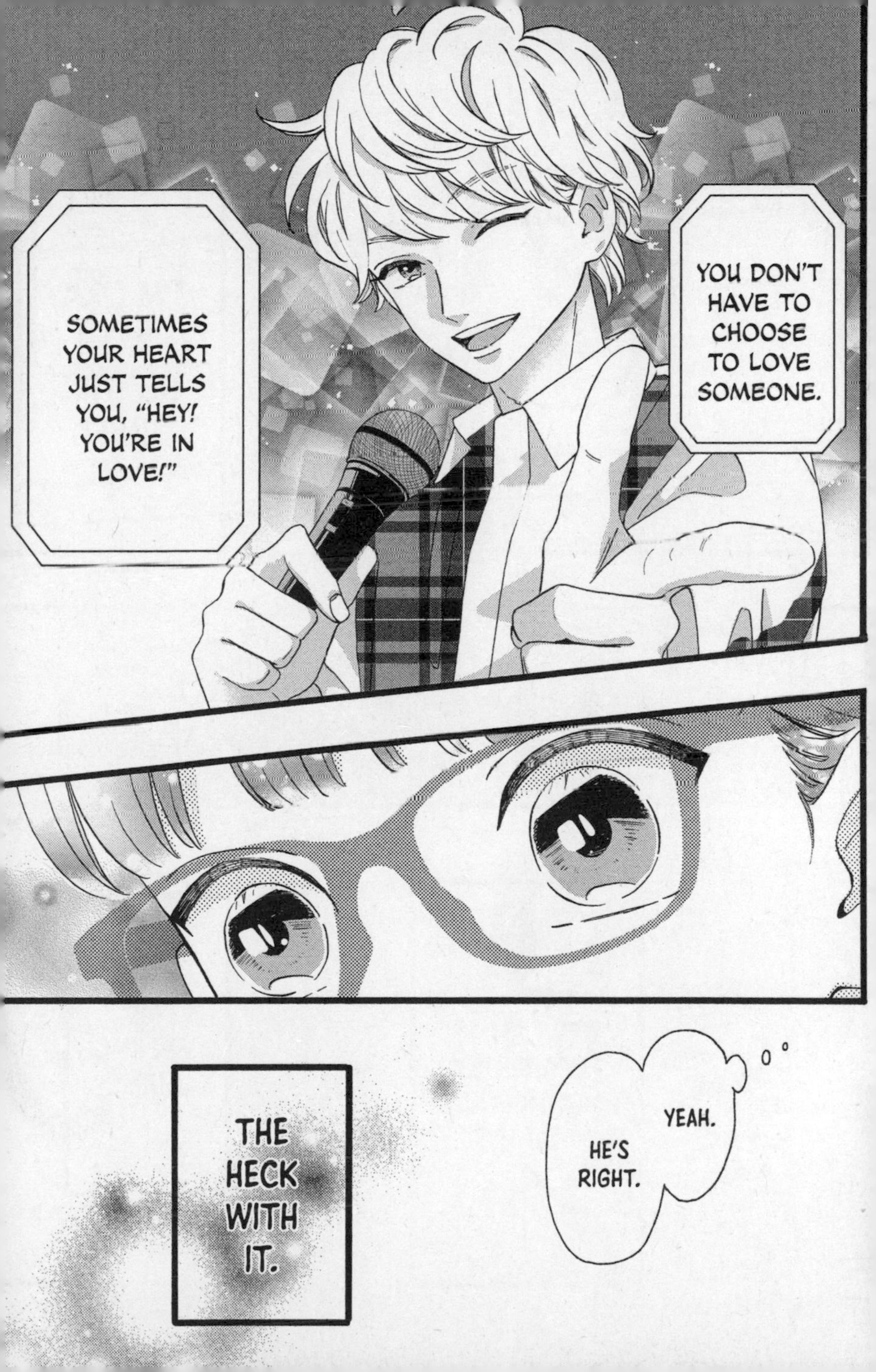
YOU DON'T HAVE TO CHOOSE TO LOVE SOMEONE.
SOMETIMES YOUR HEART JUST TELLS YOU, "HEY! YOU'RE IN LOVE!"
YEAH. HE'S RIGHT.
THE HECK WITH IT.

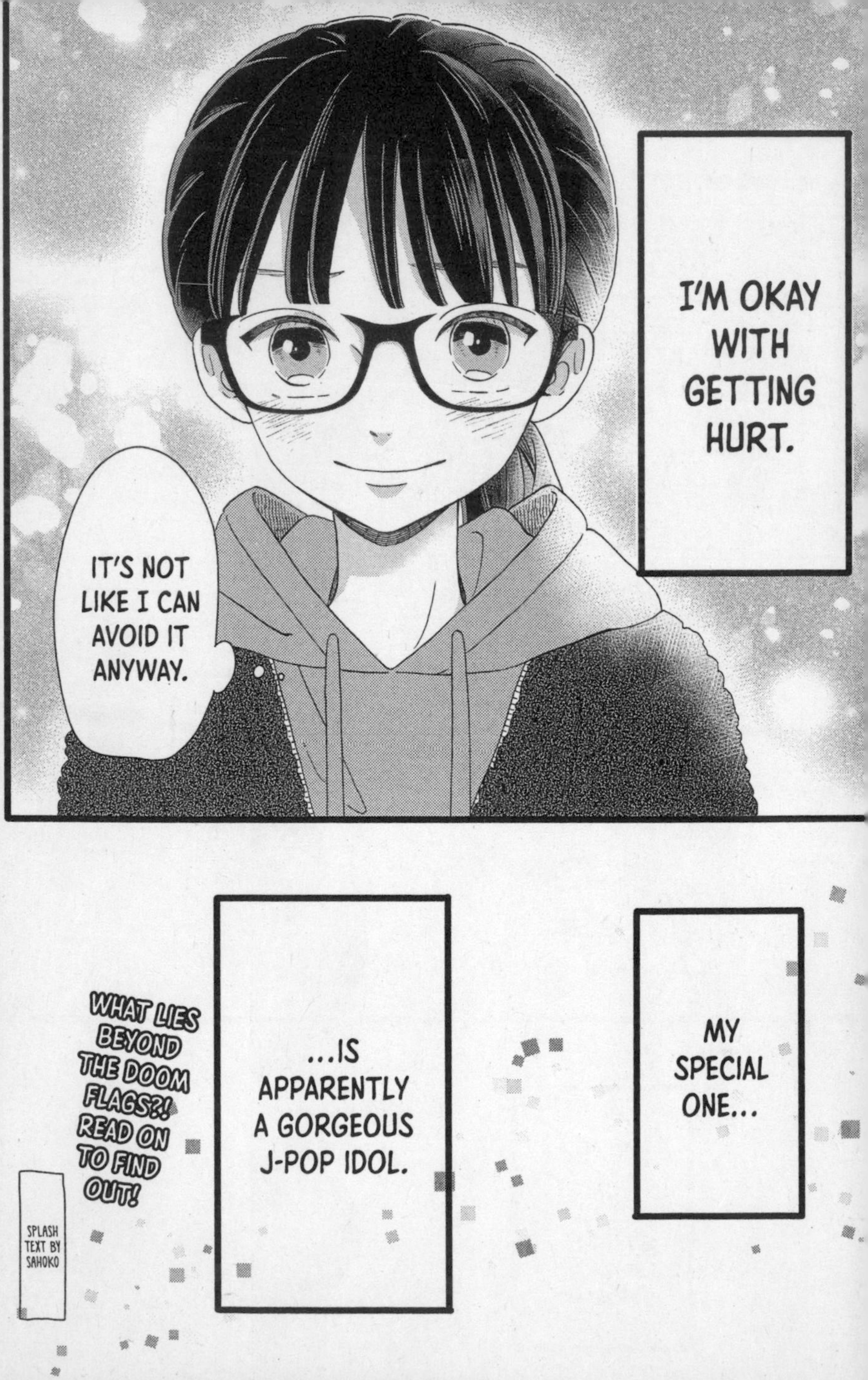
I'M OKAY WITH GETTING HURT.
IT'S NOT LIKE I CAN AVOID IT ANYWAY.
MY SPECIAL ONE...
...IS APPARENTLY A GORGEOUS J-POP IDOL.
WHAT LIES BEYOND THE DOOM FLAGS?! READ ON TO FIND OUT!
SPLASH TEXT BY SAHOKO

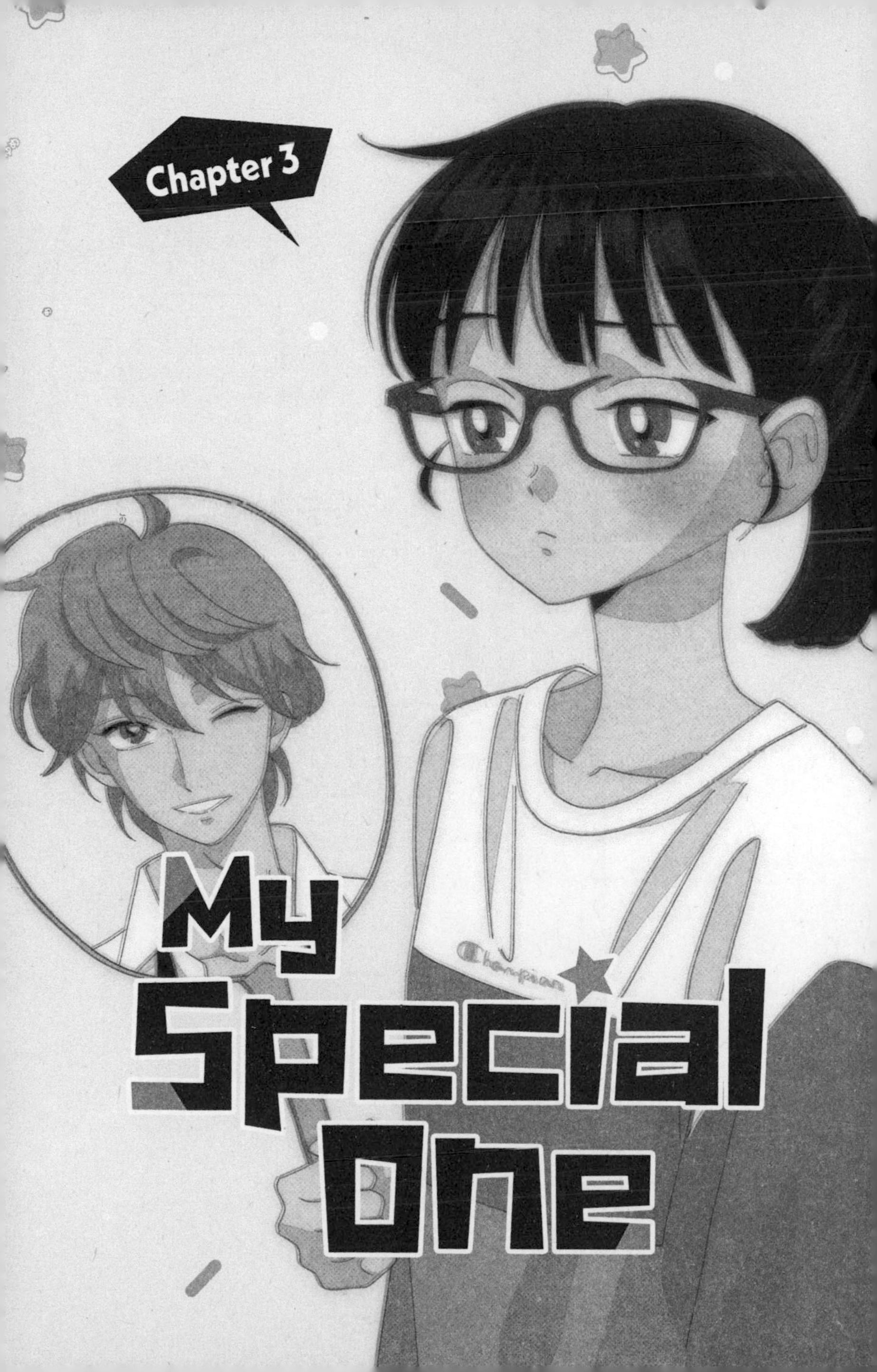
Chapter 3
My Special One
Champion

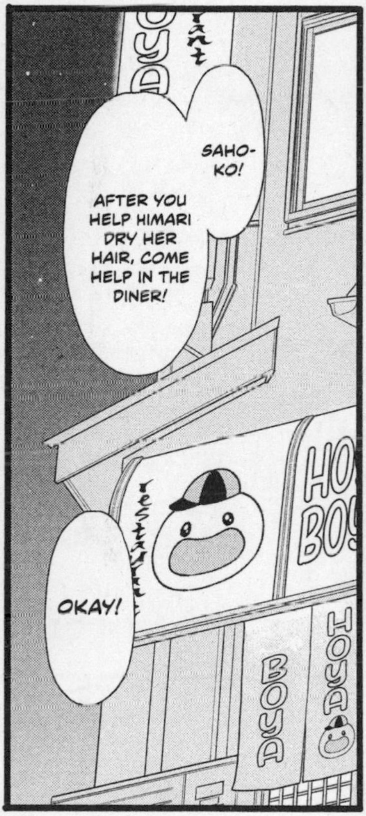
SAHO-KO!
AFTER YOU HELP HIMARI DRY HER HAIR, COME HELP IN THE DINER!
OKAY!

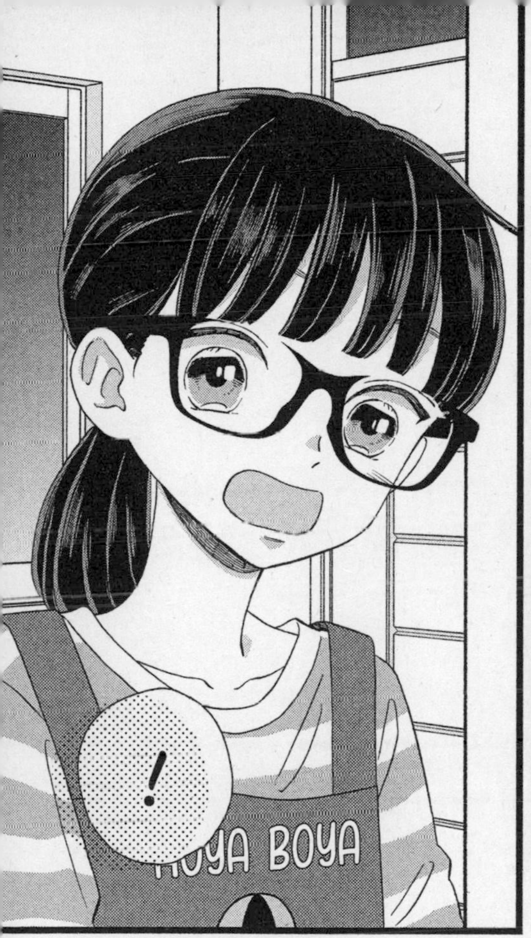
!

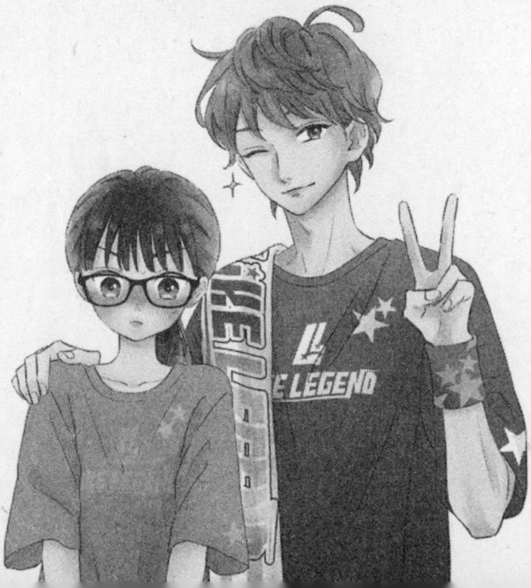

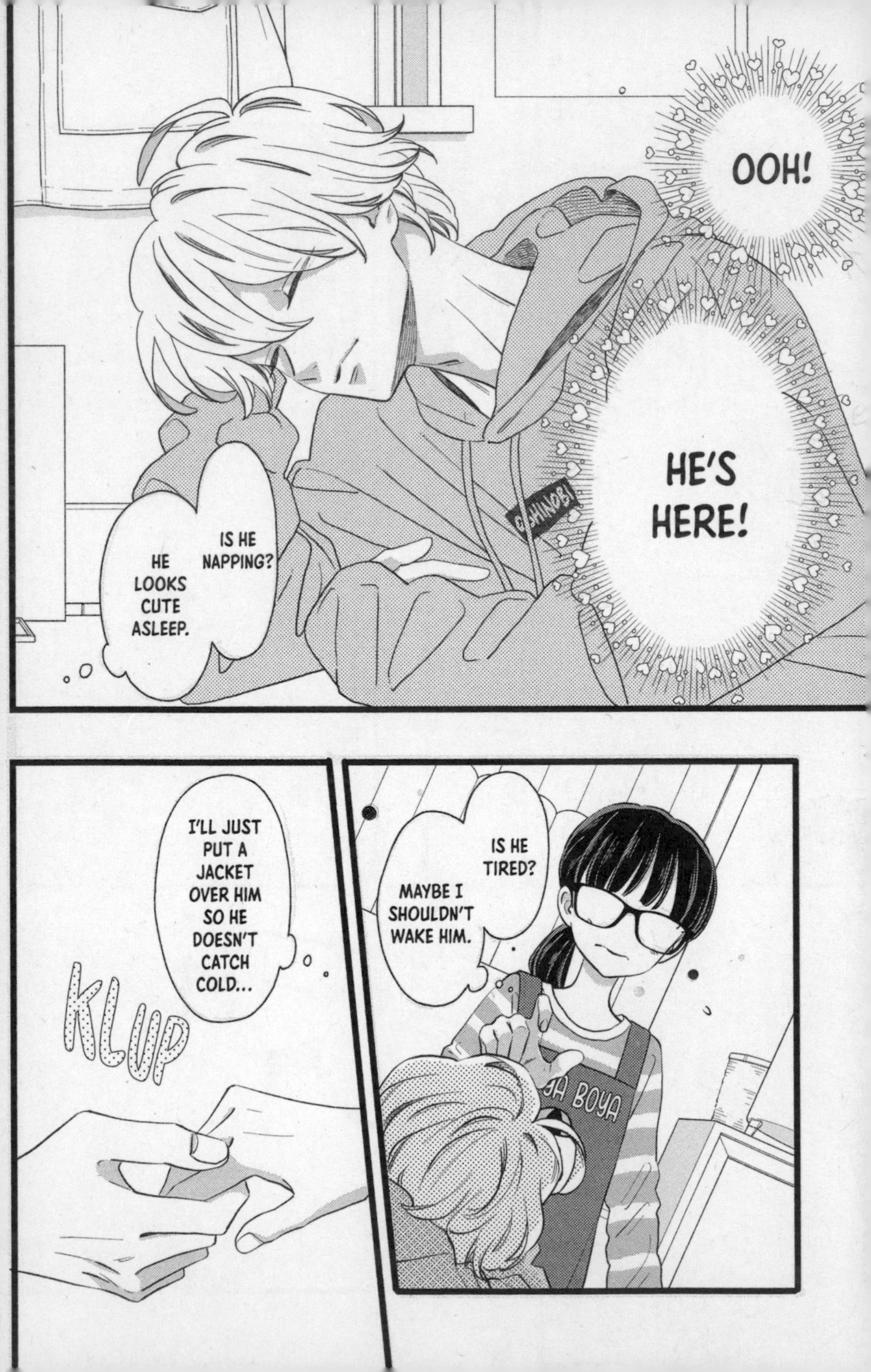
OOH!
HE'S HERE!
IS HE NAPPING? HE LOOKS CUTE ASLEEP.
IS HE TIRED? MAYBE I SHOULDN'T WAKE HIM.
I'LL JUST PUT A JACKET OVER HIM SO HE DOESN'T CATCH COLD...
KLUP

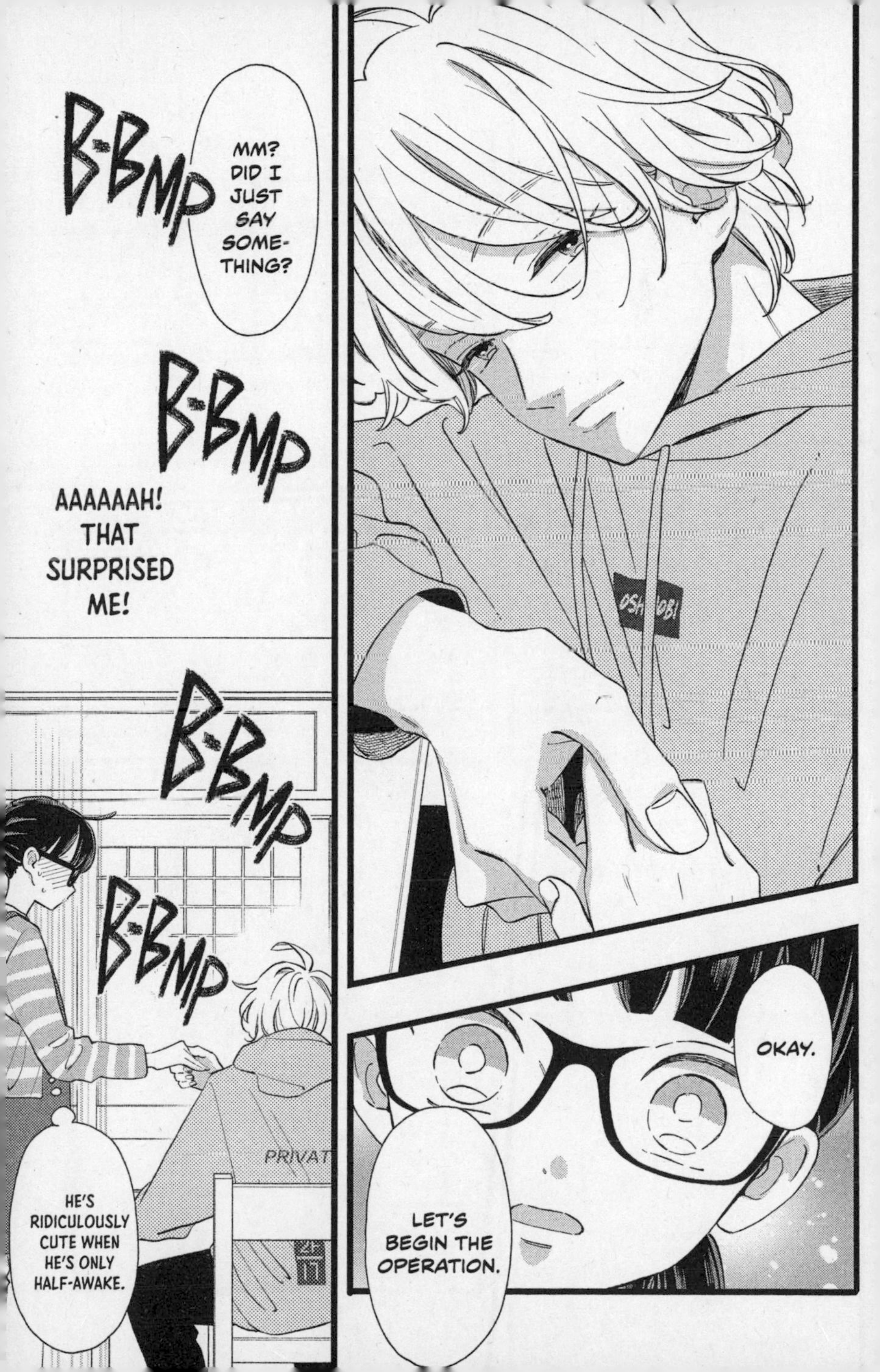
OKAY.
LET'S BEGIN THE OPERATION.
MM? DID I JUST SAY SOME-THING?
B-BMP
B-BMP
AAAAAAH! THAT SURPRISED ME!
B-BMP
B-BMP
HE'S RIDICULOUSLY CUTE WHEN HE'S ONLY HALF-AWAKE.

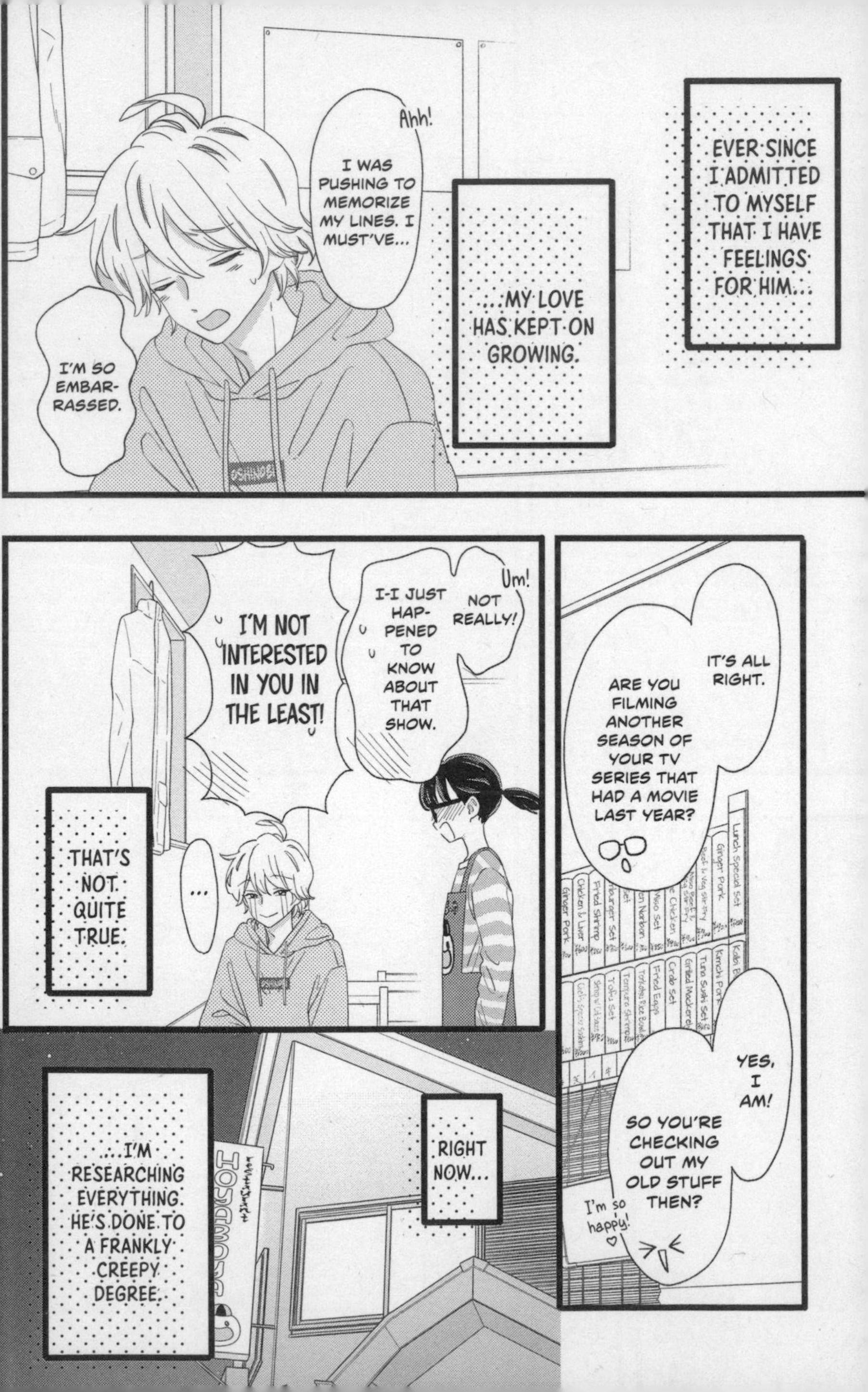
EVER SINCE I ADMITTED TO MYSELF THAT I HAVE FEELINGS FOR HIM...
...MY LOVE HAS KEPT ON GROWING.
Ahh!
I WAS PUSHING TO MEMORIZE MY LINES. I MUST'VE...
I'M SO EMBARRASSED.
IT'S ALL RIGHT.
ARE YOU FILMING ANOTHER SEASON OF YOUR TV SERIES THAT HAD A MOVIE LAST YEAR?
YES, I AM!
SO YOU'RE CHECKING OUT MY OLD STUFF THEN?
I'm so happy! ♡
Um!
NOT REALLY!
I-I JUST HAPPENED TO KNOW ABOUT THAT SHOW.
I'M NOT INTERESTED IN YOU IN THE LEAST!
...
THAT'S NOT QUITE TRUE.
RIGHT NOW...
...I'M RESEARCHING EVERYTHING HE'S DONE TO A FRANKLY CREEPY DEGREE.

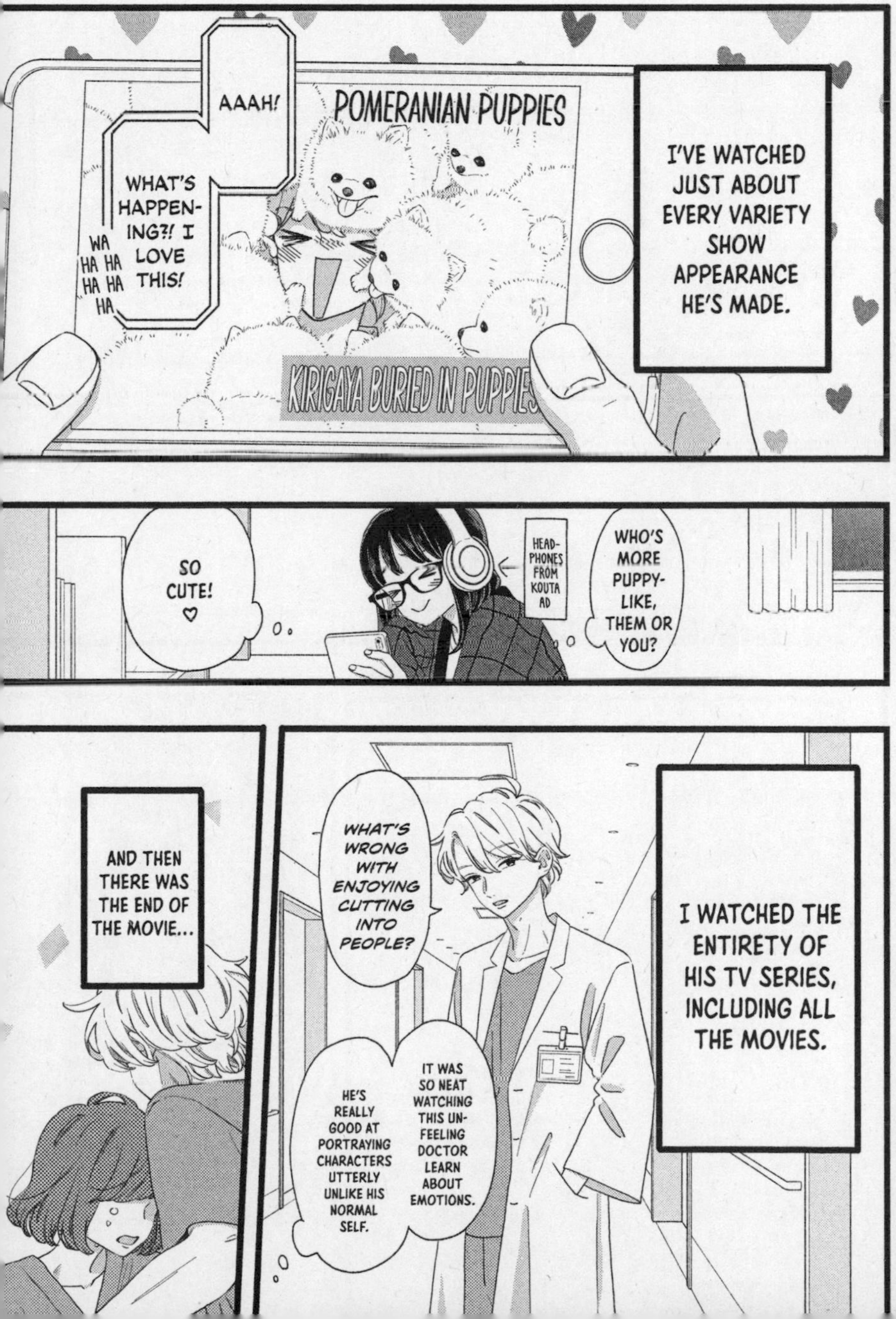
I'VE WATCHED JUST ABOUT EVERY VARIETY SHOW APPEARANCE HE'S MADE.
POMERANIAN PUPPIES
AAAH!
WHAT'S HAPPEN-ING?! I LOVE THIS!
WA HA HA HA HA HA
KIRIGAYA BURIED IN PUPPIES
WHO'S MORE PUPPY-LIKE, THEM OR YOU?
HEAD-PHONES FROM KOUTA AD
SO CUTE! ♡
I WATCHED THE ENTIRETY OF HIS TV SERIES, INCLUDING ALL THE MOVIES.
WHAT'S WRONG WITH ENJOYING CUTTING INTO PEOPLE?
IT WAS SO NEAT WATCHING THIS UN-FEELING DOCTOR LEARN ABOUT EMOTIONS.
HE'S REALLY GOOD AT PORTRAYING CHARACTERS UTTERLY UNLIKE HIS NORMAL SELF.
AND THEN THERE WAS THE END OF THE MOVIE...

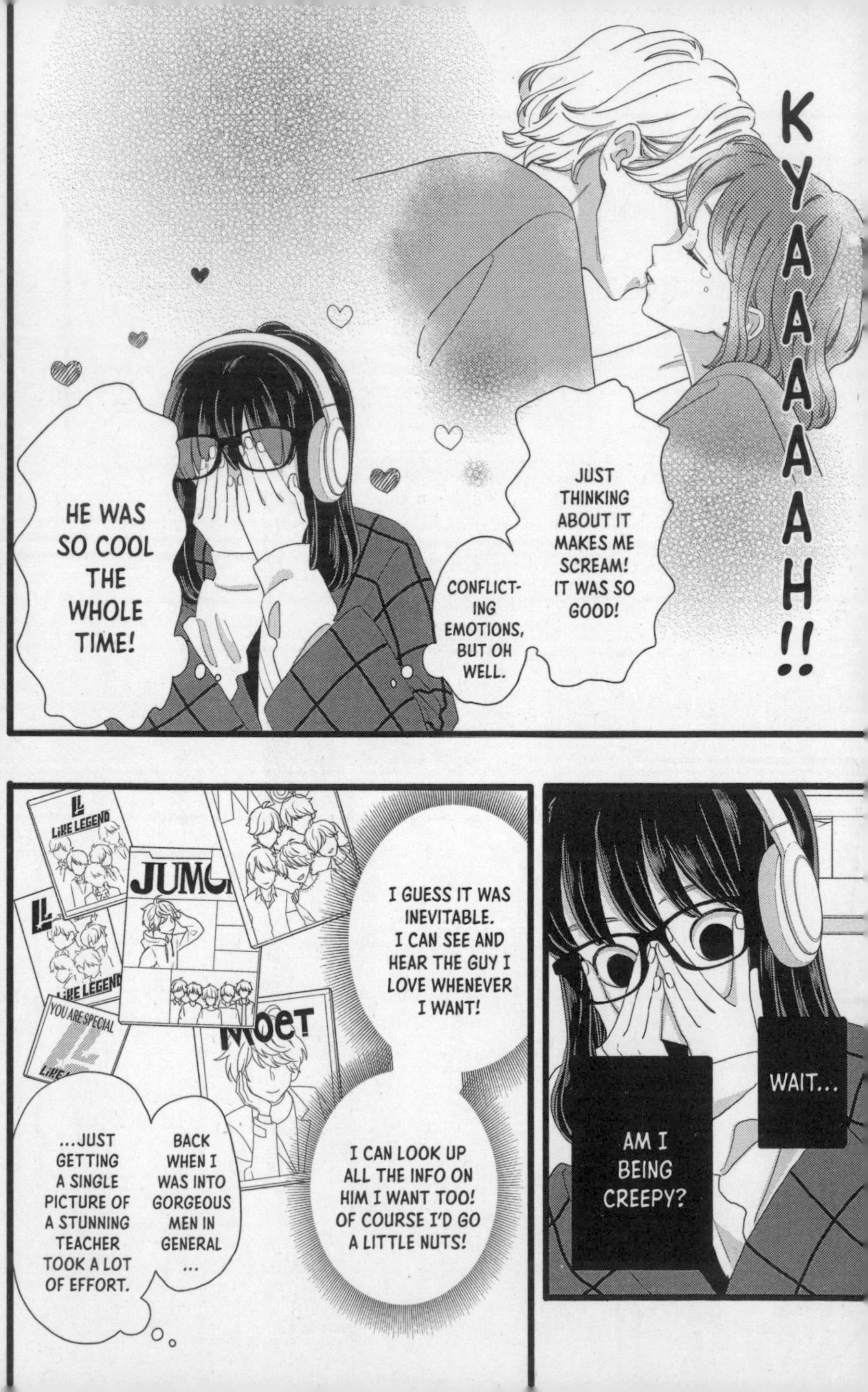
KYAAAAAH!!
JUST THINKING ABOUT IT MAKES ME SCREAM! IT WAS SO GOOD!
CONFLICT-ING EMOTIONS, BUT OH WELL.
HE WAS SO COOL THE WHOLE TIME!
WAIT...
AM I BEING CREEPY?
LIKE LEGEND
LIKE LEGEND
YOU ARE SPECIAL
Moet
I GUESS IT WAS INEVITABLE. I CAN SEE AND HEAR THE GUY I LOVE WHENEVER I WANT!
I CAN LOOK UP ALL THE INFO ON HIM I WANT TOO! OF COURSE I'D GO A LITTLE NUTS!
BACK WHEN I WAS INTO GORGEOUS MEN IN GENERAL...
...JUST GETTING A SINGLE PICTURE OF A STUNNING TEACHER TOOK A LOT OF EFFORT.

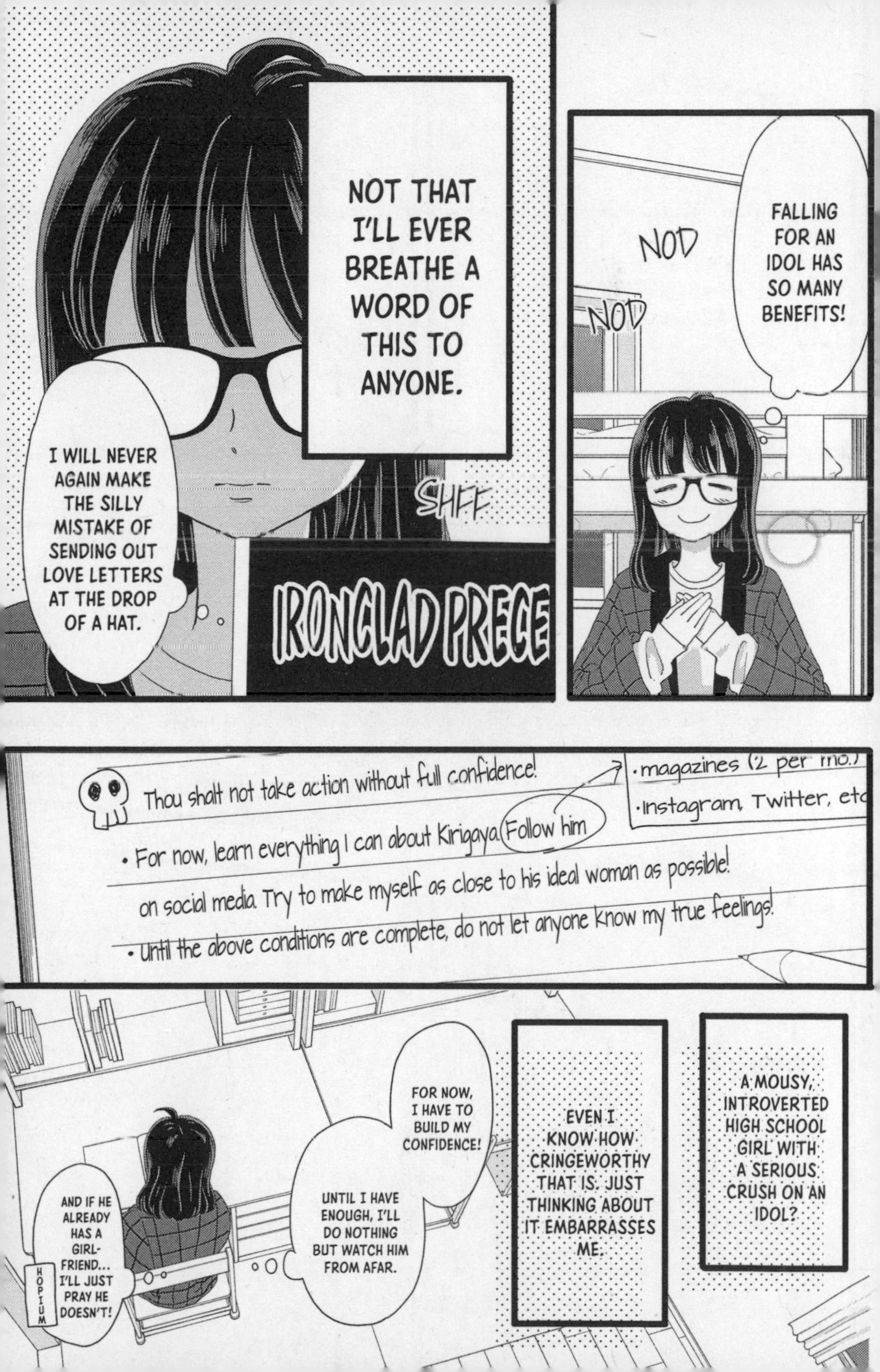
NOD
NOD
FALLING FOR AN IDOL HAS SO MANY BENEFITS!
NOT THAT I'LL EVER BREATHE A WORD OF THIS TO ANYONE.
SHFF
I WILL NEVER AGAIN MAKE THE SILLY MISTAKE OF SENDING OUT LOVE LETTERS AT THE DROP OF A HAT.
IRONCLAD PRECE
·magazines (2 per mo.)
·Instagram, Twitter, etc
Thou shalt not take action without full confidence!
• For now, learn everything I can about Kirigaya. Follow him
on social media. Try to make myself as close to his ideal woman as possible!
• Until the above conditions are complete, do not let anyone know my true feelings!
A MOUSY, INTROVERTED HIGH SCHOOL GIRL WITH A SERIOUS CRUSH ON AN IDOL?
EVEN I KNOW HOW CRINGEWORTHY THAT IS. JUST THINKING ABOUT IT EMBARRASSES ME.
FOR NOW, I HAVE TO BUILD MY CONFIDENCE!
UNTIL I HAVE ENOUGH, I'LL DO NOTHING BUT WATCH HIM FROM AFAR.
AND IF HE ALREADY HAS A GIRLFRIEND... I'LL JUST PRAY HE DOESN'T!
HOPIUM

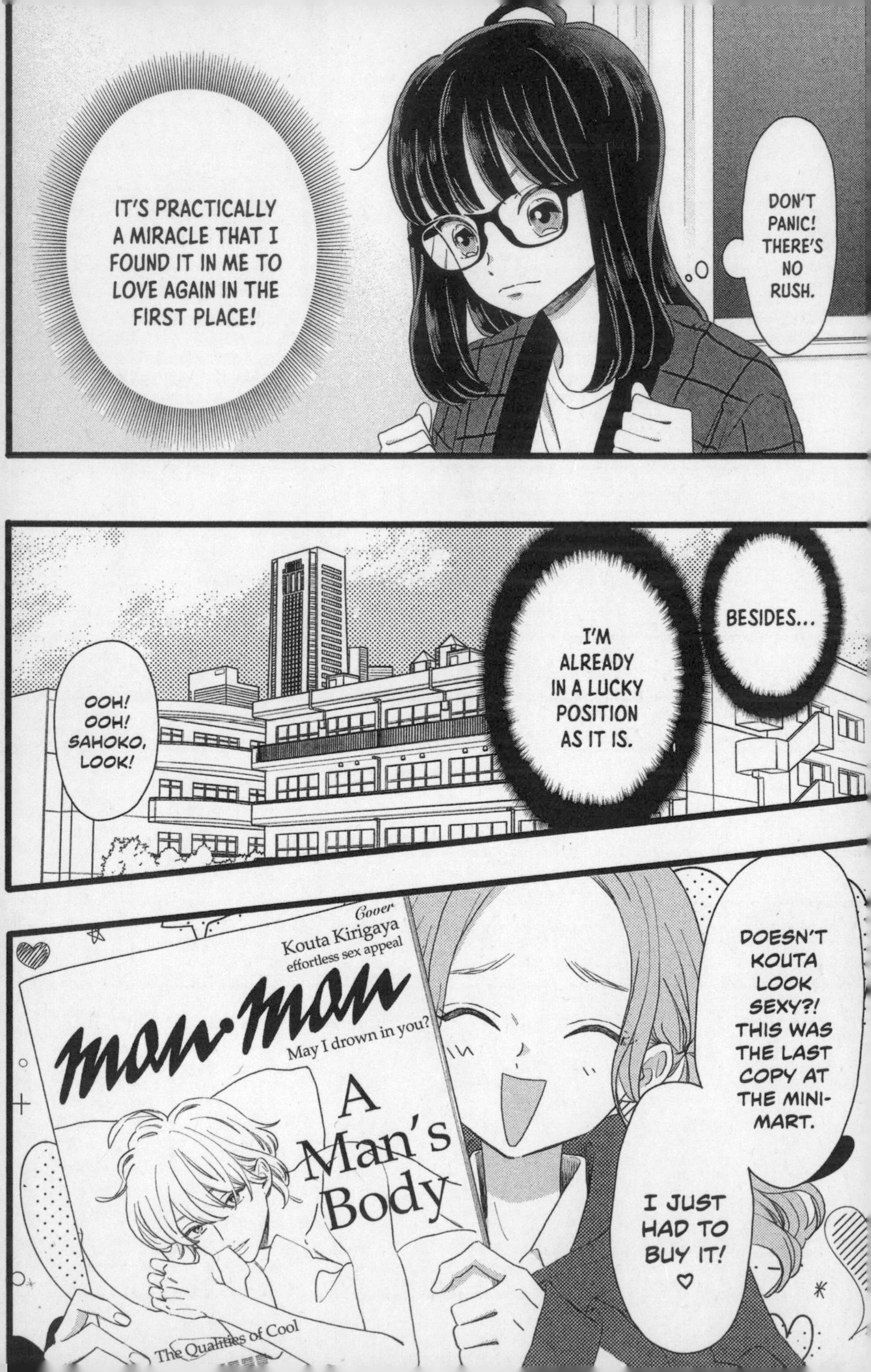
DON'T PANIC! THERE'S NO RUSH.
IT'S PRACTICALLY A MIRACLE THAT I FOUND IT IN ME TO LOVE AGAIN IN THE FIRST PLACE!
BESIDES...
I'M ALREADY IN A LUCKY POSITION AS IT IS.
OOH! OOH! SAHOKO, LOOK!
DOESN'T KOUTA LOOK SEXY?! THIS WAS THE LAST COPY AT THE MINI-MART.
I JUST HAD TO BUY IT! ♡
Cover
Kouta Kirigaya
effortless sex appeal
man-man
May I drown in you?
A Man's Body
The Qualities of Cool

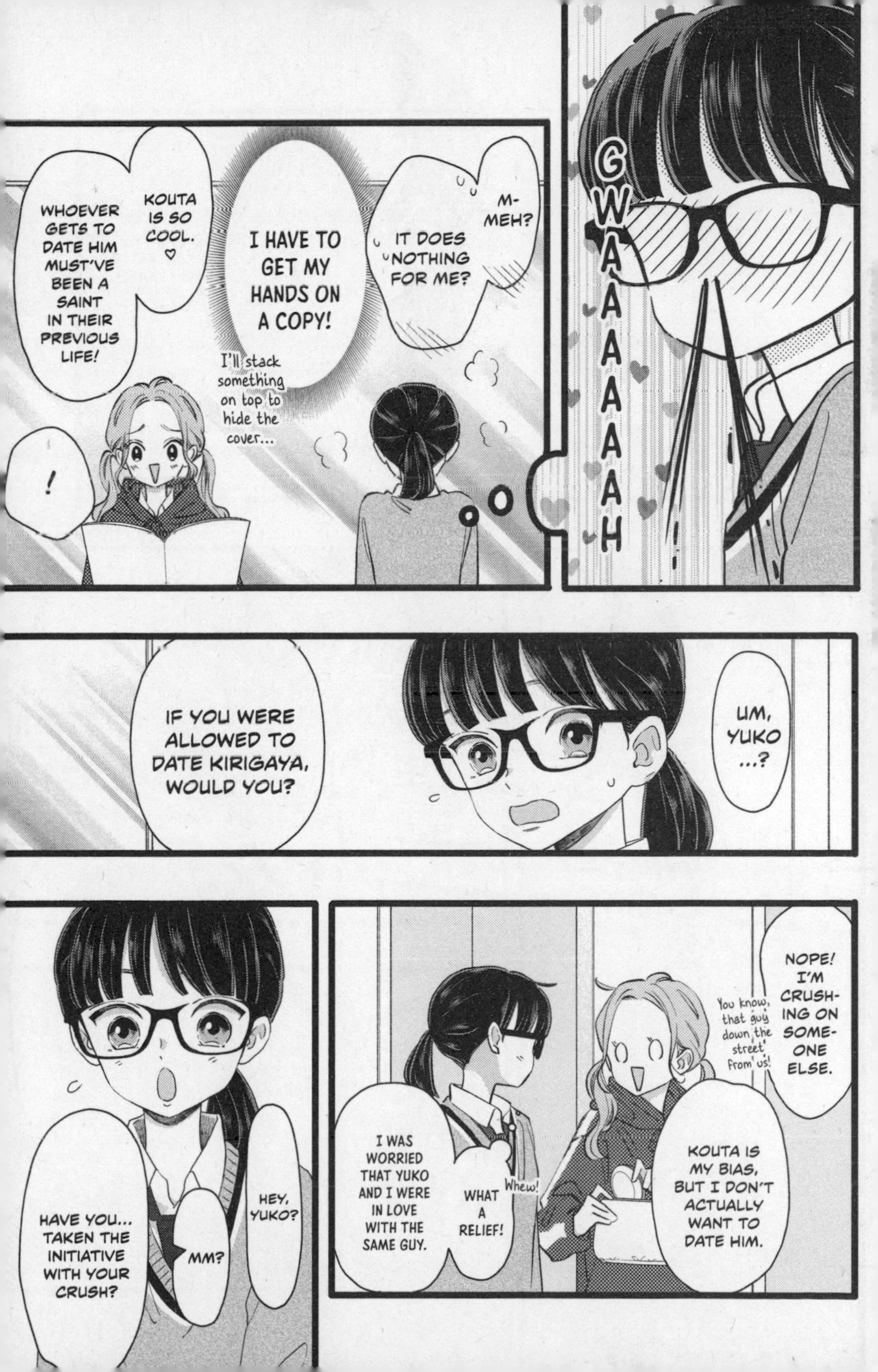
GWAAAAAAAH
M-MEH? IT DOES NOTHING FOR ME?
I HAVE TO GET MY HANDS ON A COPY!
I'll stack something on top to hide the cover...
KOUTA IS SO COOL. ♡
WHOEVER GETS TO DATE HIM MUST'VE BEEN A SAINT IN THEIR PREVIOUS LIFE!
!
UM, YUKO ...?
IF YOU WERE ALLOWED TO DATE KIRIGAYA, WOULD YOU?
NOPE! I'M CRUSHING ON SOMEONE ELSE.
You know, that guy down the street from us!
KOUTA IS MY BIAS, BUT I DON'T ACTUALLY WANT TO DATE HIM.
Whew!
WHAT A RELIEF!
I WAS WORRIED THAT YUKO AND I WERE IN LOVE WITH THE SAME GUY.
HEY, YUKO?
MM?
HAVE YOU... TAKEN THE INITIATIVE WITH YOUR CRUSH?

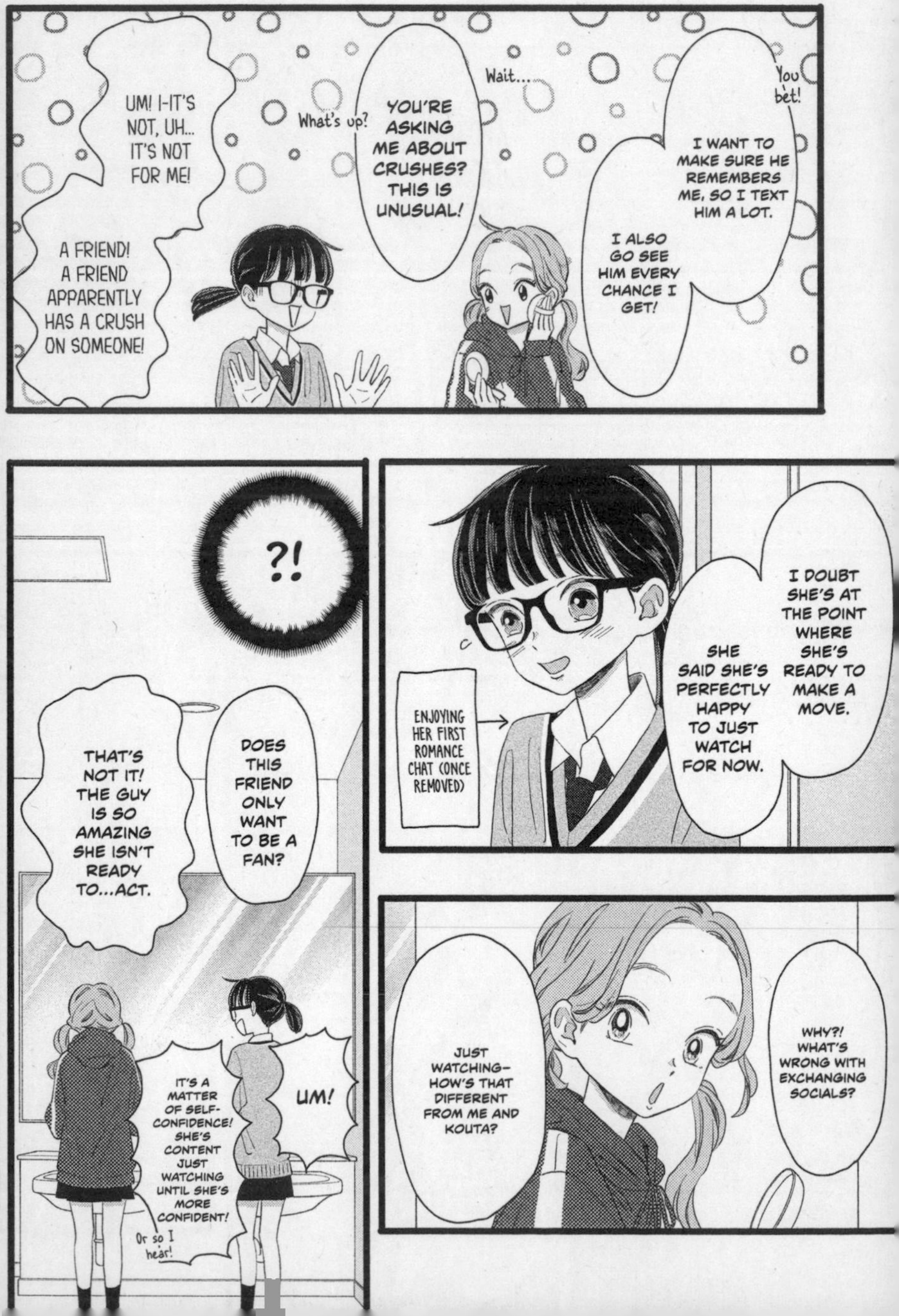
You bet!
I WANT TO MAKE SURE HE REMEMBERS ME, SO I TEXT HIM A LOT.
I ALSO GO SEE HIM EVERY CHANCE I GET!
Wait...
YOU'RE ASKING ME ABOUT CRUSHES? THIS IS UNUSUAL!
What's up?
UM! I-IT'S NOT, UH... IT'S NOT FOR ME!
A FRIEND! A FRIEND APPARENTLY HAS A CRUSH ON SOMEONE!
I DOUBT SHE'S AT THE POINT WHERE SHE'S READY TO MAKE A MOVE.
SHE SAID SHE'S PERFECTLY HAPPY TO JUST WATCH FOR NOW.
ENJOYING HER FIRST ROMANCE CHAT (ONCE REMOVED)
WHY?! WHAT'S WRONG WITH EXCHANGING SOCIALS?
JUST WATCHING—HOW'S THAT DIFFERENT FROM ME AND KOUTA?
?!
DOES THIS FRIEND ONLY WANT TO BE A FAN?
THAT'S NOT IT! THE GUY IS SO AMAZING SHE ISN'T READY TO...ACT.
UM!
IT'S A MATTER OF SELF-CONFIDENCE! SHE'S CONTENT JUST WATCHING UNTIL SHE'S MORE CONFIDENT!
Or so I hear!

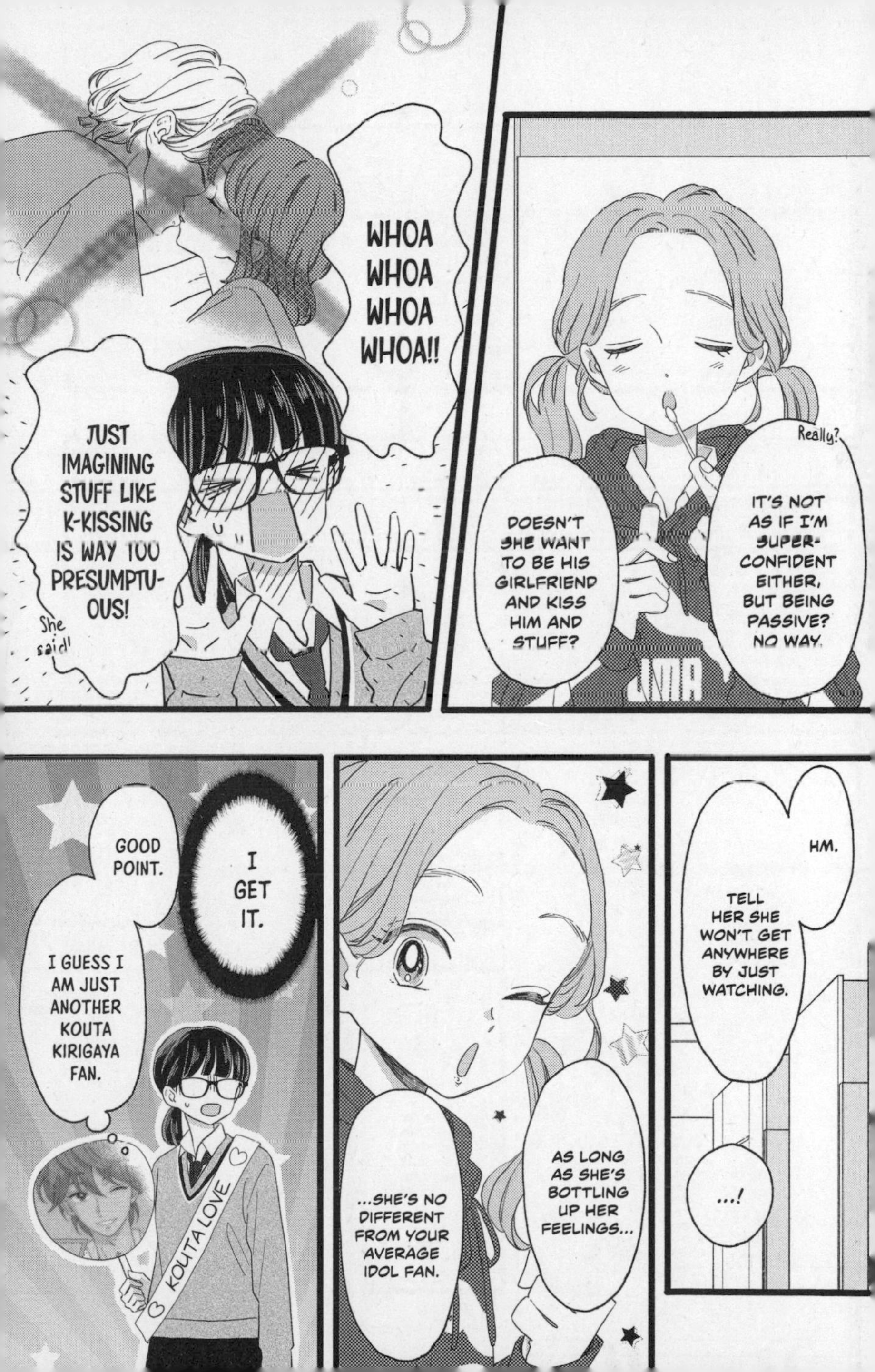
Really?
IT'S NOT AS IF I'M SUPER-CONFIDENT EITHER, BUT BEING PASSIVE? NO WAY.
DOESN'T SHE WANT TO BE HIS GIRLFRIEND AND KISS HIM AND STUFF?
WHOA WHOA WHOA WHOA!!
JUST IMAGINING STUFF LIKE K-KISSING IS WAY TOO PRESUMPTU-OUS!
She said!
HM.
TELL HER SHE WON'T GET ANYWHERE BY JUST WATCHING.
...!
AS LONG AS SHE'S BOTTLING UP HER FEELINGS...
...SHE'S NO DIFFERENT FROM YOUR AVERAGE IDOL FAN.
I GET IT.
GOOD POINT.
I GUESS I AM JUST ANOTHER KOUTA KIRIGAYA FAN.
KOUTA LOVE

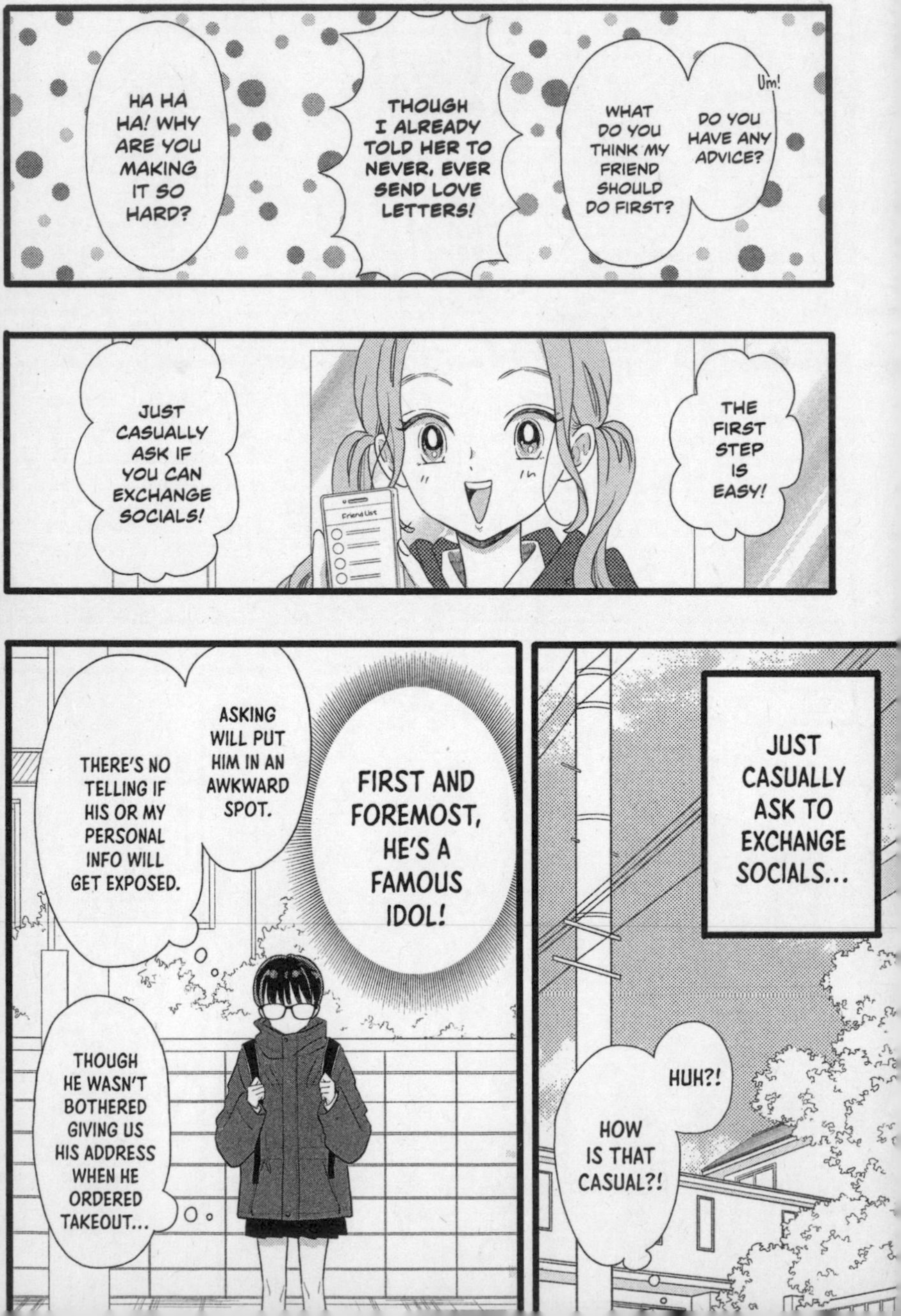
Um!
DO YOU HAVE ANY ADVICE?
WHAT DO YOU THINK MY FRIEND SHOULD DO FIRST?
THOUGH I ALREADY TOLD HER TO NEVER, EVER SEND LOVE LETTERS!
HA HA HA! WHY ARE YOU MAKING IT SO HARD?
THE FIRST STEP IS EASY!
Friend List
JUST CASUALLY ASK IF YOU CAN EXCHANGE SOCIALS!
JUST CASUALLY ASK TO EXCHANGE SOCIALS...
HUH?!
HOW IS THAT CASUAL?!
FIRST AND FOREMOST, HE'S A FAMOUS IDOL!
ASKING WILL PUT HIM IN AN AWKWARD SPOT.
THERE'S NO TELLING IF HIS OR MY PERSONAL INFO WILL GET EXPOSED.
THOUGH HE WASN'T BOTHERED GIVING US HIS ADDRESS WHEN HE ORDERED TAKEOUT...

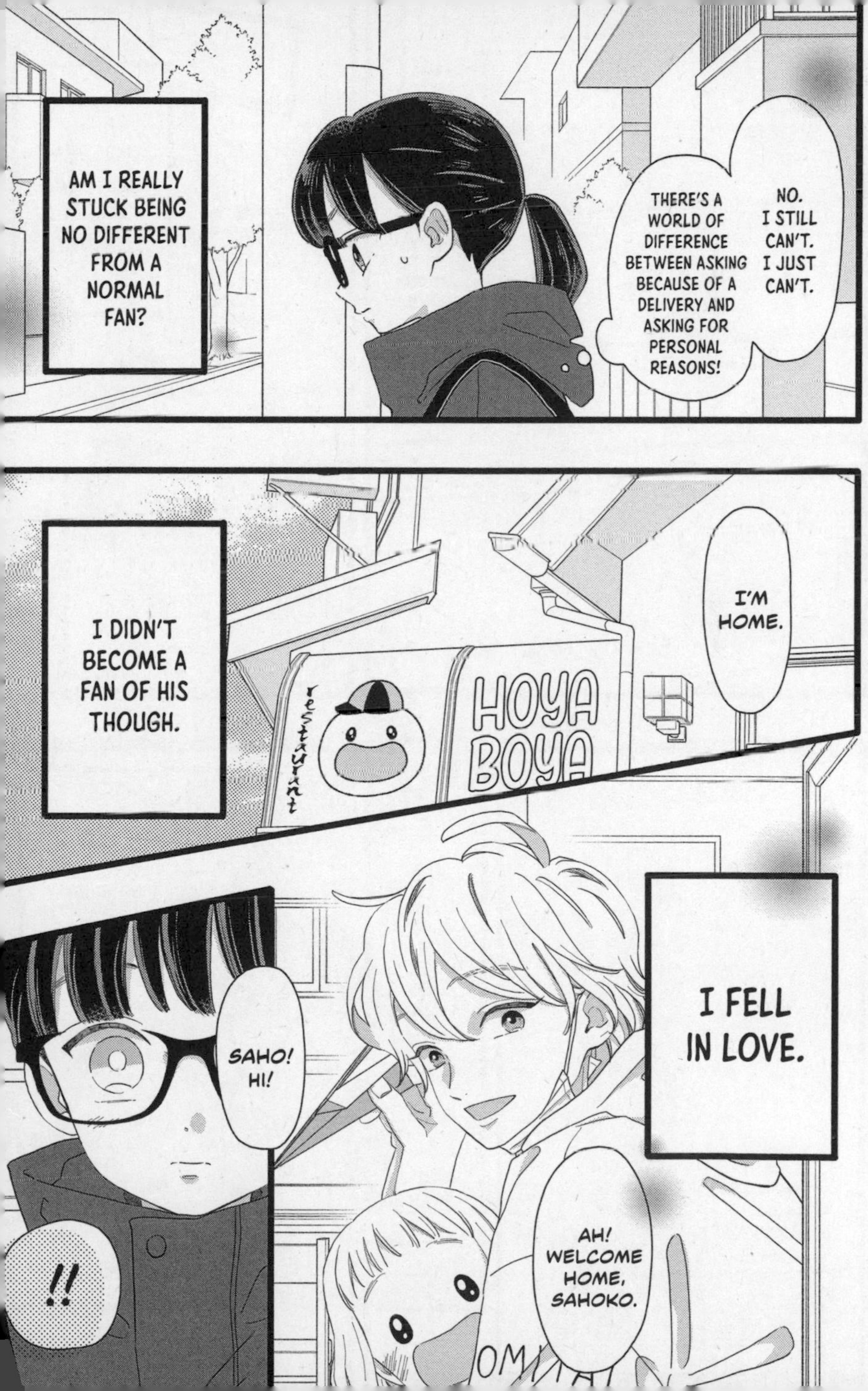
NO. I STILL CAN'T. I JUST CAN'T.
THERE'S A WORLD OF DIFFERENCE BETWEEN ASKING BECAUSE OF A DELIVERY AND ASKING FOR PERSONAL REASONS!
AM I REALLY STUCK BEING NO DIFFERENT FROM A NORMAL FAN?
I'M HOME.
HOYA BOYA
restaurant
I DIDN'T BECOME A FAN OF HIS THOUGH.
I FELL IN LOVE.
AH! WELCOME HOME, SAHOKO.
SAHO! HI!
!!

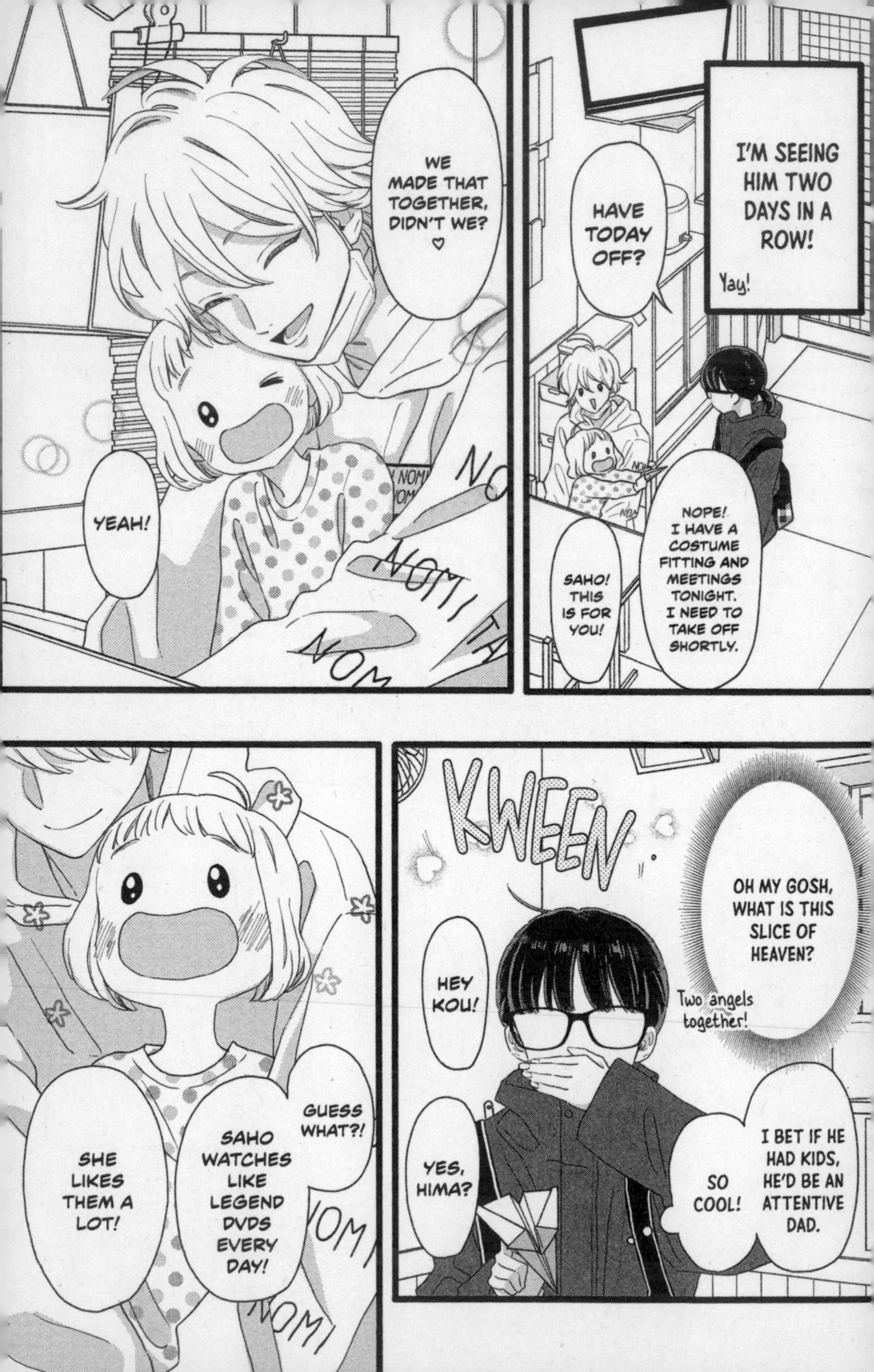
I'M SEEING HIM TWO DAYS IN A ROW!
Yay!
HAVE TODAY OFF?
NOPE! I HAVE A COSTUME FITTING AND MEETINGS TONIGHT. I NEED TO TAKE OFF SHORTLY.
SAHO! THIS IS FOR YOU!
WE MADE THAT TOGETHER, DIDN'T WE? ♡
YEAH!
KWEEN
OH MY GOSH, WHAT IS THIS SLICE OF HEAVEN?
Two angels together!
HEY KOU!
I BET IF HE HAD KIDS, HE'D BE AN ATTENTIVE DAD.
SO COOL!
YES, HIMA?
GUESS WHAT?!
SAHO WATCHES LIKE LEGEND DVDS EVERY DAY!
SHE LIKES THEM A LOT!

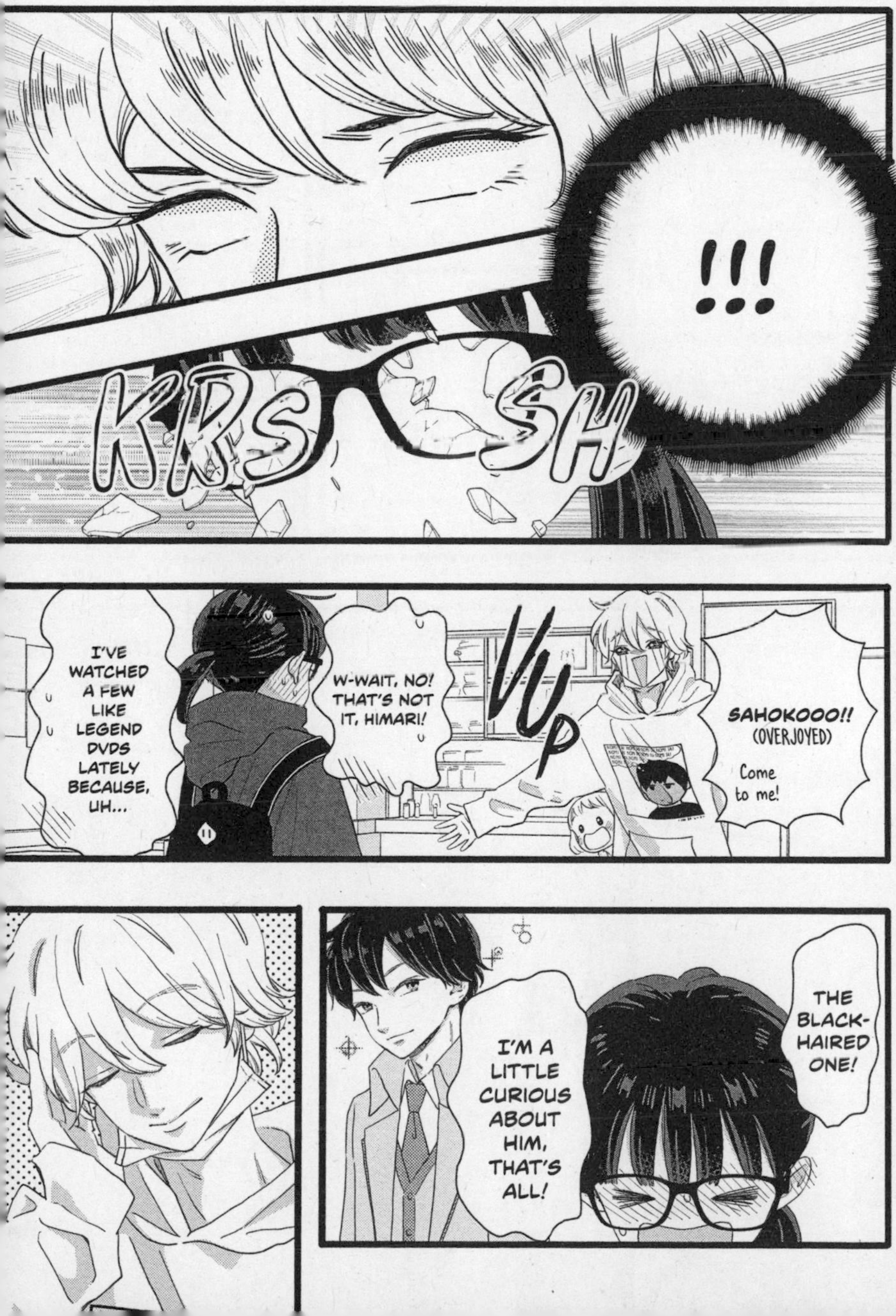
!!!
KRSSH
SAHOKOOO!! (OVERJOYED)
Come to me!
VUP
W-WAIT, NO! THAT'S NOT IT, HIMARI!
I'VE WATCHED A FEW LIKE LEGEND DVDS LATELY BECAUSE, UH...
THE BLACK-HAIRED ONE!
I'M A LITTLE CURIOUS ABOUT HIM, THAT'S ALL!

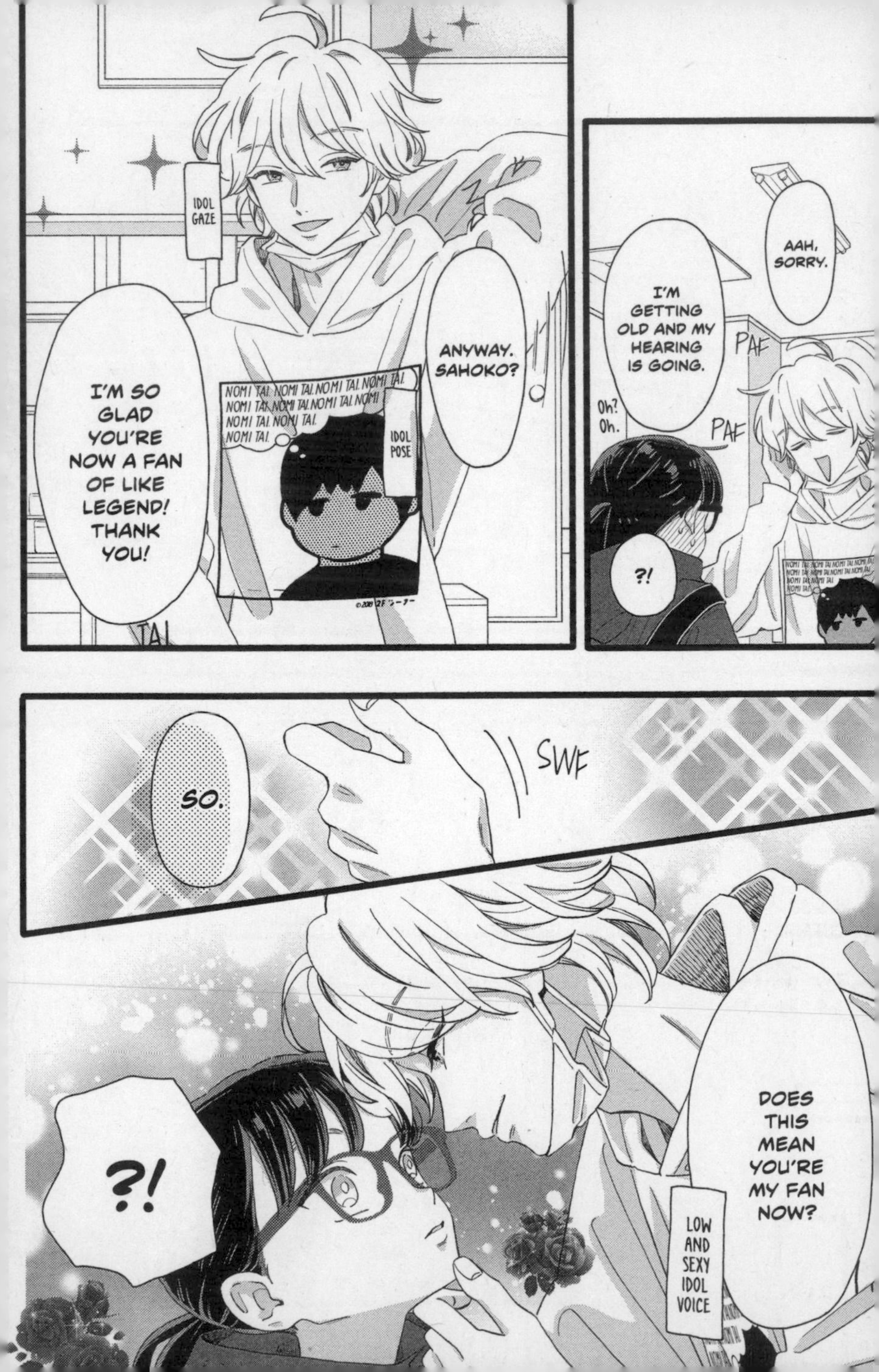
AAH, SORRY.
I'M GETTING OLD AND MY HEARING IS GOING.
PAF
PAF
Oh? Oh.
?!
ANYWAY. SAHOKO?
IDOL GAZE
I'M SO GLAD YOU'RE NOW A FAN OF LIKE LEGEND! THANK YOU!
NOMI TAI. NOMI TAI. NOMI TAI. NOMI TAI. NOMI TAI. NOMI TAI. NOMI TAI. NOMI NOMI TAI. NOMI TAI. NOMI TAI.
IDOL POSE
TAI
SWF
SO.
DOES THIS MEAN YOU'RE MY FAN NOW?
LOW AND SEXY IDOL VOICE
?!

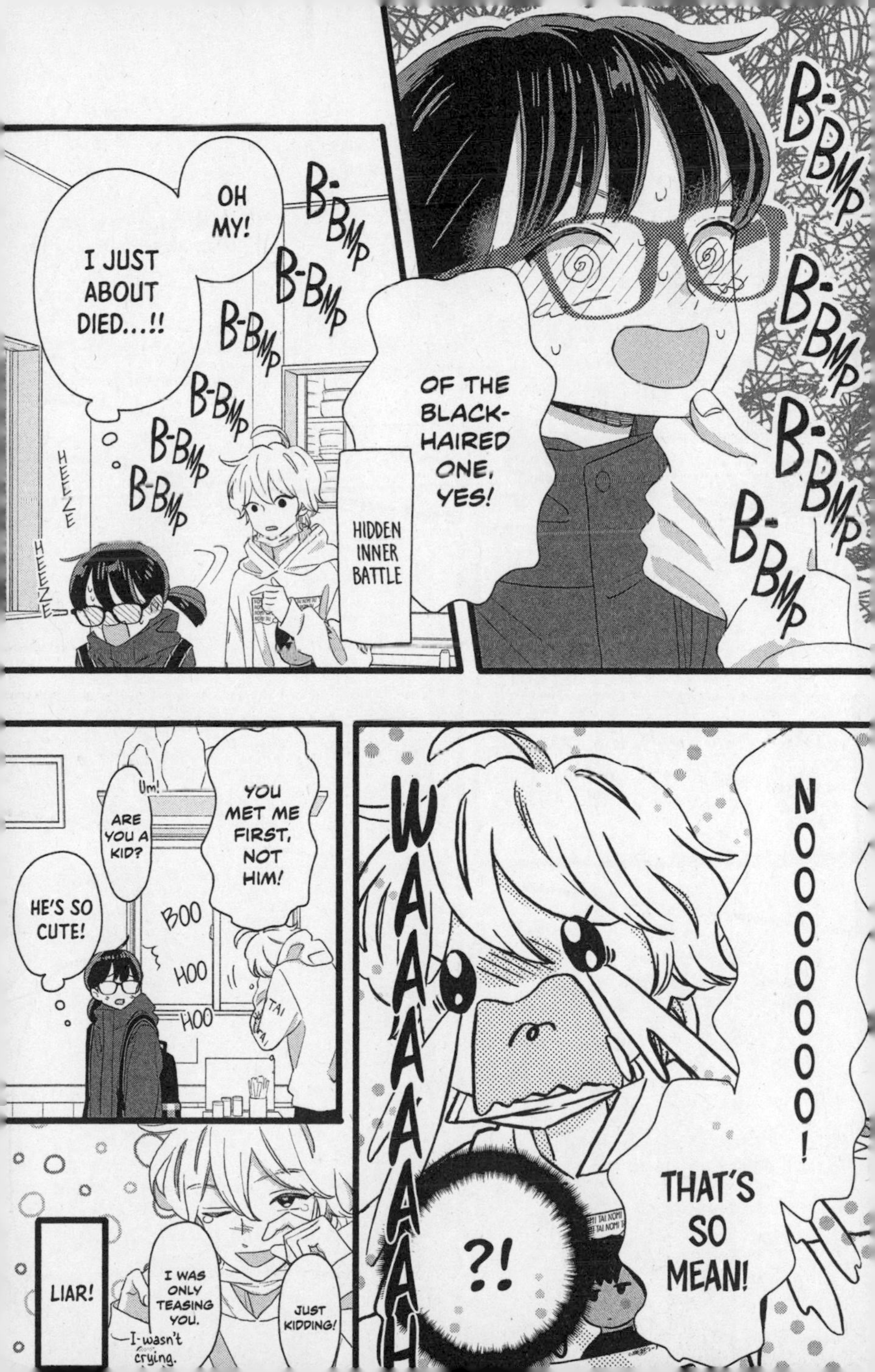
B-BMP B-BMP B-BMP B-BMP B-BMP
OF THE BLACK-HAIRED ONE, YES!
HIDDEN INNER BATTLE
B-BMP B-BMP B-BMP B-BMP B-BMP B-BMP
OH MY!
I JUST ABOUT DIED...!!
HEEZE
HEEZE
NOOOOOOOO!
THAT'S SO MEAN!
?!
WAAAAAAAH
YOU MET ME FIRST, NOT HIM!
Um!
ARE YOU A KID?
HE'S SO CUTE!
BOO
HOO
HOO
JUST KIDDING!
I WAS ONLY TEASING YOU.
—I wasn't crying.
LIAR!

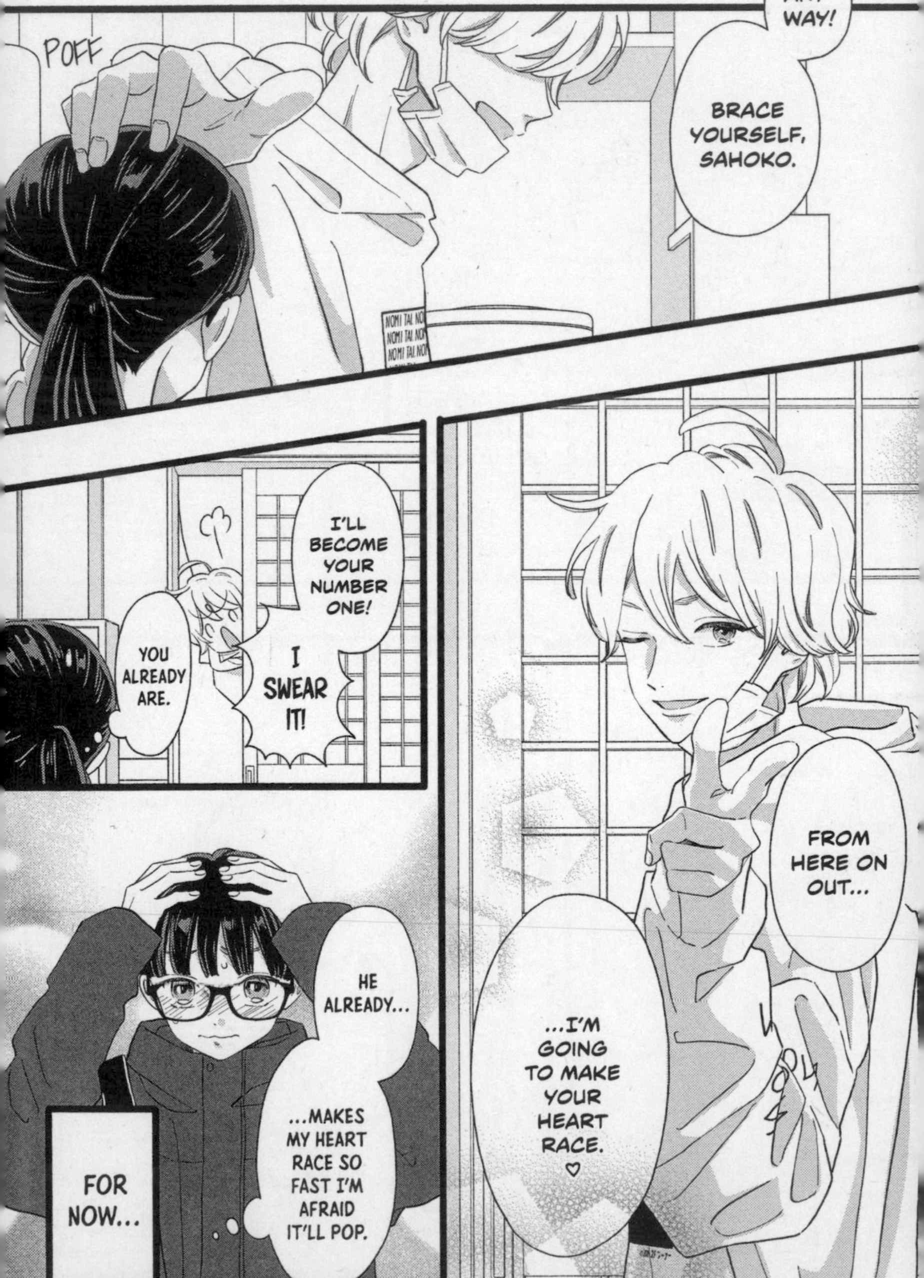
ANY-WAY!
BRACE YOURSELF, SAHOKO.
POFF
NOMI TAI NO
NOMI TAI NO
NOMI TAI NO
FROM HERE ON OUT...
...I'M GOING TO MAKE YOUR HEART RACE. ♡
I'LL BECOME YOUR NUMBER ONE!
I SWEAR IT!
YOU ALREADY ARE.
HE ALREADY...
...MAKES MY HEART RACE SO FAST I'M AFRAID IT'LL POP.
FOR NOW...

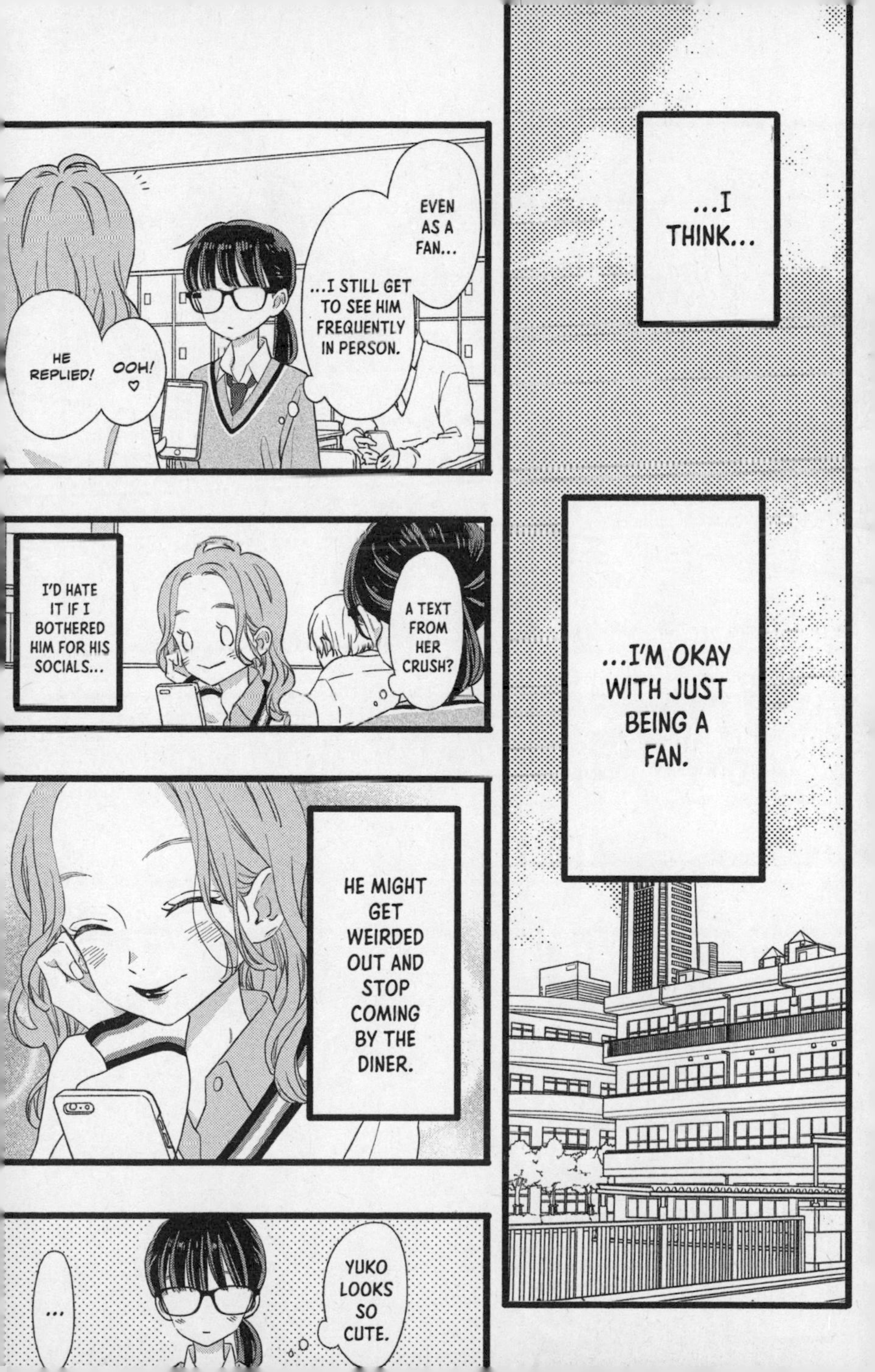
...I THINK...
...I'M OKAY WITH JUST BEING A FAN.
EVEN AS A FAN...
...I STILL GET TO SEE HIM FREQUENTLY IN PERSON.
OOH! ♡
HE REPLIED!
A TEXT FROM HER CRUSH?
I'D HATE IT IF I BOTHERED HIM FOR HIS SOCIALS...
HE MIGHT GET WEIRDED OUT AND STOP COMING BY THE DINER.
YUKO LOOKS SO CUTE.
...

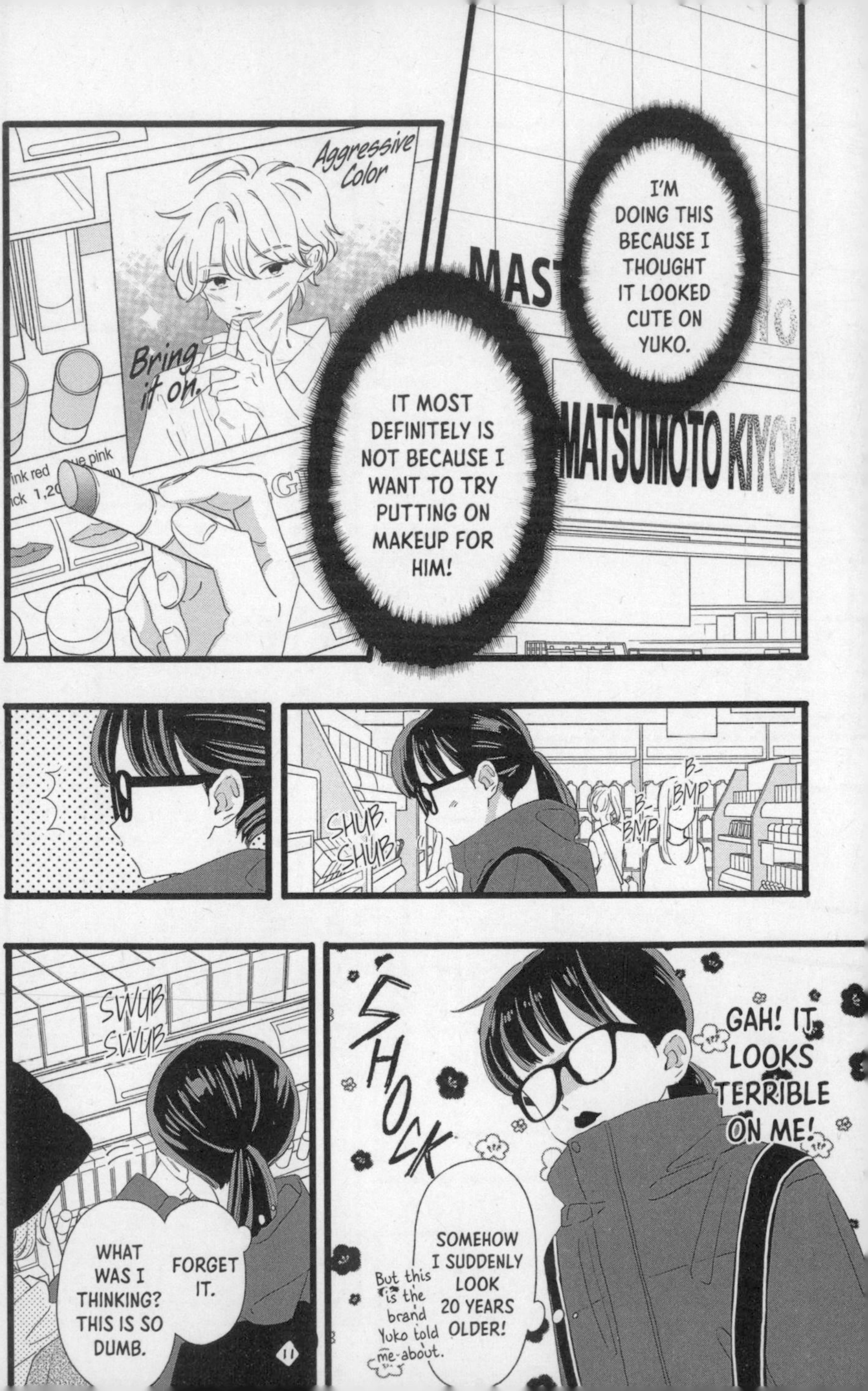
I'M DOING THIS BECAUSE I THOUGHT IT LOOKED CUTE ON YUKO.
IT MOST DEFINITELY IS NOT BECAUSE I WANT TO TRY PUTTING ON MAKEUP FOR HIM!
Aggressive Color
Bring it on.
SHUB SHUB
B-BMP
B-BMP
SHOCK
GAH! IT LOOKS TERRIBLE ON ME!
SOMEHOW I SUDDENLY LOOK 20 YEARS OLDER!
But this is the brand Yuko told me about.
SWUB SWUB
FORGET IT.
WHAT WAS I THINKING? THIS IS SO DUMB.

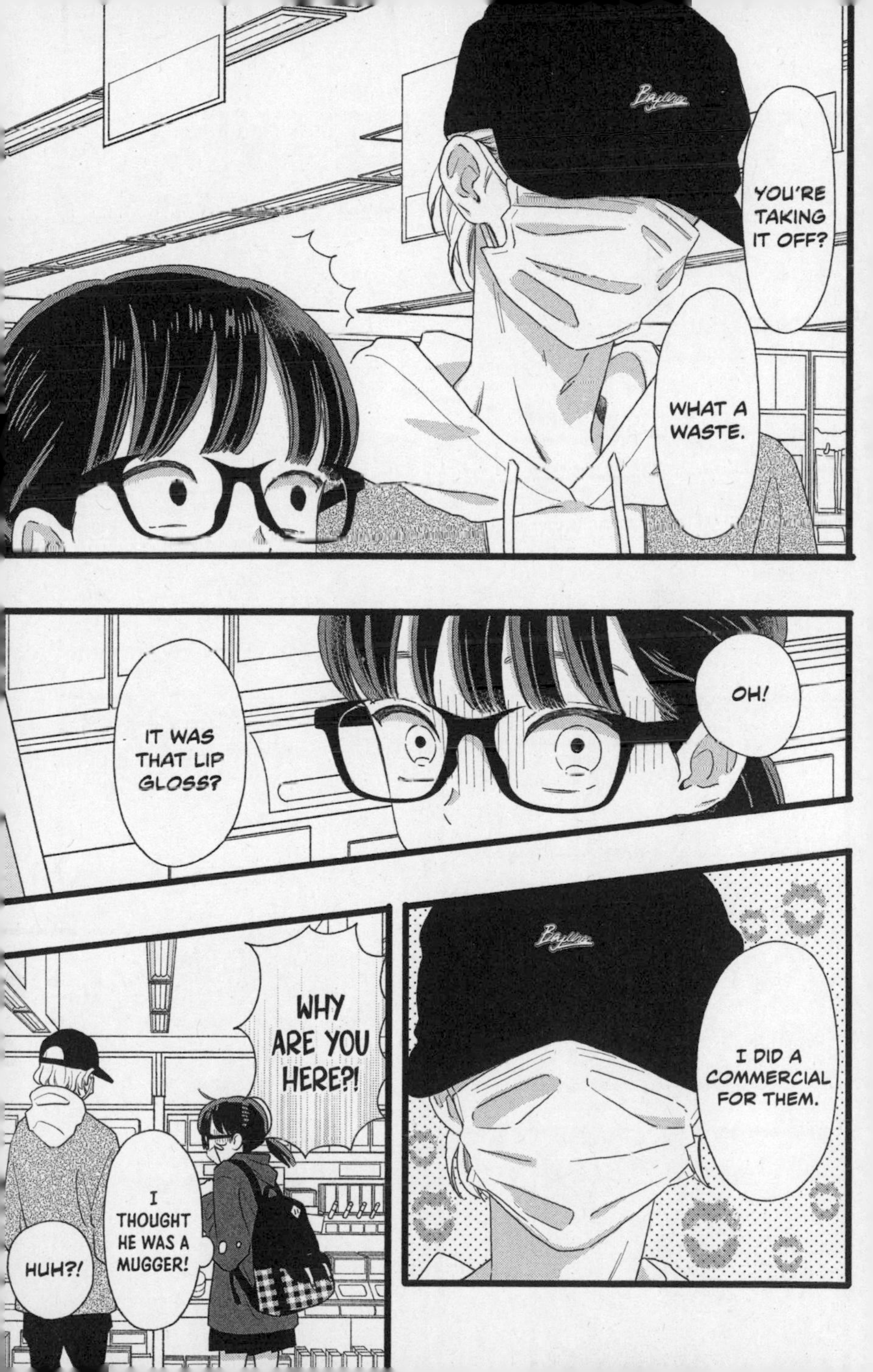
YOU'RE TAKING IT OFF?
WHAT A WASTE.
OH!
IT WAS THAT LIP GLOSS?
I DID A COMMERCIAL FOR THEM.
WHY ARE YOU HERE?!
I THOUGHT HE WAS A MUGGER!
HUH?!

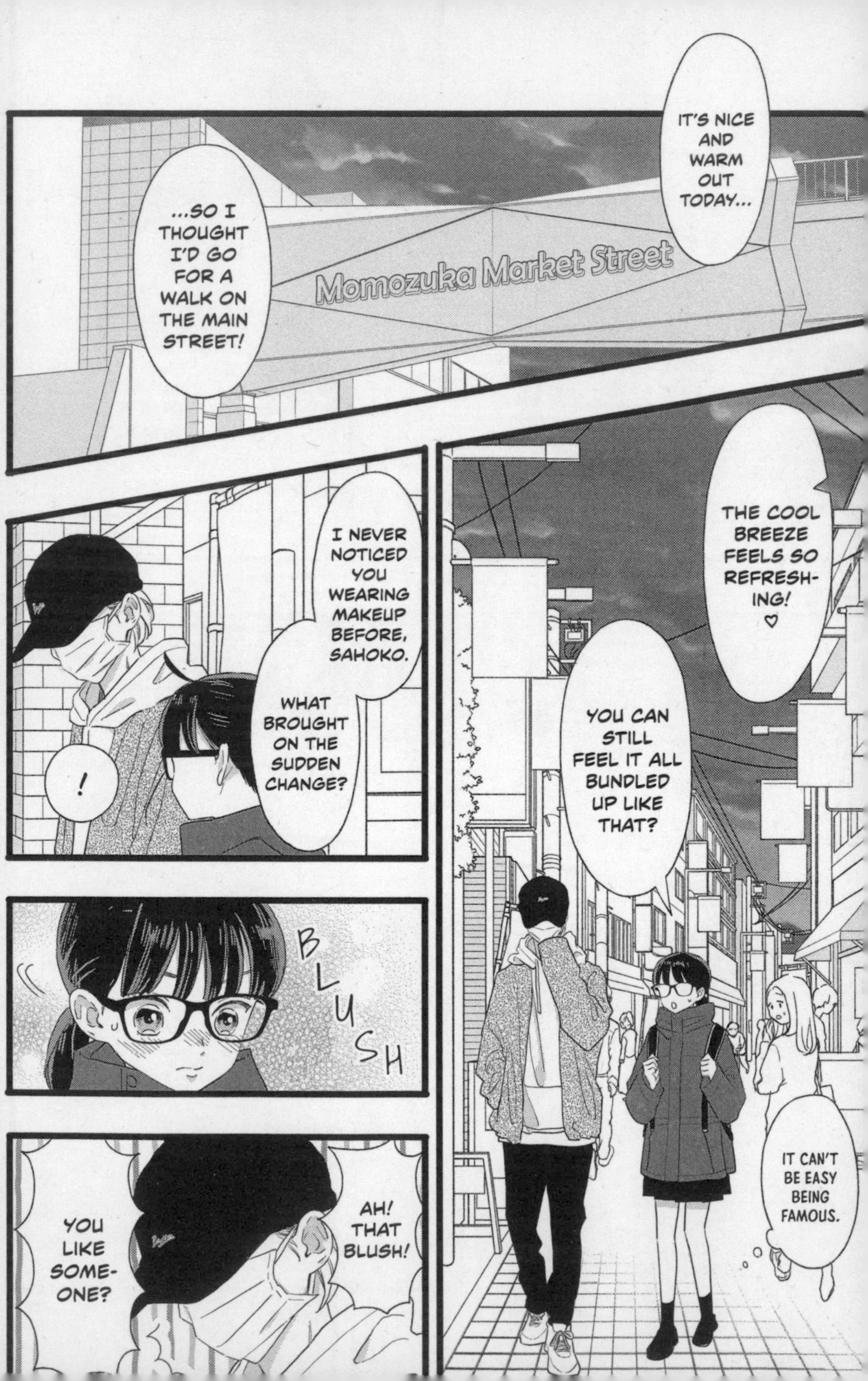
IT'S NICE AND WARM OUT TODAY...
Momozuka Market Street
...SO I THOUGHT I'D GO FOR A WALK ON THE MAIN STREET!
THE COOL BREEZE FEELS SO REFRESH-ING! ♡
YOU CAN STILL FEEL IT ALL BUNDLED UP LIKE THAT?
IT CAN'T BE EASY BEING FAMOUS.
I NEVER NOTICED YOU WEARING MAKEUP BEFORE, SAHOKO.
WHAT BROUGHT ON THE SUDDEN CHANGE?
!
BLUSH
AH! THAT BLUSH!
YOU LIKE SOME-ONE?

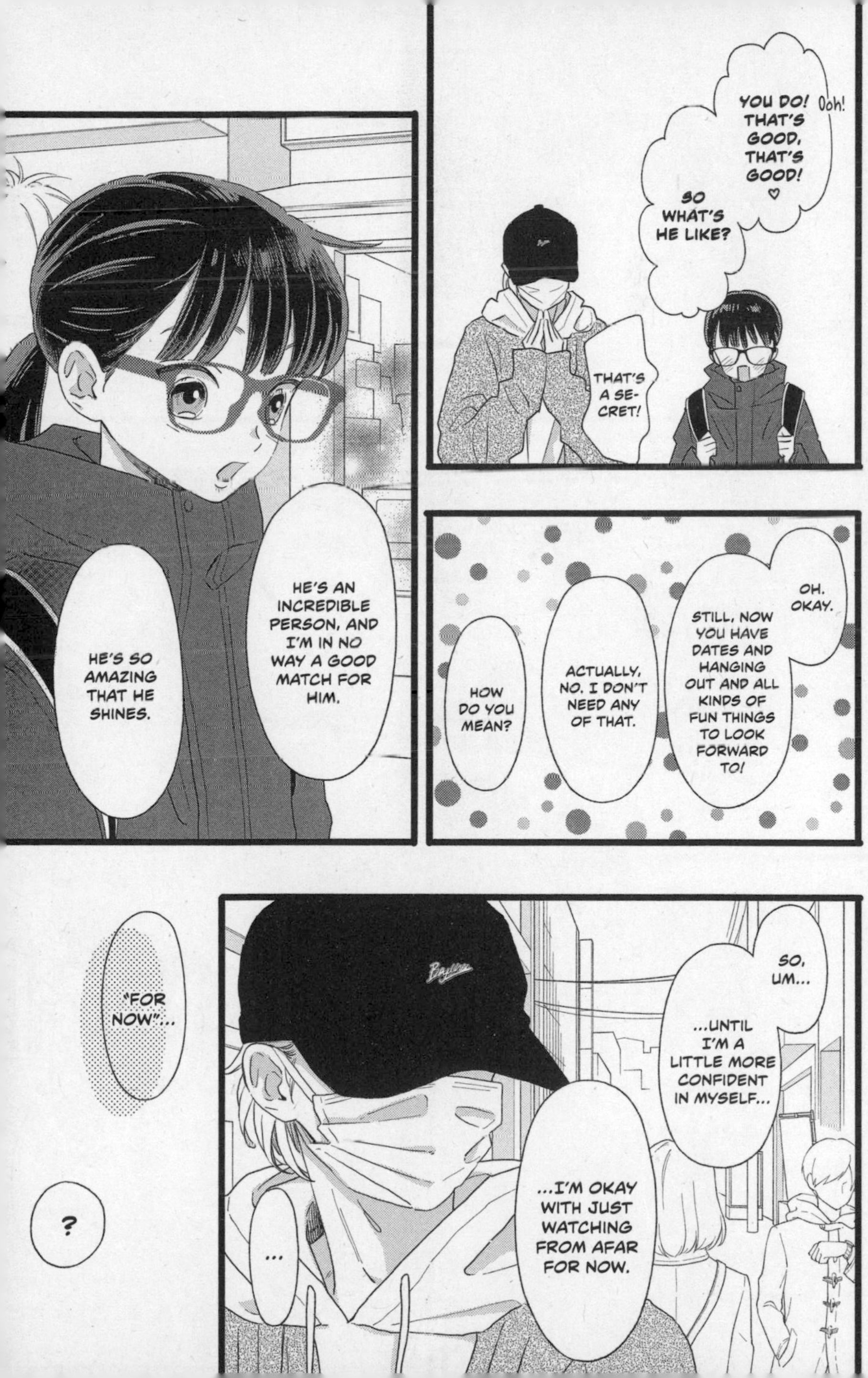

Ooh!
YOU DO! THAT'S GOOD, THAT'S GOOD! ♡
SO WHAT'S HE LIKE?
THAT'S A SE-CRET!
OH. OKAY.
STILL, NOW YOU HAVE DATES AND HANGING OUT AND ALL KINDS OF FUN THINGS TO LOOK FORWARD TO!
ACTUALLY, NO. I DON'T NEED ANY OF THAT.
HOW DO YOU MEAN?
HE'S AN INCREDIBLE PERSON, AND I'M IN NO WAY A GOOD MATCH FOR HIM.
HE'S SO AMAZING THAT HE SHINES.
SO, UM...
...UNTIL I'M A LITTLE MORE CONFIDENT IN MYSELF...
...I'M OKAY WITH JUST WATCHING FROM AFAR FOR NOW.
...
"FOR NOW"...
?

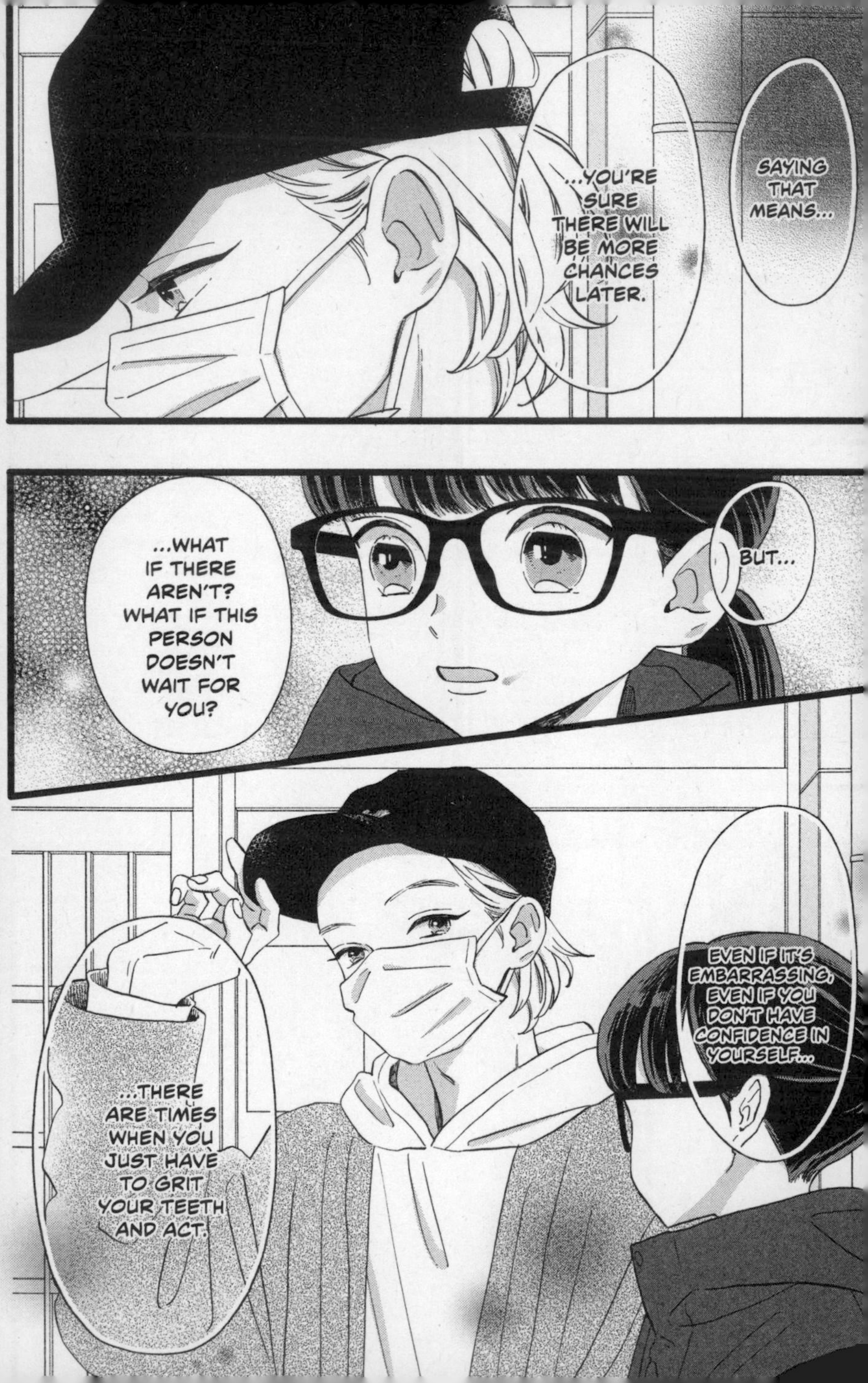
SAYING THAT MEANS...
...YOU'RE SURE THERE WILL BE MORE CHANCES LATER.
BUT...
...WHAT IF THERE AREN'T? WHAT IF THIS PERSON DOESN'T WAIT FOR YOU?
EVEN IF IT'S EMBARRASSING, EVEN IF YOU DON'T HAVE CONFIDENCE IN YOURSELF...
...THERE ARE TIMES WHEN YOU JUST HAVE TO GRIT YOUR TEETH AND ACT.

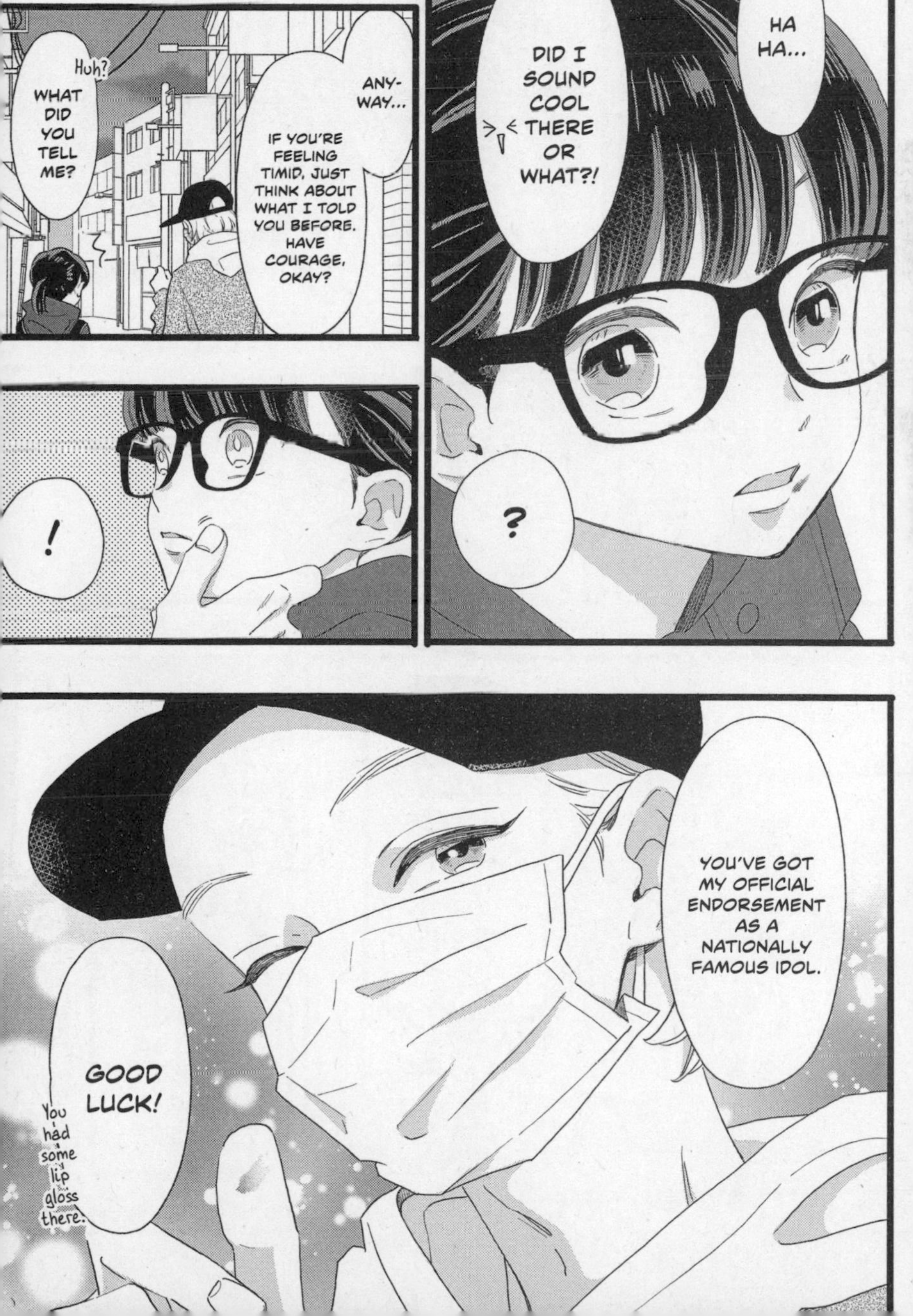
HA HA...
DID I SOUND COOL THERE OR WHAT?!
?
ANY-WAY...
IF YOU'RE FEELING TIMID, JUST THINK ABOUT WHAT I TOLD YOU BEFORE. HAVE COURAGE, OKAY?
Huh?
WHAT DID YOU TELL ME?
!
YOU'VE GOT MY OFFICIAL ENDORSEMENT AS A NATIONALLY FAMOUS IDOL.
GOOD LUCK!
You had some lip gloss there.

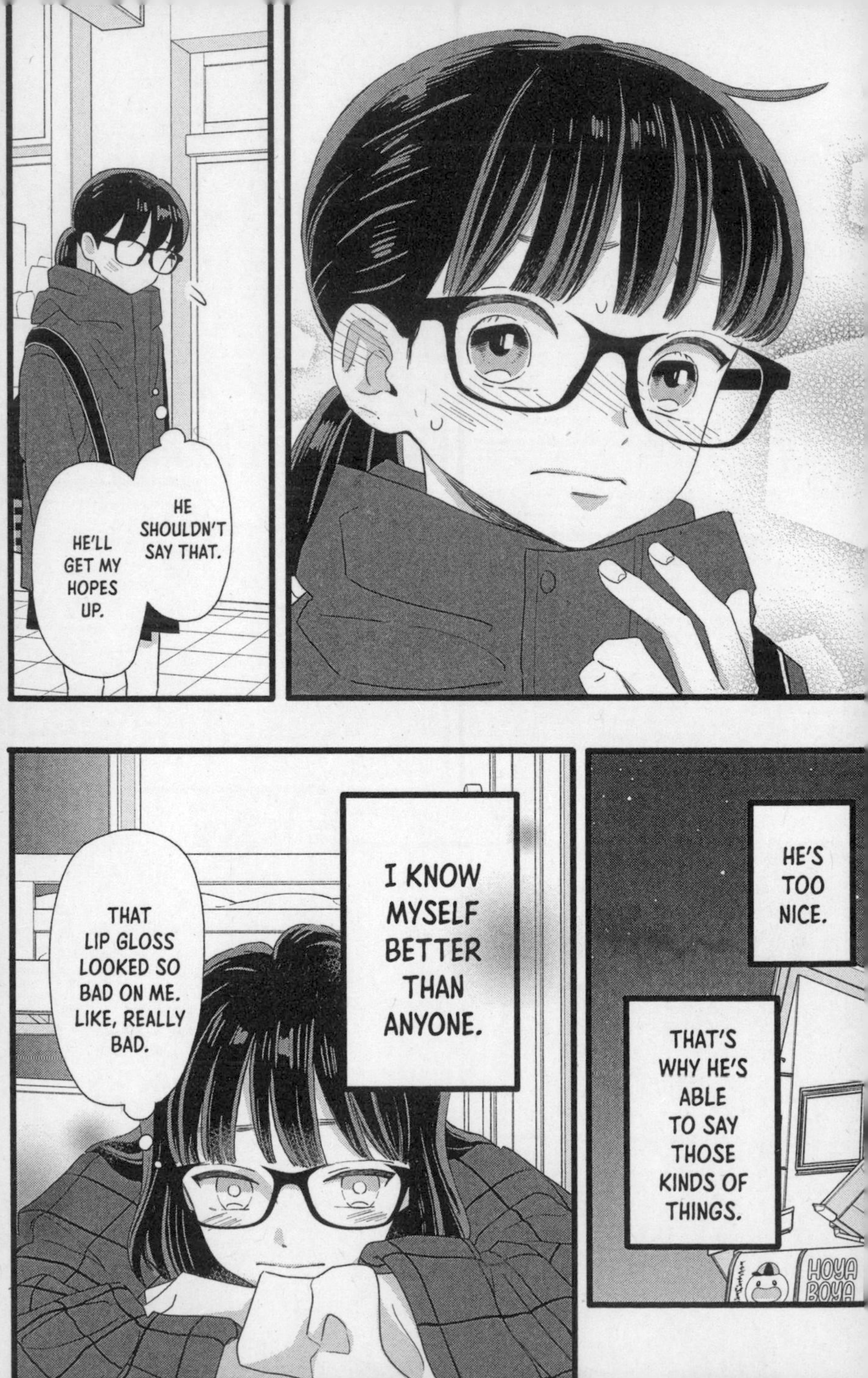
HE SHOULDN'T SAY THAT.
HE'LL GET MY HOPES UP.
HE'S TOO NICE.
THAT'S WHY HE'S ABLE TO SAY THOSE KINDS OF THINGS.
HOYA BOYA
I KNOW MYSELF BETTER THAN ANYONE.
THAT LIP GLOSS LOOKED SO BAD ON ME. LIKE, REALLY BAD.

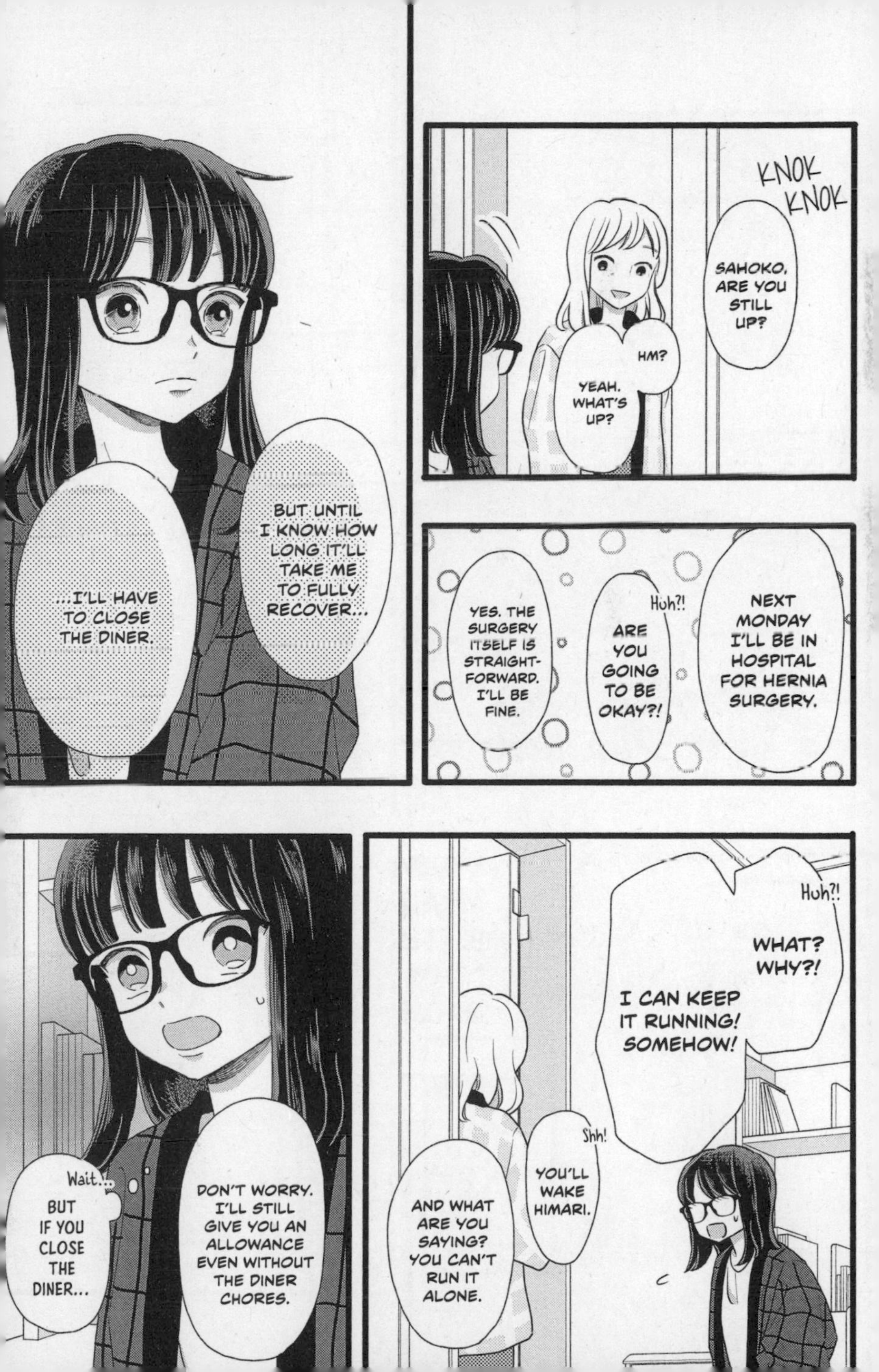
KNOK KNOK
SAHOKO, ARE YOU STILL UP?
HM?
YEAH. WHAT'S UP?
NEXT MONDAY I'LL BE IN HOSPITAL FOR HERNIA SURGERY.
Huh?!
ARE YOU GOING TO BE OKAY?!
YES. THE SURGERY ITSELF IS STRAIGHT-FORWARD. I'LL BE FINE.
BUT UNTIL I KNOW HOW LONG IT'LL TAKE ME TO FULLY RECOVER...
...I'LL HAVE TO CLOSE THE DINER.
Huh?!
WHAT? WHY?!
I CAN KEEP IT RUNNING! SOMEHOW!
Shh!
YOU'LL WAKE HIMARI.
AND WHAT ARE YOU SAYING? YOU CAN'T RUN IT ALONE.
DON'T WORRY. I'LL STILL GIVE YOU AN ALLOWANCE EVEN WITHOUT THE DINER CHORES.
Wait...
BUT IF YOU CLOSE THE DINER...

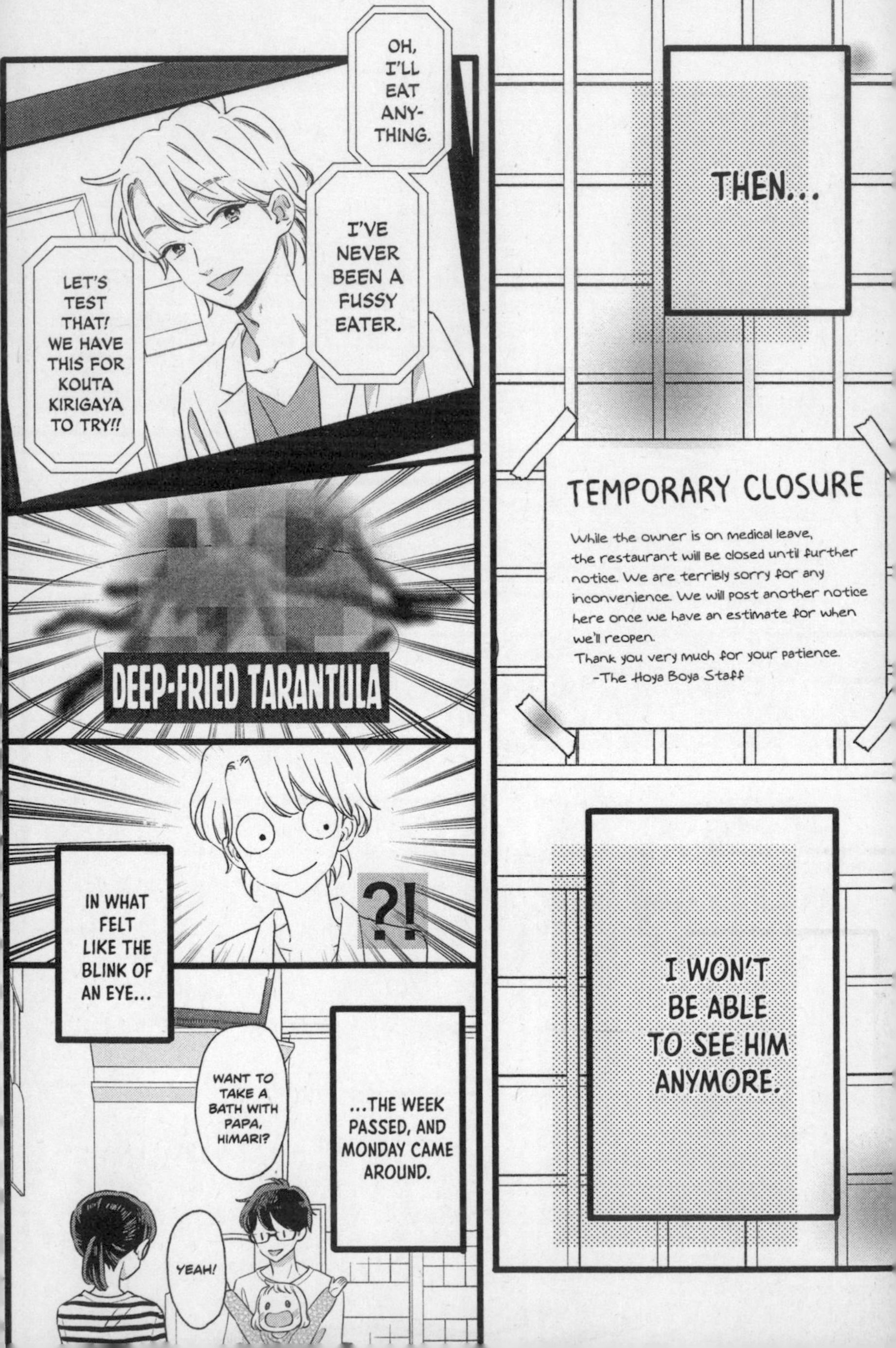
OH, I'LL EAT ANY-THING.
I'VE NEVER BEEN A FUSSY EATER.
LET'S TEST THAT! WE HAVE THIS FOR KOUTA KIRIGAYA TO TRY!!
DEEP-FRIED TARANTULA
?!
IN WHAT FELT LIKE THE BLINK OF AN EYE...
...THE WEEK PASSED, AND MONDAY CAME AROUND.
WANT TO TAKE A BATH WITH PAPA, HIMARI?
YEAH!
THEN...
TEMPORARY CLOSURE
While the owner is on medical leave, the restaurant will be closed until further notice. We are terribly sorry for any inconvenience. We will post another notice here once we have an estimate for when we'll reopen.
Thank you very much for your patience.
-The Hoya Boya Staff
I WON'T BE ABLE TO SEE HIM ANYMORE.

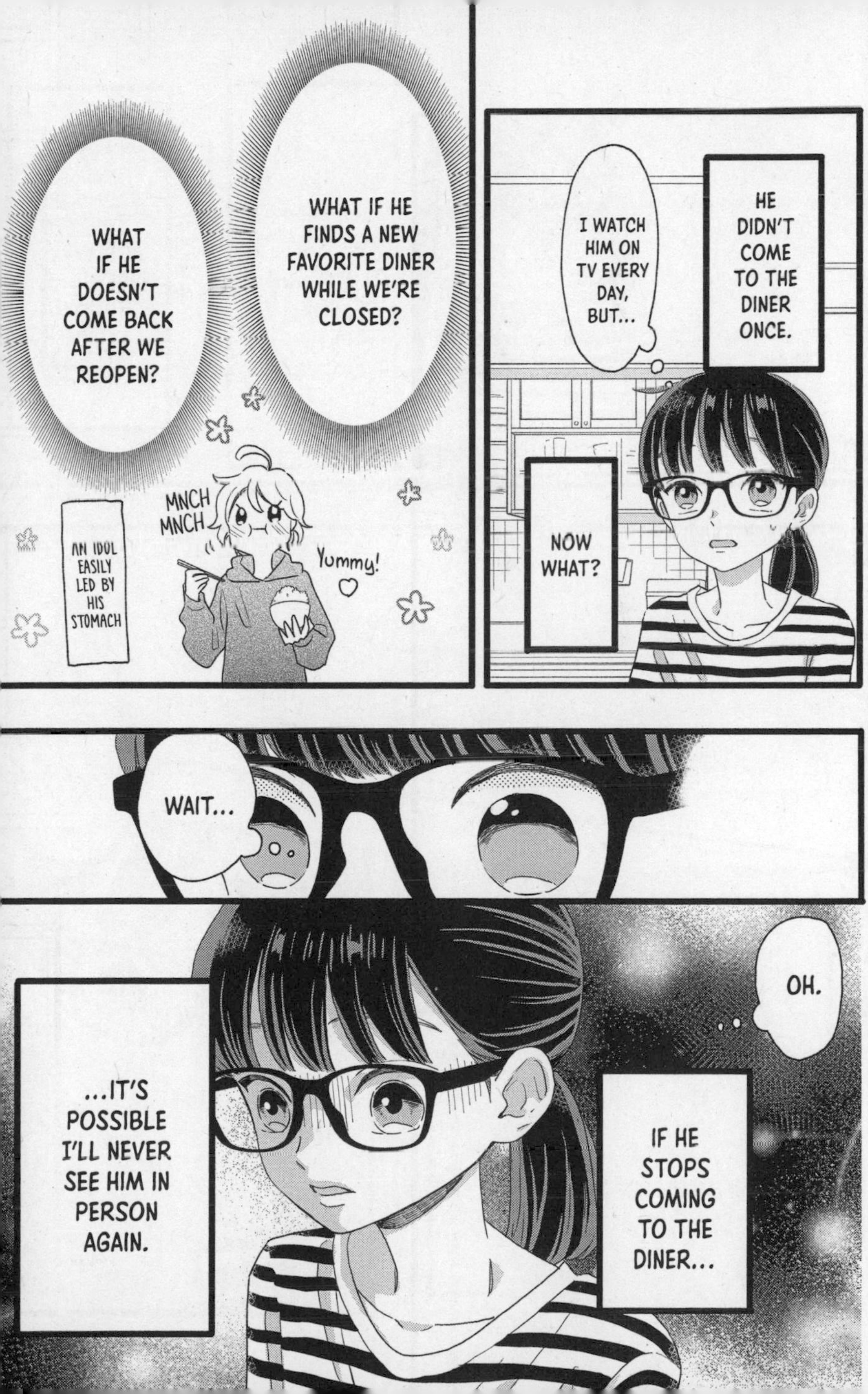
HE DIDN'T COME TO THE DINER ONCE.
I WATCH HIM ON TV EVERY DAY, BUT...
NOW WHAT?
WHAT IF HE FINDS A NEW FAVORITE DINER WHILE WE'RE CLOSED?
WHAT IF HE DOESN'T COME BACK AFTER WE REOPEN?
MNCH MNCH
Yummy!
AN IDOL EASILY LED BY HIS STOMACH
WAIT...
OH.
IF HE STOPS COMING TO THE DINER...
...IT'S POSSIBLE I'LL NEVER SEE HIM IN PERSON AGAIN.

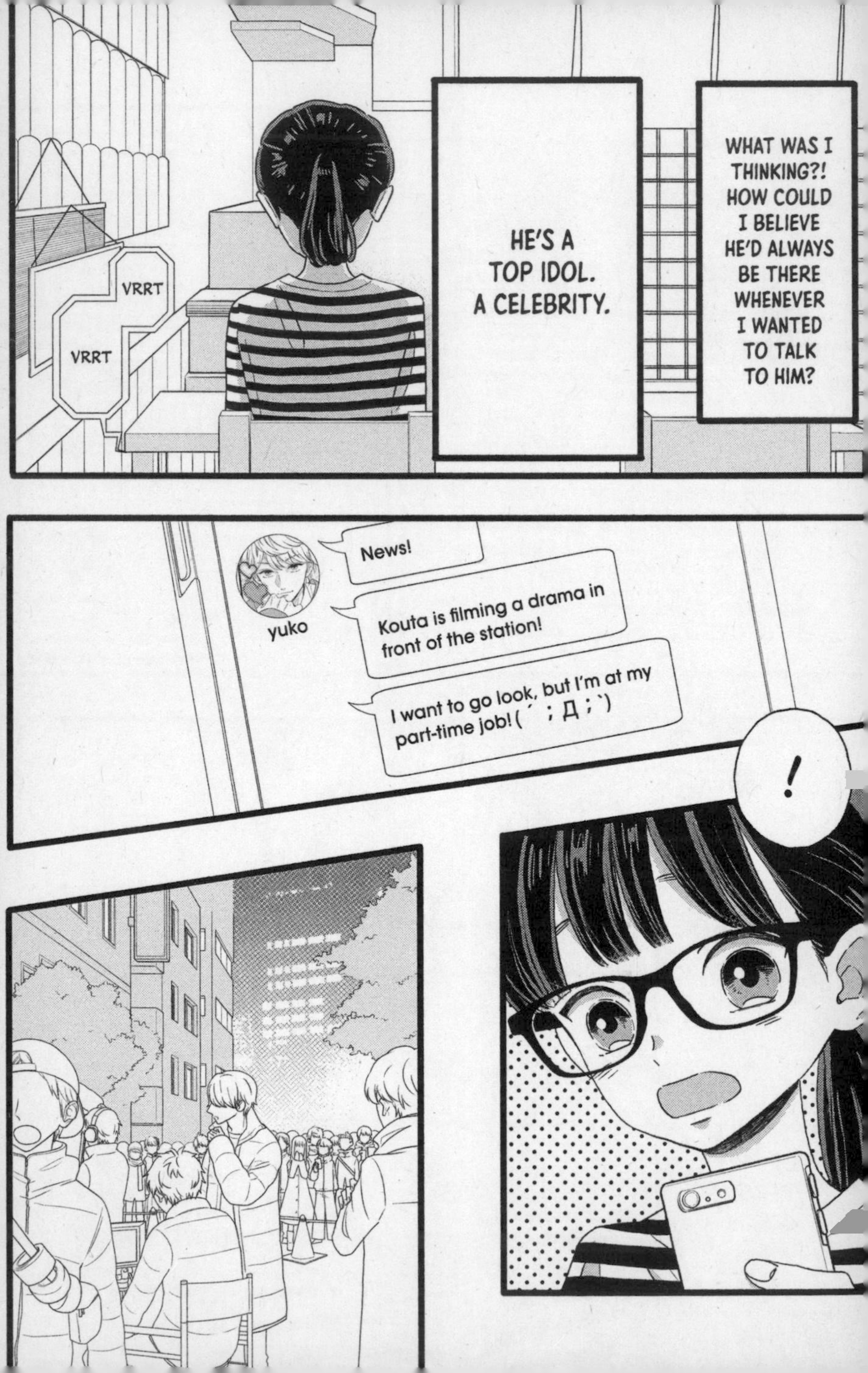
WHAT WAS I THINKING?! HOW COULD I BELIEVE HE'D ALWAYS BE THERE WHENEVER I WANTED TO TALK TO HIM?
HE'S A TOP IDOL. A CELEBRITY.
VRRT
VRRT
yuko
News!
Kouta is filming a drama in front of the station!
I want to go look, but I'm at my part-time job! (´ ; Д ; `)
!

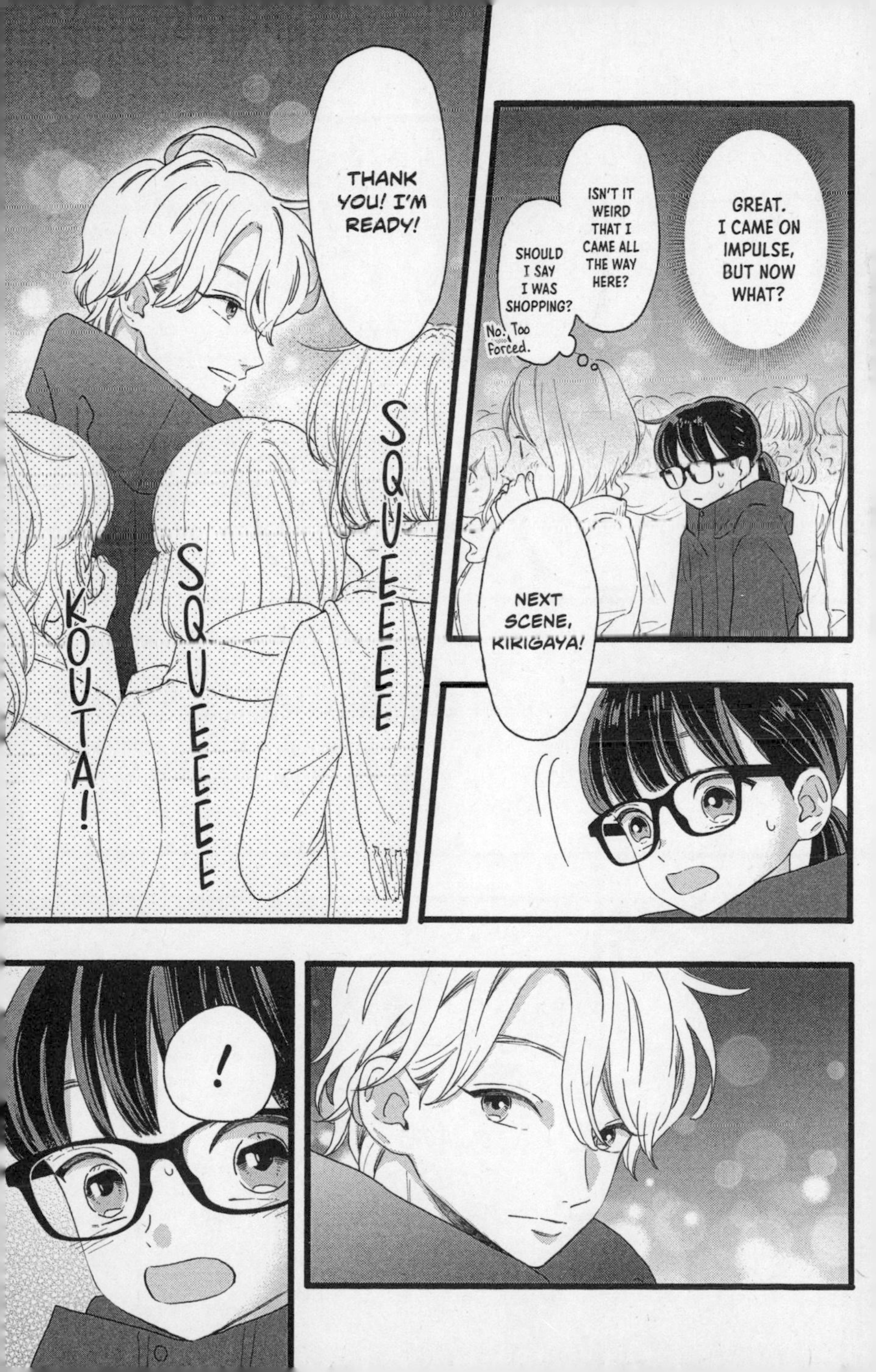
GREAT. I CAME ON IMPULSE, BUT NOW WHAT?
ISN'T IT WEIRD THAT I CAME ALL THE WAY HERE?
SHOULD I SAY I WAS SHOPPING?
No. Too Forced.
NEXT SCENE, KIRIGAYA!
THANK YOU! I'M READY!
SQUEEEE
SQUEEEE
KOUTA!
!

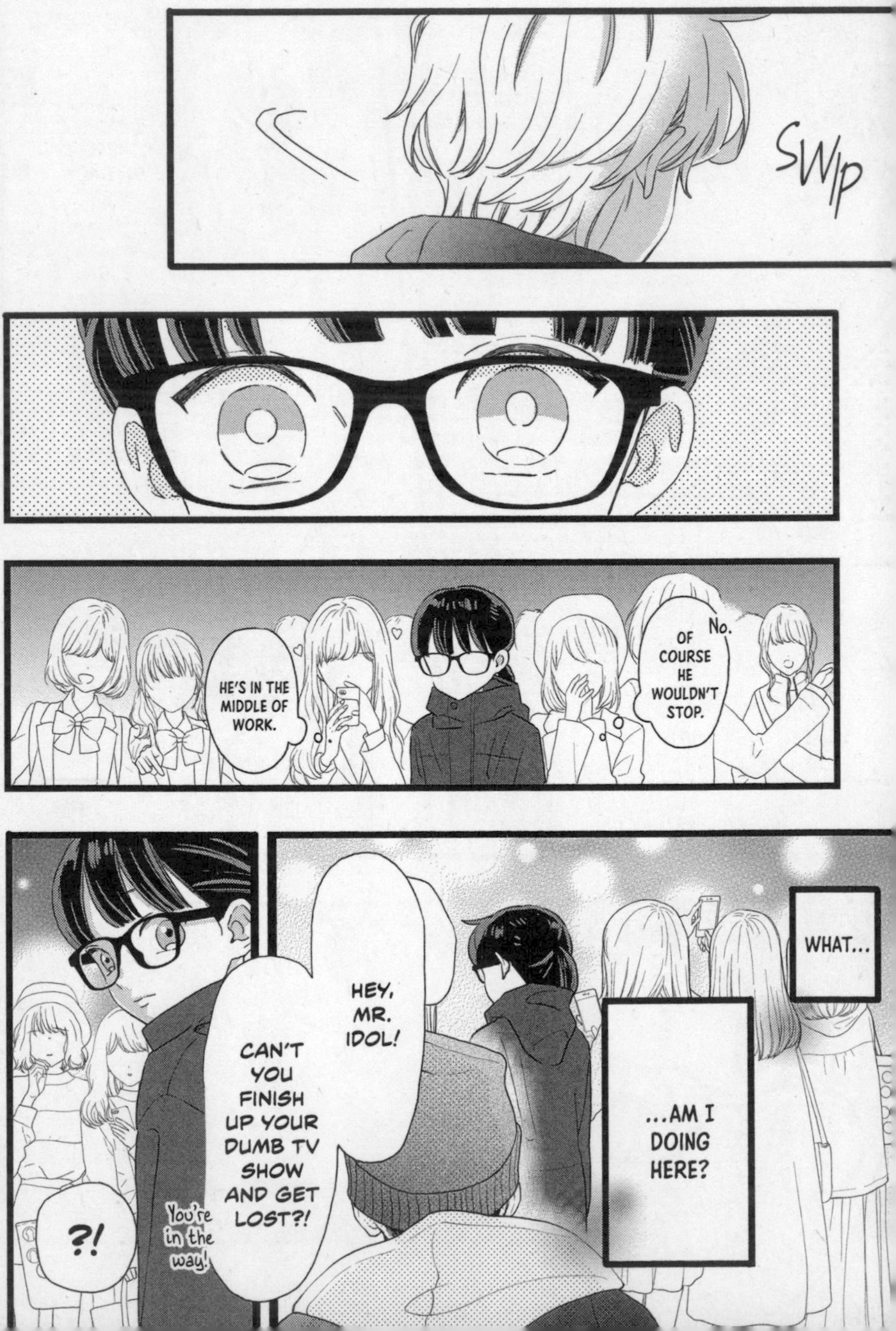
SWIP
No.
OF COURSE HE WOULDN'T STOP.
HE'S IN THE MIDDLE OF WORK.
WHAT...
...AM I DOING HERE?
HEY, MR. IDOL!
CAN'T YOU FINISH UP YOUR DUMB TV SHOW AND GET LOST?!
You're in the way!
?!

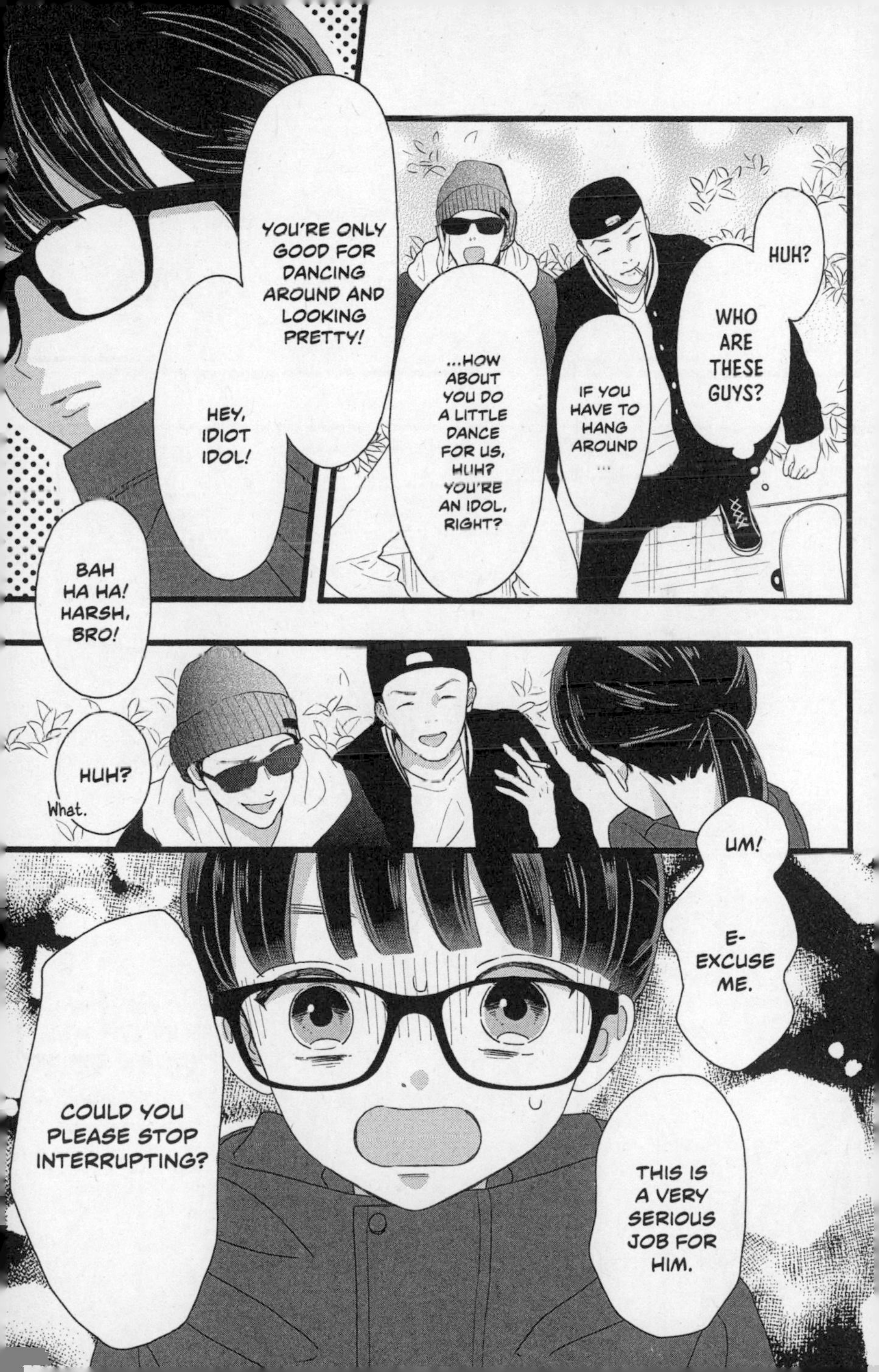
HUH?
WHO ARE THESE GUYS?
IF YOU HAVE TO HANG AROUND ...
...HOW ABOUT YOU DO A LITTLE DANCE FOR US, HUH? YOU'RE AN IDOL, RIGHT?
YOU'RE ONLY GOOD FOR DANCING AROUND AND LOOKING PRETTY!
HEY, IDIOT IDOL!
BAH HA HA! HARSH, BRO!
HUH?
What.
UM!
E-EXCUSE ME.
THIS IS A VERY SERIOUS JOB FOR HIM.
COULD YOU PLEASE STOP INTERRUPTING?

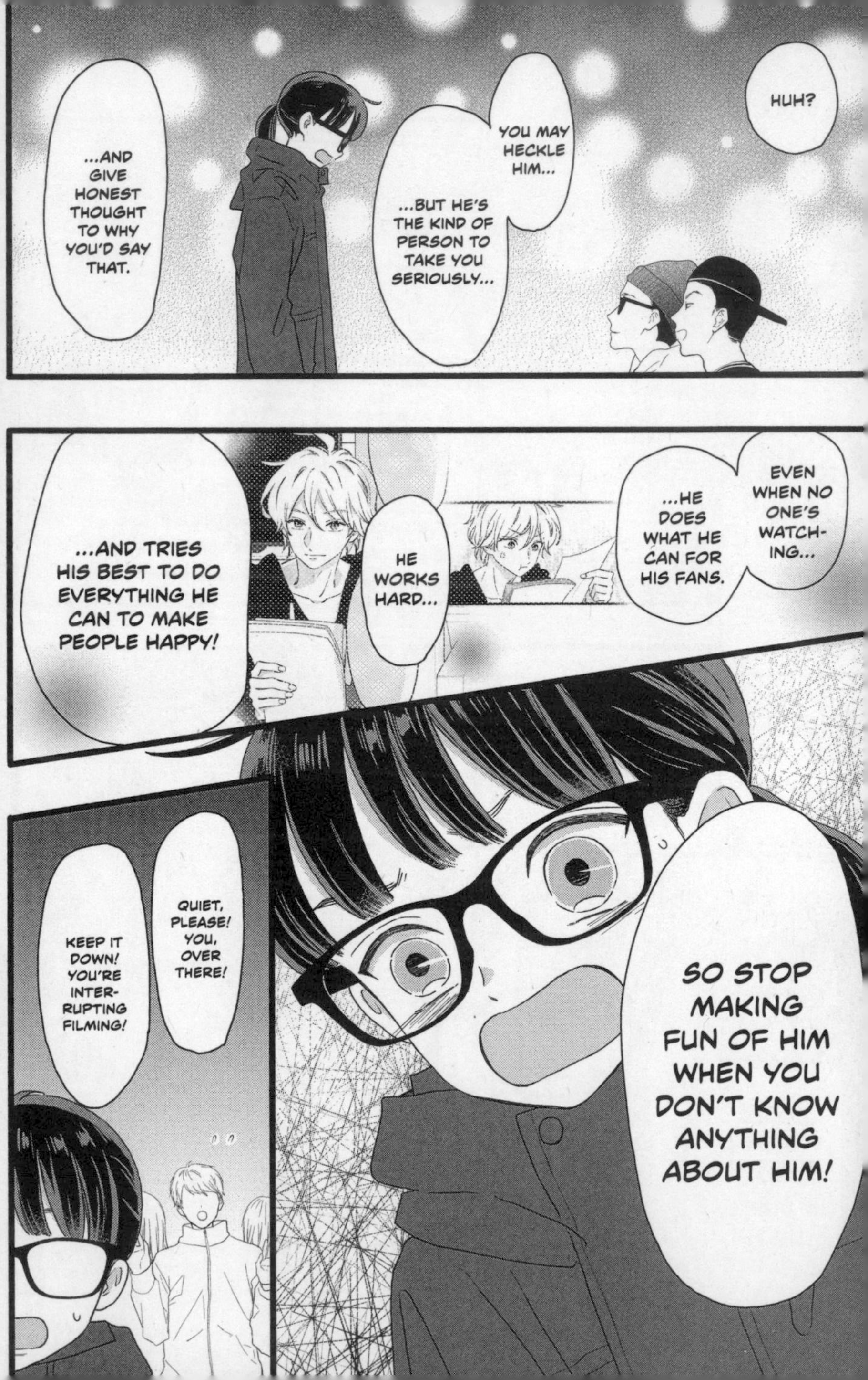
HUH?
YOU MAY HECKLE HIM...
...BUT HE'S THE KIND OF PERSON TO TAKE YOU SERIOUSLY...
...AND GIVE HONEST THOUGHT TO WHY YOU'D SAY THAT.
EVEN WHEN NO ONE'S WATCH-ING...
...HE DOES WHAT HE CAN FOR HIS FANS.
HE WORKS HARD...
...AND TRIES HIS BEST TO DO EVERYTHING HE CAN TO MAKE PEOPLE HAPPY!
SO STOP MAKING FUN OF HIM WHEN YOU DON'T KNOW ANYTHING ABOUT HIM!
QUIET, PLEASE! YOU, OVER THERE!
KEEP IT DOWN! YOU'RE INTER-RUPTING FILMING!

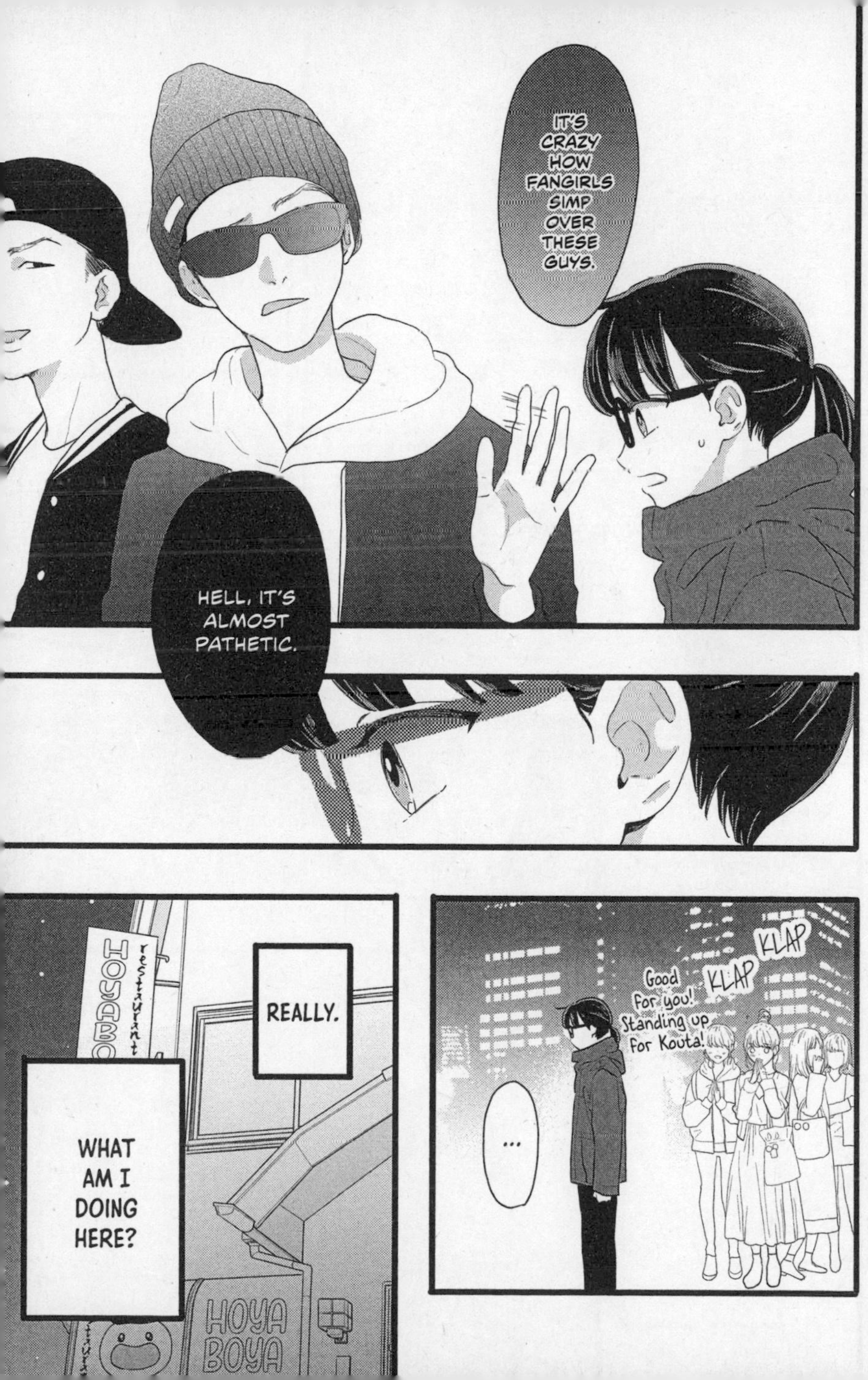
IT'S CRAZY HOW FANGIRLS SIMP OVER THESE GUYS.
HELL, IT'S ALMOST PATHETIC.
KLAP
KLAP
Good for you! Standing up for Kouta!
...
REALLY.
HOYABO
restaurant
WHAT AM I DOING HERE?
HOYA BOYA

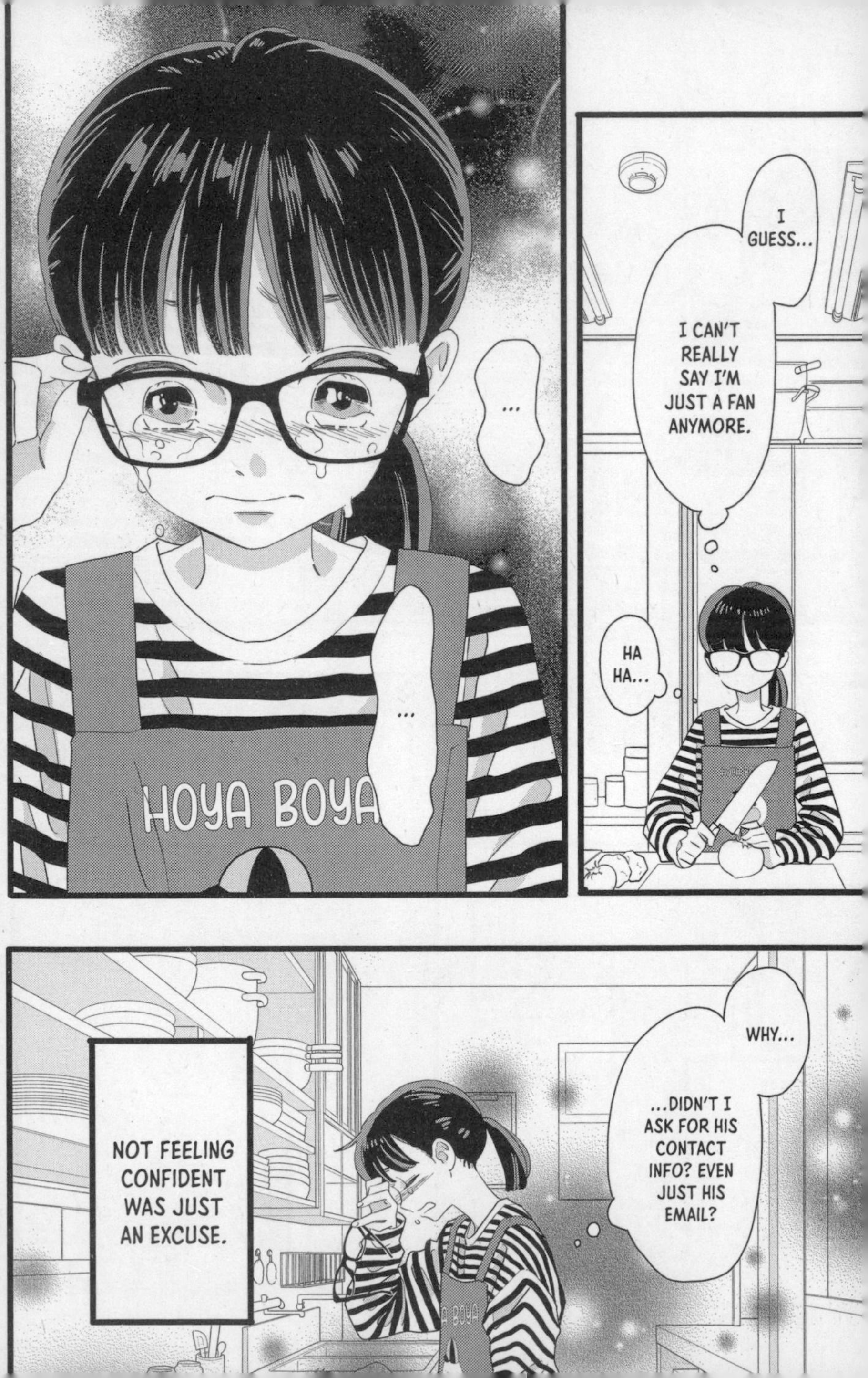
I GUESS...
I CAN'T REALLY SAY I'M JUST A FAN ANYMORE.
HA HA...
...
...
HOYA BOYA
WHY...
...DIDN'T I ASK FOR HIS CONTACT INFO? EVEN JUST HIS EMAIL?
NOT FEELING CONFIDENT WAS JUST AN EXCUSE.

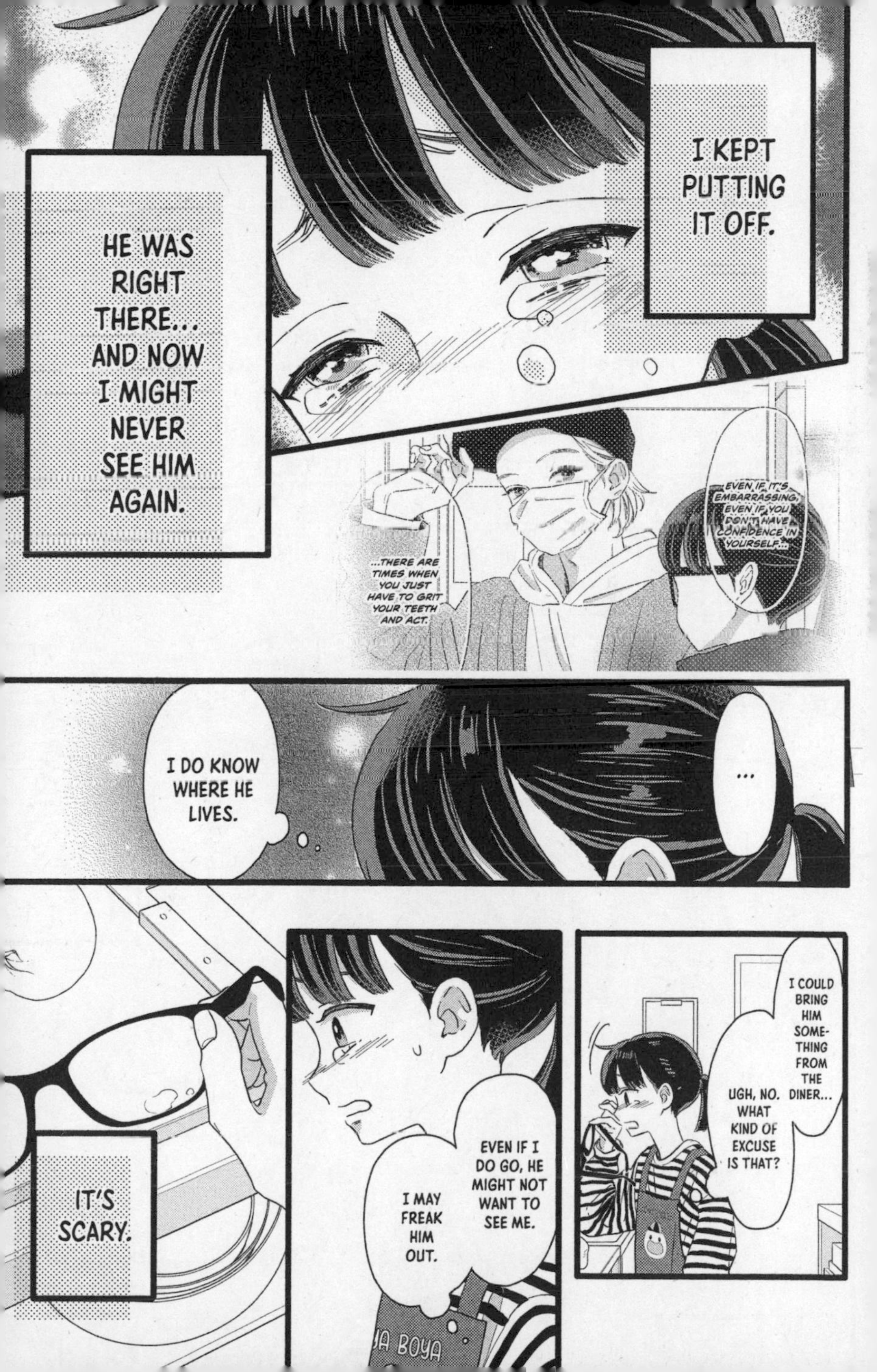
I KEPT PUTTING IT OFF.
HE WAS RIGHT THERE... AND NOW I MIGHT NEVER SEE HIM AGAIN.
EVEN IF IT'S EMBARRASSING, EVEN IF YOU DON'T HAVE CONFIDENCE IN YOURSELF...
...THERE ARE TIMES WHEN YOU JUST HAVE TO GRIT YOUR TEETH AND ACT.
...
I DO KNOW WHERE HE LIVES.
I COULD BRING HIM SOMETHING FROM THE DINER...
UGH, NO. WHAT KIND OF EXCUSE IS THAT?
EVEN IF I DO GO, HE MIGHT NOT WANT TO SEE ME.
I MAY FREAK HIM OUT.
IT'S SCARY.

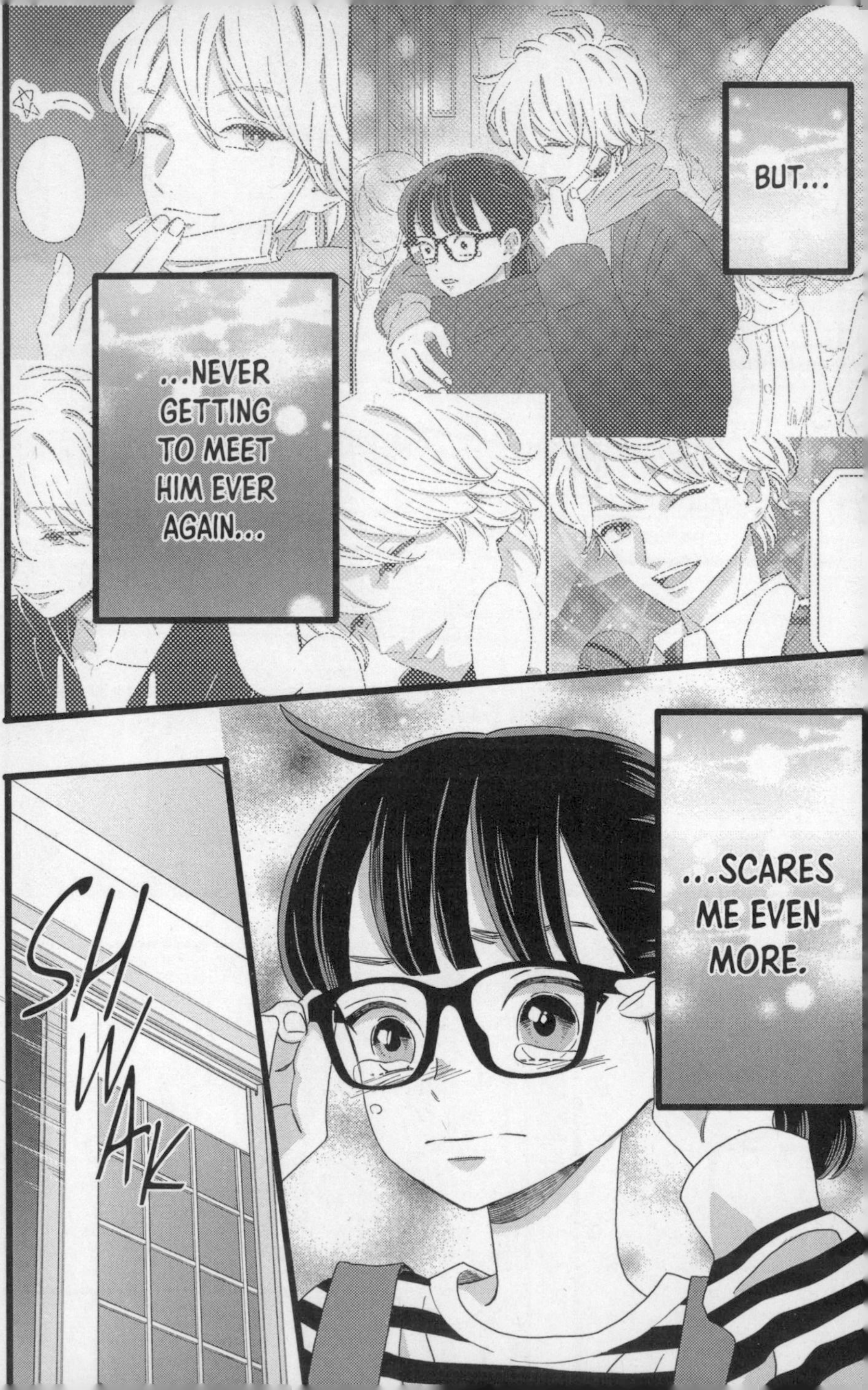
BUT...
...NEVER GETTING TO MEET HIM EVER AGAIN...
...SCARES ME EVEN MORE.
SHWAK

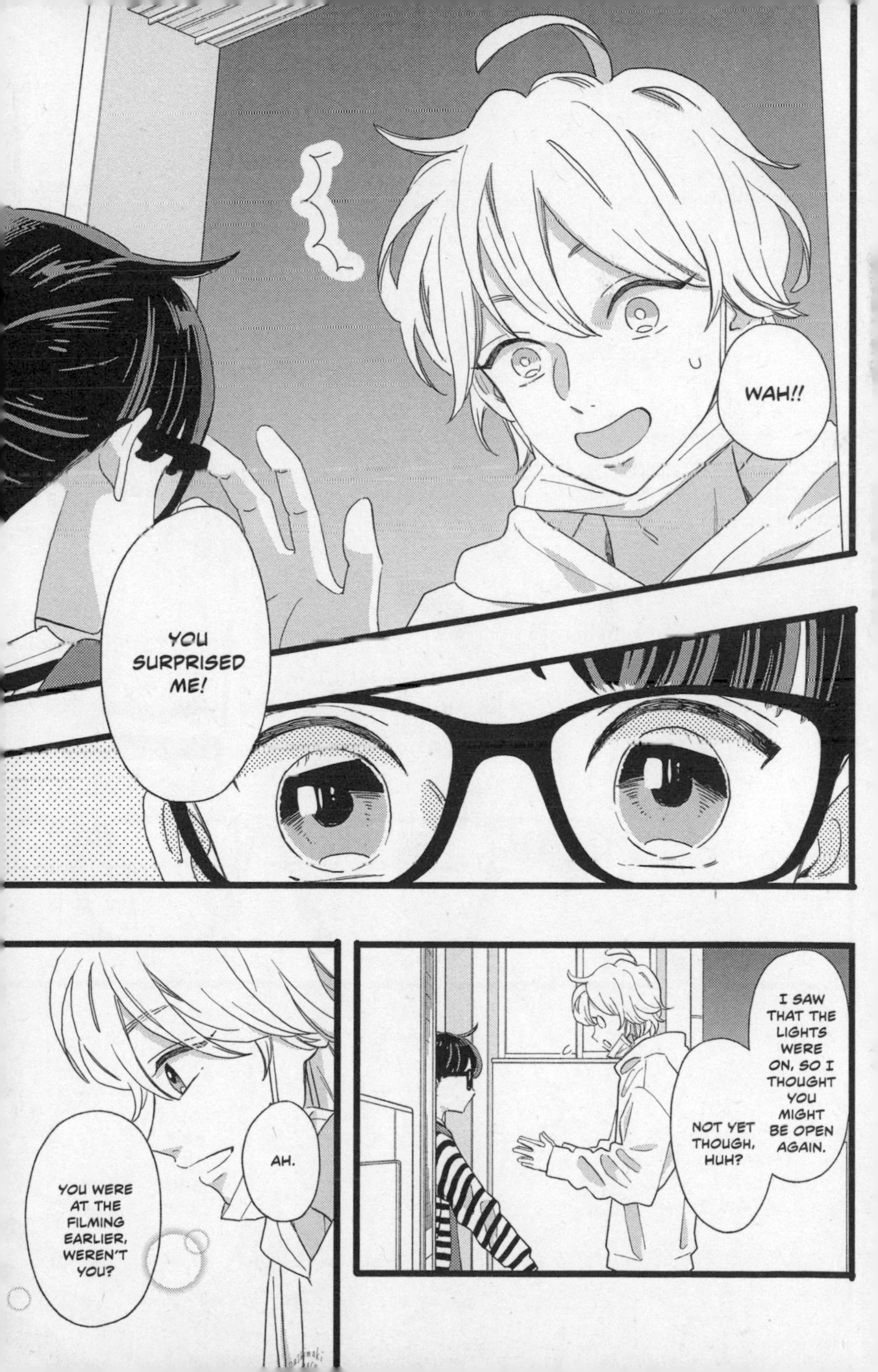
WAH!!
YOU SURPRISED ME!
I SAW THAT THE LIGHTS WERE ON, SO I THOUGHT YOU MIGHT BE OPEN AGAIN.
NOT YET THOUGH, HUH?
AH.
YOU WERE AT THE FILMING EARLIER, WEREN'T YOU?

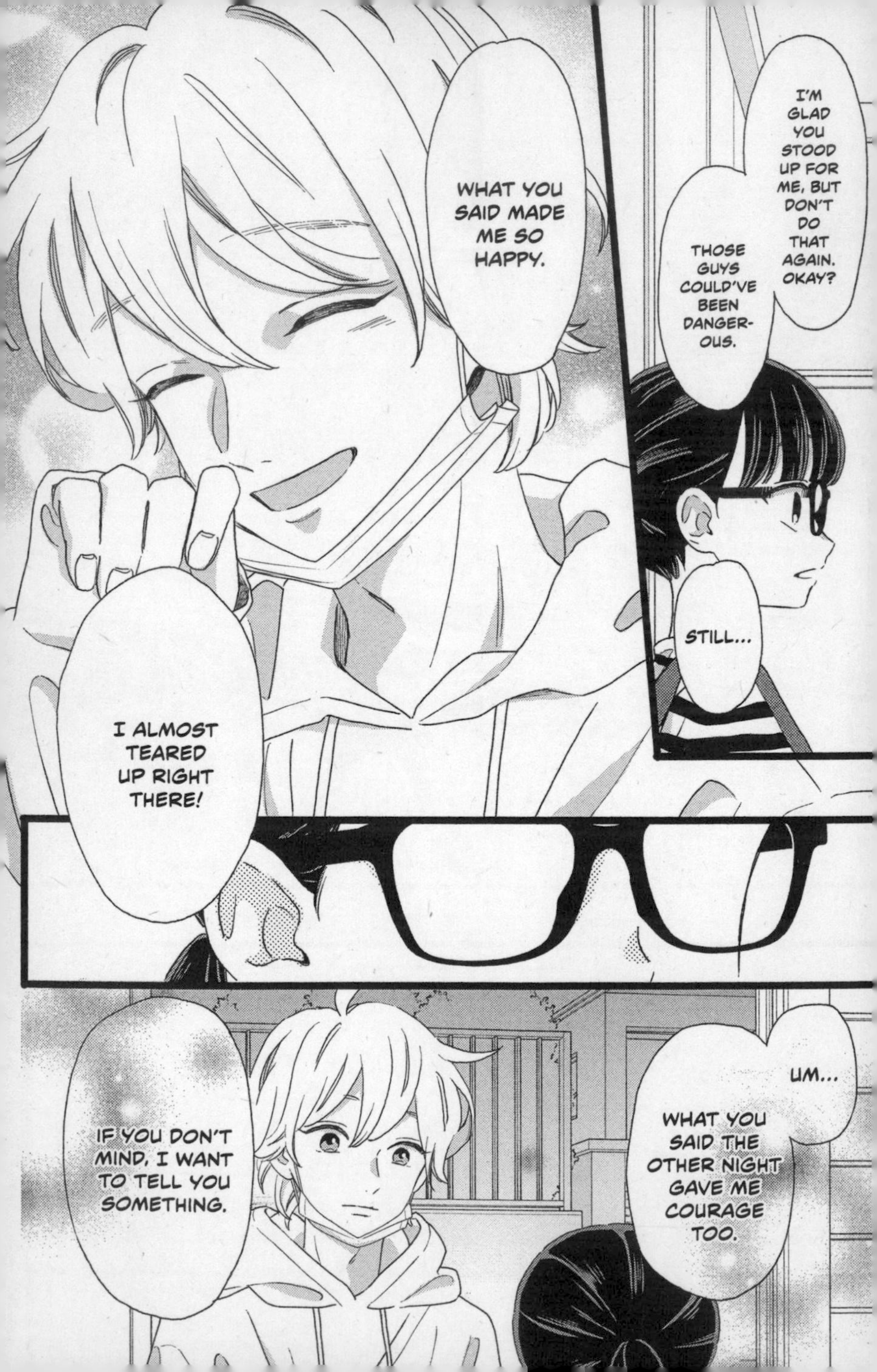
I'M GLAD YOU STOOD UP FOR ME, BUT DON'T DO THAT AGAIN. OKAY?
THOSE GUYS COULD'VE BEEN DANGER-OUS.
STILL...
WHAT YOU SAID MADE ME SO HAPPY.
I ALMOST TEARED UP RIGHT THERE!
UM...
WHAT YOU SAID THE OTHER NIGHT GAVE ME COURAGE TOO.
IF YOU DON'T MIND, I WANT TO TELL YOU SOMETHING.

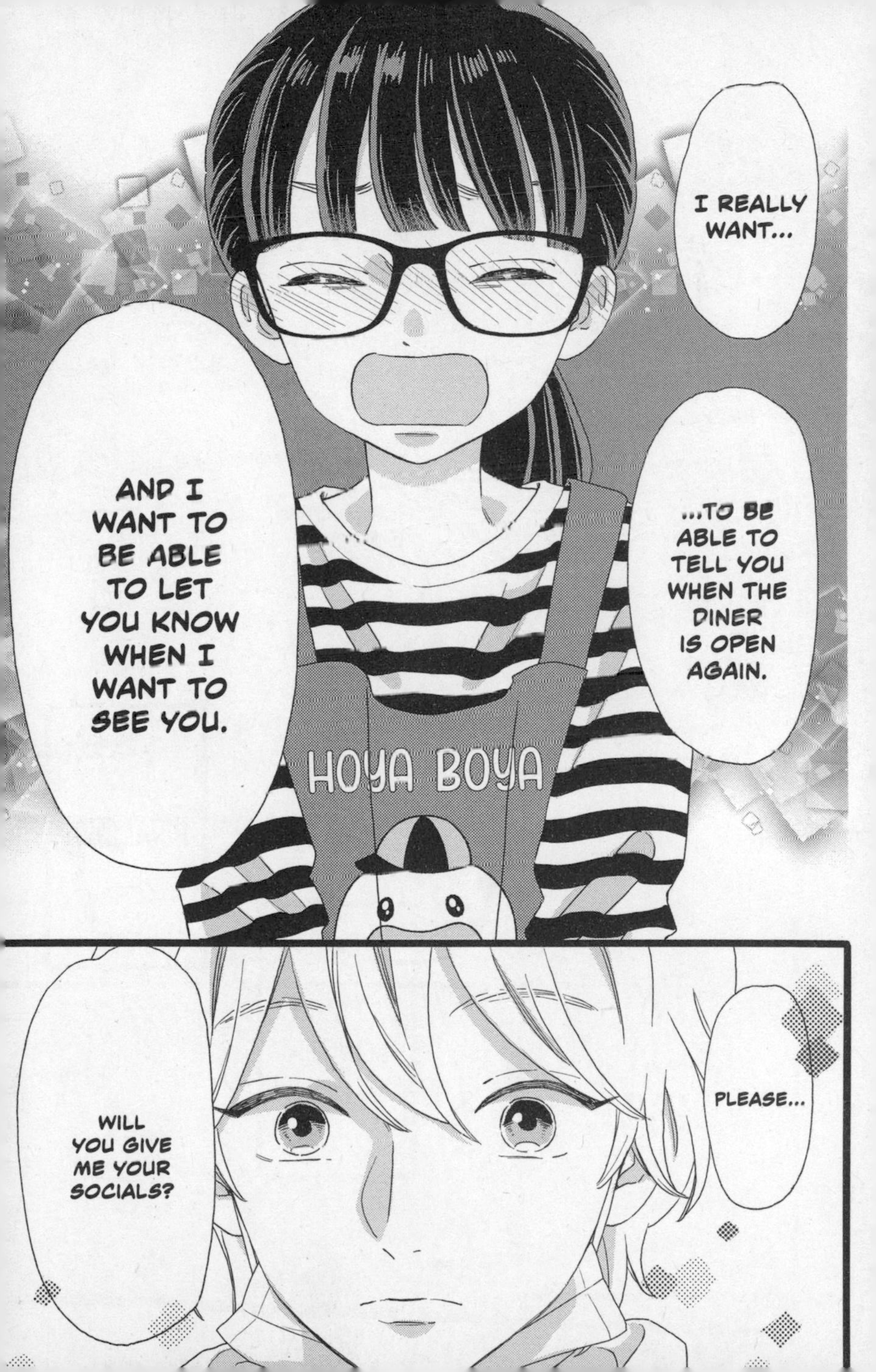
I REALLY WANT...
...TO BE ABLE TO TELL YOU WHEN THE DINER IS OPEN AGAIN.
AND I WANT TO BE ABLE TO LET YOU KNOW WHEN I WANT TO SEE YOU.
HOYA BOYA
PLEASE...
WILL YOU GIVE ME YOUR SOCIALS?

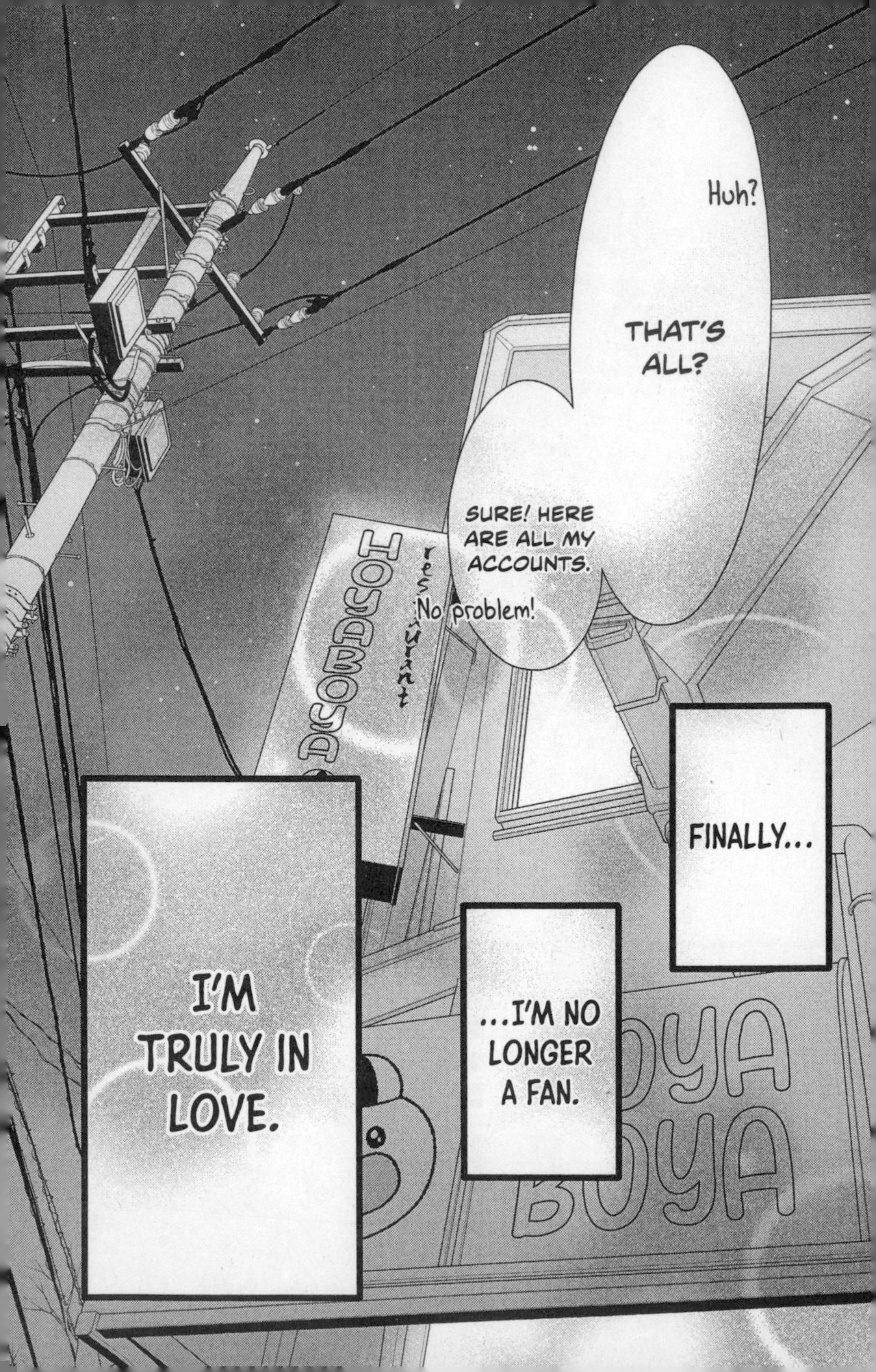
Huh?
THAT'S ALL?
SURE! HERE ARE ALL MY ACCOUNTS.
No problem!
HOYABOYA
FINALLY...
...I'M NO LONGER A FAN.
I'M TRULY IN LOVE.

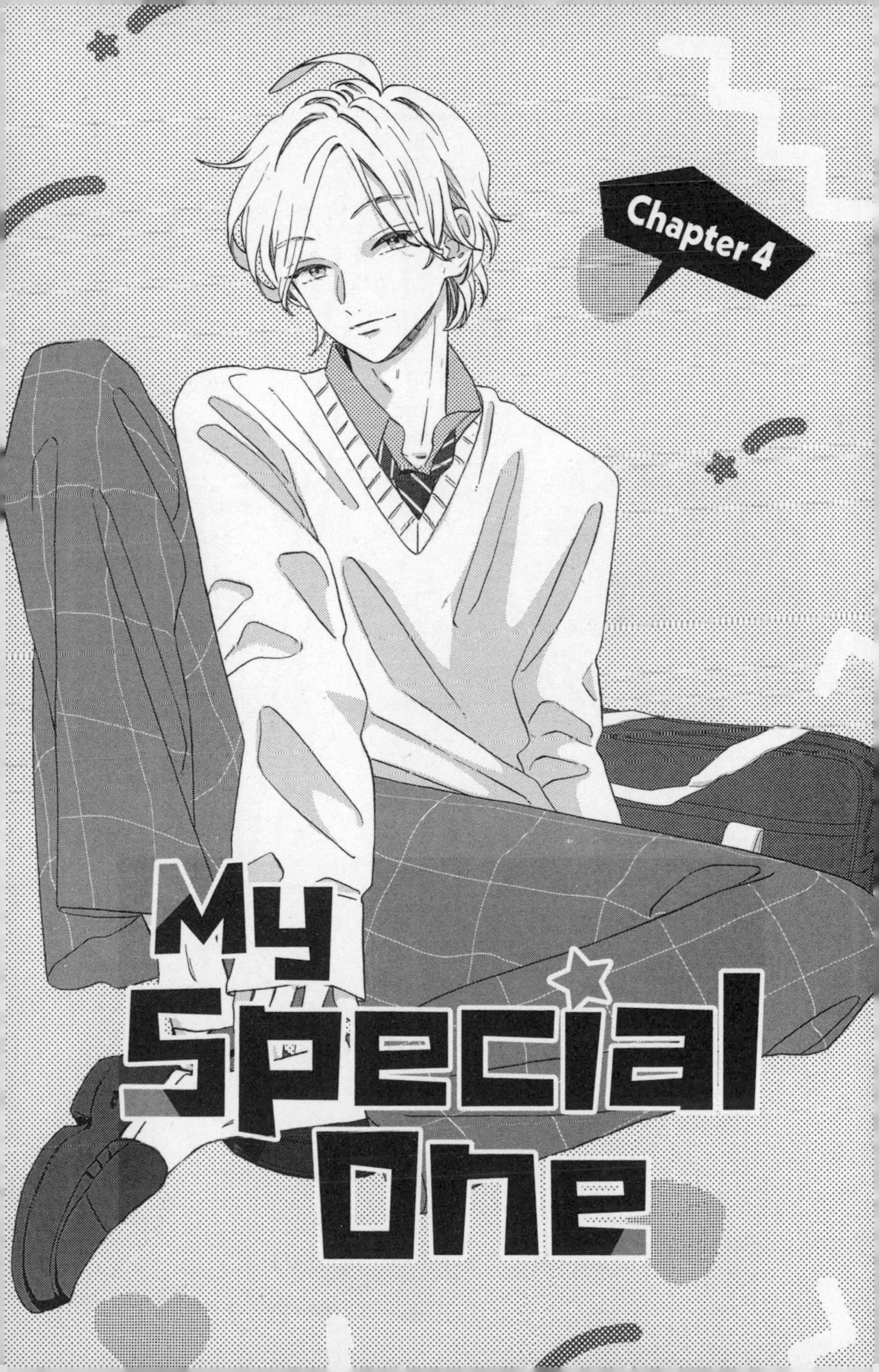
Chapter 4
My Special One

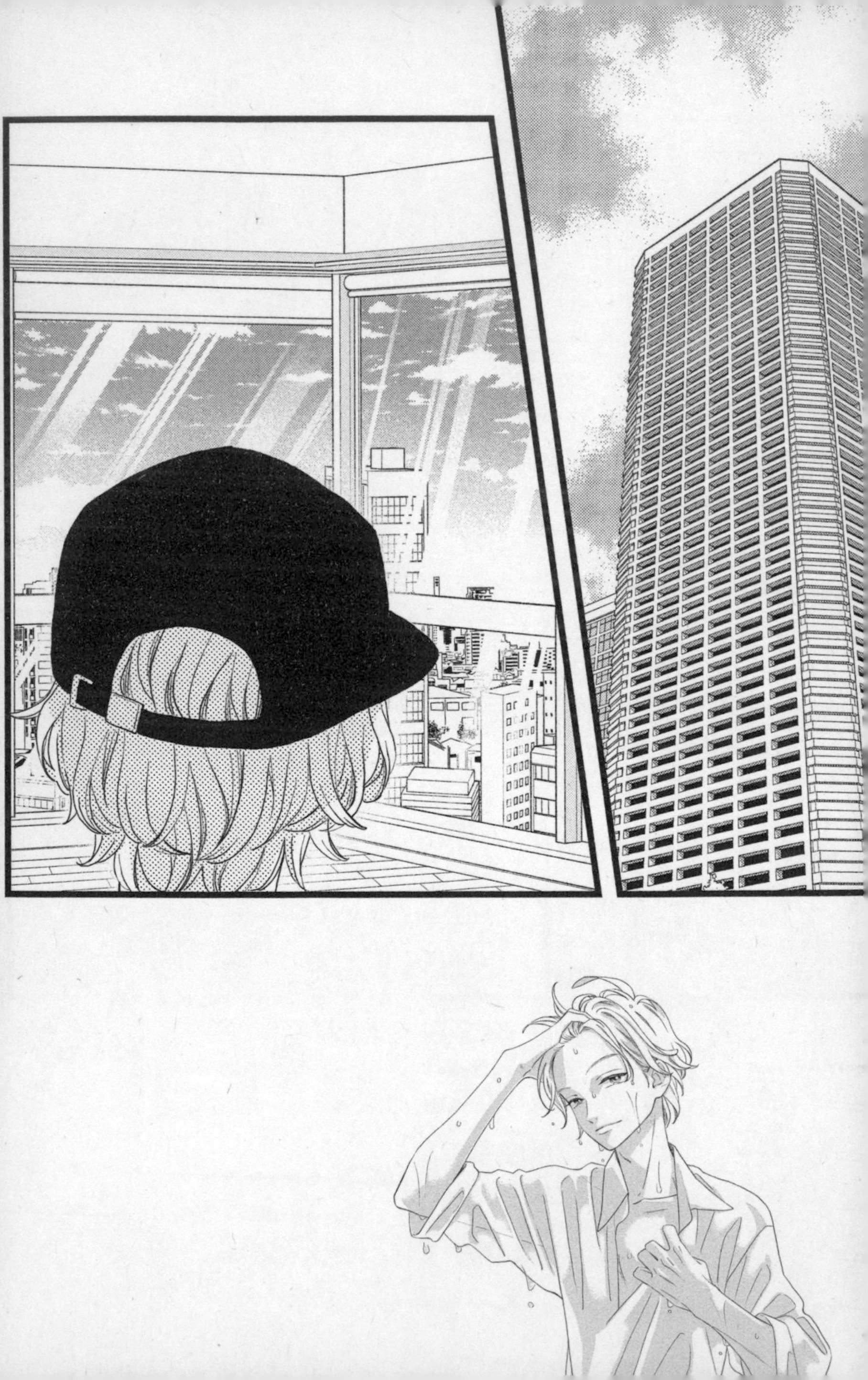

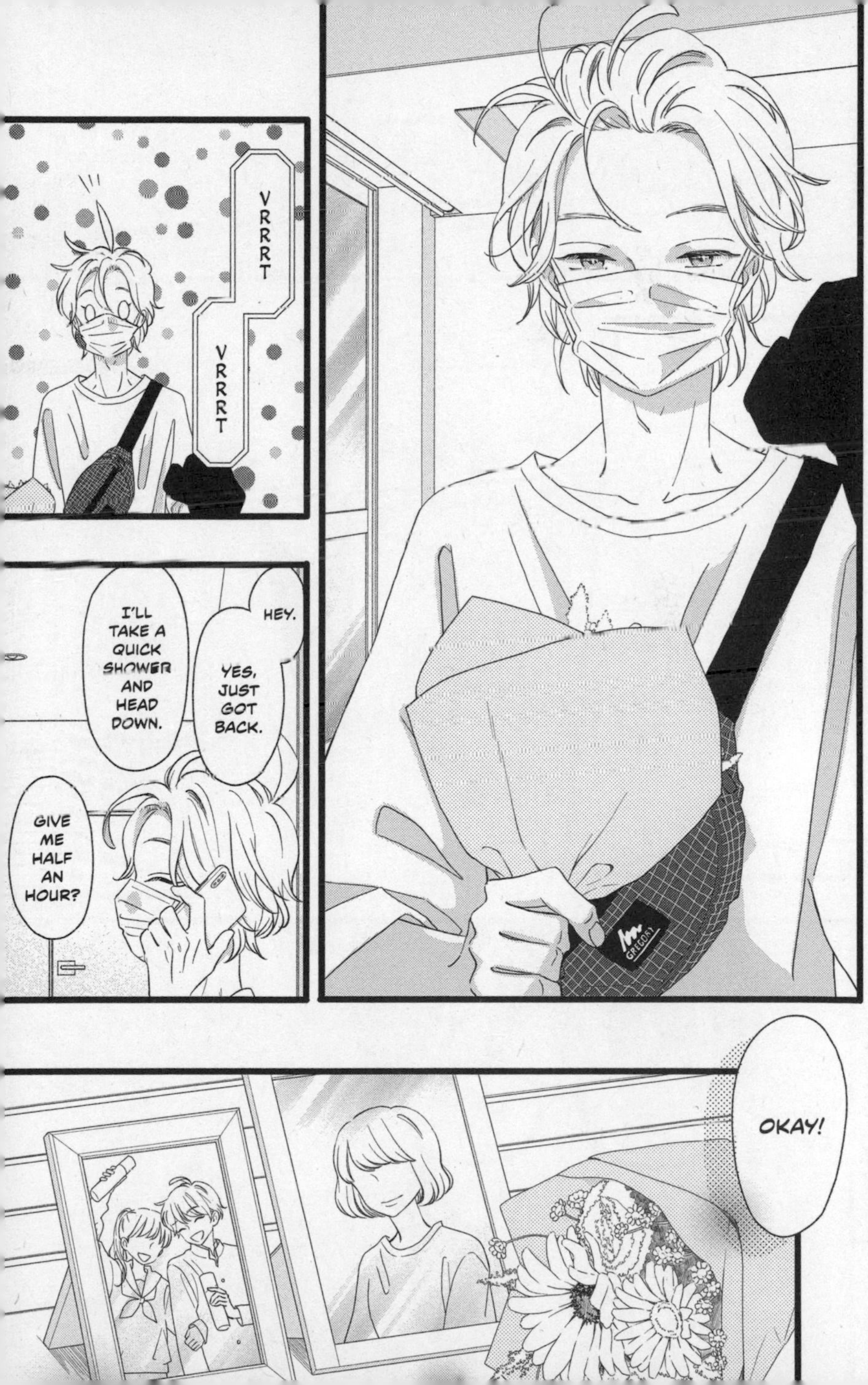
GREGORY
VRRRT
VRRRT
HEY.
YES, JUST GOT BACK.
I'LL TAKE A QUICK SHOWER AND HEAD DOWN.
GIVE ME HALF AN HOUR?
OKAY!

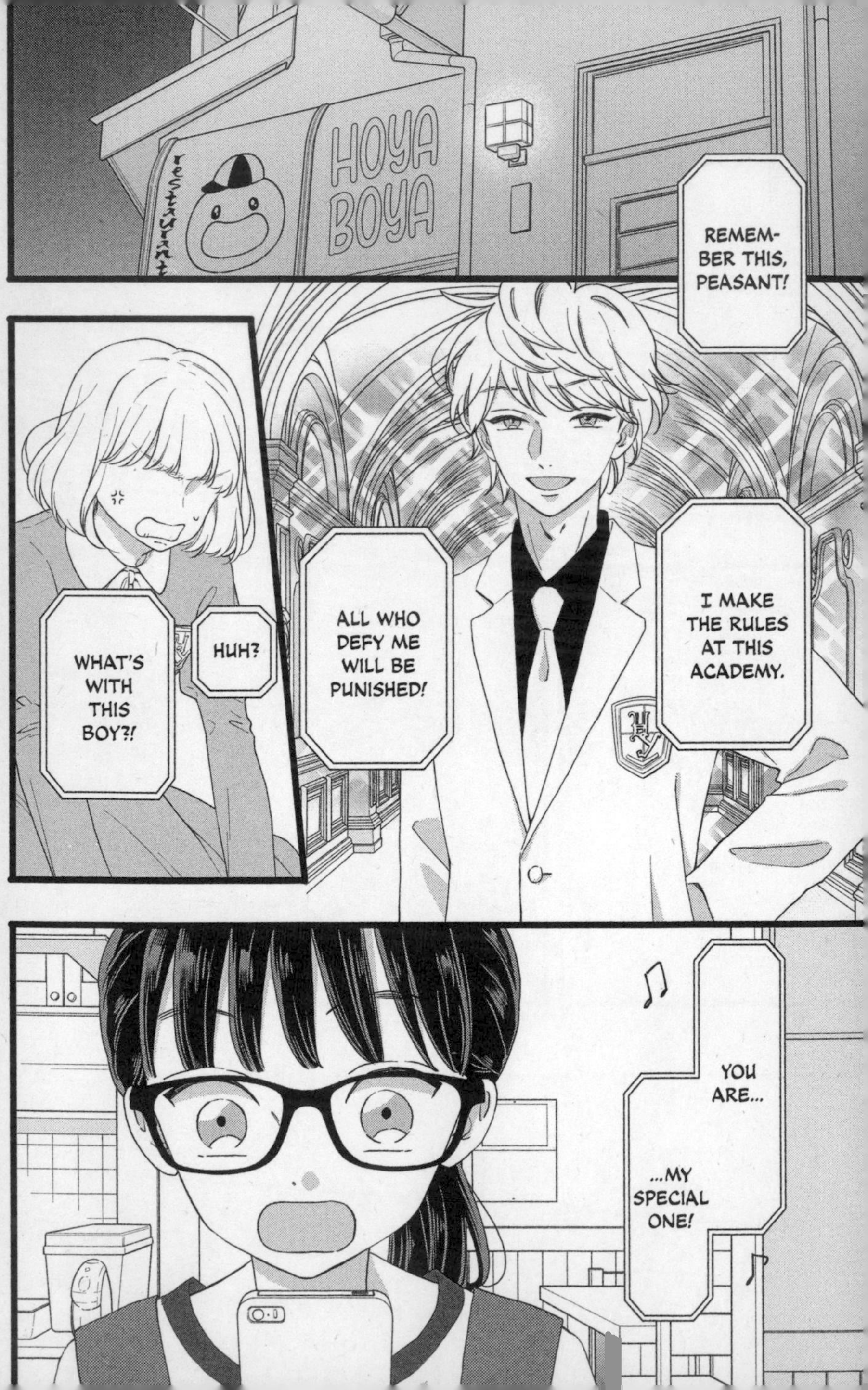
HOYA BOYA
REMEMBER THIS, PEASANT!
I MAKE THE RULES AT THIS ACADEMY.
ALL WHO DEFY ME WILL BE PUNISHED!
HUH?
WHAT'S WITH THIS BOY?!
YOU ARE...
...MY SPECIAL ONE!

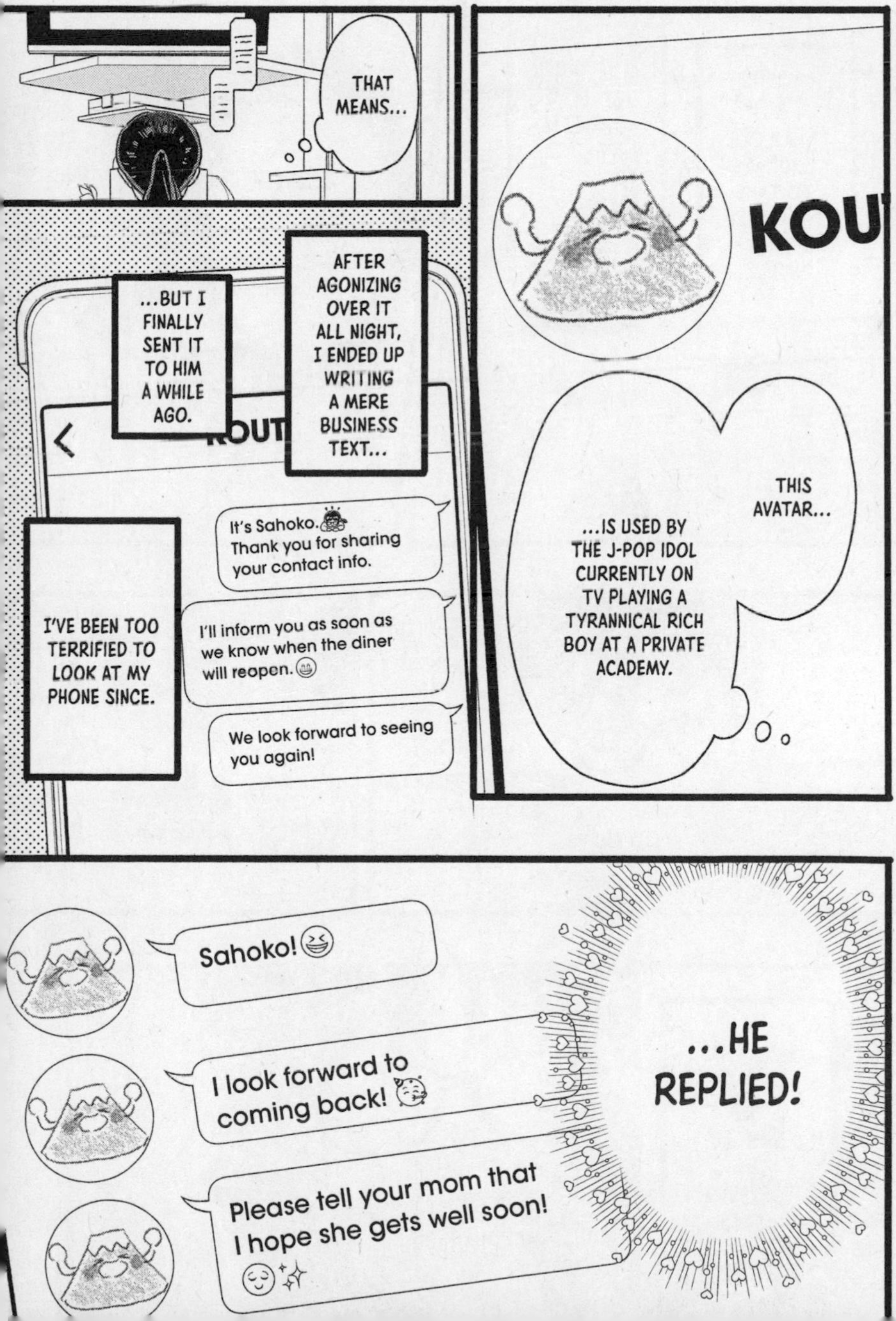
KOU
THIS AVATAR...
...IS USED BY THE J-POP IDOL CURRENTLY ON TV PLAYING A TYRANNICAL RICH BOY AT A PRIVATE ACADEMY.
THAT MEANS...
AFTER AGONIZING OVER IT ALL NIGHT, I ENDED UP WRITING A MERE BUSINESS TEXT...
...BUT I FINALLY SENT IT TO HIM A WHILE AGO.
KOUT
It's Sahoko. Thank you for sharing your contact info.
I'll inform you as soon as we know when the diner will reopen.
We look forward to seeing you again!
I'VE BEEN TOO TERRIFIED TO LOOK AT MY PHONE SINCE.
...HE REPLIED!
Sahoko!
I look forward to coming back!
Please tell your mom that I hope she gets well soon!

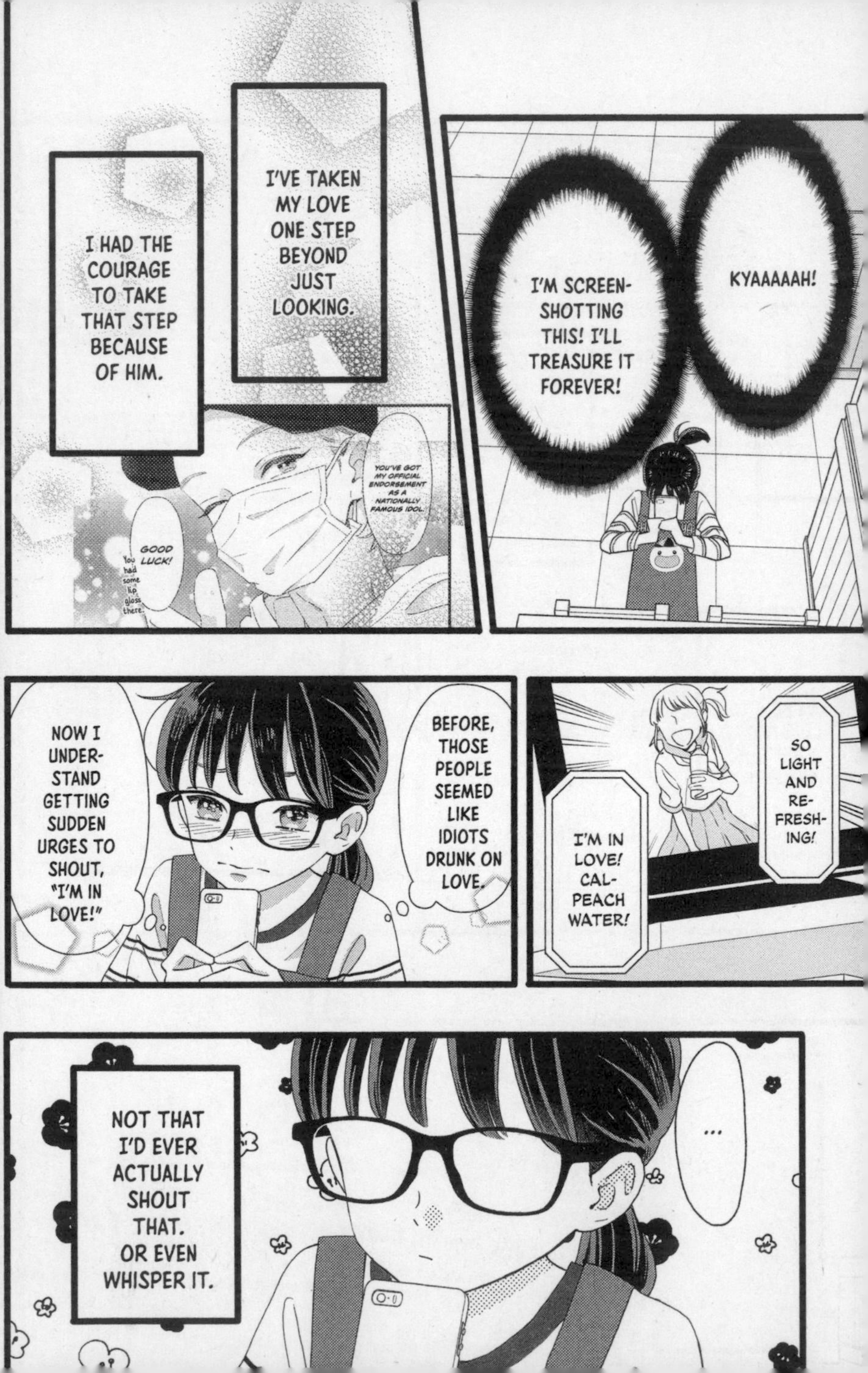
KYAAAAAH!
I'M SCREEN-SHOTTING THIS! I'LL TREASURE IT FOREVER!
I'VE TAKEN MY LOVE ONE STEP BEYOND JUST LOOKING.
I HAD THE COURAGE TO TAKE THAT STEP BECAUSE OF HIM.
YOU'VE GOT MY OFFICIAL ENDORSEMENT AS A NATIONALLY FAMOUS IDOL.
GOOD LUCK!
You had some lip gloss there.
SO LIGHT AND RE-FRESH-ING!
I'M IN LOVE! CAL-PEACH WATER!
BEFORE, THOSE PEOPLE SEEMED LIKE IDIOTS DRUNK ON LOVE.
NOW I UNDER-STAND GETTING SUDDEN URGES TO SHOUT, "I'M IN LOVE!"
...
NOT THAT I'D EVER ACTUALLY SHOUT THAT. OR EVEN WHISPER IT.

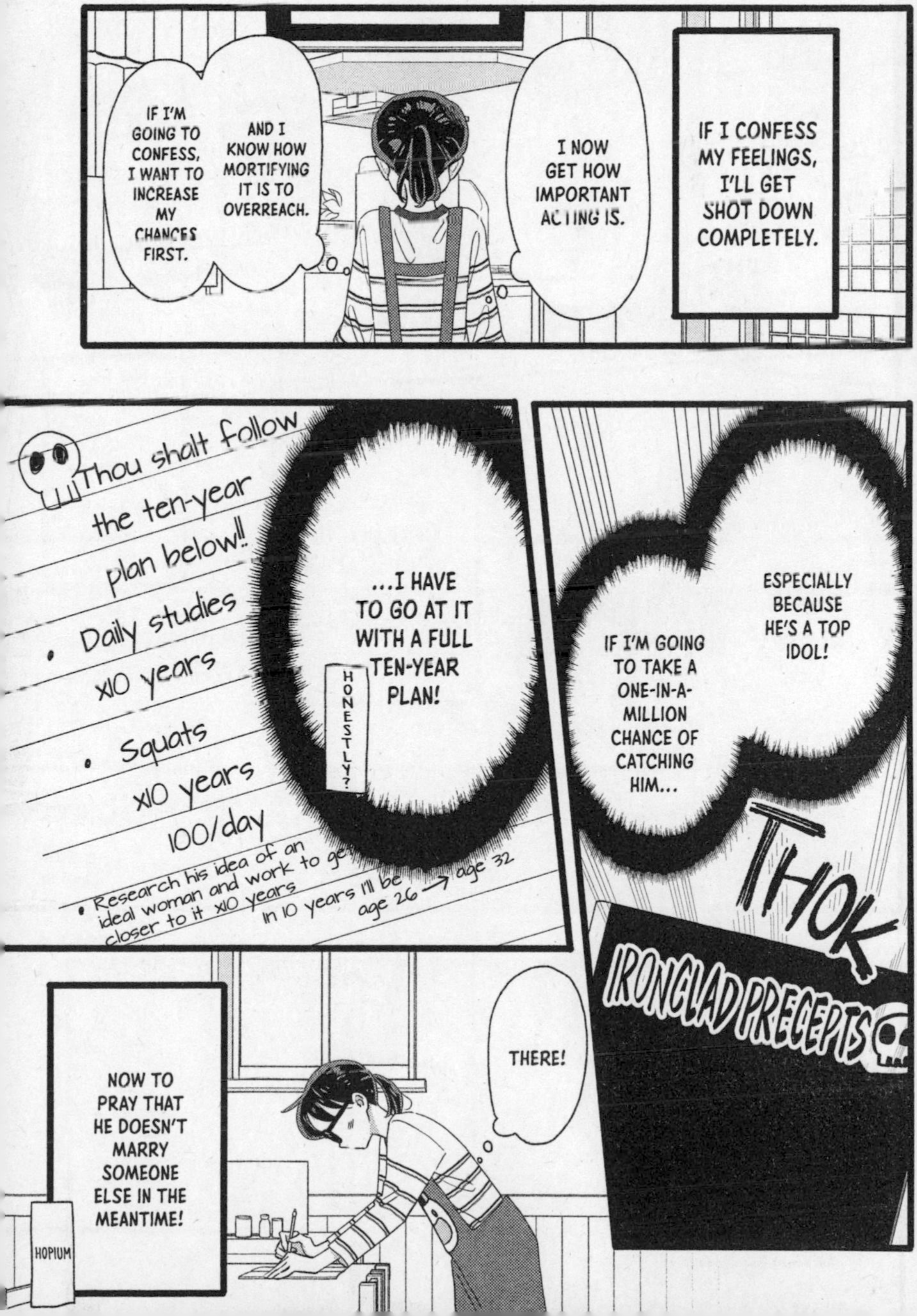
IF I CONFESS MY FEELINGS, I'LL GET SHOT DOWN COMPLETELY.
I NOW GET HOW IMPORTANT ACTING IS.
AND I KNOW HOW MORTIFYING IT IS TO OVERREACH.
IF I'M GOING TO CONFESS, I WANT TO INCREASE MY CHANCES FIRST.
ESPECIALLY BECAUSE HE'S A TOP IDOL!
IF I'M GOING TO TAKE A ONE-IN-A-MILLION CHANCE OF CATCHING HIM...
THOK
IRONCLAD PRECEPTS
...I HAVE TO GO AT IT WITH A FULL TEN-YEAR PLAN!
HONESTLY?
Thou shalt follow the ten-year plan below!!
• Daily studies x10 years
• Squats x10 years 100/day
• Research his idea of an ideal woman and work to get closer to it x10 years
In 10 years I'll be age 26 → age 32
THERE!
NOW TO PRAY THAT HE DOESN'T MARRY SOMEONE ELSE IN THE MEANTIME!
HOPIUM

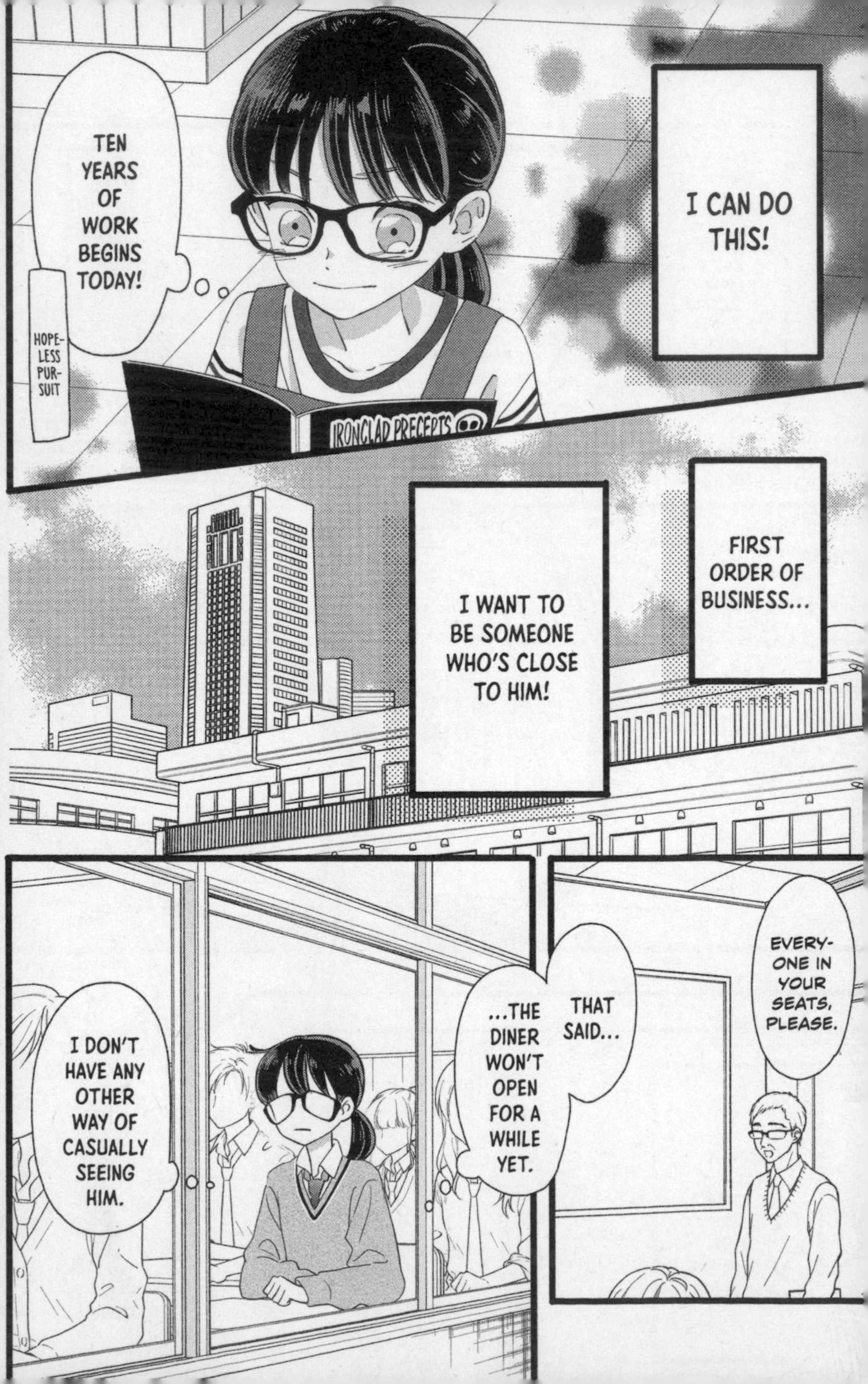
I CAN DO THIS!
TEN YEARS OF WORK BEGINS TODAY!
HOPELESS PURSUIT
IRONCLAD PRECEPTS
FIRST ORDER OF BUSINESS...
I WANT TO BE SOMEONE WHO'S CLOSE TO HIM!
EVERYONE IN YOUR SEATS, PLEASE.
THAT SAID...
...THE DINER WON'T OPEN FOR A WHILE YET.
I DON'T HAVE ANY OTHER WAY OF CASUALLY SEEING HIM.

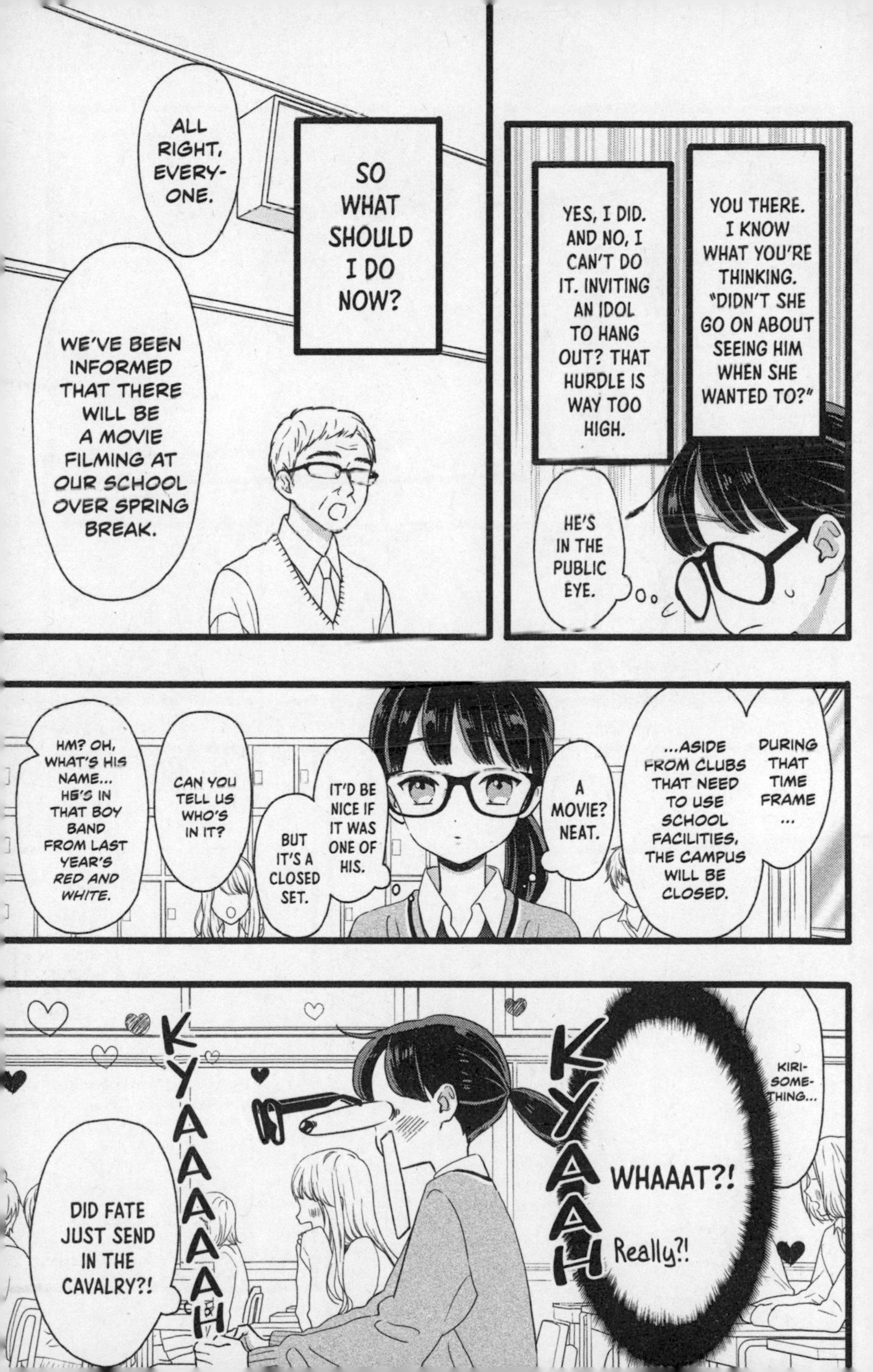
YOU THERE. I KNOW WHAT YOU'RE THINKING. "DIDN'T SHE GO ON ABOUT SEEING HIM WHEN SHE WANTED TO?"
YES, I DID. AND NO, I CAN'T DO IT. INVITING AN IDOL TO HANG OUT? THAT HURDLE IS WAY TOO HIGH.
HE'S IN THE PUBLIC EYE.
SO WHAT SHOULD I DO NOW?
ALL RIGHT, EVERYONE.
WE'VE BEEN INFORMED THAT THERE WILL BE A MOVIE FILMING AT OUR SCHOOL OVER SPRING BREAK.
DURING THAT TIME FRAME ...
...ASIDE FROM CLUBS THAT NEED TO USE SCHOOL FACILITIES, THE CAMPUS WILL BE CLOSED.
A MOVIE? NEAT.
IT'D BE NICE IF IT WAS ONE OF HIS.
BUT IT'S A CLOSED SET.
CAN YOU TELL US WHO'S IN IT?
HM? OH, WHAT'S HIS NAME... HE'S IN THAT BOY BAND FROM LAST YEAR'S *RED AND WHITE.*
KIRI-SOMETHING...
KYAAAAH
WHAAAT?!
Really?!
KYAAAAAAH
DID FATE JUST SEND IN THE CAVALRY?!

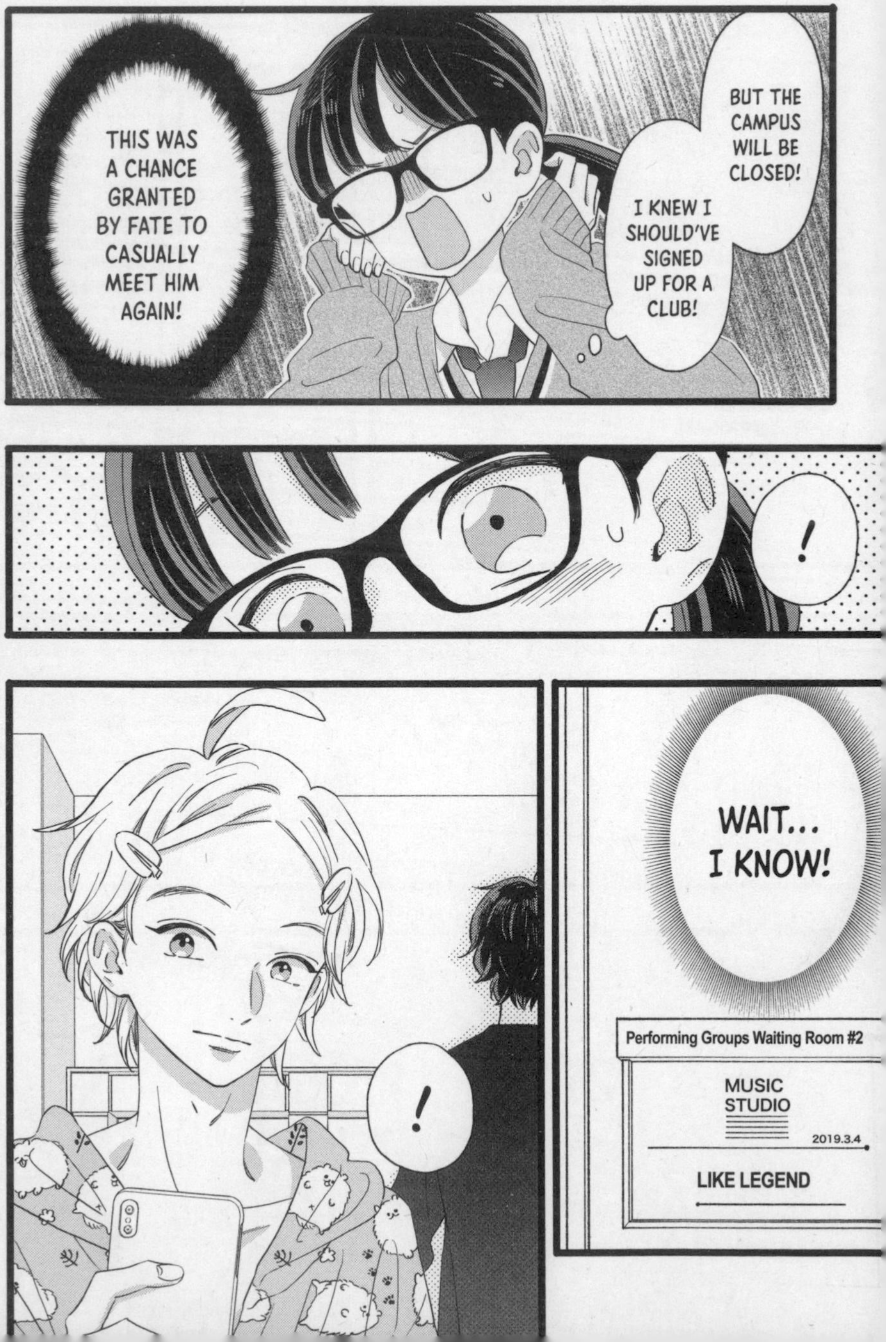
BUT THE CAMPUS WILL BE CLOSED!
I KNEW I SHOULD'VE SIGNED UP FOR A CLUB!
THIS WAS A CHANCE GRANTED BY FATE TO CASUALLY MEET HIM AGAIN!
!
WAIT... I KNOW!
Performing Groups Waiting Room #2
MUSIC STUDIO
2019.3.4
LIKE LEGEND
!

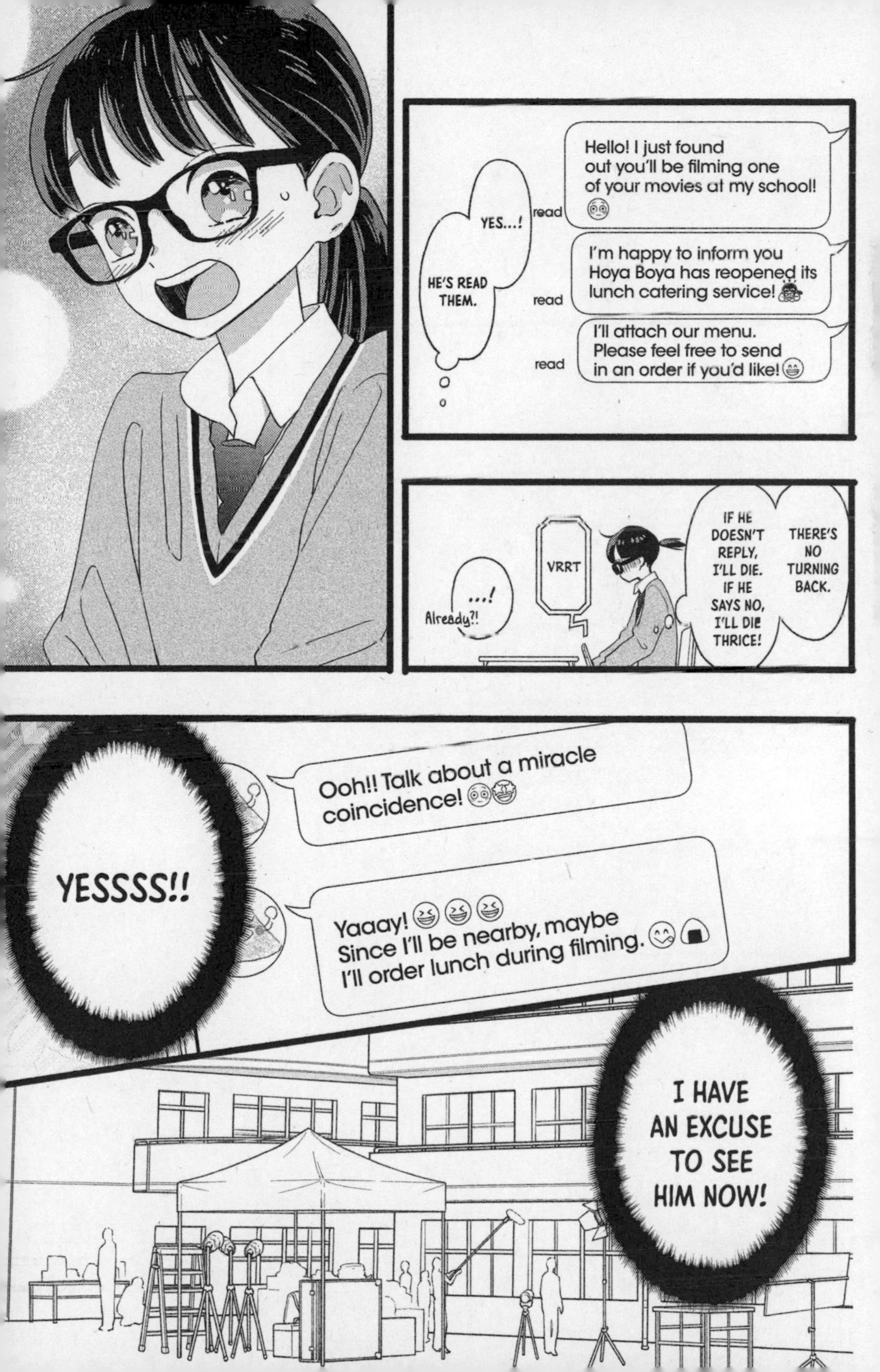
Hello! I just found out you'll be filming one of your movies at my school!
read
I'm happy to inform you Hoya Boya has reopened its lunch catering service!
read
I'll attach our menu. Please feel free to send in an order if you'd like!
read
YES...!
HE'S READ THEM.
THERE'S NO TURNING BACK.
IF HE DOESN'T REPLY, I'LL DIE. IF HE SAYS NO, I'LL DIE THRICE!
VRRT
...!
Already?!
Ooh!! Talk about a miracle coincidence!
Yaaay!
Since I'll be nearby, maybe I'll order lunch during filming.
YESSSS!!
I HAVE AN EXCUSE TO SEE HIM NOW!

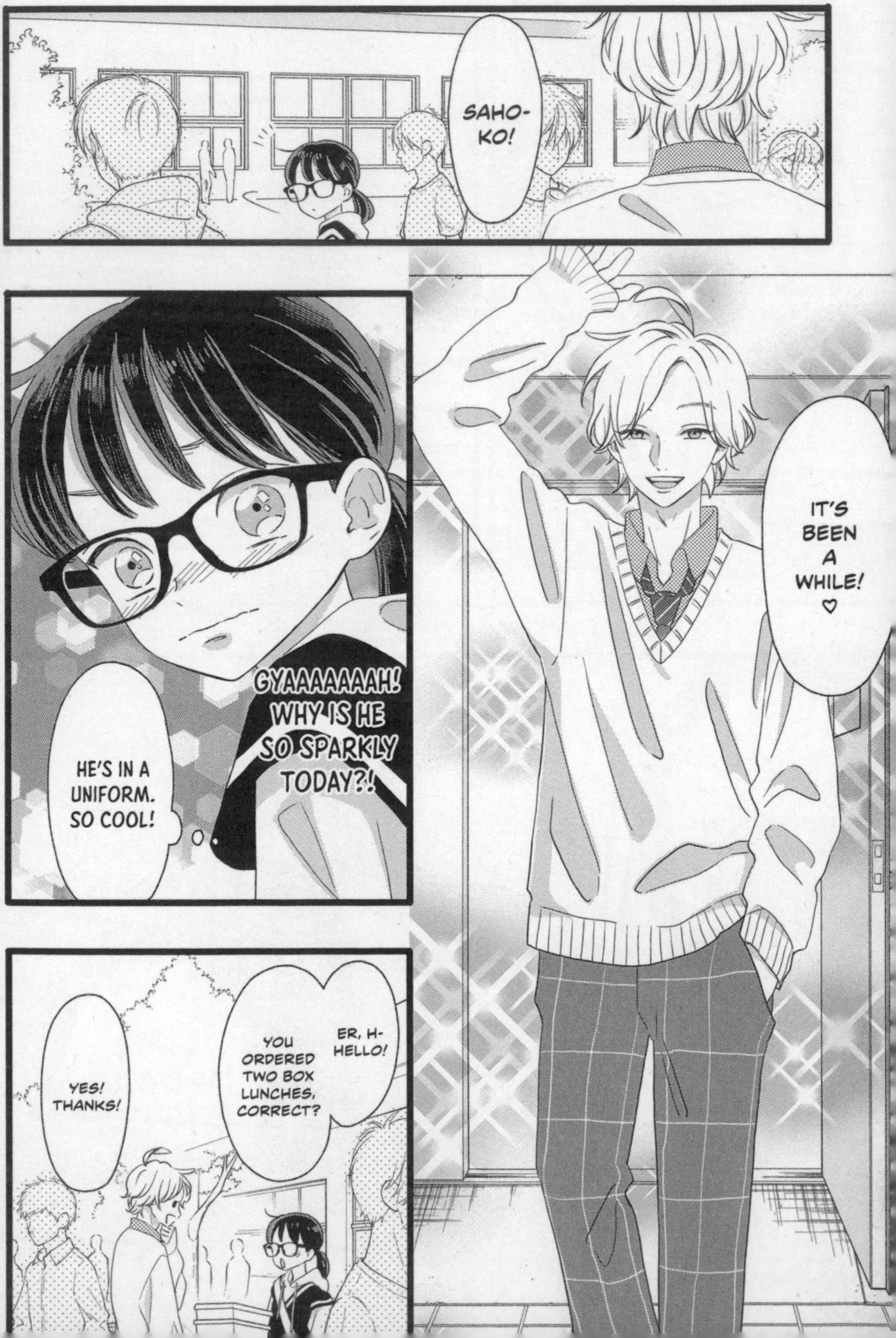
SAHO-KO!
IT'S BEEN A WHILE! ♡
GYAAAAAAAH! WHY IS HE SO SPARKLY TODAY?!
HE'S IN A UNIFORM. SO COOL!
ER, H-HELLO!
YOU ORDERED TWO BOX LUNCHES, CORRECT?
YES! THANKS!

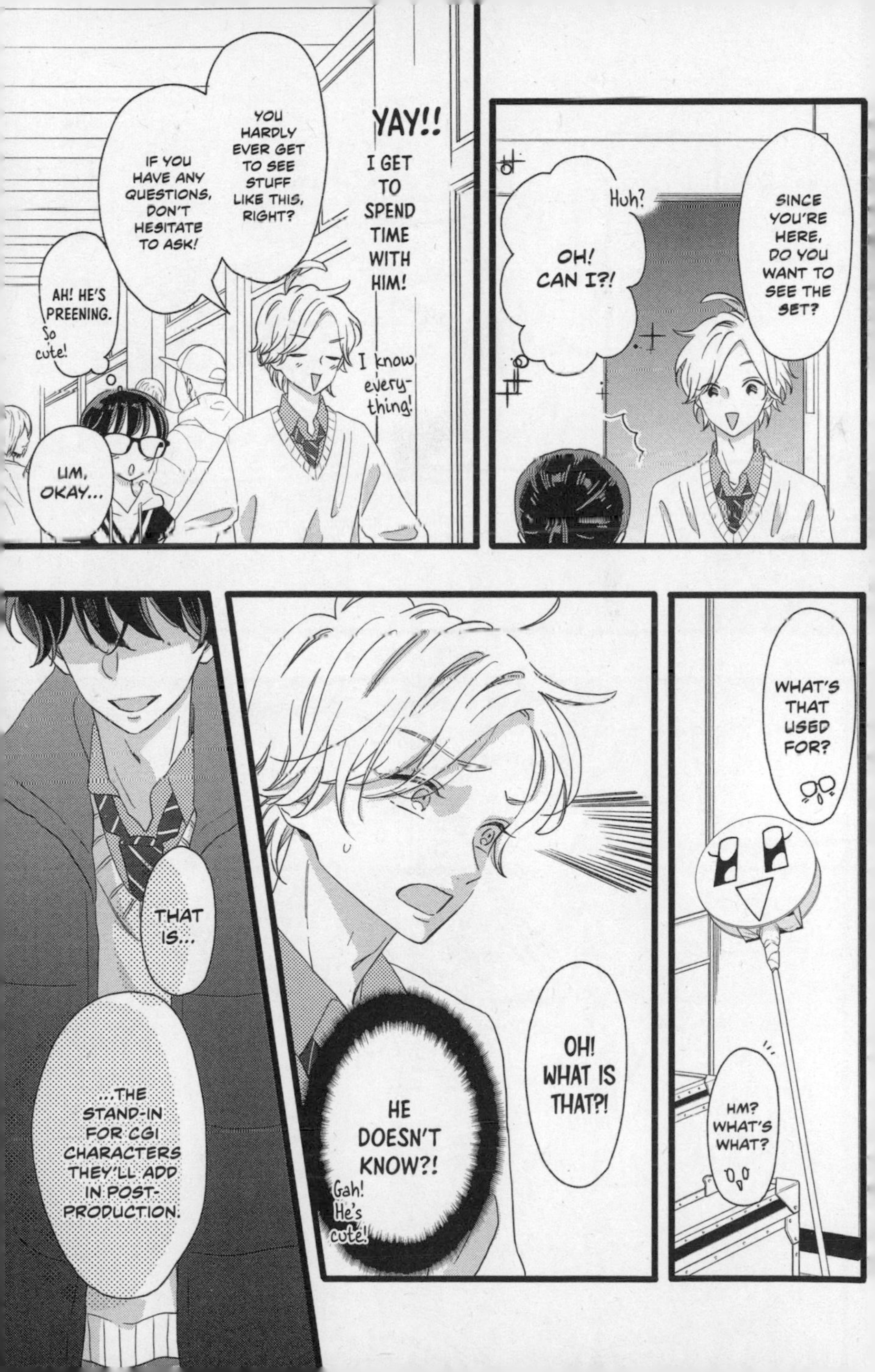
SINCE YOU'RE HERE, DO YOU WANT TO SEE THE SET?
Huh?
OH! CAN I?!
YAY!!
I GET TO SPEND TIME WITH HIM!
YOU HARDLY EVER GET TO SEE STUFF LIKE THIS, RIGHT?
IF YOU HAVE ANY QUESTIONS, DON'T HESITATE TO ASK!
I know everything!
AH! HE'S PREENING.
So cute!
UM, OKAY...
WHAT'S THAT USED FOR?
HM? WHAT'S WHAT?
OH! WHAT IS THAT?!
HE DOESN'T KNOW?!
Gah! He's cute!
THAT IS...
...THE STAND-IN FOR CGI CHARACTERS THEY'LL ADD IN POST-PRODUCTION.

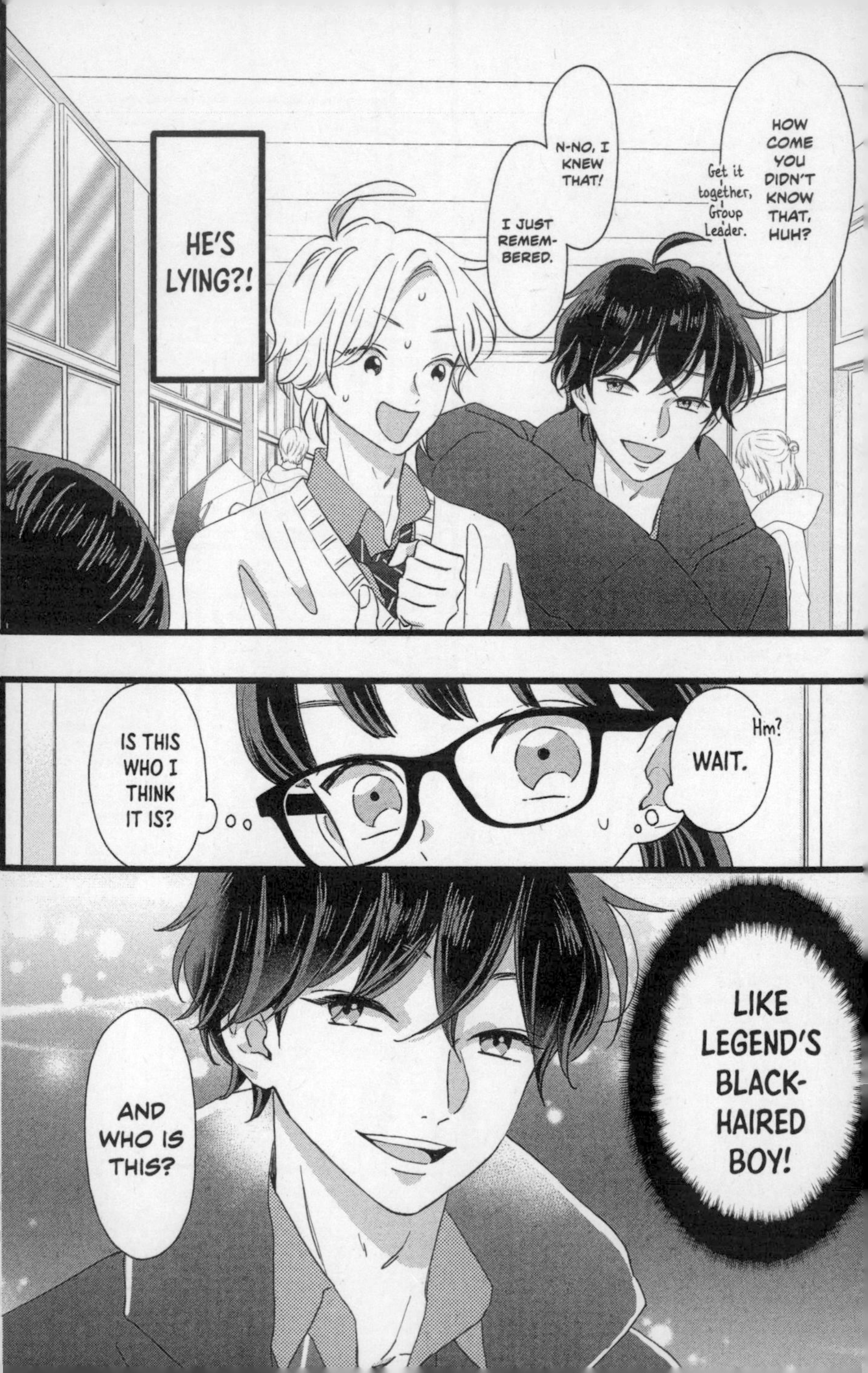
HOW COME YOU DIDN'T KNOW THAT, HUH?
Get it together, Group Leader.
N-NO, I KNEW THAT!
I JUST REMEMBERED.
HE'S LYING?!
Hm?
WAIT.
IS THIS WHO I THINK IT IS?
LIKE LEGEND'S BLACK-HAIRED BOY!
AND WHO IS THIS?

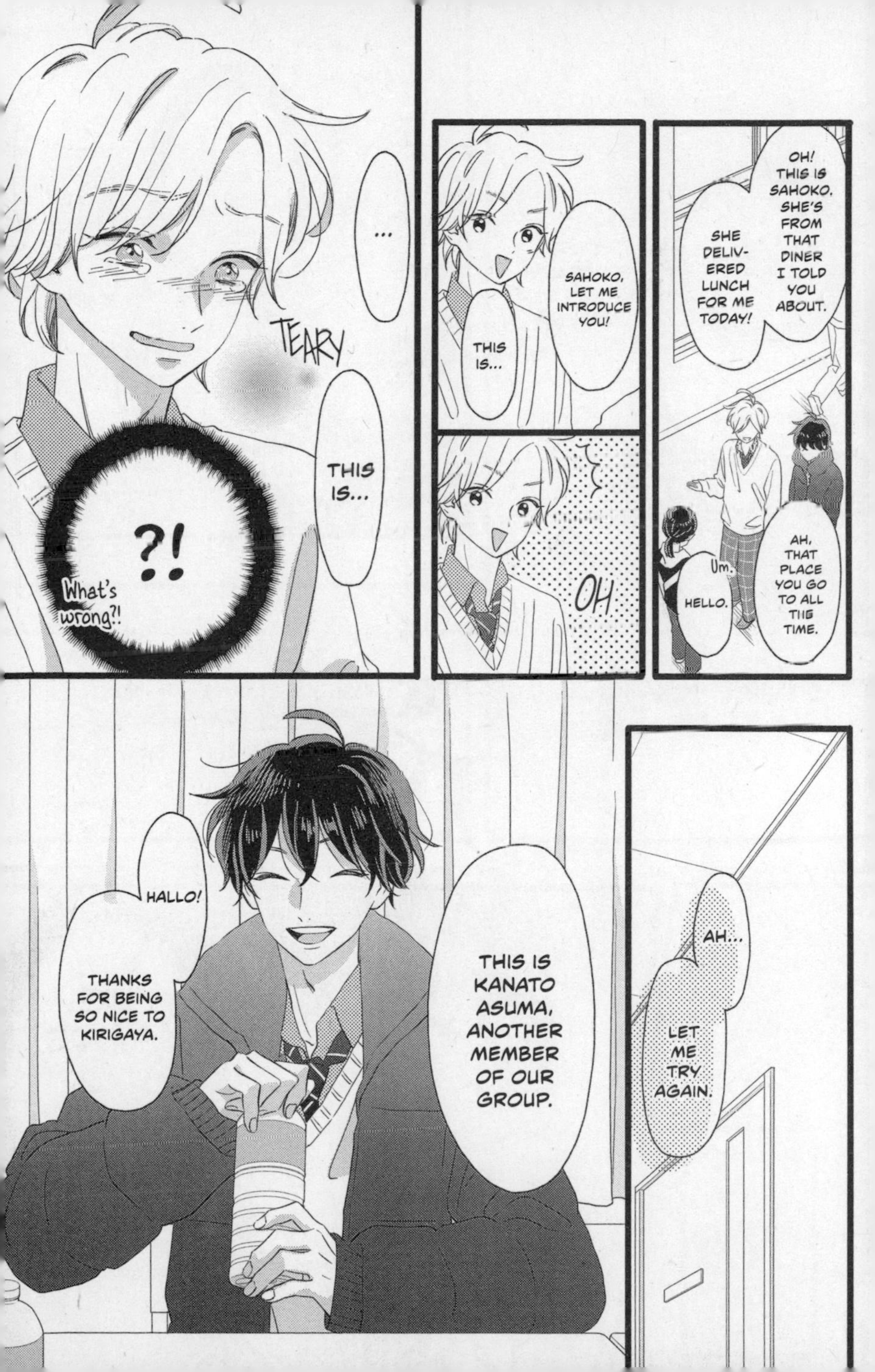
OH! THIS IS SAHOKO. SHE'S FROM THAT DINER I TOLD YOU ABOUT.
SHE DELIV-ERED LUNCH FOR ME TODAY!
AH, THAT PLACE YOU GO TO ALL THE TIME.
Um.
HELLO.
SAHOKO, LET ME INTRODUCE YOU!
THIS IS...
OH
...
TEARY
THIS IS...
?!
What's wrong?!
AH...
LET ME TRY AGAIN.
THIS IS KANATO ASUMA, ANOTHER MEMBER OF OUR GROUP.
HALLO!
THANKS FOR BEING SO NICE TO KIRIGAYA.

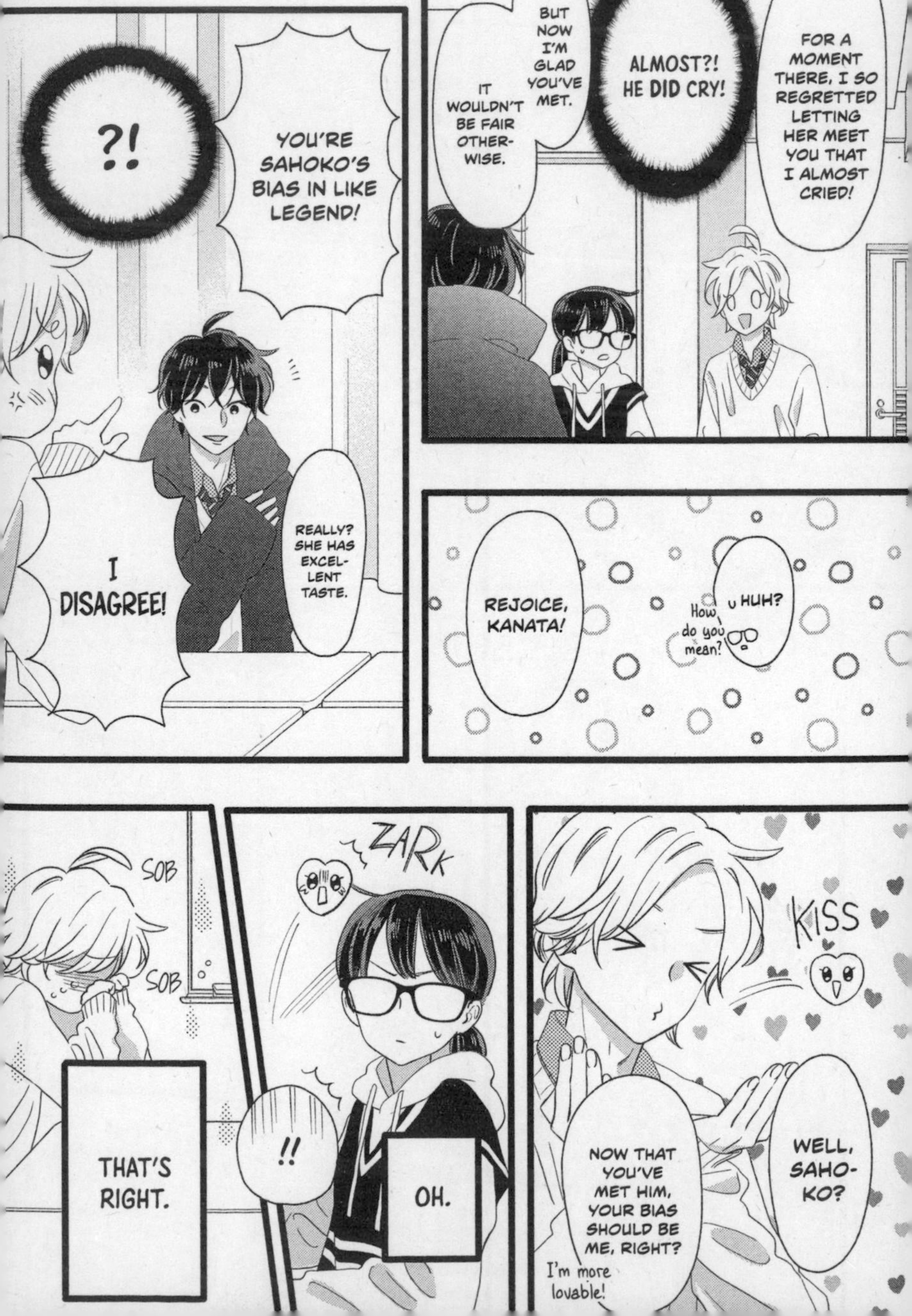
FOR A MOMENT THERE, I SO REGRETTED LETTING HER MEET YOU THAT I ALMOST CRIED!
ALMOST?! HE DID CRY!
BUT NOW I'M GLAD YOU'VE MET.
IT WOULDN'T BE FAIR OTHERWISE.
HUH?
How do you mean?
REJOICE, KANATA!
YOU'RE SAHOKO'S BIAS IN LIKE LEGEND!
?!
REALLY? SHE HAS EXCELLENT TASTE.
I DISAGREE!
WELL, SAHOKO?
KISS
NOW THAT YOU'VE MET HIM, YOUR BIAS SHOULD BE ME, RIGHT?
I'm more lovable!
ZARK
!!
OH.
SOB
SOB
THAT'S RIGHT.

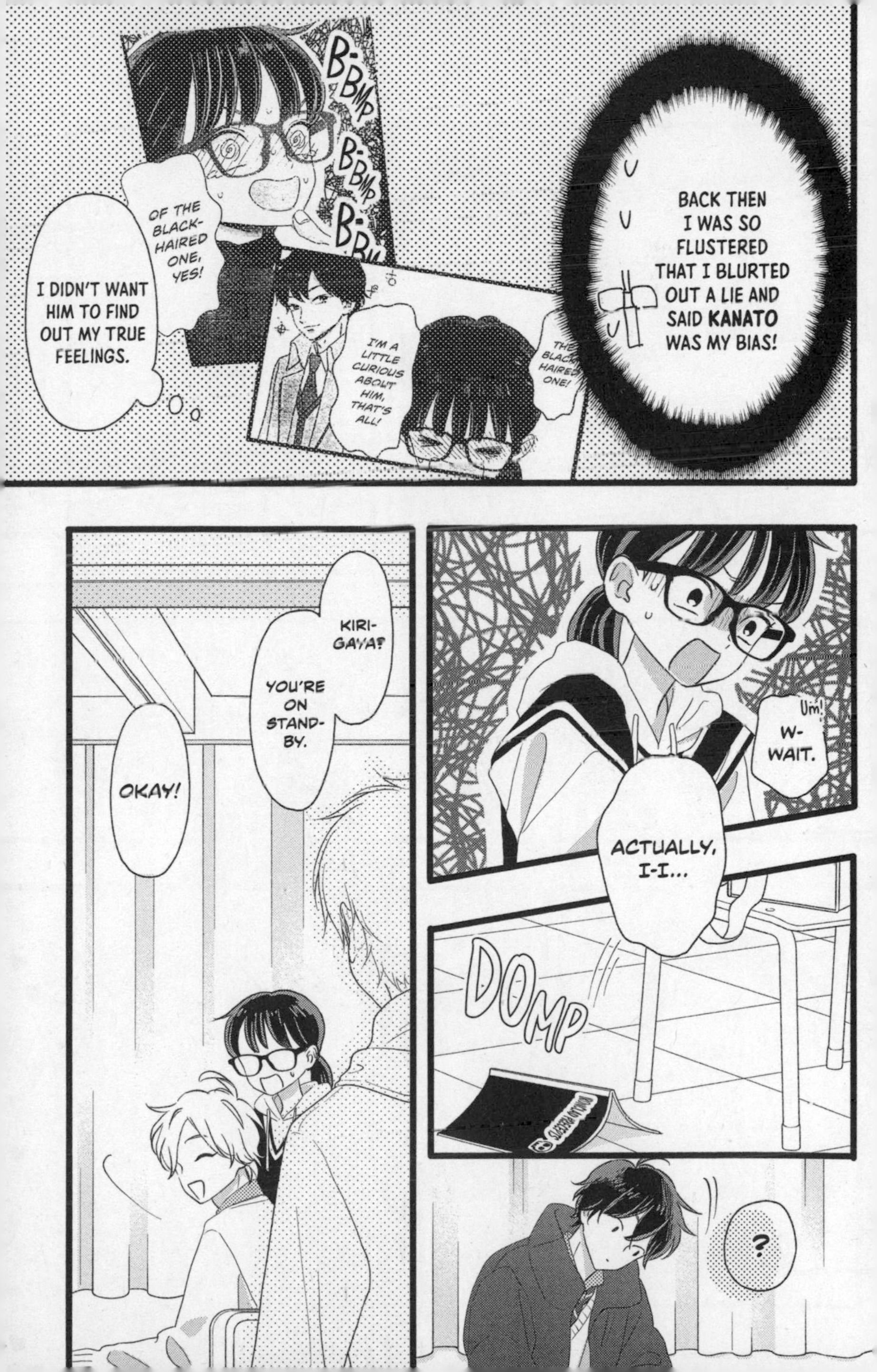
BACK THEN I WAS SO FLUSTERED THAT I BLURTED OUT A LIE AND SAID KANATO WAS MY BIAS!
B-BMP B-BMP B-BU
OF THE BLACK-HAIRED ONE, YES!
THE BLACK-HAIRED ONE!
I'M A LITTLE CURIOUS ABOUT HIM, THAT'S ALL!
I DIDN'T WANT HIM TO FIND OUT MY TRUE FEELINGS.
Um!
W-WAIT.
ACTUALLY, I-I...
DOMP
?
KIRI-GAYA?
YOU'RE ON STAND-BY.
OKAY!

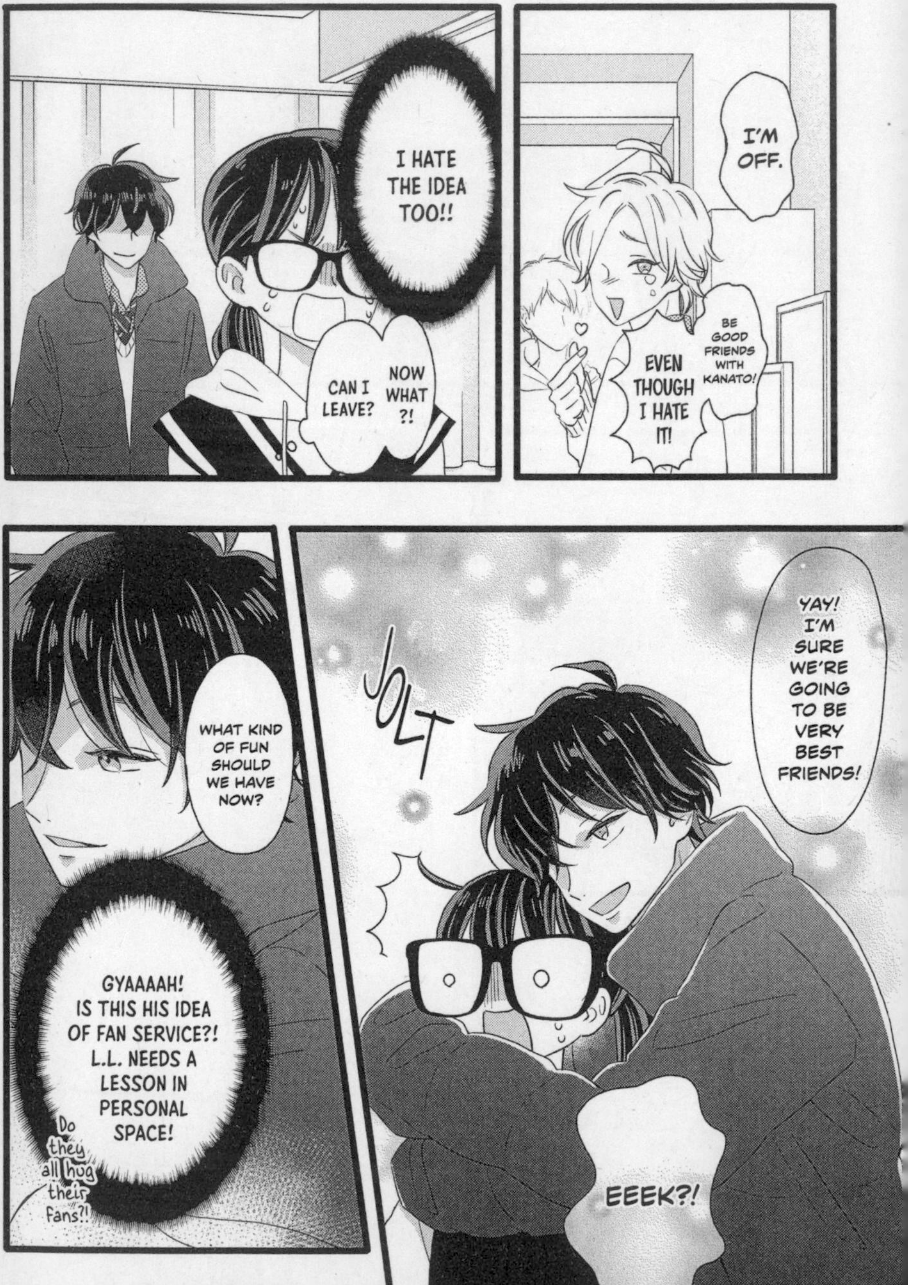
I'M OFF.
BE GOOD FRIENDS WITH KANATO!
EVEN THOUGH I HATE IT!
I HATE THE IDEA TOO!!
NOW WHAT?!
CAN I LEAVE?
YAY! I'M SURE WE'RE GOING TO BE VERY BEST FRIENDS!
JOLT
EEEK?!
WHAT KIND OF FUN SHOULD WE HAVE NOW?
GYAAAAH! IS THIS HIS IDEA OF FAN SERVICE?! L.L. NEEDS A LESSON IN PERSONAL SPACE!
Do they all hug their fans?!

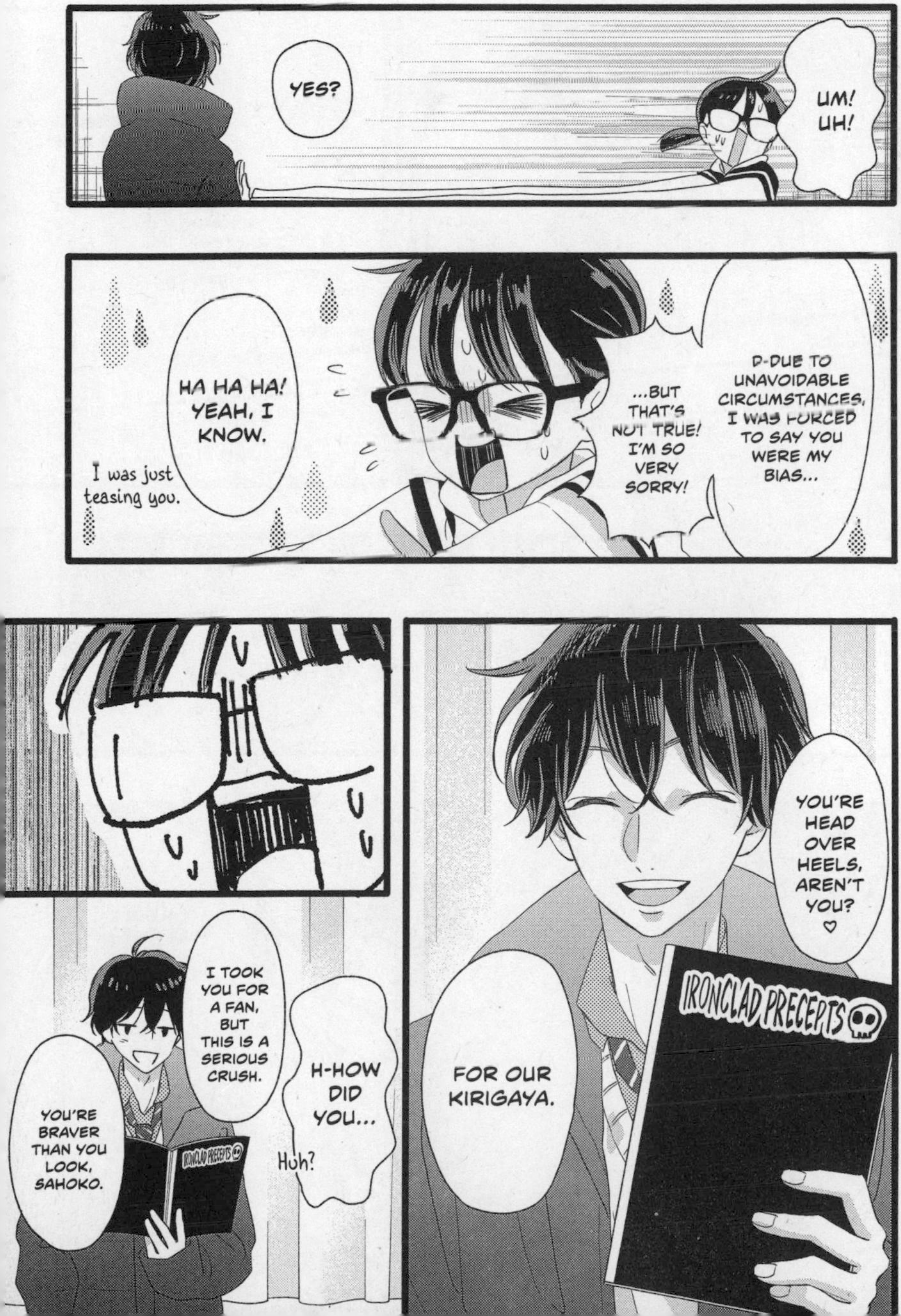
UM! UH!
YES?
D-DUE TO UNAVOIDABLE CIRCUMSTANCES, I WAS FORCED TO SAY YOU WERE MY BIAS...
...BUT THAT'S NOT TRUE! I'M SO VERY SORRY!
HA HA HA! YEAH, I KNOW.
I was just teasing you.
YOU'RE HEAD OVER HEELS, AREN'T YOU? ♡
FOR OUR KIRIGAYA.
IRONCLAD PRECEPTS
I TOOK YOU FOR A FAN, BUT THIS IS A SERIOUS CRUSH.
H-HOW DID YOU...
Huh?
YOU'RE BRAVER THAN YOU LOOK, SAHOKO.
IRONCLAD PRECEPTS

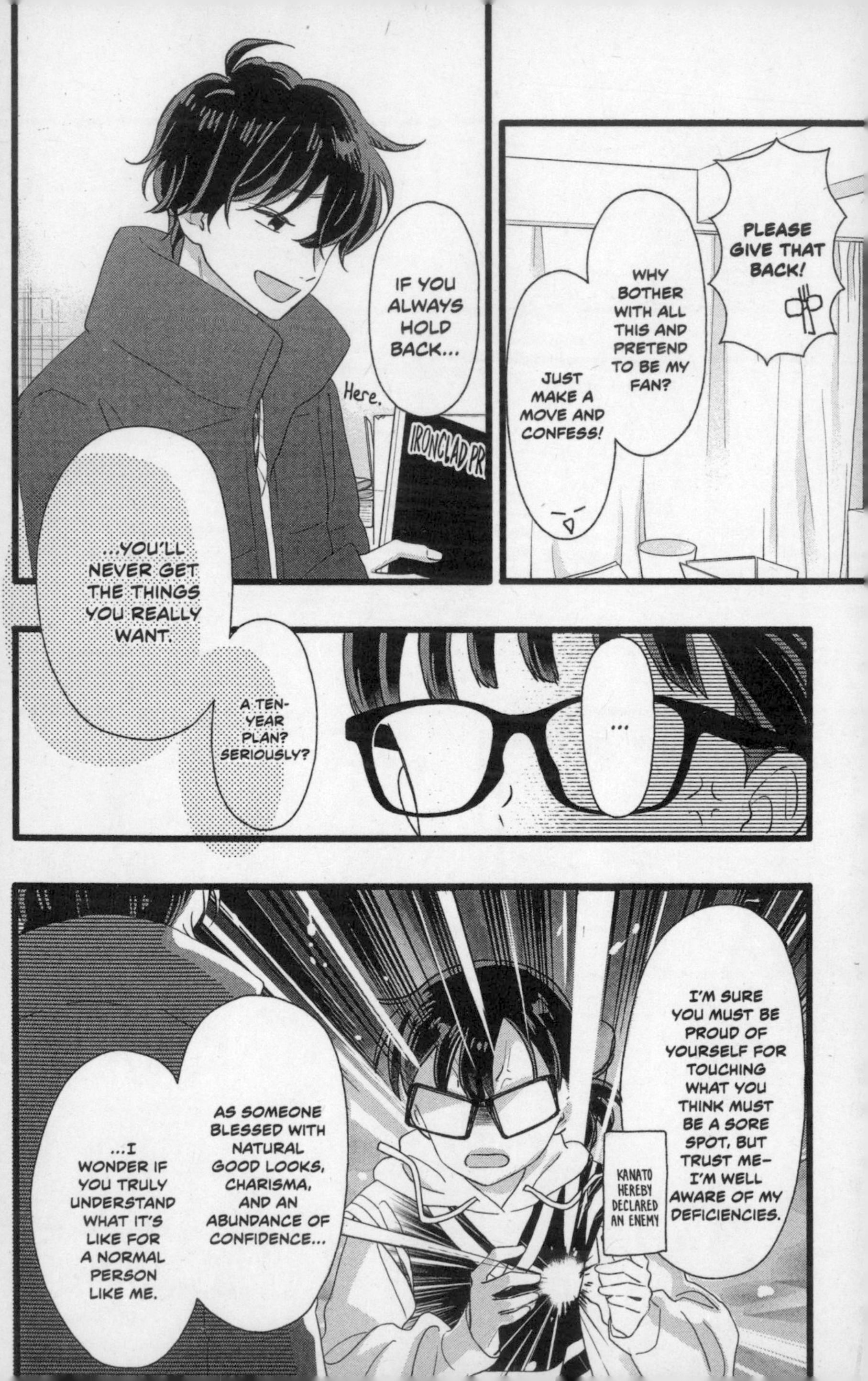
PLEASE GIVE THAT BACK!
WHY BOTHER WITH ALL THIS AND PRETEND TO BE MY FAN?
JUST MAKE A MOVE AND CONFESS!
IF YOU ALWAYS HOLD BACK...
Here.
IRONCLAD PR
...YOU'LL NEVER GET THE THINGS YOU REALLY WANT.
...
A TEN-YEAR PLAN? SERIOUSLY?
I'M SURE YOU MUST BE PROUD OF YOURSELF FOR TOUCHING WHAT YOU THINK MUST BE A SORE SPOT, BUT TRUST ME—I'M WELL AWARE OF MY DEFICIENCIES.
KANATO HEREBY DECLARED AN ENEMY
AS SOMEONE BLESSED WITH NATURAL GOOD LOOKS, CHARISMA, AND AN ABUNDANCE OF CONFIDENCE...
...I WONDER IF YOU TRULY UNDERSTAND WHAT IT'S LIKE FOR A NORMAL PERSON LIKE ME.

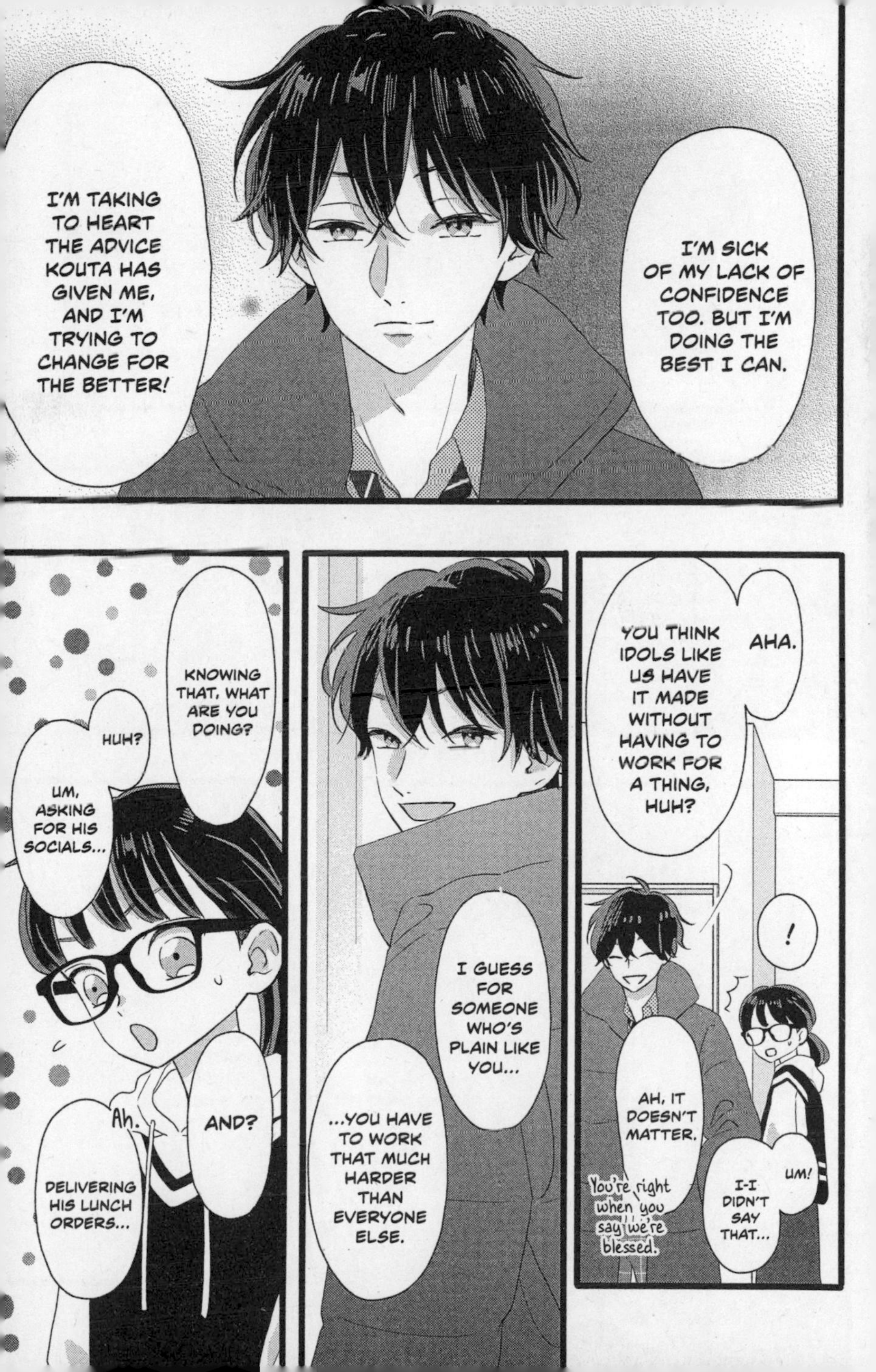
I'M SICK OF MY LACK OF CONFIDENCE TOO. BUT I'M DOING THE BEST I CAN.
I'M TAKING TO HEART THE ADVICE KOUTA HAS GIVEN ME, AND I'M TRYING TO CHANGE FOR THE BETTER!
AHA.
YOU THINK IDOLS LIKE US HAVE IT MADE WITHOUT HAVING TO WORK FOR A THING, HUH?
!
UM!
I-I DIDN'T SAY THAT...
AH, IT DOESN'T MATTER.
You're right when you say we're blessed.
I GUESS FOR SOMEONE WHO'S PLAIN LIKE YOU...
...YOU HAVE TO WORK THAT MUCH HARDER THAN EVERYONE ELSE.
KNOWING THAT, WHAT ARE YOU DOING?
HUH?
UM, ASKING FOR HIS SOCIALS...
AND?
Ah.
DELIVERING HIS LUNCH ORDERS...

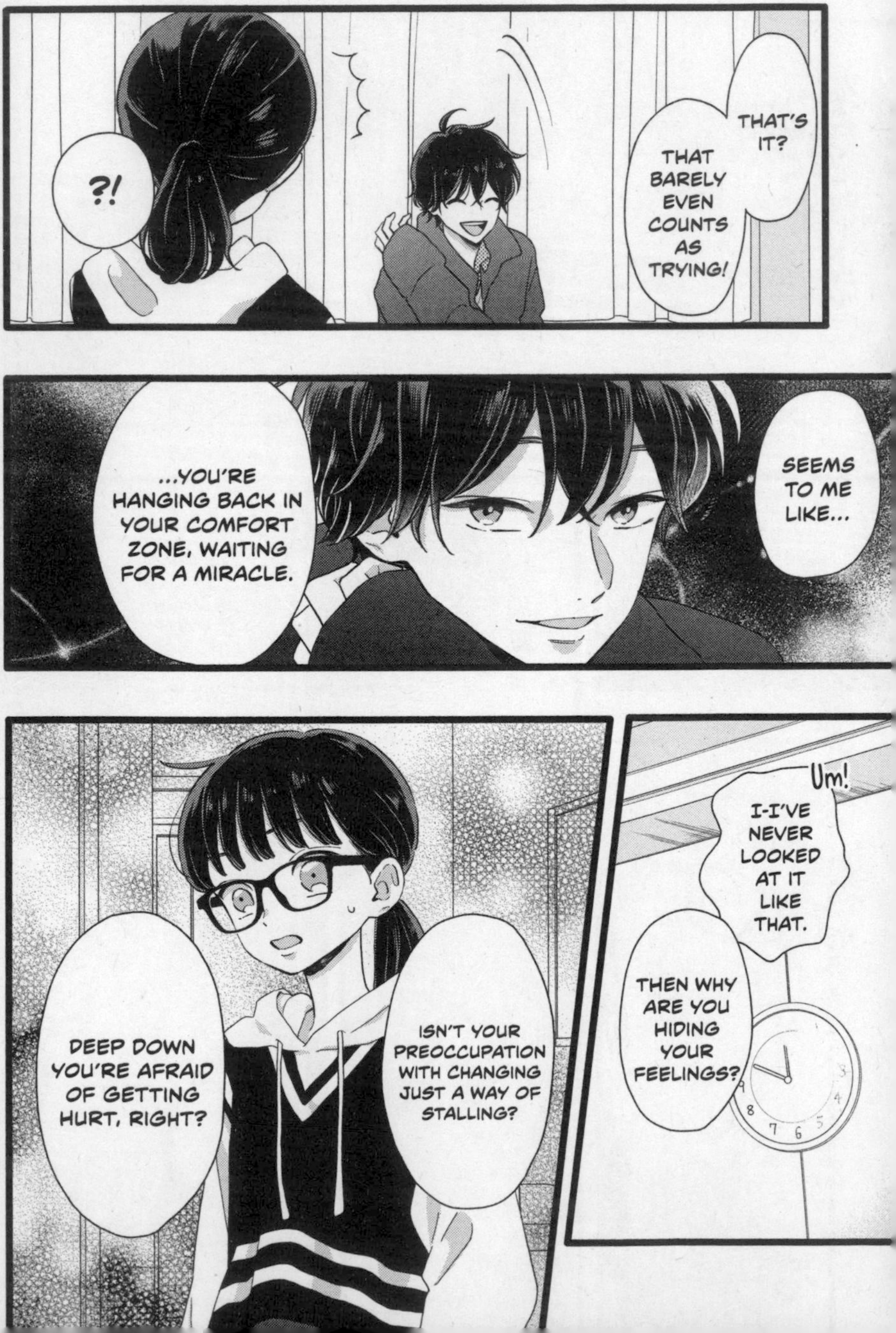
THAT'S IT?
THAT BARELY EVEN COUNTS AS TRYING!
?!
SEEMS TO ME LIKE...
...YOU'RE HANGING BACK IN YOUR COMFORT ZONE, WAITING FOR A MIRACLE.
Um!
I-I'VE NEVER LOOKED AT IT LIKE THAT.
THEN WHY ARE YOU HIDING YOUR FEELINGS?
ISN'T YOUR PREOCCUPATION WITH CHANGING JUST A WAY OF STALLING?
DEEP DOWN YOU'RE AFRAID OF GETTING HURT, RIGHT?

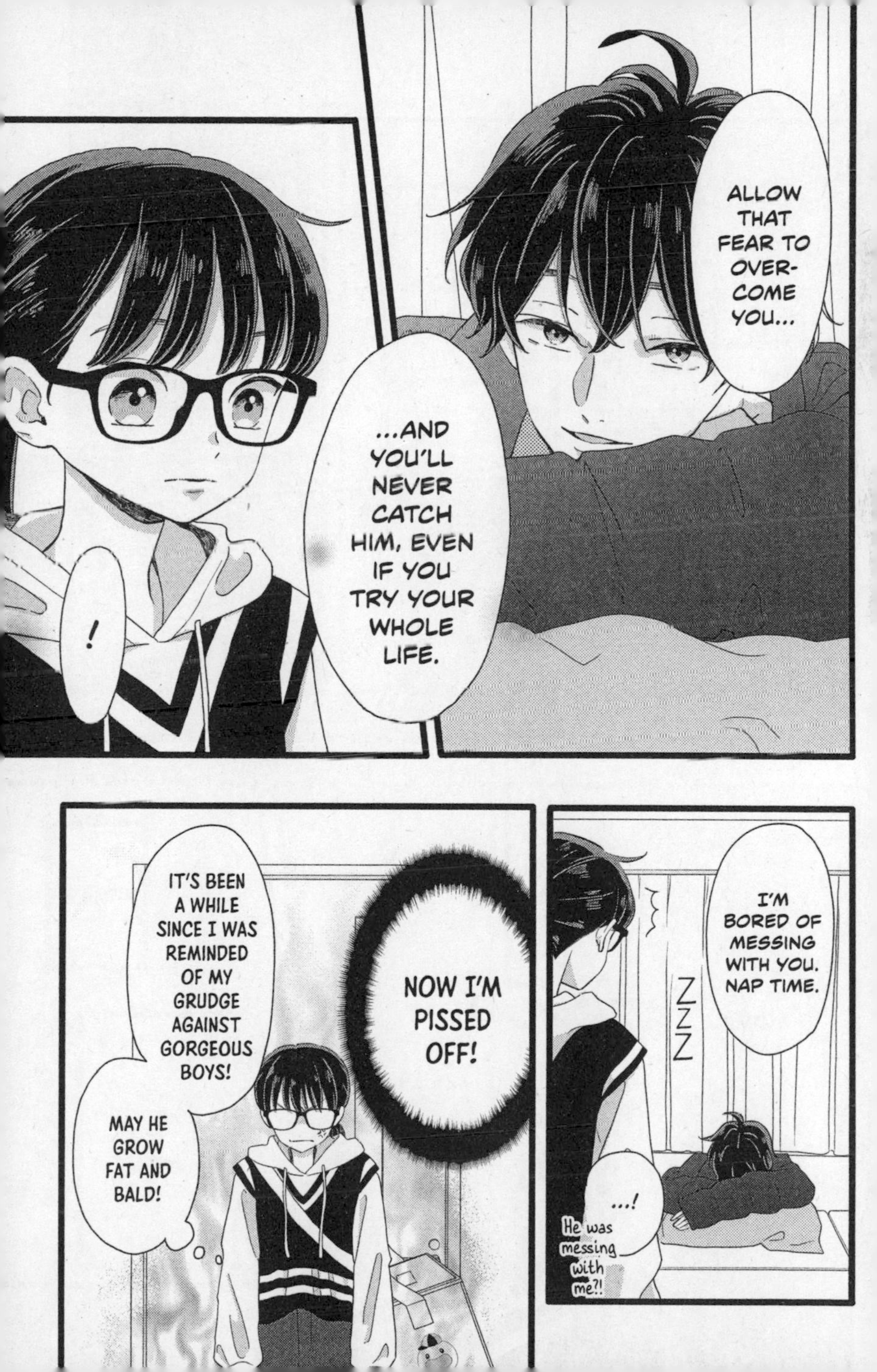
ALLOW THAT FEAR TO OVER-COME YOU...
...AND YOU'LL NEVER CATCH HIM, EVEN IF YOU TRY YOUR WHOLE LIFE.
!
I'M BORED OF MESSING WITH YOU. NAP TIME.
ZZZ
...!
He was messing with me?!
NOW I'M PISSED OFF!
IT'S BEEN A WHILE SINCE I WAS REMINDED OF MY GRUDGE AGAINST GORGEOUS BOYS!
MAY HE GROW FAT AND BALD!

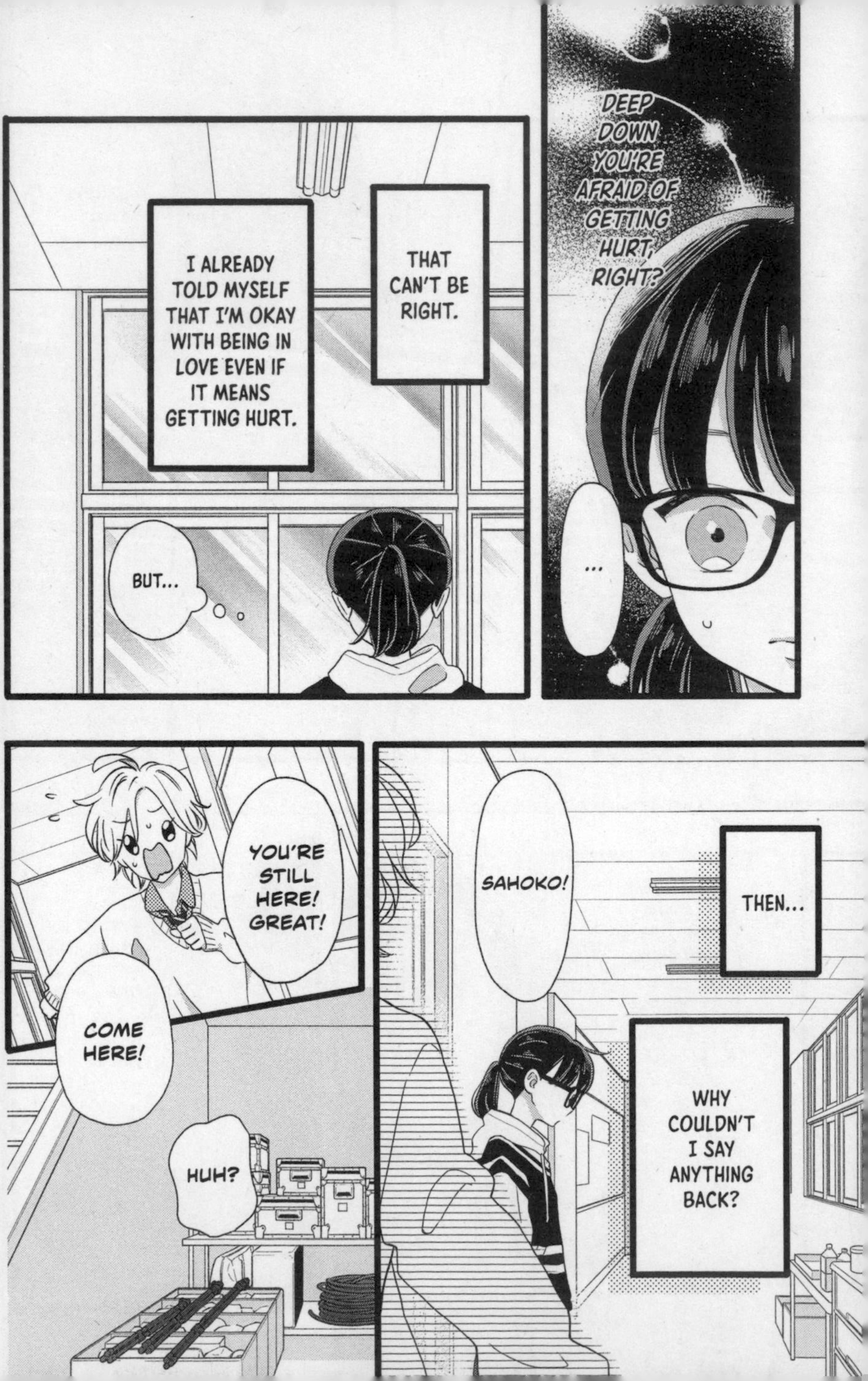
DEEP DOWN YOU'RE AFRAID OF GETTING HURT, RIGHT?
...
THAT CAN'T BE RIGHT.
I ALREADY TOLD MYSELF THAT I'M OKAY WITH BEING IN LOVE EVEN IF IT MEANS GETTING HURT.
BUT...
THEN...
WHY COULDN'T I SAY ANYTHING BACK?
SAHOKO!
YOU'RE STILL HERE! GREAT!
COME HERE!
HUH?

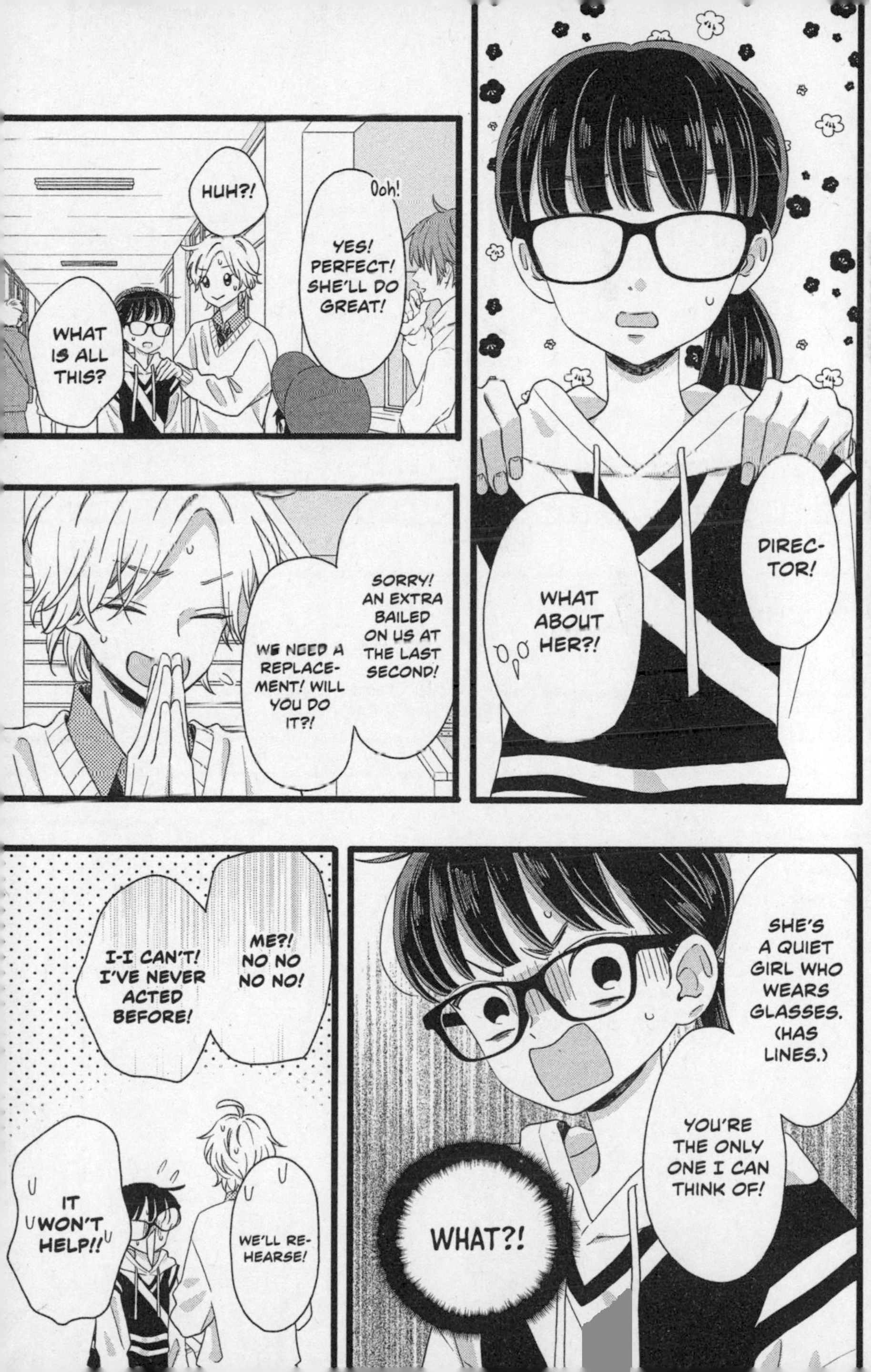
DIRECTOR!
WHAT ABOUT HER?!
Ooh!
YES! PERFECT! SHE'LL DO GREAT!
HUH?!
WHAT IS ALL THIS?
SORRY! AN EXTRA BAILED ON US AT THE LAST SECOND!
WE NEED A REPLACEMENT! WILL YOU DO IT?!
SHE'S A QUIET GIRL WHO WEARS GLASSES. (HAS LINES.)
YOU'RE THE ONLY ONE I CAN THINK OF!
WHAT?!
ME?! NO NO NO NO!
I-I CAN'T! I'VE NEVER ACTED BEFORE!
WE'LL REHEARSE!
IT WON'T HELP!!

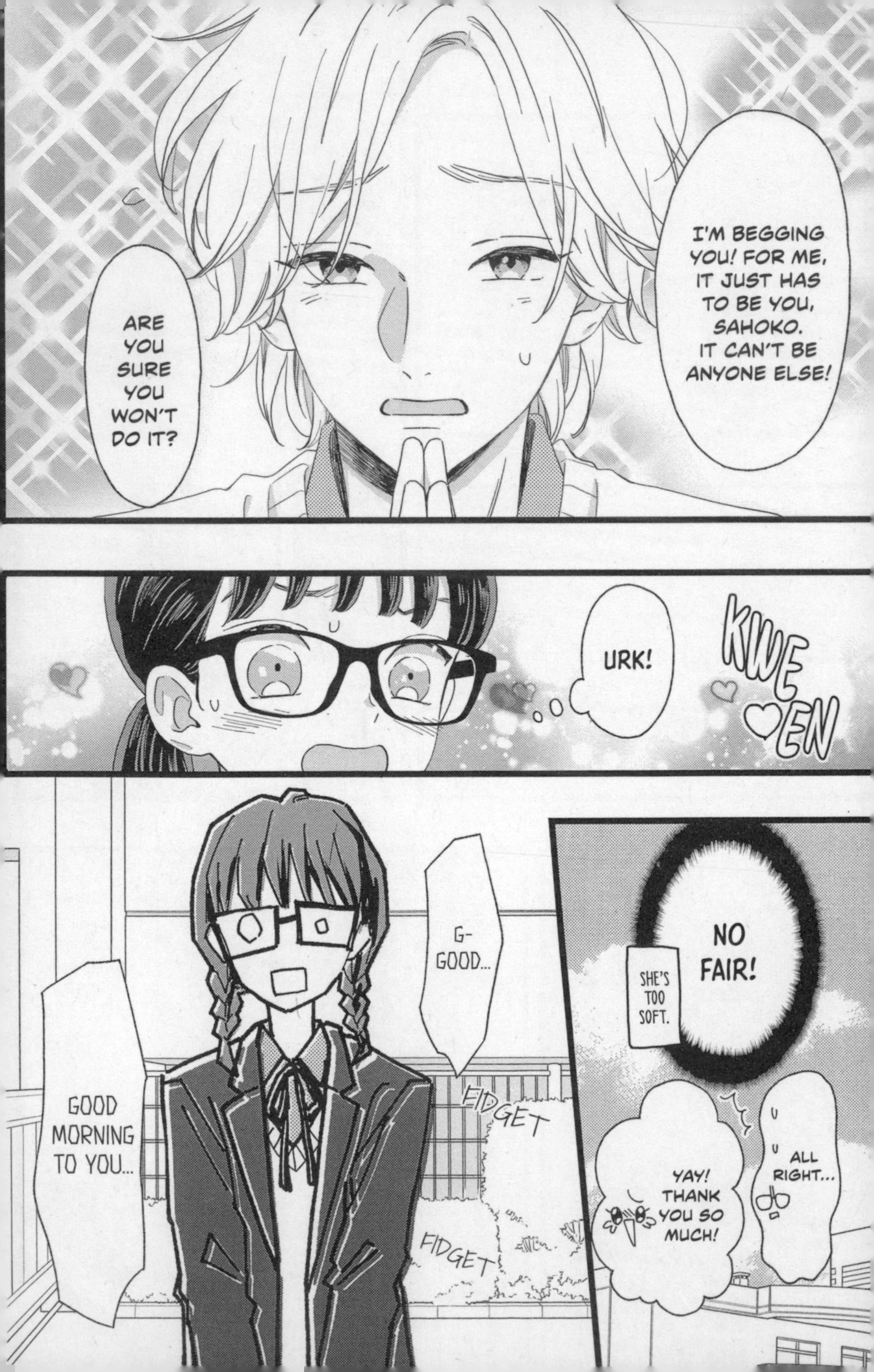
I'M BEGGING YOU! FOR ME, IT JUST HAS TO BE YOU, SAHOKO. IT CAN'T BE ANYONE ELSE!
ARE YOU SURE YOU WON'T DO IT?
KWEEN
URK!
NO FAIR!
SHE'S TOO SOFT.
ALL RIGHT...
YAY! THANK YOU SO MUCH!
G-GOOD...
FIDGET
FIDGET
GOOD MORNING TO YOU...

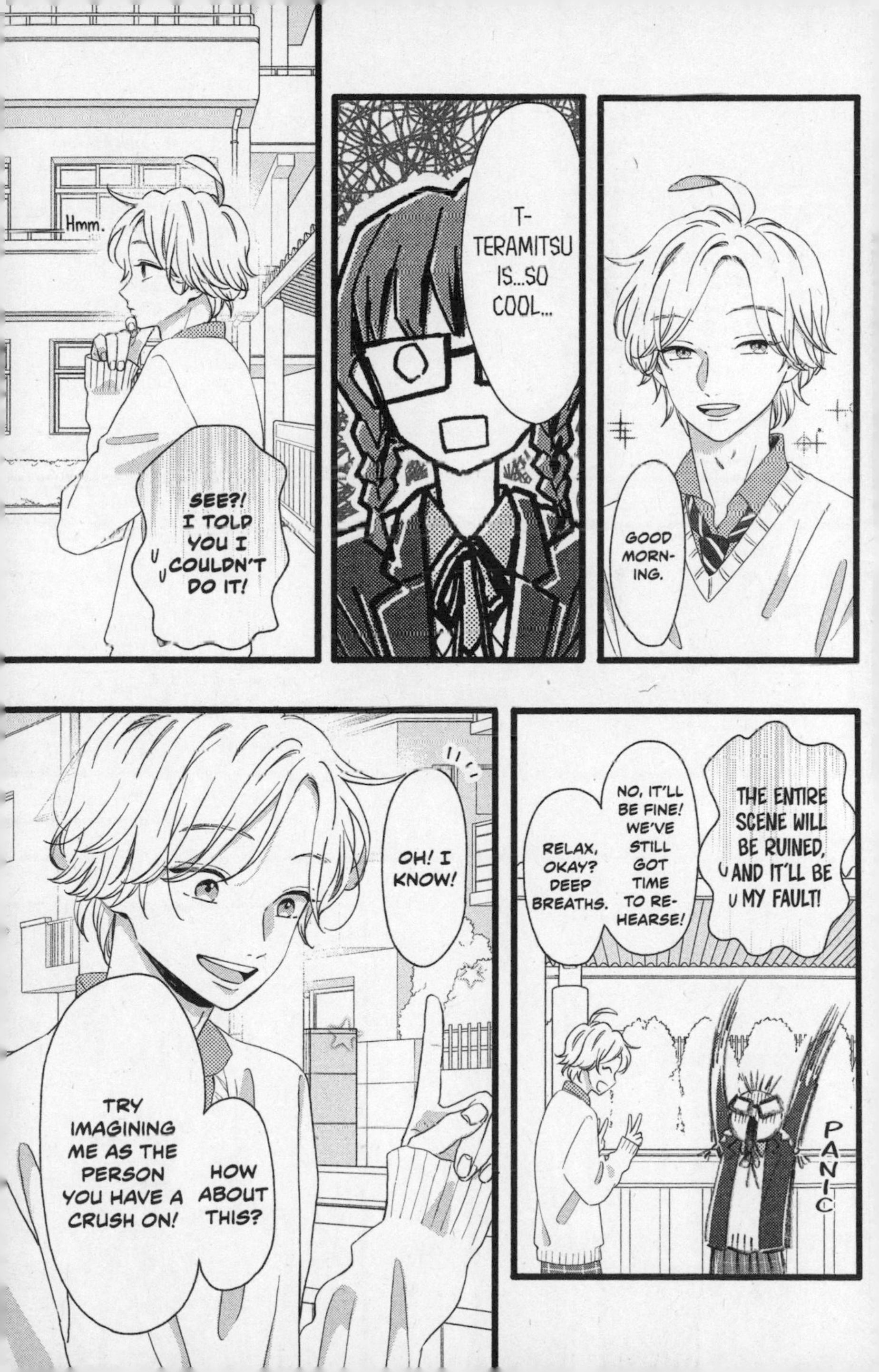
GOOD MORNING.
T-TERAMITSU IS...SO COOL...
Hmm.
SEE?! I TOLD YOU I COULDN'T DO IT!
THE ENTIRE SCENE WILL BE RUINED, AND IT'LL BE MY FAULT!
NO, IT'LL BE FINE! WE'VE STILL GOT TIME TO REHEARSE!
RELAX, OKAY? DEEP BREATHS.
PANIC
OH! I KNOW!
HOW ABOUT THIS?
TRY IMAGINING ME AS THE PERSON YOU HAVE A CRUSH ON!

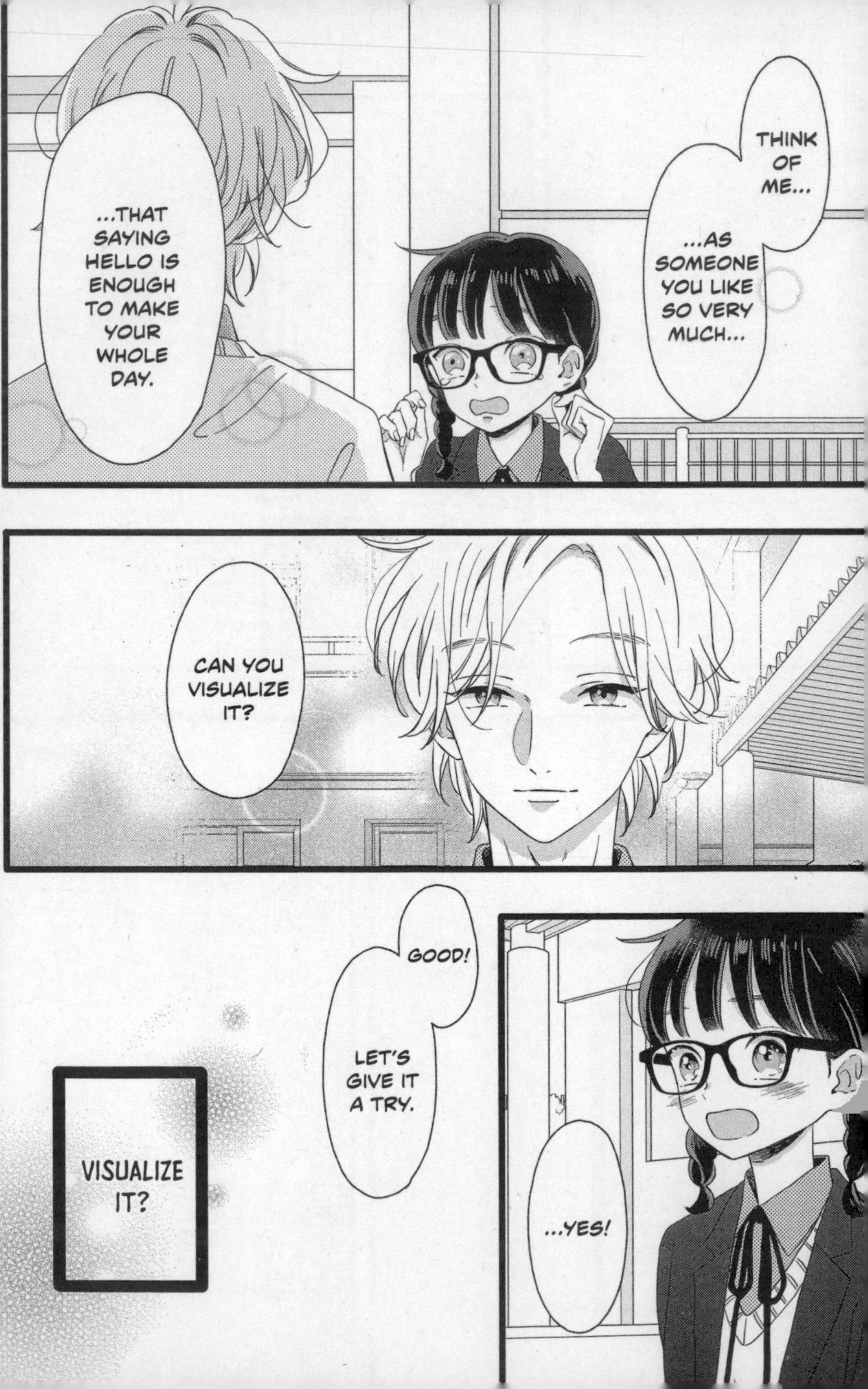
THINK OF ME...
...AS SOMEONE YOU LIKE SO VERY MUCH...
...THAT SAYING HELLO IS ENOUGH TO MAKE YOUR WHOLE DAY.
CAN YOU VISUALIZE IT?
...YES!
GOOD!
LET'S GIVE IT A TRY.
VISUALIZE IT?

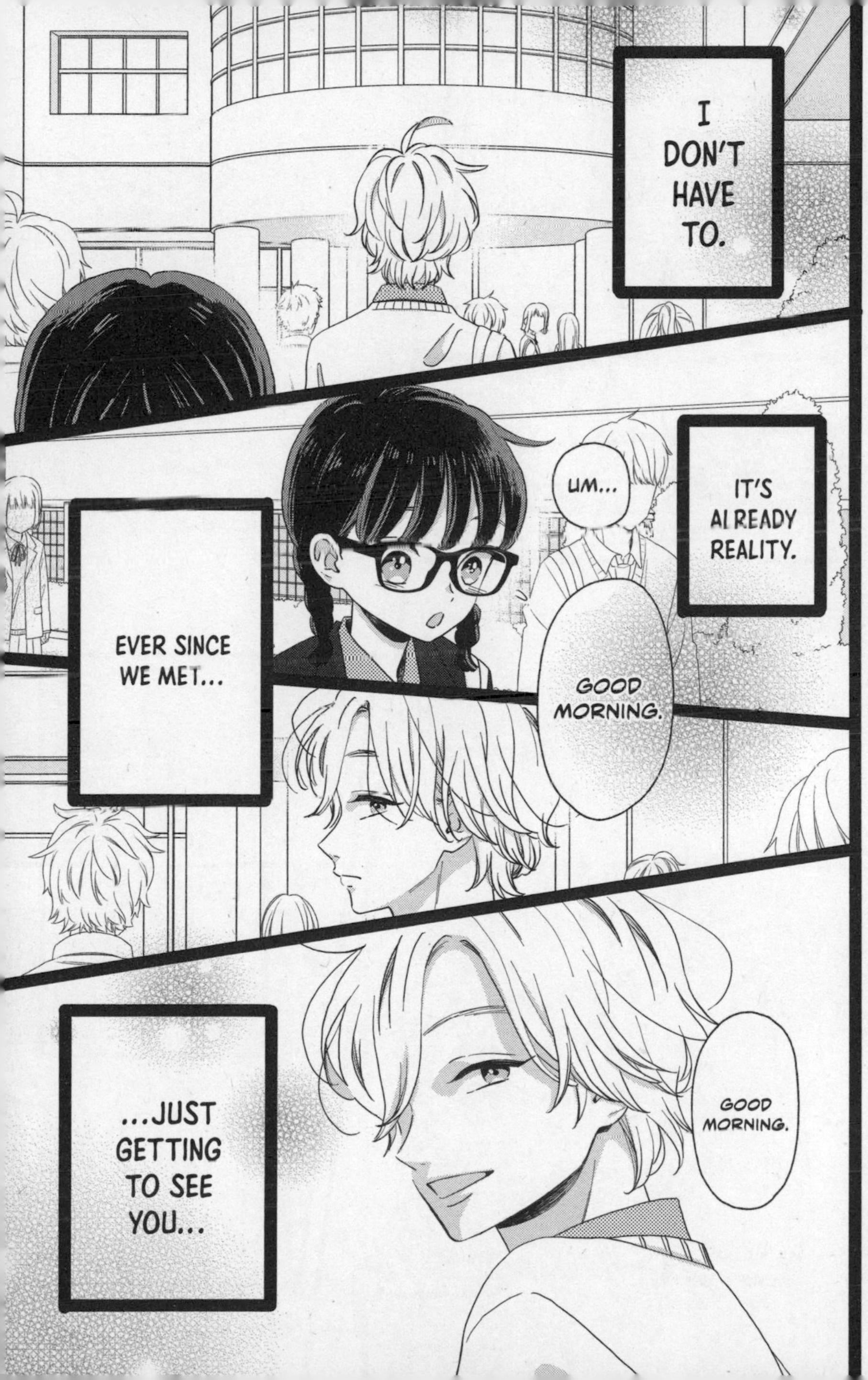
I DON'T HAVE TO.
IT'S ALREADY REALITY.
UM...
EVER SINCE WE MET...
GOOD MORNING.
GOOD MORNING.
...JUST GETTING TO SEE YOU...

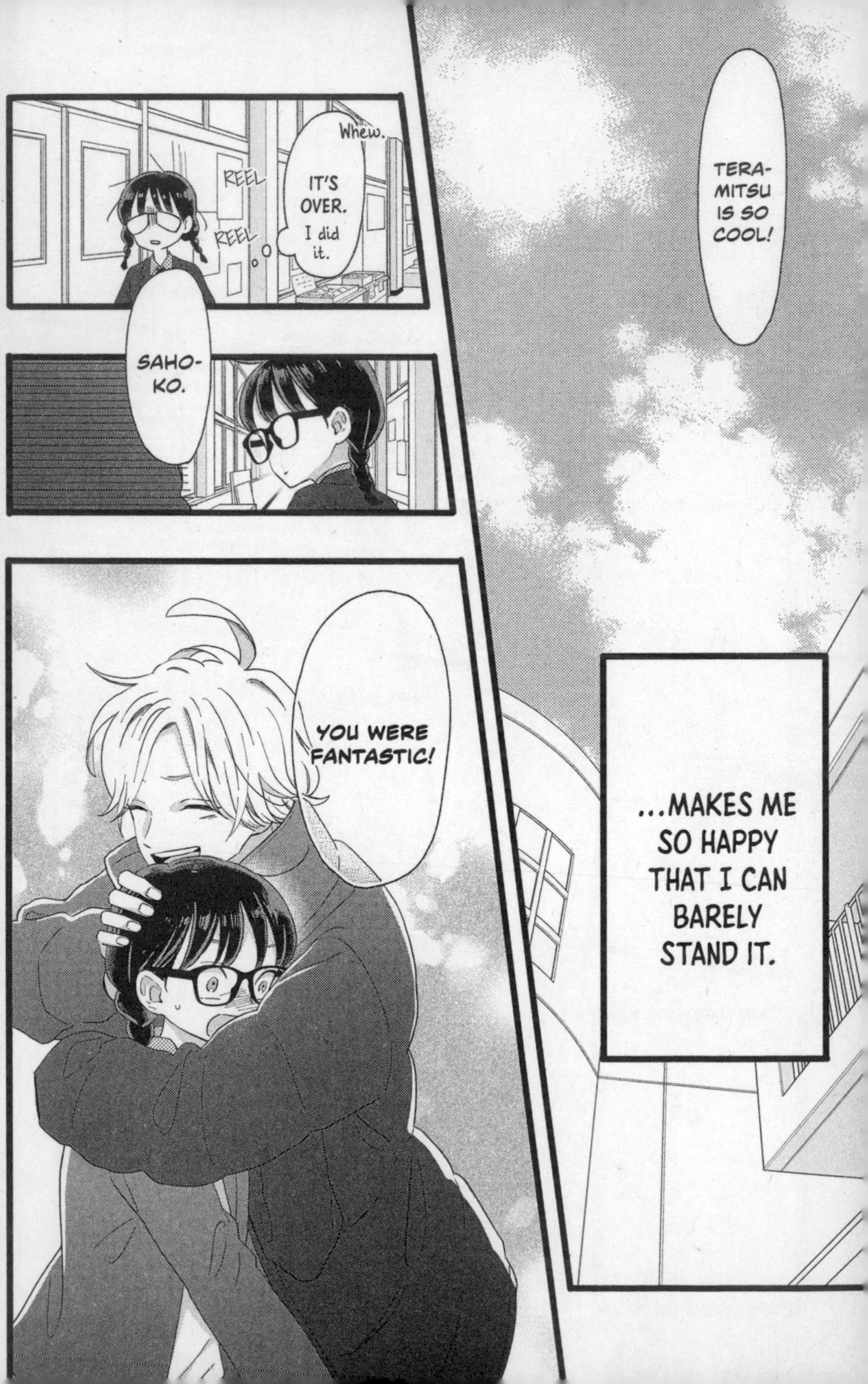
TERA-MITSU IS SO COOL!
...MAKES ME SO HAPPY THAT I CAN BARELY STAND IT.
Whew.
IT'S OVER.
I did it.
REEL
REEL
SAHO-KO.
YOU WERE FANTASTIC!

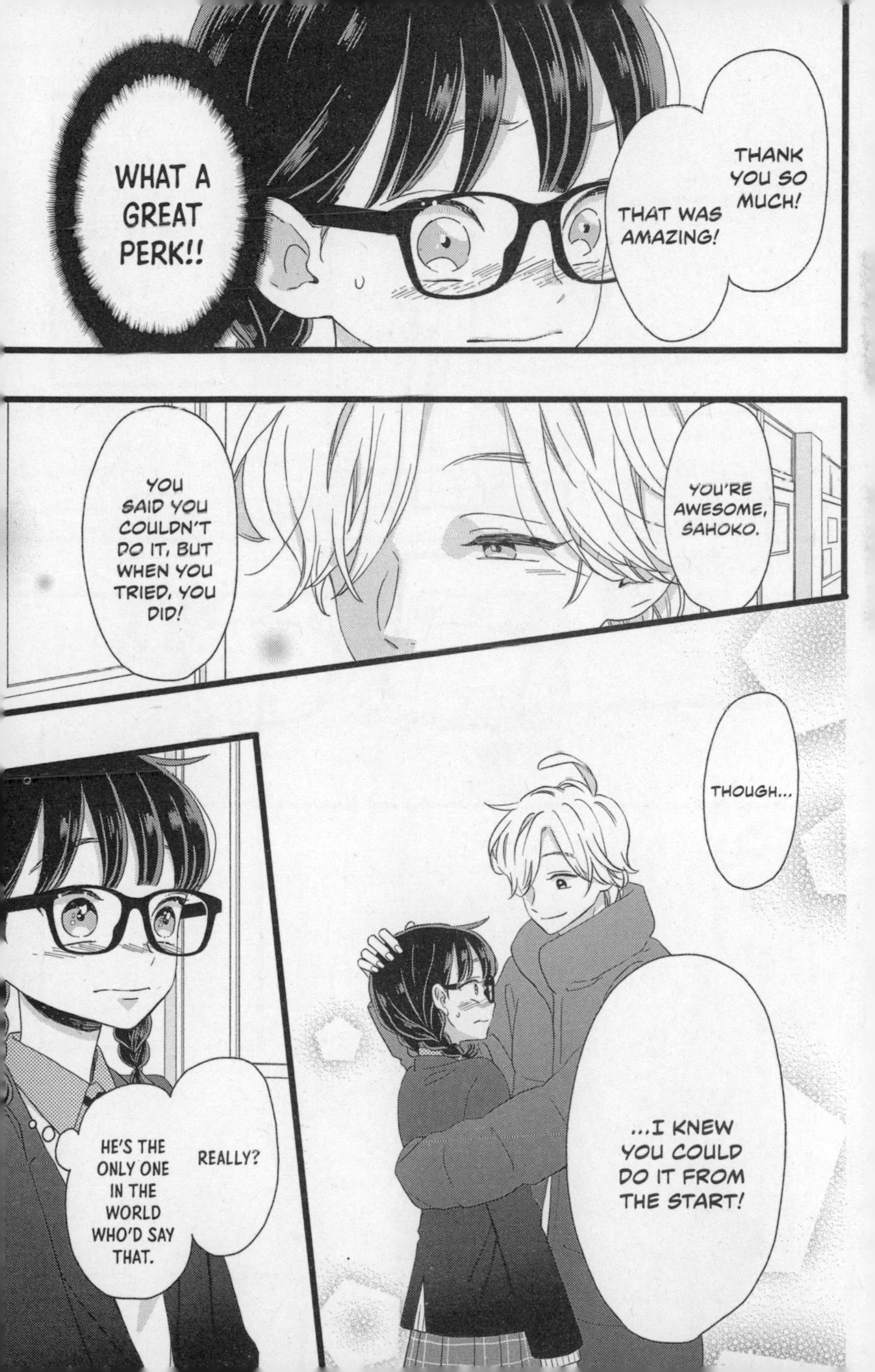
THANK YOU SO MUCH!
THAT WAS AMAZING!
WHAT A GREAT PERK!!
YOU'RE AWESOME, SAHOKO.
YOU SAID YOU COULDN'T DO IT, BUT WHEN YOU TRIED, YOU DID!
THOUGH...
...I KNEW YOU COULD DO IT FROM THE START!
REALLY?
HE'S THE ONLY ONE IN THE WORLD WHO'D SAY THAT.

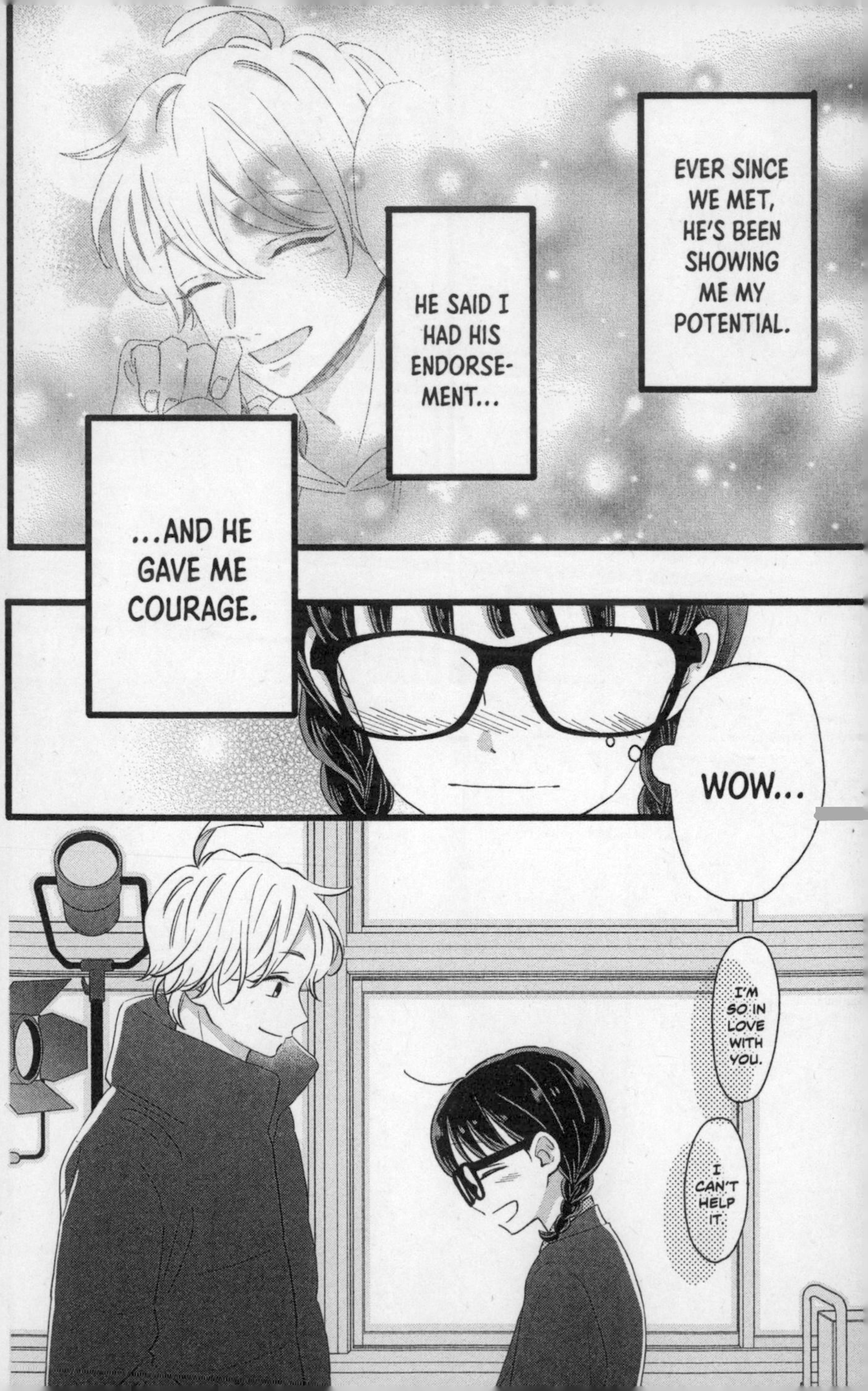
EVER SINCE WE MET, HE'S BEEN SHOWING ME MY POTENTIAL.
HE SAID I HAD HIS ENDORSE-MENT...
...AND HE GAVE ME COURAGE.
WOW...
I'M SO IN LOVE WITH YOU.
I CAN'T HELP IT.

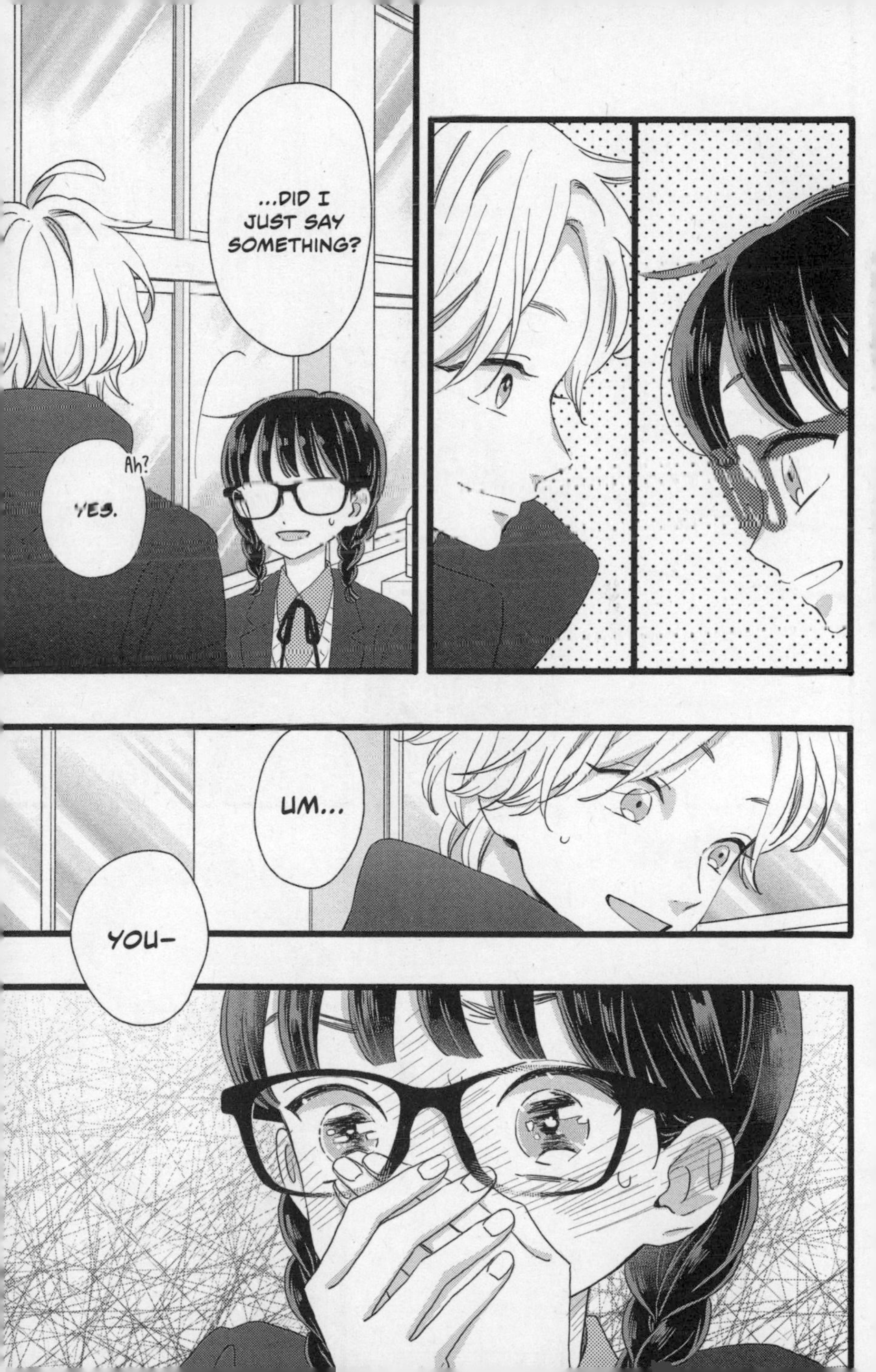
...DID I JUST SAY SOMETHING?
Ah?
YES.
UM...
YOU-

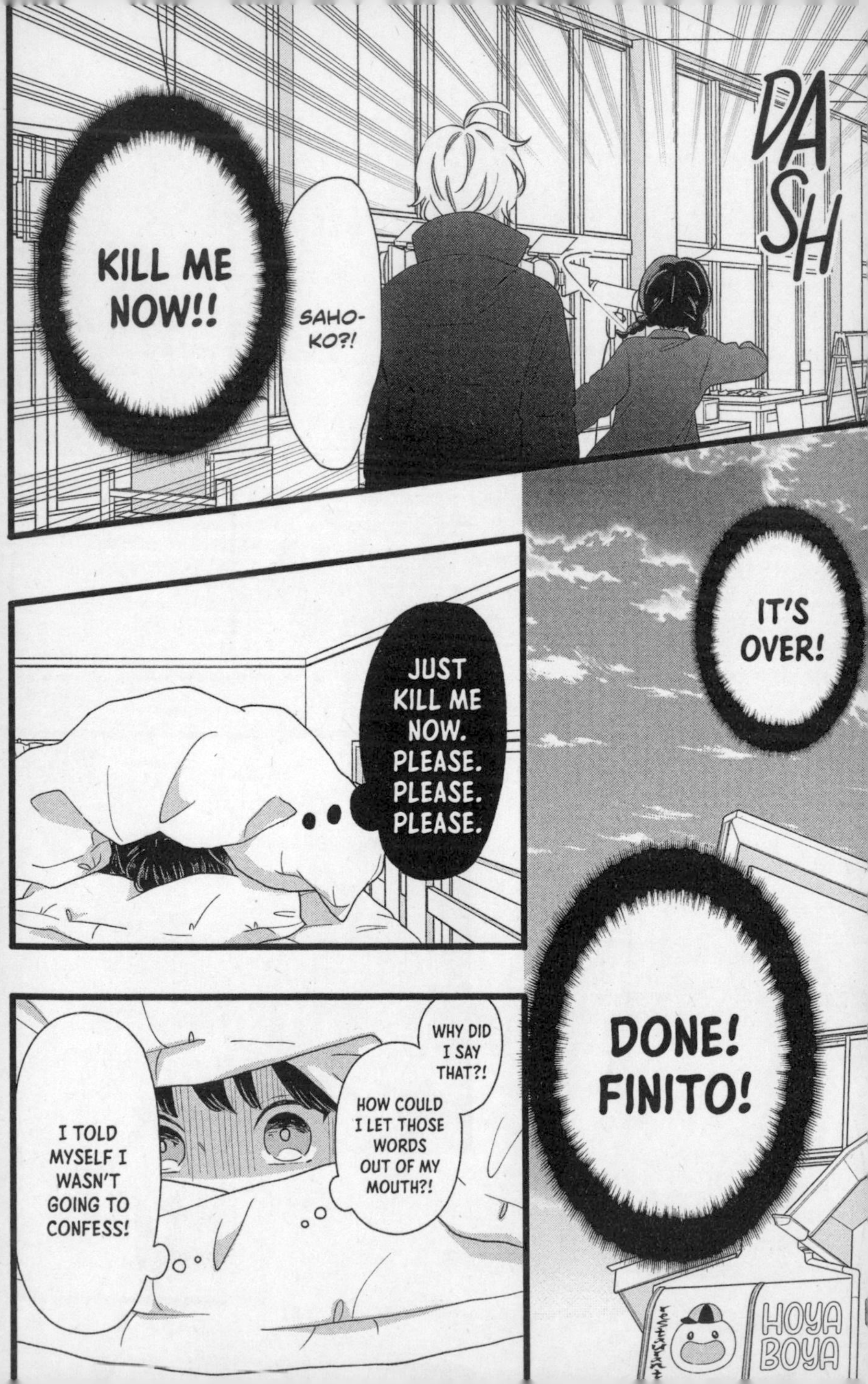
DASH
SAHO-KO?!
KILL ME NOW!!
IT'S OVER!
DONE! FINITO!
HOYA BOYA
JUST KILL ME NOW. PLEASE. PLEASE. PLEASE.
WHY DID I SAY THAT?!
HOW COULD I LET THOSE WORDS OUT OF MY MOUTH?!
I TOLD MYSELF I WASN'T GOING TO CONFESS!

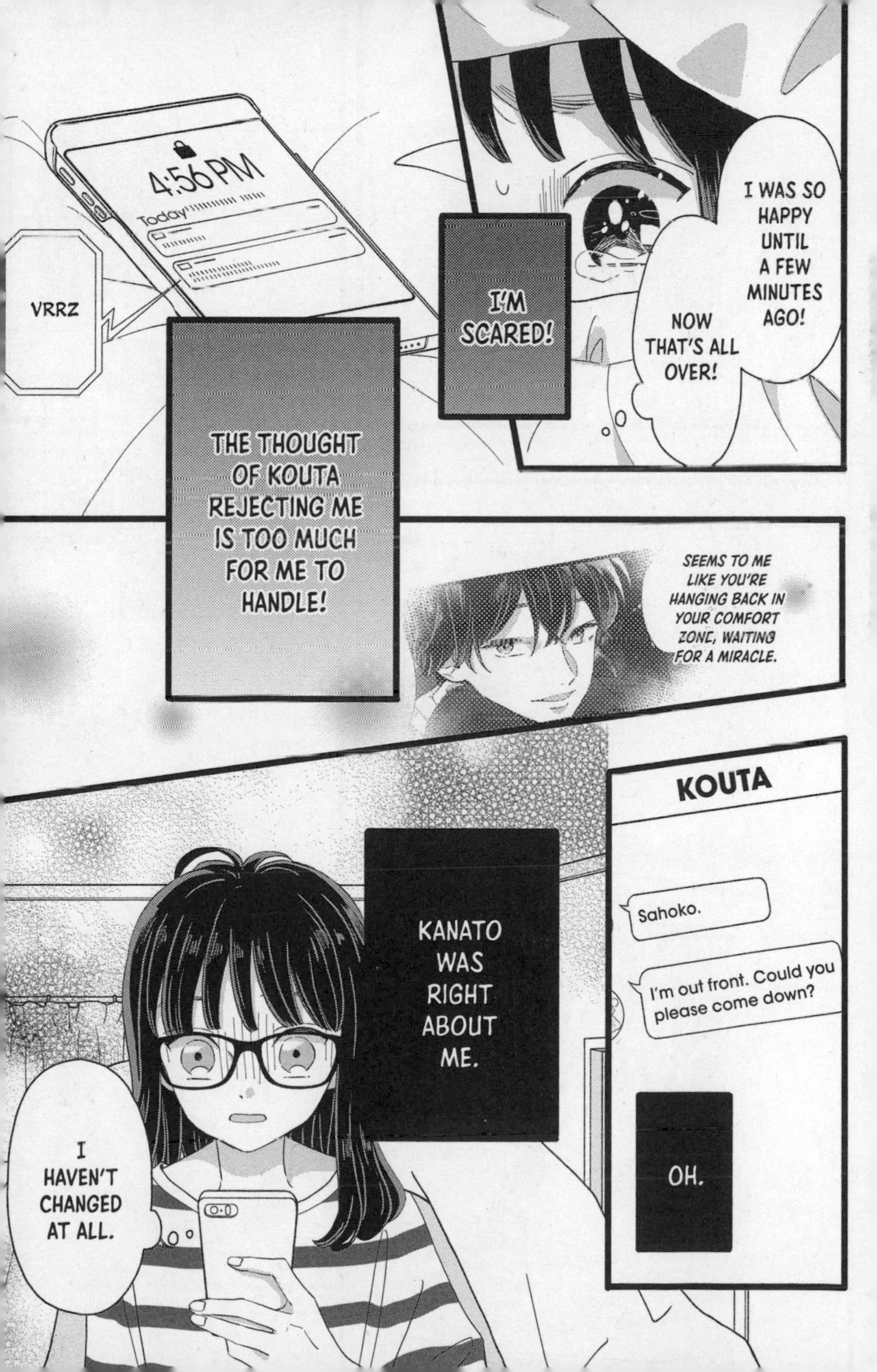

I WAS SO HAPPY UNTIL A FEW MINUTES AGO!
NOW THAT'S ALL OVER!
I'M SCARED!
4:56PM
Today
VRRZ
THE THOUGHT OF KOUTA REJECTING ME IS TOO MUCH FOR ME TO HANDLE!
SEEMS TO ME LIKE YOU'RE HANGING BACK IN YOUR COMFORT ZONE, WAITING FOR A MIRACLE.
KOUTA
Sahoko.
I'm out front. Could you please come down?
OH.
KANATO WAS RIGHT ABOUT ME.
I HAVEN'T CHANGED AT ALL.

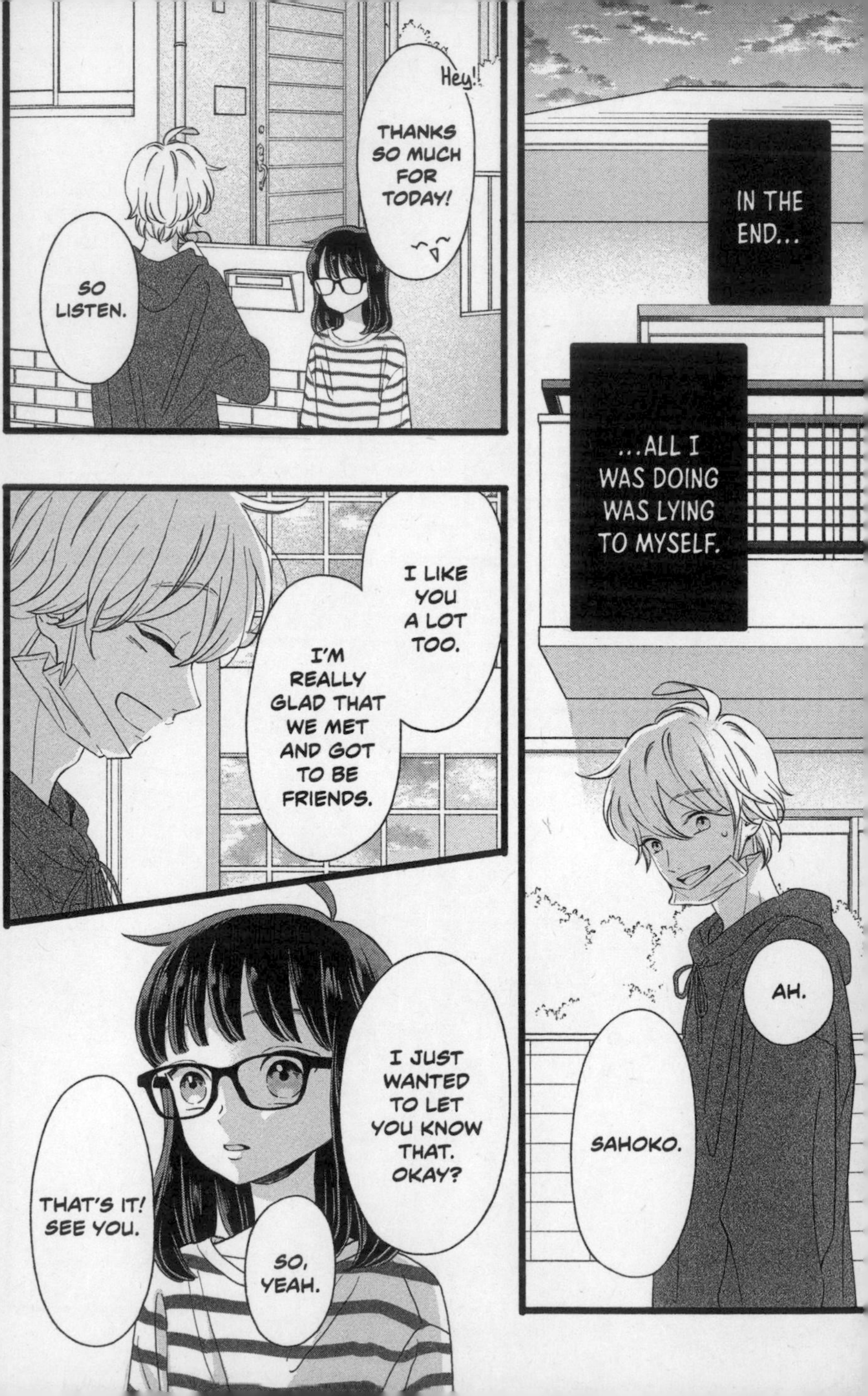
IN THE END...
...ALL I WAS DOING WAS LYING TO MYSELF.
AH.
SAHOKO.
Hey!
THANKS SO MUCH FOR TODAY!
SO LISTEN.
I LIKE YOU A LOT TOO.
I'M REALLY GLAD THAT WE MET AND GOT TO BE FRIENDS.
I JUST WANTED TO LET YOU KNOW THAT. OKAY?
SO, YEAH.
THAT'S IT! SEE YOU.

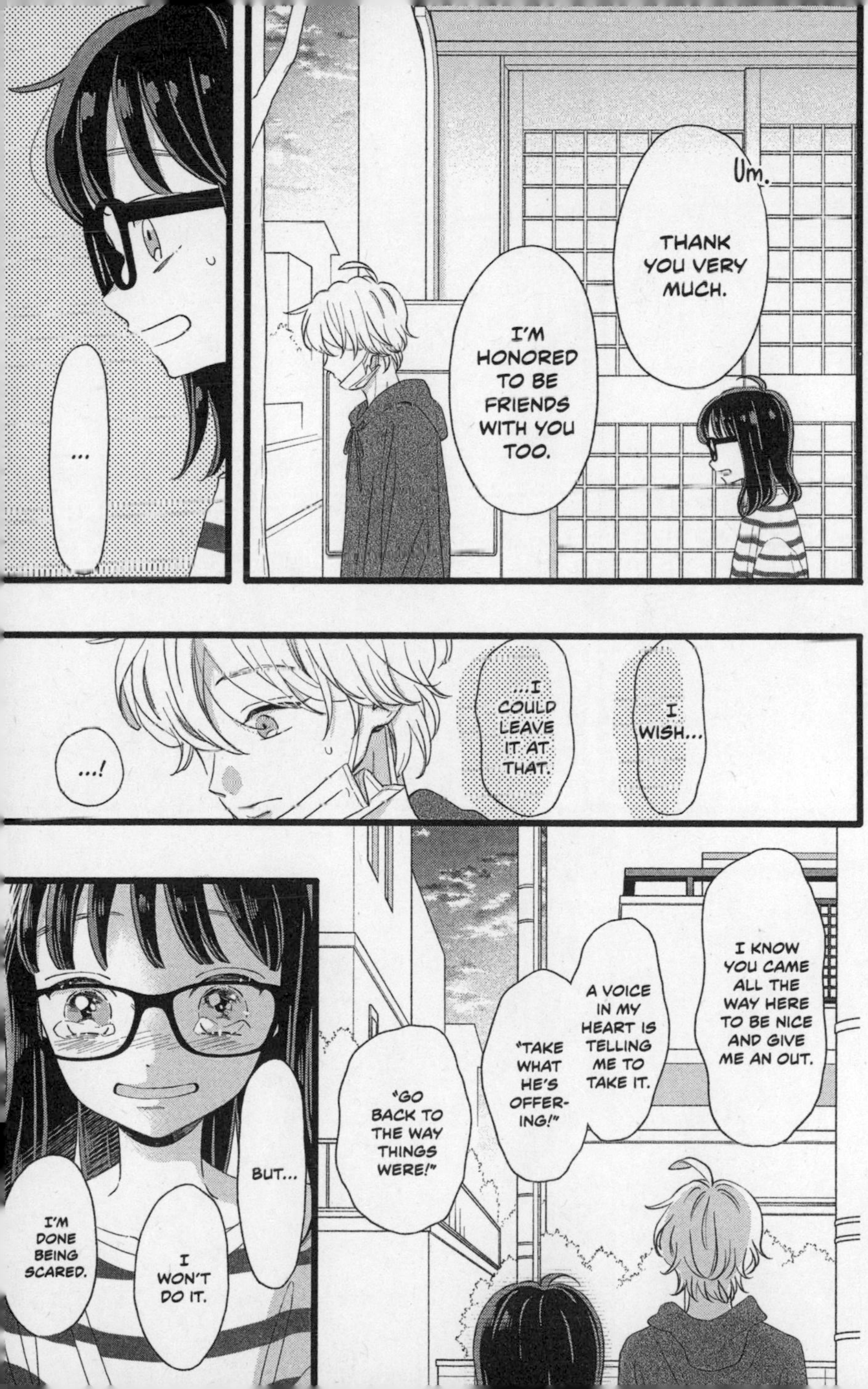
Um.
THANK YOU VERY MUCH.
I'M HONORED TO BE FRIENDS WITH YOU TOO.
...
I WISH...
...I COULD LEAVE IT AT THAT.
...!
I KNOW YOU CAME ALL THE WAY HERE TO BE NICE AND GIVE ME AN OUT.
A VOICE IN MY HEART IS TELLING ME TO TAKE IT.
"TAKE WHAT HE'S OFFER-ING!"
"GO BACK TO THE WAY THINGS WERE!"
BUT...
I WON'T DO IT.
I'M DONE BEING SCARED.

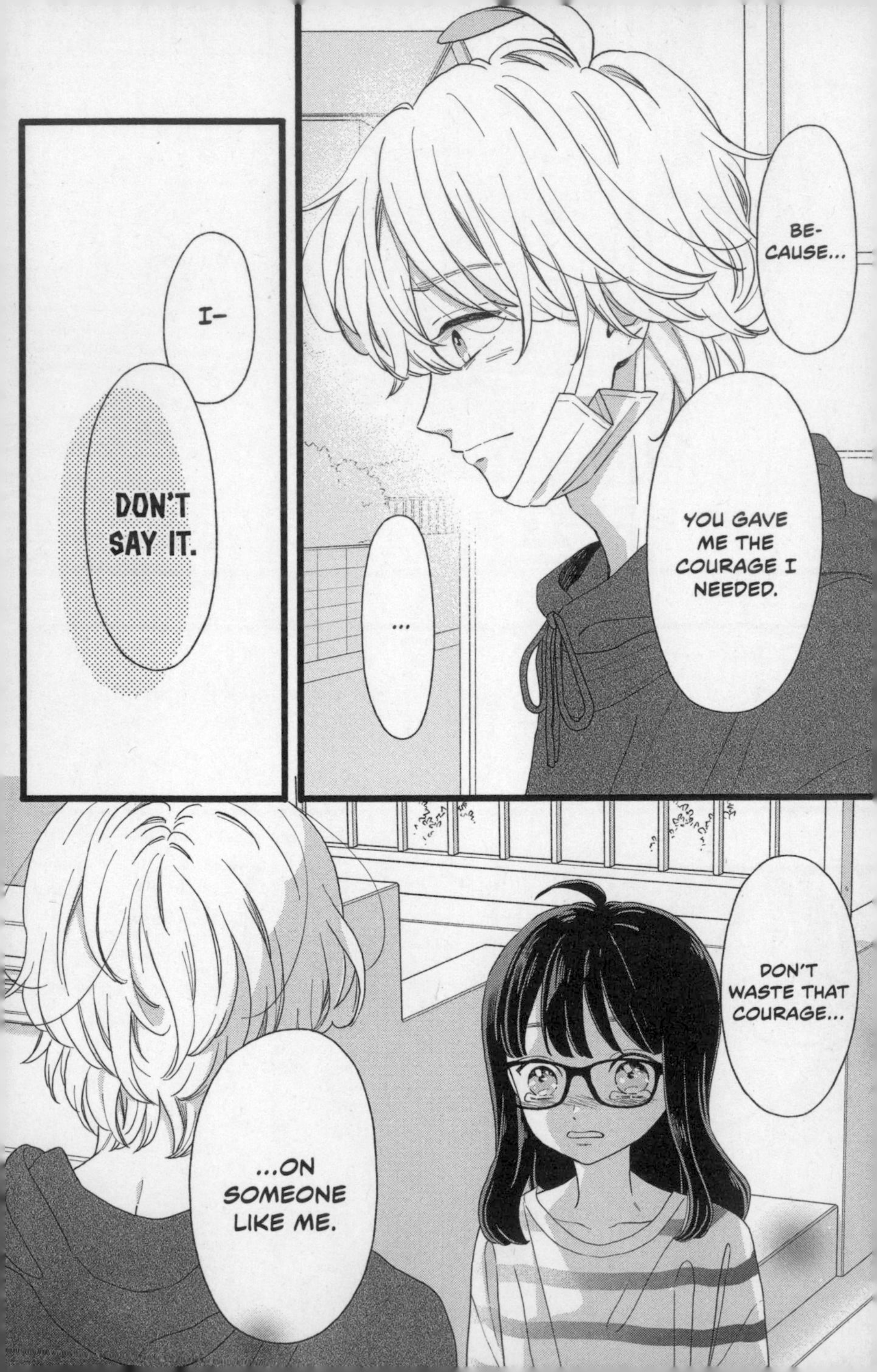
BE-CAUSE...
YOU GAVE ME THE COURAGE I NEEDED.
...
I-
DON'T SAY IT.
DON'T WASTE THAT COURAGE...
...ON SOMEONE LIKE ME.

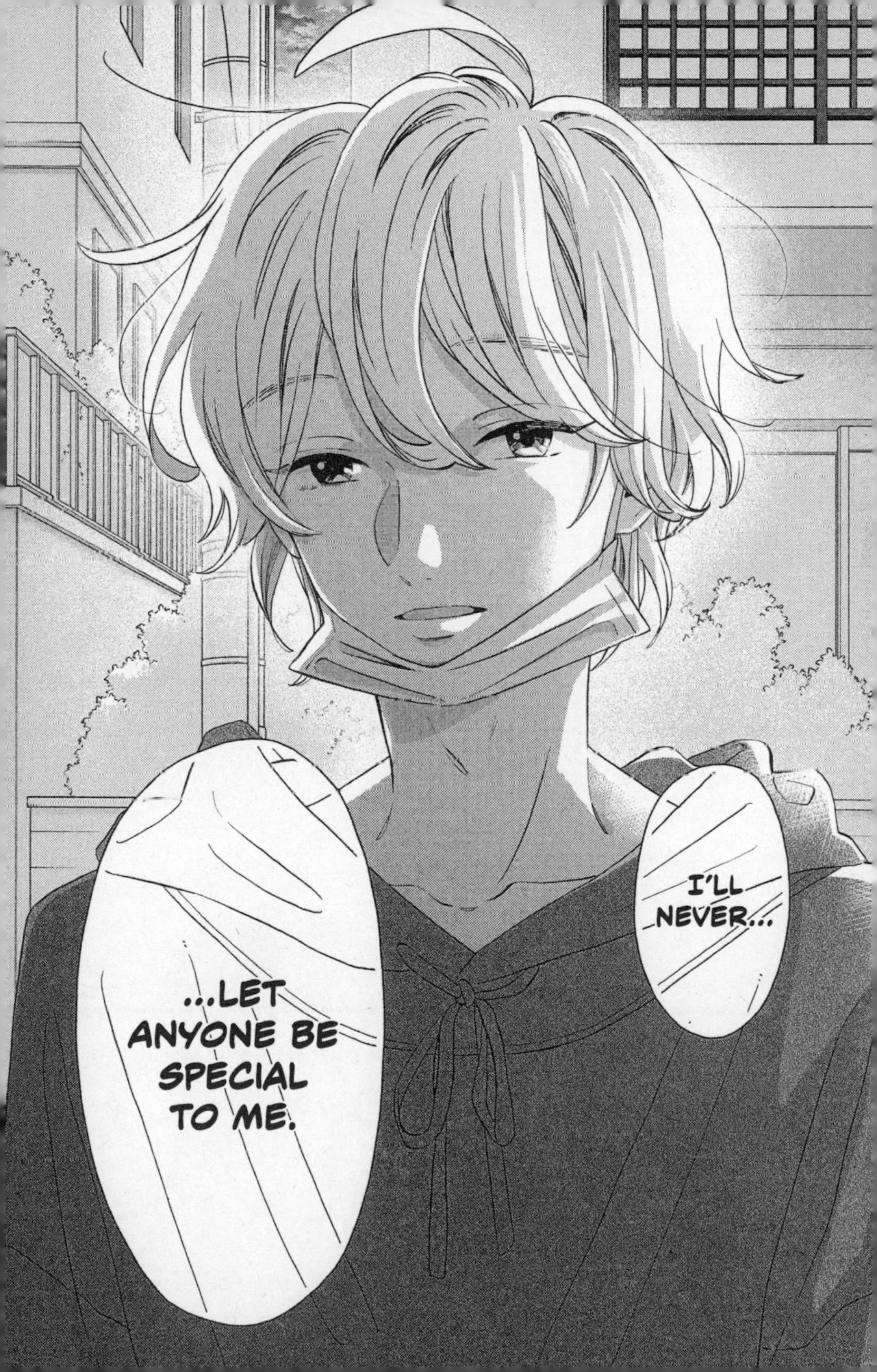
I'LL NEVER...
...LET ANYONE BE SPECIAL TO ME.

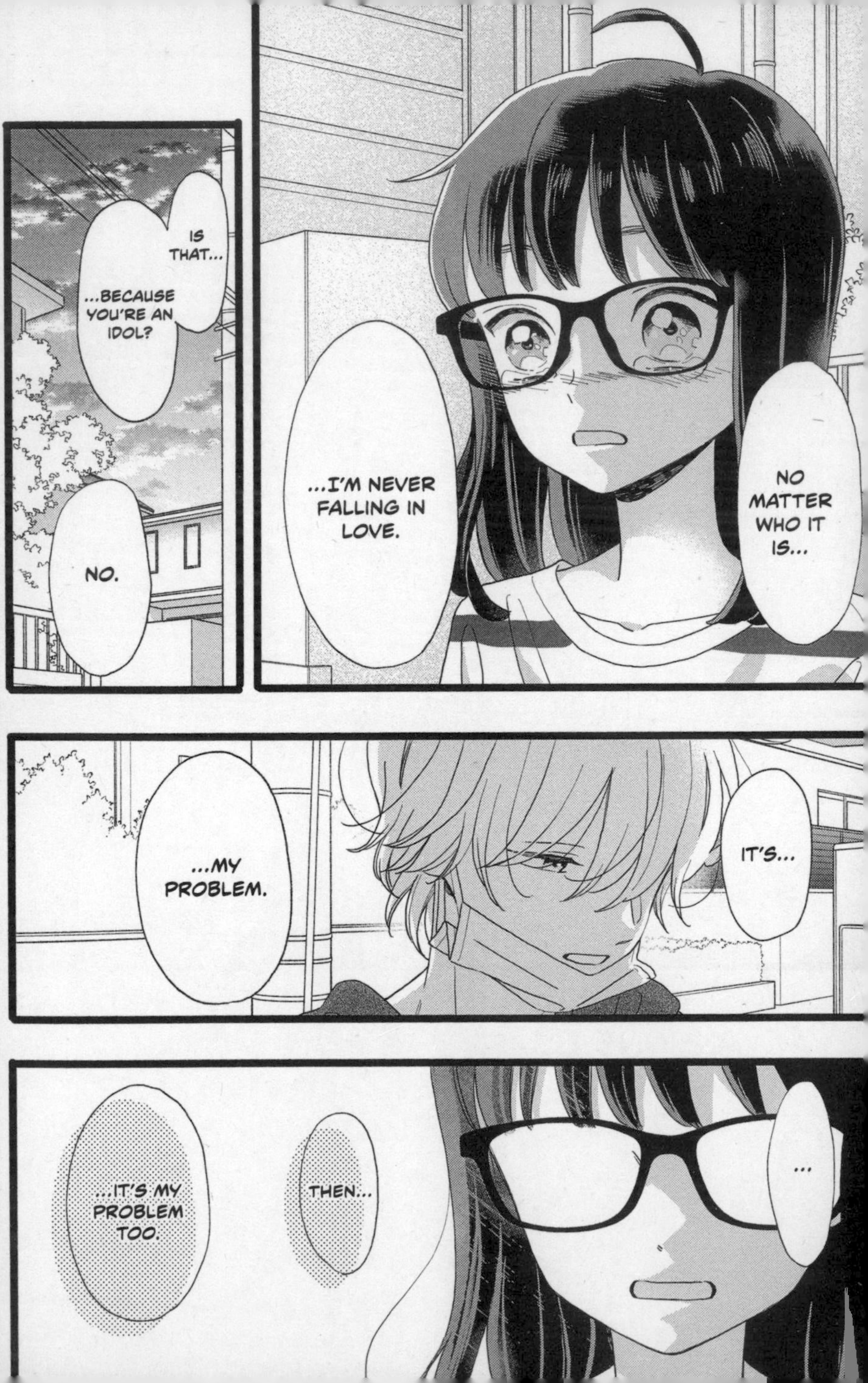
NO MATTER WHO IT IS...
...I'M NEVER FALLING IN LOVE.
IS THAT...
...BECAUSE YOU'RE AN IDOL?
NO.
IT'S...
...MY PROBLEM.
...
THEN...
...IT'S MY PROBLEM TOO.

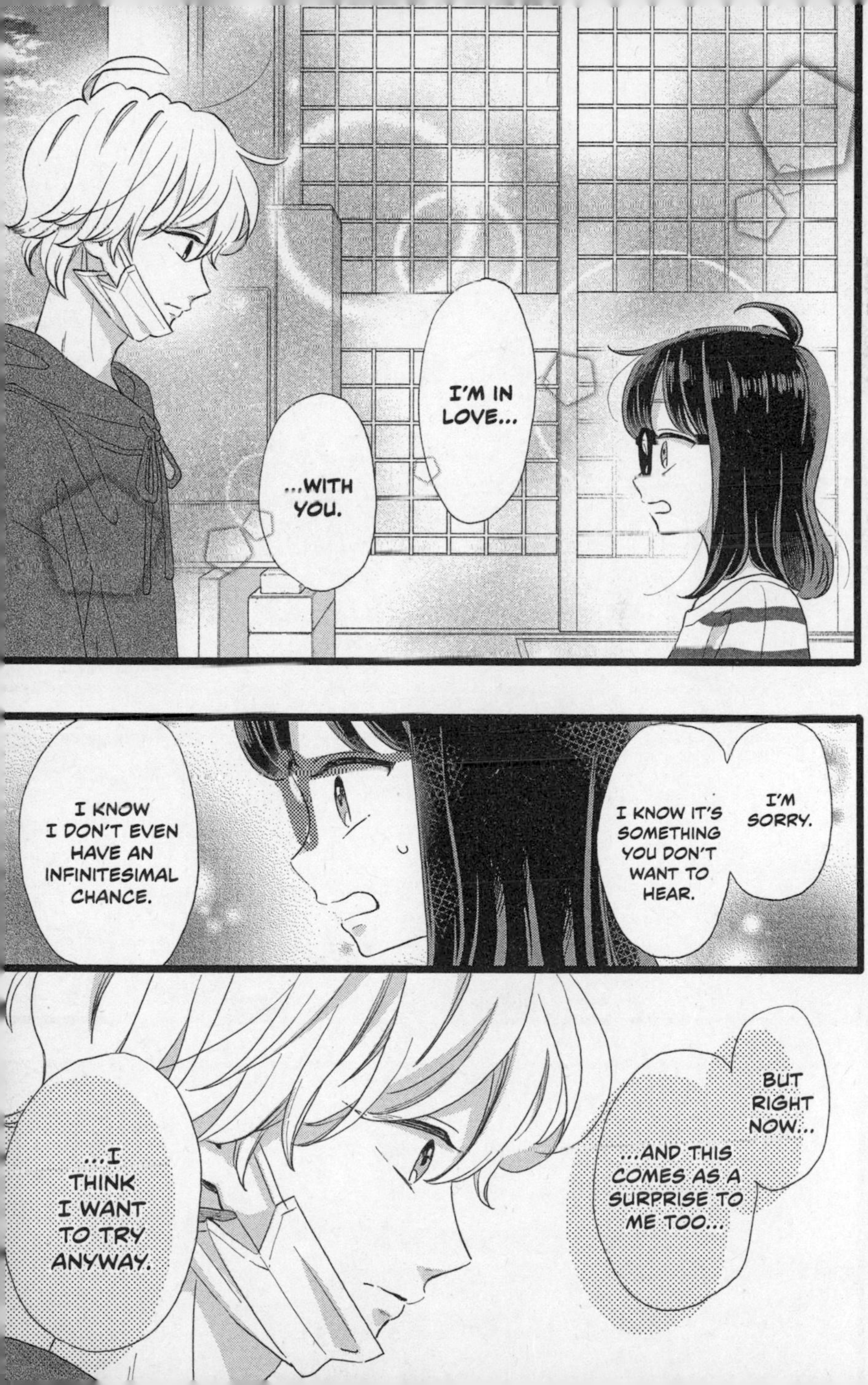
I'M IN LOVE...
...WITH YOU.
I'M SORRY.
I KNOW IT'S SOMETHING YOU DON'T WANT TO HEAR.
I KNOW I DON'T EVEN HAVE AN INFINITESIMAL CHANCE.
BUT RIGHT NOW...
...AND THIS COMES AS A SURPRISE TO ME TOO...
...I THINK I WANT TO TRY ANYWAY.

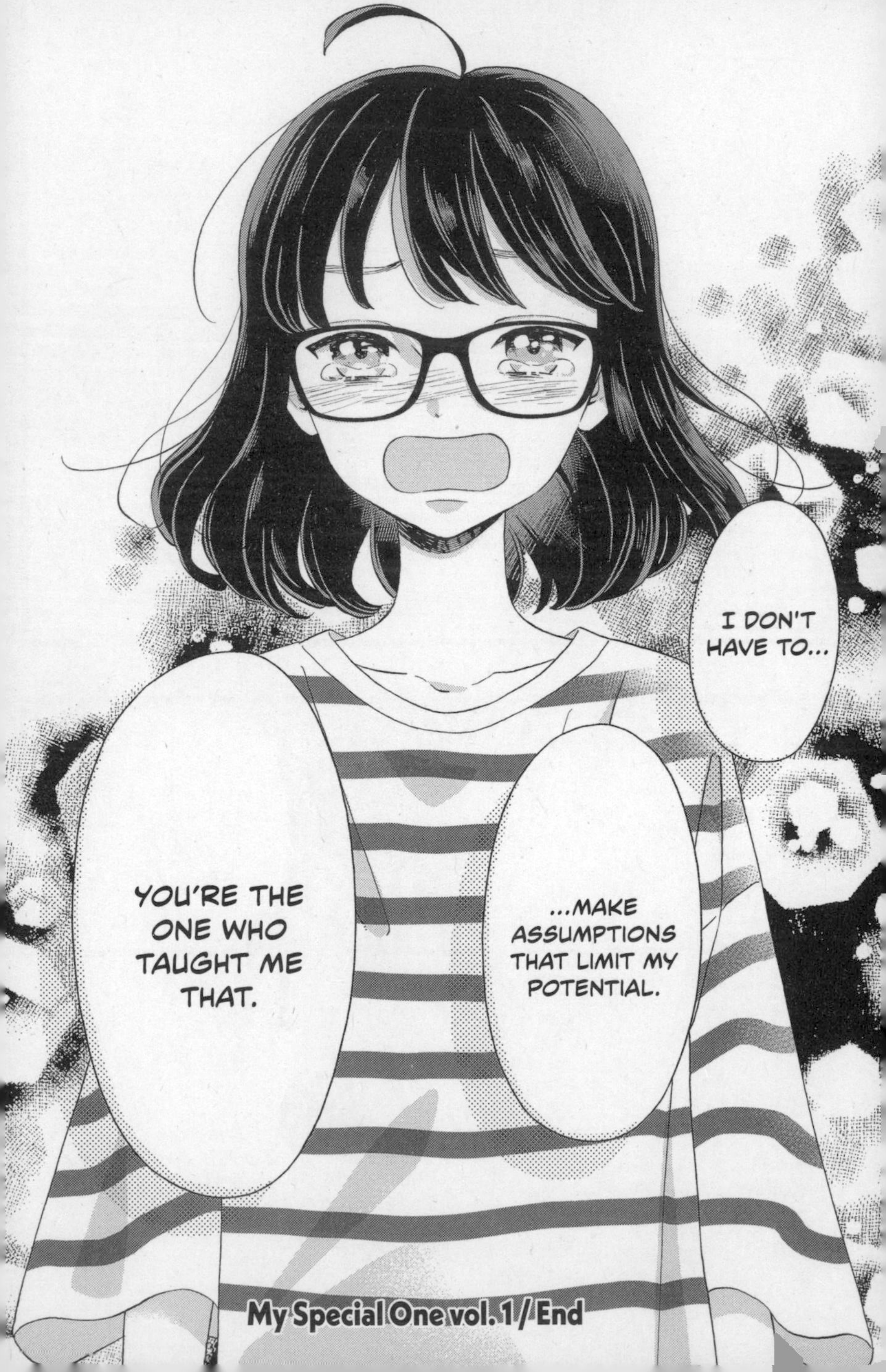
I DON'T HAVE TO...
...MAKE ASSUMPTIONS THAT LIMIT MY POTENTIAL.
YOU'RE THE ONE WHO TAUGHT ME THAT.
My Special One vol. 1 / End

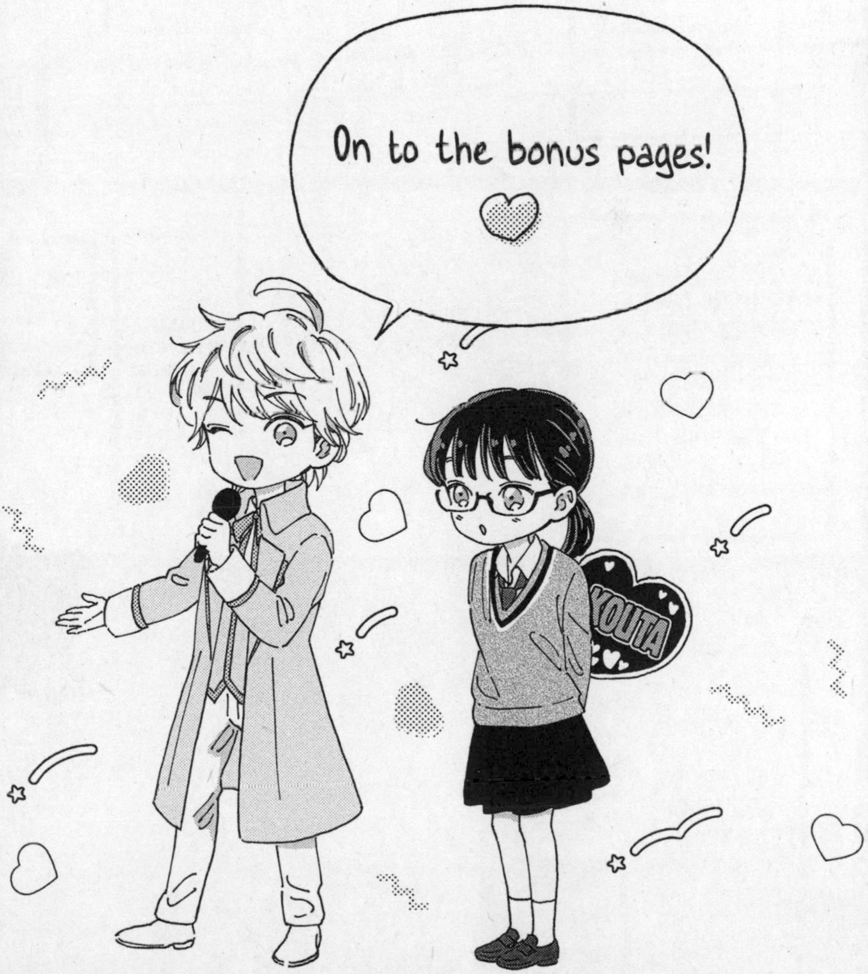
On to the bonus pages!
KOUTA

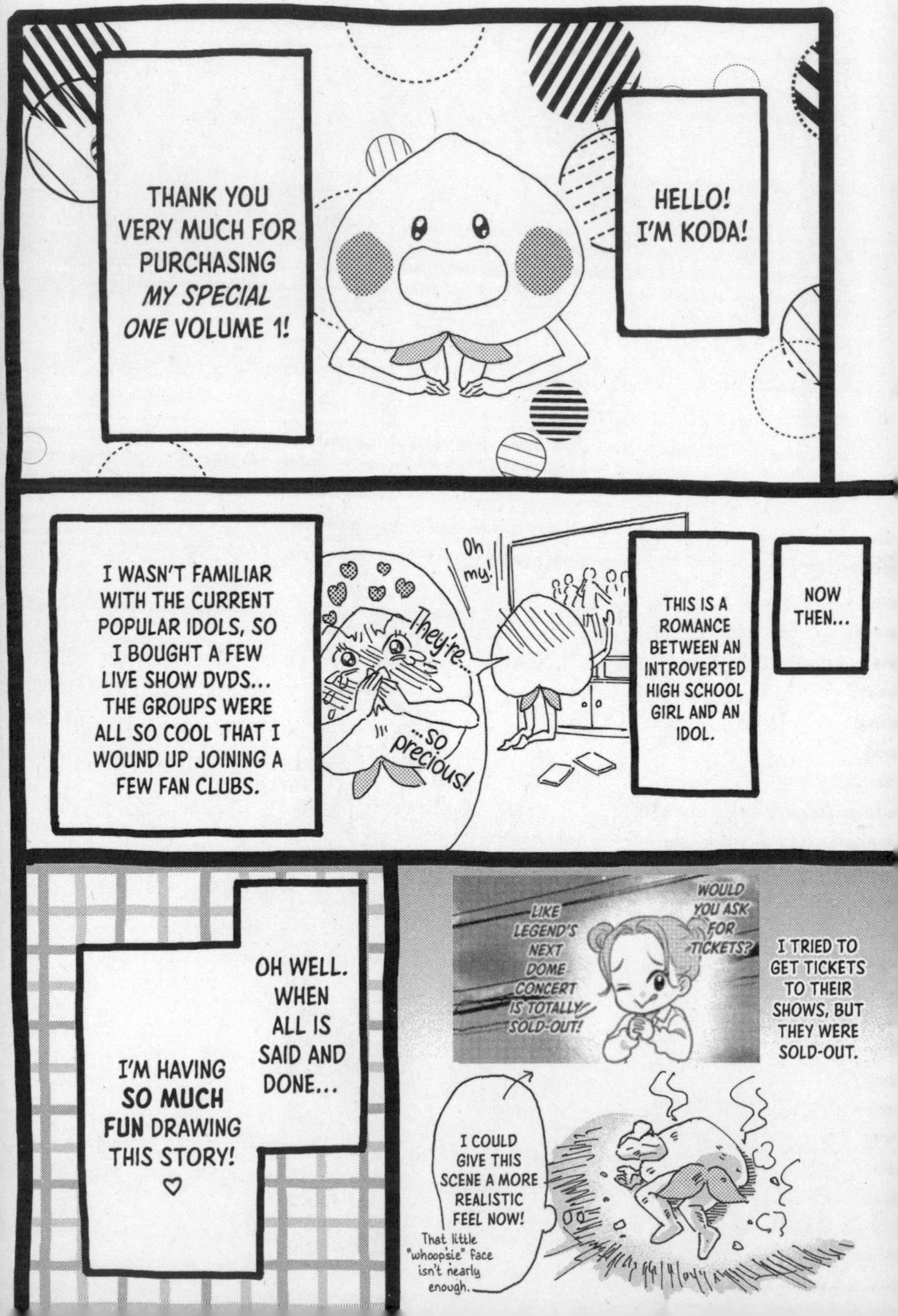
HELLO! I'M KODA!
THANK YOU VERY MUCH FOR PURCHASING MY SPECIAL ONE VOLUME 1!
NOW THEN...
THIS IS A ROMANCE BETWEEN AN INTROVERTED HIGH SCHOOL GIRL AND AN IDOL.
Oh my!
They're...
...so precious!
I WASN'T FAMILIAR WITH THE CURRENT POPULAR IDOLS, SO I BOUGHT A FEW LIVE SHOW DVDS... THE GROUPS WERE ALL SO COOL THAT I WOUND UP JOINING A FEW FAN CLUBS.
I TRIED TO GET TICKETS TO THEIR SHOWS, BUT THEY WERE SOLD-OUT.
WOULD YOU ASK FOR TICKETS?
LIKE LEGEND'S NEXT DOME CONCERT IS TOTALLY SOLD-OUT!
I COULD GIVE THIS SCENE A MORE REALISTIC FEEL NOW!
That little "whoopsie" face isn't nearly enough.
OH WELL. WHEN ALL IS SAID AND DONE...
I'M HAVING SO MUCH FUN DRAWING THIS STORY! ♡

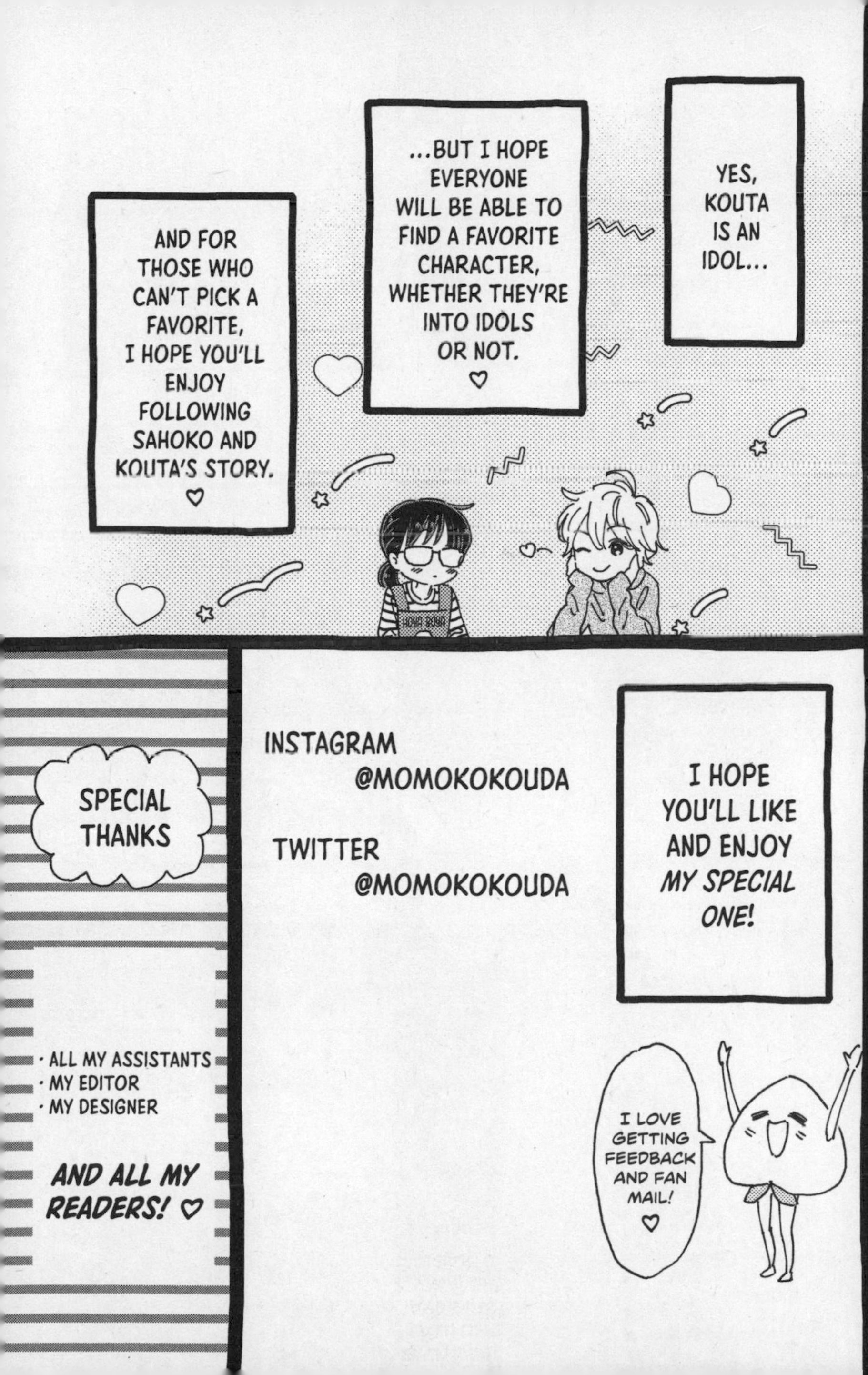
YES, KOUTA IS AN IDOL...
...BUT I HOPE EVERYONE WILL BE ABLE TO FIND A FAVORITE CHARACTER, WHETHER THEY'RE INTO IDOLS OR NOT. ♡
AND FOR THOSE WHO CAN'T PICK A FAVORITE, I HOPE YOU'LL ENJOY FOLLOWING SAHOKO AND KOUTA'S STORY. ♡
I HOPE YOU'LL LIKE AND ENJOY *MY SPECIAL ONE!*
INSTAGRAM @MOMOKOKOUDA
TWITTER @MOMOKOKOUDA
I LOVE GETTING FEEDBACK AND FAN MAIL! ♡
SPECIAL THANKS
· ALL MY ASSISTANTS
· MY EDITOR
· MY DESIGNER
AND ALL MY READERS! ♡

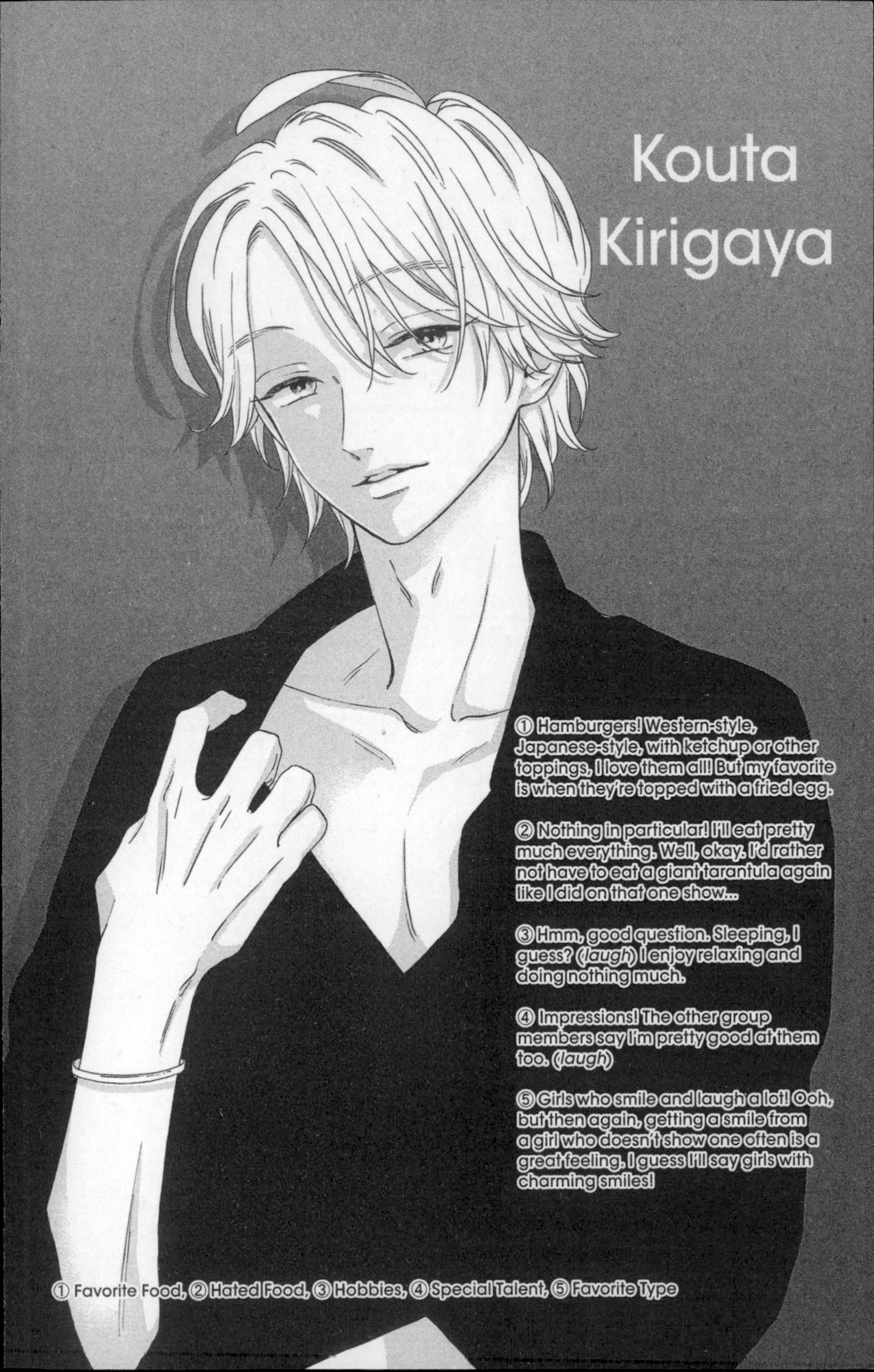

Kouta Kirigaya

① Hamburgers! Western-style, Japanese-style, with ketchup or other toppings, I love them all! But my favorite is when they're topped with a fried egg.

② Nothing in particular! I'll eat pretty much everything. Well, okay. I'd rather not have to eat a giant tarantula again like I did on that one show...

③ Hmm, good question. Sleeping, I guess? (*laugh*) I enjoy relaxing and doing nothing much.

④ Impressions! The other group members say I'm pretty good at them too. (*laugh*)

⑤ Girls who smile and laugh a lot! Ooh, but then again, getting a smile from a girl who doesn't show one often is a great feeling. I guess I'll say girls with charming smiles!

① Favorite Food, ② Hated Food, ③ Hobbies, ④ Special Talent, ⑤ Favorite Type

This is my new series.
I hope you like it! Recently I've
noticed myself starting to plan for a
single future like Sahoko is doing. But
this is something I've done since *No Longer
Heroine*, so let me declare it proudly here:
**May a hot, younger Prince Charming find
me and sweep me off my feet before this
series ends!** (makes matters worse)

MOMOKO KODA

Momoko Koda's birthday is September 24.
She began her professional manga career in 2002 with
"Tamagoyaki" (Rolled Omelet) in *Bessatsu Margaret* magazine.
In 2015, her series *No Longer Heroine* was made into a live-
action film. *My Special One* began serialization in 2019.

Volume 1
SHOJO BEAT EDITION

STORY & ART BY
MOMOKO KODA

TRANSLATION & ADAPTATION
ADRIENNE BECK

TOUCH-UP ART & LETTERING
BRANDON BOVIA

DESIGN
ALICE LEWIS

EDITOR
NANCY THISTLETHWAITE

KIMI GA TOKUBETSU © 2019 by Momoko Koda
All rights reserved.
First published in Japan in 2019 by SHUEISHA Inc., Tokyo.
English translation rights arranged by SHUEISHA Inc.

The stories, characters, and incidents mentioned in this publication are entirely fictional.

Printed in the U.S.A.

Published by VIZ Media, LLC
P.O. Box 77010
San Francisco, CA 94107

10 9 8 7 6 5 4 3 2 1
First printing, February 2023

PARENTAL ADVISORY
MY SPECIAL ONE is rated T+ for Older Teen
and is recommended for ages 16 and up.
This volume may contain suggestive situations.

viz.com

shojobeat.com

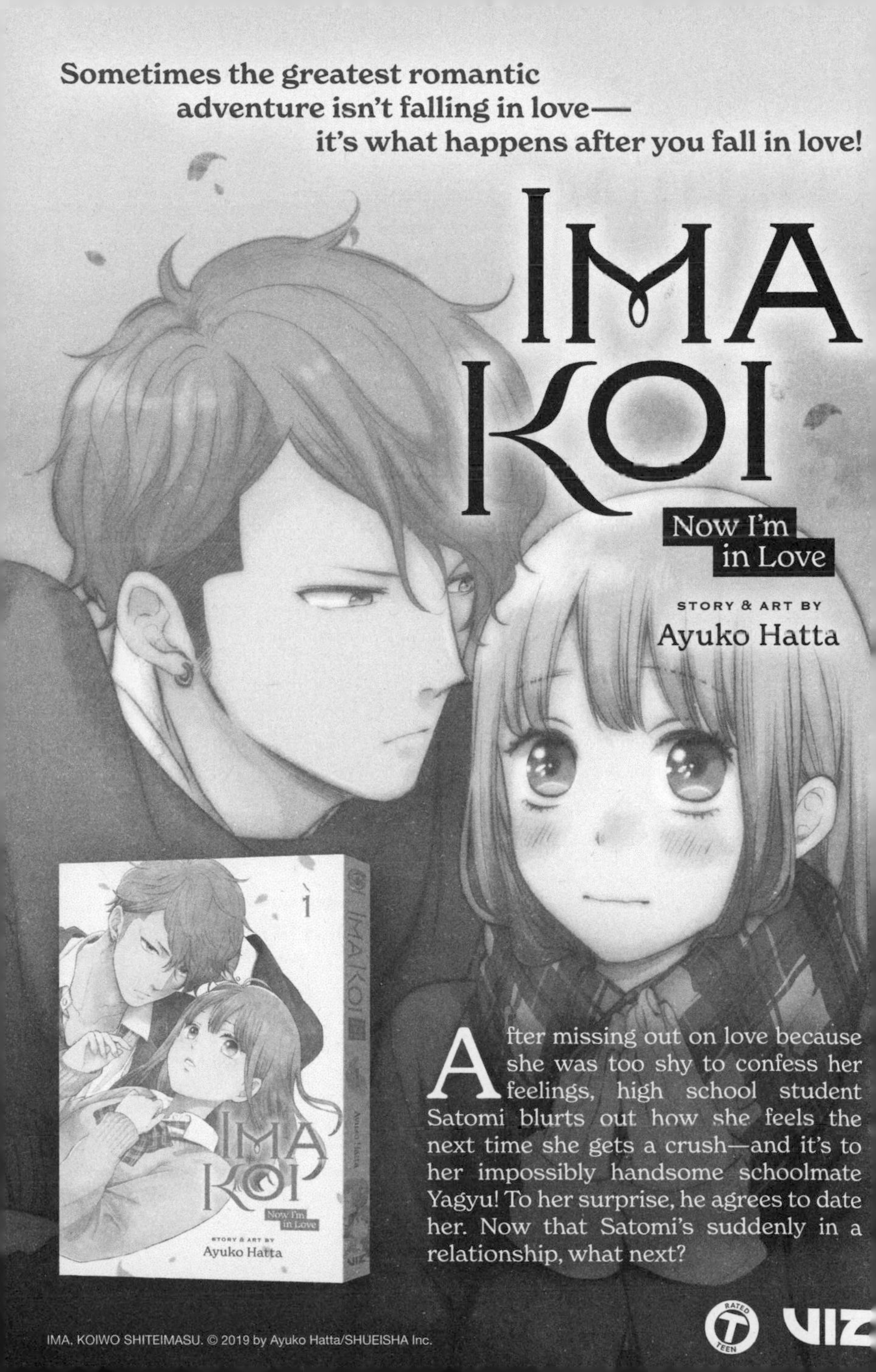
Sometimes the greatest romantic adventure isn't falling in love—it's what happens after you fall in love!
IMA KOI
Now I'm in Love
STORY & ART BY
Ayuko Hatta
IMA KOI
Now I'm in Love
STORY & ART BY
Ayuko Hatta
After missing out on love because she was too shy to confess her feelings, high school student Satomi blurts out how she feels the next time she gets a crush—and it's to her impossibly handsome schoolmate Yagyu! To her surprise, he agrees to date her. Now that Satomi's suddenly in a relationship, what next?
RATED T TEEN
VIZ
IMA, KOIWO SHITEIMASU. © 2019 by Ayuko Hatta/SHUEISHA Inc.

DAYTIME SHOOTING STAR

Story & Art by
Mika Yamamori

Small town girl Suzume moves to Tokyo and finds her heart caught between two men!

After arriving in Tokyo to live with her uncle, Suzume collapses in a nearby park when she remembers once seeing a shooting star during the day. A handsome stranger brings her to her new home and tells her they'll meet again. Suzume starts her first day at her new high school sitting next to a boy who blushes furiously at her touch. And her homeroom teacher is none other than the handsome stranger!

T RATED TEEN **VIZ**

IDOL dreams

STORY & ART BY
ARINA TANEMURA

At age 31, office worker Chikage Deguchi feels she missed her chances at love and success. When word gets out that she's a virgin, Chikage is humiliated and wishes she could turn back time to when she was still young and popular. She takes an experimental drug that changes her appearance back to when she was 15. Now Chikage is determined to pursue everything she missed out on all those years ago—including becoming a star!

YOU'RE READING THE WRONG WAY!

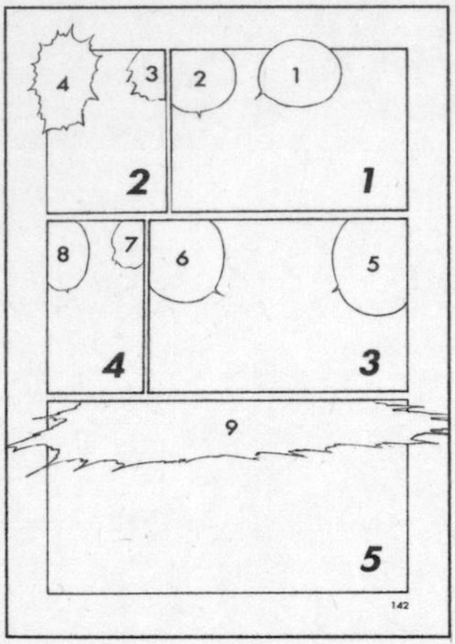

My Special One reads from right to left, starting in the upper-right corner. Japanese is read from right to left, meaning that action, sound effects, and word-balloon order are completely reversed from English order. Check out the diagram shown here to get the hang of things, and then turn to the other side of the book to get started!

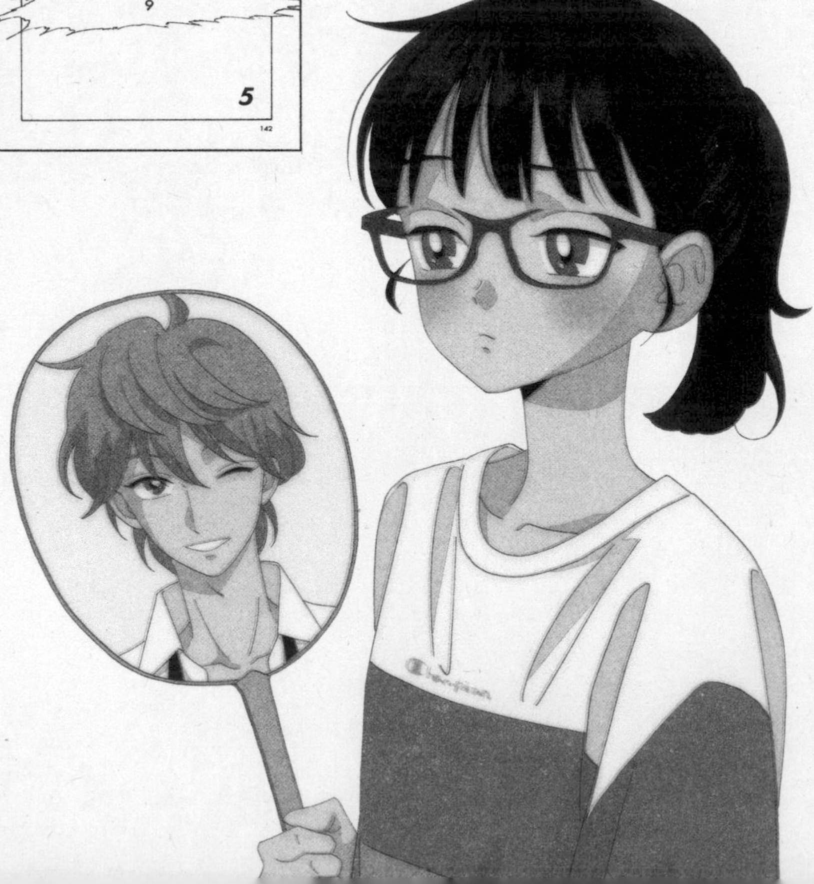